WHEN RUSTLING
BECAME AN ART

WHEN RUSTLING BECAME AN ART:

Pilane's Kgatla and the Transvaal Frontier 1820–1902

FRED MORTON

Published in 2009 in southern Africa
by David Philip Publishers,
an imprint of New Africa Books (Pty) Ltd,
99 Garfield Road, Claremont 7700, South Africa

© in text: Fred Morton
© in published edition: New Africa Books (Pty) Ltd

All rights reserved. No part of this publication may be
reproduced, stored in a retrieval system, or transmitted in
any form or by any means, electronic, mechanical or otherwise,
without prior written permission of the publishers.

ISBN: 978-0-86486-724-7

Editor: Helen Hacksley
Design and typesetting: Nazli Jacobs
Illustrator: Lemington Muzhingi, Munya Art, Gaborone
Cartographer: Elmari Kuyler
Cover design: Peter Bosman
Proofreader: James McFarlane

Printed and bound in South Africa by SED Printing Solutions

To Barry

CONTENTS

List of Abbreviations	viii
List of Maps and Illustrations	x
Acknowledgements	x
Preface	xi
Terms and Designations	xvi
Kgatla Rules of Rustling	xviii

Introduction: Rustlers' Heir		xix
Chapters		
1.	*Mmadinale* ('The Clawer'): Pilane Pheto	1
2.	Kgamanyane Pilane and Paul Kruger	28
3.	Saulspoort	55
4.	Emigration	89
5.	War	110
6.	Consolidation	149
7.	Threat from the South	167
8.	Love, Duty	209
9.	The Last Raid	237
Epilogue: The Eclipse of Isang		274

List of Male Regiments	288
Pilane's Genealogy	289
Glossary of Kgatla terms	290
Bibliography	294
Index	308

ABBREVIATIONS

ALFPT	*Alphabetical List of Farms in the Province of Transvaal*
BBP	Bechuanaland Border Police
BM	British Museum
BNA	Botswana National Archives
BPBC	*British Bechuanaland. Proceedings of the Bechuanaland Protectorate Boundary Commission.*
CAD	Central Archives Depot, Pretoria
CO	Colonial Office Series, Public Record Office, Kew Gardens, U.K.
COCP	Colonial Office Confidential Prints
CUL	Cambridge University Library
DRC	Dutch Reformed Church (Nederduitse Gereformeerde Kerk)
DRCA	Dutch Reformed Church Archives, Cape Town
DSAB	Dictionary of South African Biography
HC	High Commissioner
HMG	Her Majesty's Government
HMSR	Hermannsburger Mission Society Records (Transcripts, Botswana National Achives, Gaborone)
HSRC	Human Sciences Research Council
LMS	London Missionary Society
MSS	Manuscripts
NAC	Native Advisory Council
PP	Parliamentary Papers
PRO	Public Record Office, Kew Gardens
RCS	Royal Commonwealth Society Collection
RH	Rhodes House, Oxford University, U.K.
SAA	South African Archives, Pretoria
SAAR	*South African Archival Records*
SAM	South African Museum, Cape Town
SP	Schapera Papers
SPUP	Shepstone Papers, University of Pretoria
TA	Transvaal Archives, National Archives Repository, National Archives of South Africa, Pretoria

ABBREVIATIONS

WP Willoughby Papers
ZAR *Zuid-Afrikaansche Republiek* (South African Republic)

Transvaal Archives, National Archives Repository, National Archives of South Africa, Pretoria (TA)

AG Auditor General (1867-1900)
ATG Attorney General (1902-1939)
ATC Administrator of the Transvaal Colony (1877-1881)
BR British Resident, Transvaal (1880-1885)
CT Colonial Treasurer, Transvaal (1900-1910)
GOV Secretary of the Governor of the Transvaal (1900-1910)
KG Kommandant General (1880-1900)
KRB Native Commissioner, Rustenburg (1910-1968)
LD Law Department, Transvaal (1900-1925)
LRB Landdrost, Rustenburg (1902-1980)
LTG Lieutenant Governor of the Transvaal Colony (1902-1907)
MGP Military Governor, Pretoria (1900-1902)
PMG Postmaster General (1892-1904)
PWD Public Works Department (1901-1914)
RAK Land Registers
SN Superintendent of Native Affairs (1877-1900)
SNA Superintendent of Native Affairs (1900-1911)
SP State Attorney (1864-1900)
SS State Secretary, ZAR (1829-1900)
SSA State Secretary, Foreign Affairs Section (1894-1900)
TAD Transvaal Agriculture Department (1900-1919)
ZRB Landdrost, Rustenburg (1873-1890)
ZTPD Supreme Court of the ZAR and of the Transvaal Colony (1877-1910)

South African Archives, Pretoria (SAA)

GG Governor General (1907-1974)
NTS Native Affairs (1880-1972)

LIST OF MAPS AND ILLUSTRATIONS

MAPS

1.	Pilane's World ca. 1840	xxx
2.	Rustenburg District ca. 1868	56
3.	Bechuanaland and the South Africa Republic ca. 1880	90
4.	Bakgatla Reserve, ca. 1899	238

ILLUSTRATIONS

5.	Isang Pilane	xxi
6.	Stephanus Johannes Paulus Kruger	29
7.	Henri Gonin and Family	62
8.	Sidney Godolphin Alexander Shippard	175
9.	Ramono Pilane	215
10.	Hercules Malan and Associates	249
11.	Linchwe, 1902	266

ACKNOWLEDGEMENTS

I wish to thank the staff members at the National Archives of Botswana, Gaborone; the University of Botswana library, Gaborone; the Phuthadikobo Museum, Mochudi; the Academic Resource Center, Loras College, Dubuque; the Wartburg Seminary Library, Dubuque; the National Archives of South Africa, Pretoria; the University of Pretoria Library, Pretoria; the University of Witwatersrand Library, Johannesburg; the Dutch Reformed Church Archives, Cape Town; the South African Museum Library, Cape Town; the National Archives of Zimbabwe, Harare; the Public Records Office, Kew Gardens; the British Museum, London; the Library, University of Cambridge; and the Rhodes House Library, Oxford.

PREFACE

History is just the fanciest way possible of wanting to deny or distract attention from what's happening now.
(Maureen Dowd)

When, as a Yankee with a new doctorate, I flew in to Gaborone to teach at the new University College of Botswana (UCB) in February 1976, I arrived with hardly any knowledge of Botswana or South Africa. My task was to teach East African history (my Syracuse thesis being on nineteenth-century Kenyan coastal slavery). But soon my seniors Thomas Tlou and Leonard Ngcongco had me walk the coals as a supervisor of fourth-year research essays on Botswana history. One of my first students was Rrenyane S. Dikole, who wrote on 'Kgosi Isang Pilane's Modernising Programme' (1978). The following year, the department, then larger, sent all researchers to one area. The destination was Mochudi and the Kgatleng district, where 14 students majoring in history fanned out to do interviews. The three in my care – Bagele Kenosi, Philip Monnatsie and Phanuel Richard – chose diverse paths: economic history, the Zionist church and Bushmen cattle-post labourers. Following them around the Kgatleng and into the national archives also led me chest-deep into the massive published record of the inimitable Professor Isaac Schapera.

By 1980 I was hooked. I started with a research project on cattle and Kgatla cross-border relations, funded by the university and assisted by Mochudi resident and UCB student in political administration, Bruce Palai. Other recruits helped the blind man see. Mmamosadinyana Molefhe and Keoagile Kebilwe guided me through interviews in Mochudi and Saulspoort between December 1981 and January 1982. Not long after that I located the Pretoria Archives in the basement of the Union Buildings, and in 1984, thanks again to a grant from the now University of Botswana travelled to Harare and Cape Town to tap more archival sources. As disabled with Dutch and Afrikaans as I was with Setswana, another again was needed to come to the rescue: nineteenth-century European literature specialist Wom van den Akker, miraculously idle in Gaborone, was dragooned into translating piles of Dutch correspondence among missionaries of the Dutch

Reformed Church in Mochudi and Saulspoort. Mochudi elder Edwin Gare led me to Ratshegana Sebeke, the gold seam of Kgatla history; William Sentshebeng transcribed and translated the hours-long interview with Sebeke. By 1985 some pieces started to come together in the form of journal articles and conference papers.

In 1987 my time in Botswana ran out. I returned to the States, landing with luck at Loras College in Iowa, and slowly plotted my return. Conferencing and editing with Betsy Eldredge and working with Jim Zaffiro to create the Iowa African Studies Association kept me in the mix of things. Two Indiana University graduate students, Barry Morton and Dan Galbraith, dished me plates full of gemstones from nineteenth-century South African newspapers. In 1995 the National Endowment for the Humanities gave me a stipend for research in Botswana and South Africa, topped up by a Loras College Faculty Development Committee travel grant. This was my chance to dive into the new Pretoria Archives facility and to meet Bernard Mbenga, Tlou Makhura, Justin Erasmus and Johan Bergh at the South African Historical Association conference in Grahamstown. In Gaborone Jacqueline Tabane, Part and Rebecca Mgadla and Jeff and Sekgabo Ramsay made me feel at home, while the legendary Mmua Raditladi led me around Sikwane, Mathubudukwane and Malolwane. *Kgosi* Linchwe II graced me with lunch, frank recollections and access to family portraits. Loras College helped me get back to southern Africa in 1997. Two years later, Loras again backed my quest with a six-month sabbatical, while the US Department of Education awarded me a generous Faculty Research Abroad grant. I converted my good fortune into archival sleuthing in England, and with the support of the Department of Historical and Heritage Studies at the University of Pretoria I was able to work for a sustained period in the Pretoria Archives. Professor Bergh opened to me his vault of translated archival and published material and invited me into a joint publication project. As dependent as ever on others, I made key finds in nineteenth-century correspondence with the assistance of Ria Groenewald.

Along the way, I received a great deal that on my own I could not have unearthed. Professor Schapera gave me genealogies, ward lists and correspondence from his collection and donated to the Botswana National Archives a rich trove of his research materials. My son Barry Morton offered me a tall stack of notes from his survey of nineteenth-century literature on Botswana and South Africa that he had used to publish his excellent articles and annotated bibliography. Jan Boeyens corrected my erring reproduction of nineteenth-century Dutch, led me to valuable sources, introduced me to the granddaughter of Henri Gonin and kept me abreast of the latest developments in Transvaal archaeology. Elisabeth Viljoen generously provided copies of the Henri Gonin family photographs and with the help of her family identified all of the children. Neil Parsons shunted numerous obscure articles and his notes from British press and the Ellenberger papers in my direction.

My work with Jeff Ramsay, Part Mgadla, Barry Morton and Andy Murray on three editions of the *Historical Dictionary of Botswana* kept me abreast of the growing field of Botswana history, and collaboration with Johannes Du Bruyn, Lizé Kriel and Jackie Grobler enabled me to participate in opening up the study of the Transvaal in the nineteenth century. Correspondence over the years with Sandy Grant, Mochudi's closest observer, engaged me with always thoughtful comments on my work. At Loras College, Jens Werner translated Lutheran mission correspondence in German, Barry van Wyk translated an extensive Afrikaans text, while Andy Auge, John and Kristin Anderson-Bricker and other members of the Redactors scrutinised my drafts for most of the chapters in this volume and kept me motivated during my 18-year residence in Iowa and until my retirement from teaching. In 2006, with my library scanned onto CDs by Bernie Giese, I returned to Botswana with my wife Sue, settled near Gaborone and peacefully finished this book.

What follows is a (pray readable) history. Though it is about a people few will recognise at the outset and about persons very few who live in their vicinity are likely to admit resemble themselves or their forbearers, the story of Pilane's Kgatla is ultimately about fairly ordinary souls who lived in a difficult age, kept their wits and made the best of it. That is not to say that what they did was unexceptional – on the contrary. Their achievements were substantial, more so because of the odds stacked against human endeavour in the Transvaal and Bechuanaland during the nineteenth century. Their world required endurance beyond the capacity of modern people. None of us would be up to its physical rigours or the repeated trials of survival they faced.

In piecing together their history I came to the conclusion that, at the point where the story leaves off, the Kgatla had come a long way from where they started and had created a life that made them better off than many other people in the region. Theirs is a triumph of sorts, though the account below is less interested in the eventual outcome or how success is measured (except on their terms), but in the long and uneven journey the Kgatla took from their beleaguered position in the early nineteenth century to their much more independent and self-respecting circumstances in the early twentieth century.

My aim has been to keep out of the way and allow the Kgatla, insofar as the scattered record makes possible, to speak and act for themselves. My sketches of their world are an attempt to describe matters as they might have seen or heard about them, though at times I have failed to resist inserting my own opinions. In the footnotes are listed the varied sources used to reconstruct the scenes described and an occasional comment on the narrative. However, this history is not intended to prove a theory or overturn any interpretation. Its casting of individuals or depicting groups may rankle with some, but my wish rather has been to serve readers wanting to imagine what it was like for the persons found here to live with a purpose, when life offered the scantiest of rewards or guarantees.

FRED MORTON
Ruretse
14 March 2008

TERMS AND DESIGNATIONS

The reader will soon recognise that the telling of Kgatla history involves a great many place references, some historical, some contemporary and, occasionally, idiosyncratic. For example, 'trans-Vaal' is frequently used as a geographical reference rather than the standard 'Transvaal'. The reason being that 'Transvaal' was used by nineteenth-century English writers to refer to the area claimed by the Dutch-speaking Boers after the 1840s, which was governed by the British during the Annexation period (1877–1881) and after the South African War (1899–1902). In other words, it was a political reference, though English travellers adopted 'Transvaal' and 'Trans-Vaal' as a loose geographical reference after the 1860s. The 1852 Sand River Convention, which acknowledged the independence of 'emigrant farmers beyond the Vaal River', made no use of the term, and until the South African War (1899–1902), neither did the Kgatla adopt it, nor, rarely, did their Boer contemporaries, the latter preferring instead *Zuid-Afrikaansche Republiek*.

Attempts have been made to orient the reader not familiar with the historical provinces by inserting modern provincial references (Gauteng, Limpopo, etc). Thus, the important (though temporary) Kgatla settlement of Tshwene-tshwene, now located in the present North West province, was located in the Potchefstroom district between 1843 and 1871, and the Marico district from that year to 1994. In addition, local African place names (e.g. Monamaneng, Bogopana) are identified with the relevant modern farm name and number (Kafferskraal 43, Moroelasfontein 366) to assist anyone wishing to locate them precisely on topocadastral maps. Bear in mind that farm numbers follow the post-1937 numbering system. Often appearing in this book are African settlement names that in the nineteenth century were commonly associated with a kgosi/kapitein/chief and known after the kgosi himself: Sechele's, Mokgatle's, Kgamanyane's, and so forth.

African language terms are used in this book with and without proper prefixes. For example, Kgatla is often used in the place of the proper Ba-Kgatla (people of Kgatla). The same is true of any number of references to groups (BaFokeng, Fokeng, Ndebele, AmaNdebele, etc.), simply to introduce variation while recognising proper forms. I also interchange English with Dutch and SeTswana references, as in Boer with *leBuru*. This is to help readers become used to how people referred to one another and how it was heard. The term *kaffer* appears often in this book both to evoke the sound and sentiment current in the nineteenth century among Dutch speakers. As unsettling as it will be to modern ears, kaffer then was in common currency among Dutch-speakers and was well known to the BaKgatla, many of whom spoke Dutch. During the nineteenth century, early forms of Afrikaans were spoken by Boer and Griqua, among others, but Dutch was used for written correspondence.

Orthography perplexed early writers representing Tswana and Dutch/Afrikaans, occasioning wide variation. A spelling standard remained decades away. Therefore, searching nineteenth-century records for the BaKgatla's past can feel like entering a maze. Most references to them were made by Europeans, who with some exceptions had the scantest of familiarity with their language, much less the slightest agreement on how their names were to be recorded. They wrote according to how a name sounded, with no shortage of tin ears. BaKgatla was very easy to mishear, and met with considerable variation: Bakatlas, Khatlas, Kahlas, Kahltas, Cata, Kgathas, Bagatlas, and so on. Pilane was relatively unproblematic (Pilan, Pilaan, Pilanie, Pelani), but his ruling descendants Kgamanyane and Linchwe bamboozled contemporary recorders. Kgamanyane was rendered in at least ten distinct spellings (Gamjan, Gajaman, Khagamajane, Khamajane, Kamyani, Kaminyani, etc.) while Linchwe's imitators yielded more than thirty variations, arguably a world record for any historic figure (see below). Though barely literate, Linchwe had little trouble choosing his own rendition, using Linchue in his first letter (1876) and adopting Linchwe from 1902 onwards, a spelling accepted by his namesake and great-grandson, Linchwe II, *kgosi* of the BaKgatla from 1963 until his death in 2007.

Leincheu	Lenchwi	Lentsu	Linjoa	Lintsue
Leinchue	Lencoe	Lentswe	Linjua	Lintzoe
Leincue	Lencue	Leucini	Linsou	Luisou
Leinschue	Lencwe	Leucore	Linstia	Lynchwe
Lenchie	Lencwi	Lincae	Lintcue	Lyntsche
Lenchue	Lensey	Linchne	Lintshwe	
Lenchwe	Lentsoe	Linchue	Lintsoe	

KGATLA RULES OF RUSTLING

1. Always have friends – you may need them when you least expect it.

2. Learn from others – a good idea is worth thousands of cattle.

3. Don't show weakness or hesitate to be ruthless – it will encourage your enemies.

4. Never trust others – alertness to betrayal is the surest way to maintain good relations with those you need.

5. Let the men who raid on your behalf have their share – their dependence on your leadership will be a happy and thankful one.

6. Know when to raid – a good cattle rustling enterprise every ten years or so is sufficient to keep everyone together and keep your allies from worrying about your next step.

7. There are other ways to become wealthy than just rustling cattle – be open to trade, agriculture, concessions, hiring skilled people from the outside.

8. More cattle means more herders – get BaSarwa and BaKgalagadi whenever possible.

9. Be prepared to move – good territory makes for good cattle.

10. Stay abreast of events – the future is more important than the past.

11. Know your enemy – one's secrets and plans are best preserved by communicating with the enemy in *their* language.

12. Look up-to-date – no one takes seriously someone who seems to be behind the times.

Introduction

RUSTLERS' HEIR

A bundle of spears,
God with the wet nose,
A short, hot drink,
The medicine that burns the men's beards.
Cow, god of the home,
Cow that makes the nations
You have killed many men. (Kgatla initiation song; Schapera 1934: 563)

In 1931, when the Great Depression was under way, three white South Africans drove from the Transvaal into the dusty, drought-stricken Bechuanaland Protectorate (in 1966 it became Botswana), one of the poorest areas on the planet. William Ballinger, Margaret Hodgson and Leonard Barnes were liberal activists gathering evidence to show that Great Britain had been neglecting its black colonies in southern Africa. They were concerned especially about what whites called the 'High Commission Territories': Basutoland, Swaziland and the Bechuanaland Protectorate.[1] They drove into the Protectorate at the Derdepoort drift, passed through Sikwane – one of the small settlements of the Kgatla people, or BaKgatla as they called themselves – and headed for the Kgatla capital of Mochudi. Thirty years before, white officials had named this eastern corner of the Protectorate the 'Bakgatla Reserve'. As they made their way along the rutted dirt road, Ballinger, Hodgson and Barnes discussed the 'natives' they saw walking by and pieced together what little they knew of the Kgatla 'tribe'. (English speakers liked using 'native' and 'tribe' – it made them feel superior to the Afrikaners, who spoke only of *kleurlingen* and *kaffers*.) From the open window, they saw mostly acacias and grass, interspersed with large patches of stunted maize, sorghum and beans, with a broken-down hut or two at the edge of each miserable field. A harvest looked unlikely. On the other hand, cattle seemed to be everywhere – not in herds, but moving mostly about on their own, grazing along the roadside or standing on the road blocking their way and staring at them indifferently. Dust was thick in the air, flies buzzing in and out. Every kilometre or so, they came upon two or three scrawny beasts being driven by barefoot boys in rags heading in one direction or another. Eventually, they reached the outskirts of Mochudi, the main Kgatla town and headquarters of the Bakgatla Reserve. They could see it from a distance, or at least Phuthadikobo Hill, Mochudi's most prominent feature. The car slowed as Mochudi came into full view; it consisted of hundreds of rondavels nestled among the rocks at the base of Phuthadikobo.

As they pulled up to the offices of the 'chief', Ballinger and his colleagues were met by a striking figure. He was around fifty years old, but stood erect at six feet tall, had a trimmed goatee and was wearing a three-piece grey suit, neatly pressed, with white shirt, starched collar and tie. A medium-brimmed felt hat, brushed clean, sat on his head like it belonged there. The stately gentleman had been awaiting the white visitors, but later they learned he almost always dressed in this way. He walked towards them with a limp, yet with unmistakable authority in his step, barely leaning on his brass-topped cane. In perfect English, His Dignity greeted the white visitors, speaking in a natural, courteous tone. They sensed immediately that in spite of his full smile and direct look, this man was not trying to be liked or expecting to be looked down on. He introduced himself. He was Isang Pilane, Kgatla elder and advisor to his nephew Molefi Pilane, the Kgatla *kgosi* ('chief', Hodgson whispered to the others, 'that means "chief"'). Isang emphasised that before the young Molefi was installed in office less than two years ago, he, Isang, had been the regent of the Kgatla for nearly eight years. Isang Pilane cordially invited Ballinger and the others to his large compound nearby, had them served tea in the shade next to his massive thatched rondavel and answered their questions without hesitation, but with no haste in his manner. Authority exuded effortlessly from this man.

Then it was time for Isang to call for his chauffeur and escort his guests around Mochudi. Moving slowly through the tidy lanes, Isang and the white visitors passed along the wide pathways between neat, thatched rondavels with decorated walls, hand-etched courtyards and individually shaped enclosure walls, some made of rock, others of mud and sheathed in cow dung plaster. Shade trees and thatch made the hot sun look cool. Fruit hung in the tiny orange groves along the Ngotwane River, which flowed around Phuthadikobo. Men, women and children, for the most

INTRODUCTION

Isang Pilane, circa 1933. Sketch by Lemington Muzhingi.

part well clothed and in good health, watched them but took no special notice. As they toured through this orderly community, Isang drew his guests' attention to the many improvements for which he and his father, the late Linchwe Pilane (d. 1924), had been responsible. The British had been around since 1885, he reminded them, close to a half century, but only the Kgatla had made the changes around here. In fact Protectorate headquarters at Mafeking (now Mafikeng) had not bothered even to station an official in Mochudi. Hodgson and Ballinger busied themselves taking notes. Isang then showed them the borehole, which provided good water to the town year round, the new medical clinic (run by white missionaries), the tractors taking the place of oxen, the double-furrow steel ploughs, the shops and the agricultural market cooperative, which was attempting to gain better prices for the farmers so they could stay on the land and out of the mines. Isang started a discourse on bulls and cattle breeding, but these white city folks showed little understanding, and he skipped to the next subject, his showcase for outsiders. Returning to the *kgotla* (the kgosi's open court, next to where the 'chief's office' was built), they got out of the car and made their way to the top of Phuthadikobo Hill where, sitting rather majestically as it overlooked the town, was the Mochudi National School. Under Isang's direction while he was regent, it had been built and financed by the Kgatla themselves. Thousands of Kgatla had carried rocks, sand, gravel and water up Phuthadikobo in order to construct this large building, which was the finest structure in the entire Protectorate, not to mention its only post-primary school. Every day the bell on Phuthadikobo summoned hundreds of boys and girls from the town below to come for their lessons in mathematics, English, geography, agriculture, debating and other subjects. And its headmaster and teachers were all Africans. The Mochudi National School and the other projects shown to his white visitors, Isang said again, were the Kgatla's own achievements – except for the clinic, which missionaries of the Dutch Reformed Church had started.

Ballinger, Hodgson and Barnes concluded their short visit and were soon off, heading out of Mochudi towards the railway hotel at Gaberones (Gaborone since 1965), their destination for the night. There is no doubt that they departed very impressed with what they saw and in particular with Isang and reports of Linchwe, his late father. 'Between them', they wrote after touring the Protectorate, 'these two men made the Bakhatla

INTRODUCTION

the most progressive and incidentally the most prosperous tribe of the territory'.[2]

If they had spent more time in Mochudi and talked to the Kgatla about Isang, these visitors might have seen other, maybe even more fascinating, qualities in their host and thereby understood the BaKgatla better. To be sure, Isang Pilane was educated, articulate and progressive – all the hallmarks of the modern man – and one might think the Kgatla, who had nicknamed him *Ramalebanya* ('far-sighted one') mostly thought of him that way. But those qualities were not especially important to the Kgatla; Isang got that name because he always seemed to know what others were up to. He was like the parent you could never catch out. Isang was simply smarter and quicker than anyone else around. He knew every Kgatla, including children, and not just by name. He knew how each person was related by marriage and birth to others in the community, what ward they resided in and what others thought of them. No one escaped his recognition. Isang had also mastered the complexities of cattle-keeping, which historically had been the life-blood of the Kgatla as a people. Isang could identify most of the approximately 30,000 cattle in the Kgatla Reserve by their markings as well as their brands, the progeny of these beasts, and who owned which cattle or who borrowed which cattle from whom. His colossal memory made him the expert on Kgatla history, customs, religion, magic (except for rainmaking – everyone knew he was a failure at making rain) and other lore. And when it came to dealing with whites, Isang had much more than a westernised appearance, church-going habits and easy manner at his disposal – he knew English *and* Afrikaans, knew Roman-Dutch law, and he understood the white men's institutions better than most whites knew themselves. Nothing seemed mysterious to Isang.

The man was as mean and ruthless as they came. As regent he was known for his whip and the cruelty with which he used it to enforce his rules. It was not uncommon to see him at night riding his horse around town, seeking out curfew violators and sjambokking them senseless. His temper was legendary, and those whom he believed had crossed him knew it best. Isang had killed men. He had beaten others nearly to death. Women and children had died due to his violence. He had practised witchcraft trying to kill others. Many believed that one of his targets was kgosi Molefi.

And Isang was rich, really rich. At the time, most white people in south-

XXIII

ern Africa, not to mention black, were not even close to having the wealth he had accumulated. He owned several farms in the Transvaal, the first modern tractor in the Protectorate, had bank accounts in Mafeking and Rustenburg, boreholes for his cattle and shops near the railway line. By far the greatest portion of his wealth, however, was in cattle. That was because Isang was a true Kgatla, a man whose status was determined mainly by the size of his herd. Apart from kgosi Molefi, who is said to have had 5,000 head, Isang owned more cattle than anyone else by far. He was alleged to have nearly 2,000 more than the next wealthiest Kgatla. The odd thing about the Kgatla, though, and this is true of many cattle people in this region, is that cattle are not something wealthy people show off. Everyone *knew* Isang had lots of cattle, but they had never seen them and no one but a white person would ever dare ask as to how many he had. The fact is they were kept at a distance from the town in scattered *meraka* (cattle posts), and only a handful at a time were ever brought into town, when they were needed for draught purposes or to be slaughtered. There were several reasons why this was done and why no one thought it unusual. Cattle had to be kept far from town – so they would not destroy the town's surrounding vegetation and create a manure nuisance – and close to plenty of pasture and good water. A man's herd, if large, also needed to be broken up and scattered about at different meraka. This kept overgrazing down, made for better breeding and reduced the risk of disease spreading quickly. It also made it easier for the owner to ensure his herders had a manageable number to keep track of, and to prevent neighbours from helping themselves to a stray beast or two, but only an owner could know how many cattle he had altogether. With cattle at different meraka it was impossible for anyone else to know – and for the better. Knowing would just increase jealousy and lead to trouble. Isang Pilane told Isaac Schapera, a young ethnographer doing research in Mochudi, that he owned 2,500 head. It was a lie. (Whites always went for round figures.) Secrecy was the byword of a good cattleman, and Isang was the best. And more than most cattle owners, Isang had reason to be elusive.

Isang smuggled cattle into South Africa. Since 1924 South Africa had made it illegal for Protectorate cattle to enter the Union and reach the lucrative Johannesburg market. It was the white government's latest way of protecting white farmers from black competition. Rather than be shut out, Isang and his cousin Kgari Pilane, also known as 'Mussolini' (he had a weakness for black shirts) organised a smuggling ring involving several Boer farmers just across the border. The Kgatla and the Boers had been rubbing shoulders for generations, and Isang knew them well (Isang and the Kgatla called them all '*maBuru*'). The maBuru were willing to pay up-front a few pounds each for cattle they could truck straight to market. All sorts of Kgatla were willing to sign up, giving their cattle over in return for a tax receipt or Kgari's promissory note. At night, fence posts were up-rooted, the fence laid flat and Kgari and his men would then run the cattle through the opening to the maBuru waiting on the other side. No one ever got caught, and the racket went on for years. The South African police had '*Skelm* Kgari' on their wanted list seemingly forever, but somehow he always evaded arrest. When the subject of smuggling came up in public, Isang liked to chortle 'our cattle have become winged and we cannot find them'.[3]

Isang and Kgari were part of an old Kgatla tradition. They were the direct descendants of a long line of cattle entrepreneurs. The grand schemes in Mochudi that had so impressed Ballinger, Hodgson and Barnes had been paid for mostly from the proceeds of smuggled cattle – cattle that in turn were taken from the herds that had been built up over decades by cattle raiding. The odds were that most of the cattle Isang and Kgari smuggled to the maBuru were the progeny of cattle Linchwe and his brothers had stolen from the maBuru during the South African (Anglo-Boer) War of 1899–1902. The rustling business went way back. It had taken at least five generations, extending back to Isang's great-great grandfather Pheto, for the Kgatla to work their way up to become the pre-eminent cattle rustlers of the region. Pheto, who ruled from 1775 to 1810, made the Kgatla a power north of the Vaal River with their base in the Sefikele Hills. Pheto's second son Pilane (ruled 1825 to 1848), founder of Isang's line, rescued the Kgatla from internecine murder and invasions by the Kololo and Ndebele, regrouping them into a raiding force. The maBuru came in Pilane's time and named the Sefikele Hills 'Pilanesberg'. Then came Pilane's son Kgamanyane (ruled 1848–1875), the fiercest of the Kgatla raiders, who led the Kgatla from the Pilanesberg to Bechuanaland; and then his son Linchwe (ruled 1875–1920), who presided over the greatest of all Kgatla raids before whites ruled the entire region. Isang was born too late to participate in these raids, but he ran his smuggling operation by adapting the skills passed down by his forefathers.

Isang's rapacious pedigree had been hatched in some of the finest cattle country anywhere in southern Africa. In a vast, undulating plain stretching from the Vaal River to the Kalahari sandveld in the north and west, to the Waterberg, Blauwberg and Soutpansberg mountains in the north, and to the Drakensberg in the east, the highveld and bushveld of the trans-Vaal[4] offered endless grass amidst rivers and streams.[5] The trans-Vaal plain stood south of the Tropic of Capricorn and maintained altitudes in excess of a thousand metres, producing a temperate climate. Alternating mild summers and brisk winters rejuvenated the landscape annually. Cattle could be moved at short distances between abundant sweet and sour grasses. Rainfall was not all that reliable, more likely to be local than widespread, and given to extremes – floods in some years, absolute droughts in others. Agriculture was feasible, and everyone planted each spring, but drought-resistant sorghum and millet were the mainstays. Even then, crops failed three years out of ten. Only cattle, goats and sheep could keep people fed with milk – cattle most of all. Hunting was excellent, meaning meat was always nearby. Cattle-keeping and hunting had sustained the trans-Vaal highvelders since the iron age. But not until the early nineteenth century did cattle rustling come of age. That is when the trans-Vaal's vastness, its excellent grazing and the thousands of cattle moving about for the taking attracted the attention of powerful stock-grabbers surveying the view from south of the Vaal River.

They came in force, one after the other – the Kololo, the Ndebele, the half-caste *maSetedi* and the most fearsome thieves of all, the maBuru. The Kololo and Ndebele were large, mobile armies led by all-powerful military rulers (Sebitwane and Mzilikazi). The maBuru came in small family groups who formed bands of gun-toting, horseback raiders (commandos) to attack large communities and rustle their stock. They raided for slaves on the side. These black and white predators amassed huge herds, setting a standard of unsurpassed armed extortion. As is typical of invaders, their superior power was an excuse to look down on highvelders (such as the Kgatla) as aliens. They picked up their languages but shunned their cultures, and thought only about bending the human and physical landscape to their respective wills. They had arrived trying to escape troubles elsewhere and, once in the trans-Vaal, moving elsewhere was always on their mind. Except for the maBuru, they came and went (some of the maBuru went, too). They took innumerable cattle, killed lots of people and inspired much fear, but produced no imitators.

The Kgatla did not dare emulate them, and frankly did not try. Instead, it was the turmoil created by the Ndebele and maBuru, and the mistakes they made, that offered the Kgatla opportunities to set themselves up in the rustling business. These two powerhouses fought on too large a scale and constantly had to force others to serve them. In turn, each tried commanding large spaces. One after the other they failed. No matter how powerful, they were newcomers to the highveld, invaders, too impatient and greedy to blend their raiding organisations into the terrain, water, foliage and people. They always seemed to be at war with the inhabitants. Pilane and his heirs were highvelders who planned to outlast each of these invaders and build an operation where they lived. They started rustling as a small, part-time family business to supplement trade in ivory, minerals, skins and other market items. The patriarchal kgosi, his brothers and uncles ran it, passing on their knowledge and skills to their sons and nephews.

The Kgatla learned how to keep away from trouble and pick their fights. They knew when to team up with one of the juggernauts and when to steer clear. The Kgatla under Pilane and his son Kgamanyane rustled the cattle of people at a distance, but remained at peace with people in their own neighbourhood. As they grew slowly but steadily, the Kgatla became a respected force that others wanted to avoid or to join. The nineteenth-century trans-Vaal was a violent place, where raiders and raided alike lived pretty much on constant security alert. The Kgatla kept their pose as a minor, secondary threat that kept a friendly face, but showed just enough strength not to be tampered with. This, and their small-scale operation, set them apart from the juggernauts, who everyone feared and wished to see done in.

Kgatla also used geography to better advantage. Like other highveld dwellers, the Kgatla understood that it was far easier to get along with others and gain access to valuable territory than to try controlling lots of people and land. For any group wanting or having lots of cattle, the highveld was suited to shifting one's location rather than to staying in one spot and extending one's reach. Solid homes could be built in a matter of days. The territory was strewn with ready-made building materials – especially rock, clay and grass – and one of hundreds of derelict settlements could be reoccupied and quickly reconstructed. And so, as the Kgatla expanded their cattle-rustling enterprise, they thought always of remaining in the highveld and moving to the place best suited to taking them a step further in their goal of accumulating wealth and power. For years, without controlling any territory, they acquired large holdings in cattle and moved them over great distances for safe-keeping in well-watered recesses known only to a few. Eventually, when they had mastered the method of shifting livestock, the Kgatla, under Pilane's son Kgamanyane, made a calculated bid to set themselves up as a small territorial power, in the Bechuanaland bushveld, on the fringe of maBuru settlement. Choosing this spot and making it theirs was an undertaking of years involving thousands of people and costing thousands of lives. The achievement bred steeliness and self-assurance in their leaders, and a belief in the cleansing qualities of force. To know Pilane and Kgamanyane is to know Linchwe and Isang.

Such men, not the Ndebele or maBuru, introduced the art of cattle rustling to the trans-Vaal. They were not bullies and thieves like the invaders, who thought acquiring wealth meant taking other people's property. Though they may be said to have perfected the felonious crafts, the Kgatla enabled their purloined cattle to multiply. For a relatively small group in the violent and turbulent trans-Vaal, this amounted to nothing less than a remarkable, creative act. Their achievement has been overlooked as attention has been given to large, resilient kingdoms on the edges of the trans-Vaal – the BaSotho, BaPedi and AmaSwati, BaNgwato and BaKwena.[6] But these states had geography on their side, and were not obliged to move. Mountains and sandveld gave them their power to withstand invaders, whereas the Kgatla lived in open range with grass coveted by all and with only a few hills for defence. Without the luxury of natural barriers to fend off outsiders, the Kgatla built their fortunes by studying the forces contending for power in their midst (before and after the discovery of diamonds and gold), accumulating knowledge and new skills, and imagining a future in which the Kgatla could prosper. Their leaders thought together and they thought ahead. They knew the value of research, of taking calculated risks, of communicating with enemies as well as friends, and killing when it counted. So much was at stake because the Kgatla ran a social enterprise. Their enemies the maBuru were typical invaders in that they fought well as a group but quarrelled over spoils. They thought as individuals and amassed wealth each for oneself. The men who led the Kgatla had their differences, but settled them quickly and stayed together. Their purpose was strengthening the community one generation at a time, improving its ability to fend off new dangers and to displace weaker communities. At each stage, they took enough cattle to satisfy their needs but seldom more than they could protect. The BaKgatla were motivated by land and cattle hunger, but never greed. They desired prosperity and independence in the land of their ancestors.

What follows is the story of how Pilane and his heirs managed to pull off this feat as cattle rustling artists. The Kgatla took eighty years to reach their full powers, and not one of those years was easy.

ENDNOTES

1 Barnes (1932); Hodgson and Ballinger (1933).
2 Hodgson and Ballinger (1933: 52).
3 *Native Advisory Council*, 20th Session, 6–10 Mar. 1939: 68.
4 See 'Terms and Designations' for an explanation of the choice of this term.
5 Among the noteworthy: Thokwe (Sand), Madikwe (Marico), Matsukubjana (Hex), Kgetleng (Elands), Tshane (Apies), Dikgatlong (Harts), Tlokwe (Pienars), Magalikwena (Nylstrom), Oodi (Krokodil).
6 Parsons (1973); Sanders (1975); Thompson (1975); Bonner (1983); Delius (1984); Ramsay (1991).

Chapter one

MMADINALE ('THE CLAWER'): PILANE PHETO

KePilane amalosa
Mmadinale wagaMotswasejane

*[I am Pilane, the war-monger
the clawer, companion of Motswasejane]*

(Opening phrase of Pilane's praise poem (*leboko*), composed by himself; Schapera 1965: 55–57)

The centre of Pilane's world was located in the rolling bushveld and hills north of present-day Rustenburg, enclosed by the Kgetleng, Oodi and Madikwe rivers (Elands, Krokodil and Marico). This territory was ideal for grazing and hunting, because it possessed winter and summer grazing in close proximity to surface water provided by the many streams and rivers originating in the hills throughout the area and feeding the Limpopo River – except in times of prolonged drought. Its most prominent feature is Sefikile, the circular range of hills, known since Linchwe's grandfather's time as the Pilanesberg(en). Today most of these hills have been fenced in as the Pilanesberg Game Reserve and the southernmost portion has been turned into 'Sun City'. Long ago, at the base of the Pilanesberg's southeastern slopes near to the present Pilanesberg airport, Pilane established his last capital at Mmasebudule (on the farm Rhenosterfontein 86) along the Kgetleng River. Linchwe was born there in about 1858.

Pilane's predecessors had spilled blood to control this territory. Sovereignty over it was achieved through war in the time of his grandfather Molefe (d. 1790), great uncle Mmagotso (d. 1795) and father Pheto (d. 1810). The followers of these men defeated the Mabodisa, Madibana, Masiana, Modimosana and Seleka and incorporated their people. They also looted cattle from their neighbours: Fokeng, Tlhako, Mmatau, Mogopa Kwena, Ngwaketse and Hurutshe. Pheto boasted that his raiders were *lebophalaphala* ('the swelling flood') who returned as well with *tshopya* ('horn-cattle'), a euphemism for women. Augmented by war and pillaging, eto's followers were the most numerous of any group in the western trans-Vaal, and the most powerful. They called themselves BaKgatla baga Kgafela, followers of the royal descendants of Kgafela, venerators of *kgabo* ('vervet monkey').[1] Their capital was on Mabule hill, north of present Saulspoort, on the northern edge of the Pilanesberg. Applying a label such as tribe or group to Pheto's followers obscures much and conveys little as to their purpose, their structure or their methods. As best as can be understood, they appear to have formed a coalition of families of various origins operating under the direction of a single group of men tied closely together by birth, all sharing the conviction that their future hinged on acquiring people, cattle and territory. In effect they were a settled but loose community committed to raiding. Although they accepted Pheto's authority, deferring to him as kgosi ('supreme authority'), their loyalty to one another was too recent, intermarriage as yet too infrequent, and ties with neighbours still too intact to constitute anything approaching a cohesive unit.

Military success over the previous three decades had brought wealth and power to the BaKgatla, but it had also created conditions for civil war. Pheto and his predecessors reigned long enough to initiate and arm young men eager for booty, but too briefly to build a political base sturdy enough to protect the kingship from intrigue and transform a coalition of followers into a solid community. Jealousy among royal siblings had led to fighting on more than one occasion, and forced BaKgatla into taking sides. Such internal conflicts were common throughout the trans-Vaal, where tensions were heightened by growing insecurity in the region long before the *mfecane*. The significant wealth they had been accumulating in the previous decades meant that with each succession the BaKgatla who were involved in any political contest were risking ever higher stakes.[2] In some ways a MoKgatla of status was in greater danger living among his own people than in joining raids on his neighbours.

Pilane, of high royal birth, was, from the time he was a young man, close enough to power to place his life at risk. Born in about 1790 to Pheto by his second wife Sakalengwe, Pilane did not expect to succeed his father. He did not attempt either to become a rival to Letsebe, son of Pheto's first (great) wife. Pilane could not realistically have expected Letsebe to rule in his interest, and in any case Letsebe's junior brother, Thari, stood next in line. Pilane was more concerned with Letsebe's self-centeredness. Before succeeding to the throne, Letsebe dallied with women in a way that threatened to divide the royal family. His affair with the wife of his uncle Senwelo, who was regent after Pheto's death in 1810, led to a murder plot, an open fight between Kgatla regiments, and Senwelo's exile. Meanwhile Pilane was grooming himself as a military leader, with an eye to acquiring wealth. His royal birth gave him the position of second-in-command (behind Letsebe) of the fighting regiment maFiri ('hyenas'), which Pilane used to acquire cattle and safeguard his own life. Battleworthy regiments (*mephato*), and the extremely harsh initiation period used to form them, bred intense loyalty among fellow militiamen and devotion to their leaders.[3] For Pilane, it was best to serve Letsebe with such men at his back.

When Letsebe became kgosi in about 1815, Pilane was given the opportunity to show his loyalty and gain the favour of the Kgatla's youngest regiment. Letsebe was asked by Motswasele, kgosi of the BaKwena of 'Kgalagadi' (Botswana), for a regiment to aid his fight against the BaNgwaketse, who had looted Motswasele's cattle. Letsebe sent in the maFiri, who defeated the Ngwaketse, secured Motswasele's cattle, and delivered them back to the Kwena kgosi. Pilane led the maFiri, who Kgatla tradition alleges distinguished themselves in marked contrast to the Kwena fighting men. In appreciation, Motswasele granted the Kgatla the eastern, sandy portion of his territory (the *matlaba*) for use in the future if needed.[4] Pilane, still a young man, had enhanced his reputation and increased his cattle holdings. He fed his public persona with his own praise, 'I am Pilane, warmonger, the clawer, companion of Motswajane' (i.e. 'little' Motswasele). He then betrothed Morelle, and his choice is revealing. Morelle was the daughter of Magomeng, a renowned Kgatla hunter, who later played a crucial, though indirect, role in Pilane's rise to power. The trade for hunting trophies was growing in the region, and Pilane meant to take part. In later years, Pilane became an important ivory trader, but even as a man barely in his twenties, Pilane's choices of mates, and fathers-in-law, indicate that he had already seen his opportunities.

Pilane's reputation, not least of all his long-term plans, then lost its lustre. Suddenly the immediate concern became saving his life. Not long after returning from victory over the Ngwaketse, the Kgatla suffered their first invasion since the rise of Molefe fifty years prior. The forces of Thulare, leader of the BaPedi of the northeastern trans-Vaal, swept into the area and lifted thousands of cattle. The Kgatla's herds were decimated.[5] Pilane somehow managed to keep his cattle post intact, but he was not to keep it for long. By the time the Pedi attacked, Letsebe's talent for engendering hatred had led to his assassination and sent the Kgatla into a rapid descent of internecine bloodletting. In 1820, the year of the Pedi invasion, Senwelo engineered Letsebe's murder and installed himself once more as regent (Thari being too young to take over). Perhaps for his own safety, Senwelo shifted the Kgatla capital to Tlhokwane hill (Mmampana), 30 kilometres north of Mabule. But revenge soon had its day; Senwelo was killed in turn. Pilane may have been involved in his uncle's murder, but regardless, he and all the other sons of Pheto were threats to the new regent Motlotle, who soon made it obvious he intended seizing the throne for himself. With the Pedi gone, Motlotle set about killing Pheto's heirs one by one. Motlotle's brutal ambition destroyed what remained of Kgatla cohesiveness, and all but Motlotle's supporters scattered to the hills. Thari, Pilane and the other of Pheto's surviving sons fled west of the Pilanesberg and gained refuge with the BaTlhako of kgosi Mabe (Mabieskraal). Motlotle enticed Thari to return, and had him stabbed to death. Thari's demise meant that Pilane was now next in line, and being of age to succeed Letsebe, he became Motlotle's next target. When word of Thari's death reached Pilane, he fled Mabieskraal and travelled northwest towards Botswana. For the next two years, Pilane secreted himself away from all other Kgatla, trusting none of them. But he was not travelling alone. While in Mabieskraal, he had married his first wife Mankube, daughter of Bogatsu, the late kgosi of the BaTlokwa and fighting ally of the Kgatla; the Tlkowa were settled near to the Tlhako at Pilwe.[6]

Pilane put his time in exile to good use. He and Mankube made their way to the Madikwe River where, thanks to information most likely gained from Magomeng, he located Ngwako Sekgotlela, a well-known Kwena hunter. Together they trapped game in pits all along the Madikwe. Trading game trophies was no doubt part of the operation, as was Pilane's becoming acquainted with the territories on either side of the Madikwe. On the left bank was the land granted to the Kgatla by Motswasele of the Kwena, whom Pilane had aided in his fight against the Ngwaketse a few years before. Pilane also gained knowledge that he and his brother-in-law Matlapeng would share in the years to come to trade ivory to Delagoa Bay (now Maputo Bay) and to the Cape.

Pilane also escaped further turmoil in the Pilanesberg, where the mfecane had finally reached the Kgatla. In 1824 the BaKololo of Sebetwane, cattle-hungry refugees from the battle of Dithakong, invaded the Kgatla from the south.[7] They scattered the Kgatla, then moved northwest into Botswana. In the chaos, Motlotle fled with a handful of followers to Tshwene-tshwene in the Dwarsberg, where some Kgatla who had fled his tyranny, found him. They murdered him on the spot. Soon thereafter, Pilane was discovered near the Madikwe River by other scattered Kgatla, including two royal headmen, Molefi and Segale. They told Pilane of Motlotle's death and entreated him to return home to accept *bogosi*. Pilane consented, and with Mankube alongside he took back home with him the trading connections that would underpin his authority as the new head of the Kgatla.

Pilane wasted no time. In quick succession, he established four bases, each with a distinct purpose. He went first to Letlhakeng, a day's walk from the Madikwe and northeast of the Dwarsberg, where the hunter Magomeng had collected and fed many Kgatla who had gathered at his place after being scattered by Motlotle. There he was accepted as the new Kgatla kgosi, and there he finally married his first and long-betrothed Morelle, Magomeng's daughter. Then he moved away from the veld and up into the more secure Pilanesberg, settling in the hills west of Saulspoort at Monamaneng (Kafferskraal 43). Soon thereafter he shifted headquarters to the Witfontein Hills, 50 kilometres north of Saulspoort at Bogopana (Maroelasfontein 366), and then again to Mmamodimokwana (Schildpadnest 385), a few kilometres east of Bogopana. Letlhakeng and Bogopana served as hunting bases, Monamaneng as the main settlement of the Kgatla, and both Bogopana and Mmamodimokwana were near to the copper and chromite deposits mined in generations past by Pilane's ancestors, including his father Pheto.[8] Within two or three years, at least three if not more additional marriages were arranged, and several sons were born, all linking royals and commoners to Pilane's kingship and gaining them access to his multiple ventures.[9] Pilane also had a regiment (*Lomakgomo*) formed, the first since Motlotle's usurpation, and it was headed by Pilane's junior half-brother Kgotlamaswe.[10]

Pilane pronounced Mankube, daughter of the Tlokwa, as his great wife over some objections by the Kgatla, who regarded Morelle as entitled to the highest rank. Pilane overruled his people, claiming that Mankube's loyalty to him in the previous years of difficulty had earned her the position.[11] Pilane was also politically shrewd. Mankube's children would have no maternal kin nearby competing for influence in his affairs, challenging his authority or arousing the jealousies of other Kgatla. Given the precarious state of affairs in the region, and the internal strains that only recently had given rise to lethal intrigue in the Kgatla royal family, Pilane was safer having a senior wife who was an outsider and therefore had greater influence over her children and undivided loyalty to him. Moreover her royal Tlokwa descent gave her high status and entitled her to respect among the Kgatla. By taking as his junior wives the daughters of different Kgatla wards he could ask for their support at less cost.[12] Around 1830 Mankube gave birth to Kgamanyane ('little hartebeest'), Pilane's heir.

As he moved to consolidate his following and create a new ruling lineage, Pilane also connected his people to the region's developing trading networks. Pilane was aware that middlemen, linked to markets in the Cape to the south and Delagoa Bay to the northeast, were looking for products that the Kgatla could provide. Ivory in particular was in demand in both markets, while skins also reached the Cape and copper went to Delagoa Bay.[13] The trade in copper to Delagoa Bay was generations old, and the long association the Kgatla had with copper workings in the trans-Vaal suggests they were part of it.[14] By what methods or trade routes Pilane came into contact with long-distance traders is unclear, but what is likely is that Pilane re-established the Delagoa Bay connection and initiated contact with Cape traders. The Pilanesberg, located in North West province, was at the time distant from active trade routes. Those lay to the west through the North West Province and eastern Botswana, and to the north along the Limpopo River through Mozambique or overland into the present-day Mpumalanga Province, in either case extending to the Limpopo Province.[15] At the time Pilane was building his following in the Pilanesberg, the predominant trade links for the people in Botswana and in the Limpopo Province were with Delagoa Bay. Pilane was soon trading in that direction, from Bogopana and Mmamodimokwana. In the 1840s, Pilane was met by traveller d'Elegorgue passing through the Pilanesberg area, and he told d'Elegorgue 'of white men living ... in a country Mandrisse' and referred to a friend 'Mashlapire' (Matlapeng) who had visited 'the Portuguese colony after a month's march'.[16] Pilane's contact with Delagoa Bay was not recent, because d'Elegorgue mentioned that several years before he met him, Pilane had temporarily 'abandoned the area [Pilanesberg] to be on better terms with [to live nearer] the whites'.[17] D'Elegorgue was referring to the period, 1831–1837, when Pilane spent most of his time in the Limpopo Province to avoid capture by Mzilikazi, whom he had offended over issues related to trade (see below).

Early in his reign Pilane also struck up a relationship with the traders and hunters operating north of the Gariep (Orange) River.[18] In the mid-1830s, Andrew Smith, travelling through the present-day North West and Gauteng provinces, learned that 'Bastards and Corannas and Griquas had long before [i.e. before 1831, when Berends' commando raided Mzilikazi – see below] been in the habit of visiting that chief [Pilane] hunting in the country and exchanging [goods]'.[19] The maSetedi, as the Tswana speakers then referred to the brigands of mixed background, had embroiled themselves in the affairs of the Ngwaketse, Kwena, Hurutshe, Ngwato and Kaa at least since the early nineteenth century. The most noteworthy in this regard were the German-Kora Jan Bloem Jr. and the Dutch-born Coenraad de Buys.[20] But loot, rather than trade with the Cape, was their motivation. In 1826, however, at Boetsap on the Harts River, Berends Berends established a community of Griqua, Bastaards, Kora and Tlhaping and Rolong refugees; he developed agriculture and began to 'hunt and trade further into the interior'.[21] Berends' shift away from cattle and slave raids to commerce coincides with Pilane's rise to power in the Pilanesberg, and it would appear that soon both were in touch with one another.

The maSetedi–Pilane connection could not have developed without the blessing of Mzilikazi. The AmaNdebele of Mzilikazi had moved into Gauteng around August 1823 (about the time Motlotle was murdered by his own people) and centred their capital south of the Magaliesberg along the Vaal River. From there they raided in their vicinity and northwest to the Molopo River and beyond into Ngwaketse territory.[22] In the winter of 1827 they shifted their headquarters to the Apies River, close to Pilane's Kgatla. Mzilikazi is notorious in the literature for his regiments' wholesale destruction of trans-Vaal communities and stealing their cattle and people, but his role in encouraging trade is seldom acknowledged.[23] The territories his regiments controlled, and the border areas they tried to empty as buffer zones, were organised primarily to afford the Ndebele security from attack, but they also constituted a trading zone inside of which hunting and trading were permitted, and in which trade with other markets was regulated. Persons with trading connections, such as Pilane, were in a position to benefit from Mzilikazi's presence because they were of particular value to the Ndebele king. Those without them had fewer options. Many of the Kgatla's neighbours were killed or driven out by Mzilikazi's regiments, and not all for resisting.[24]

Among Pilane's first considerations in regrouping the Kgatla under his leadership was building up a following in a territory dominated by Mzilikazi. He and several of his peers chose the policy of submission.[25] Mokgatle, who was installed as kgosi of the Fokeng after his regent uncle Noge tried to rob some of Mzilikazi's cattle (and fled to escape execution for his daring), recognised Mzilikazi and was permitted to gather his people. Thus began a long and prosperous reign for this man, who accumulated wealth from serving the more powerful.[26] Mogale of the BaPo, Mabalane of the BaPhiring and Mkgosi of the BaLete took similar steps, and were allowed to keep their cattle.[27] When he was installed by his people as their new leader, Pilane had immediately to acknowledge Mzilikazi's supremacy in turn and gave him reasons for accepting it. Pilane's setting up his four capitals in the Pilanesberg, and reviving the Delagoa Bay trade connection had to have been part of the arrangement, as was rendering to Mzilikazi the proceeds of hunting and agriculture. Pilane gave Mzilikazi skins, ivory and sorghum.[28] Mzilikazi's people also had an insatiable demand for beads, which at the time were available only from Delagoa Bay, and Pilane alone among his subjects had such connections.[29] In return, Pilane's people retained their cattle, and Pilane was allowed to trade with Berends' hunters.

Mzilikazi also had reasons for wanting a few Griqua to pay the occasional visit. At a formative stage in developing defences against his enemies, Mzilikazi was interested in the Griqua's use of firearms. Soon after the Ndebele arrived in the central trans-Vaal Mzilikazi had learned from his Sotho captives how, two months previously, a few armed Griqua on horseback and two white missionaries had turned back thousands of attacking 'Mantatee' at Dithakong.[30] Berends Berends was among the defenders.[31] Mzilikazi paid close attention to the maSetedi, and soon distinguished between those who wanted his cattle and women, and those who were interested instead in hunting and trade, avocations the Ndebele were not well organised to pursue. In 1826 or 1827, Mzilikazi gave Berends' people access to the hunting areas north of the Magaliesberg and allowed them to trade with Pilane. He did so even though other maSetedi were troubling the Ndebele. Since 1823, in fact, Mzilikazi had been harassed by cattle raiders from the southwest, principally by Molitsane of the BaTaung and his Griqua and Kora allies, including the notorious cattle and slave raider Jan Bloem Jr., Mzilikazi regarded these raids as serious enough to shift his base from the Vaal River to north of the Magaliesberg in 1827, but he did not interpret them as involving Berends. Gradually, his view began to change. In July 1828, Bloem formed a large commando and, with Molitsane's support, raided a series of Mzilikazi's cattle posts on the north side of the Magaliesberg. They made off with 3,000 cattle. Bloem's success was but momentary, because the Ndebele soon tracked down the rustlers and repossessed their herds, at no little cost to Bloem's party.[32] Mzilikazi noted that his move to the Magaliesberg seemed to have the effect of emboldening, rather than discouraging, the maSetedi. Their greater familiarity with Mzilikazi's new territory than the old might have had played a part. Mzilikazi was beginning to conclude that his generosity to Berends was taken for granted and that allowing Berends' hunters into his territory increased his exposure to the maSetedi. His suspicions could only have increased when, several months after the 1828 raid, Berends allowed Jan Bloem to settle at Boetsap.[33] In the following year, Mzilikazi launched a major assault on Molitsane, dispersing his people. Then, in 1830 he banned maSetedi and European traders in his dominions without his permission.[34]

Before he lost his trade connection with Berends, Pilane was already plotting against Mzilikazi. True to character, Pilane was as decisive as he was foolhardy. In his last meeting with Berends, Pilane encouraged his trading partner to mount a commando against his Ndebele overlord. Berends returned to Boetsap, sought permission from colonial authorities to attack Mzilikazi, and then set about organising a major commando.[35] Pilane's move to engineer Mzilikazi's ouster reflects just how valuable the maSetedi–Pilane trade was to him, how highly he was regarded by Berends, and how strong Pilane's vision of an Ndebele-free Pilanesberg must have been. It would be a mistake to interpret Pilane's ready submission to Mzilikazi several years before as evidence of a lack of spirit or savvy, though giving way to the Ndebele seems now a much saner step than this new, radical move. Pilane did not look the bold type, but under pressure he evinced boldness. Perhaps it was because his short, thin physique and misshaped head commanded more amusement than respect. He would have stood looking up at, and well within the shadow of, the bulky Mzilikazi at two metres. Pilane's true aura, when provoked, was cast rather by an excitability – an energy that could border on wildness. He was capable of just about anything, and used to risking his life. One line of his boastful self-praise reveals the contrast between his harmless appearance and the impact he thought himself actually capable of creating:

> [I am] a servant who loots without a horse,
> he hasn't a horse, Pilane Pheto
> he loots only on foot, Pilane,
> the Avenger of the Ape[36]

Pilane viewed himself on the same level with the maSetedi, as capable as they of robbing their enemies, and as keen to repay injury.

Berends' commando nearly succeeded.[37] Consisting of several hundred armed Griqua, Kora and Bastaards on horseback, and as many as a thousand auxiliaries supplied by the Rolong and Hurutshe, Berends' force advanced into the Magaliesberg when Mzilikazi's main forces were away to the northwest attacking the BaNgwato. The timing could not have been better.[38] Over the span of a day commando parties, meeting no resistance, combed cattle posts along the northern foot of the Magaliesberg and gathered up thousands of head. They made off, too, with women caught in the vicinity. Mzilikazi and his depleted followers retreated to the hills, where one account states that the *inkosi* cried for the loss not only of his cattle but at being 'left with a ruined tribe'.[39] After two days of moving the cattle slowly back in the direction they had come, the commando stopped for the night and, confident that Mzilikazi could not retaliate, slept with no one standing watch. Meanwhile, the older, but able-bodied Ndebele (*madodo*) who had stayed behind during the Ngwato campaign, had mobilised and traced the rustlers' spoor. Just before dawn, they attacked, driving cattle into the encampment to break up the commando, then set upon them with their broad-bladed spears. In the chaos, maSetedi guns killed more comrades than enemies, and only a handful from the original commando of 300 to 400 escaped. It was a slaughter. Berends Berends, who had been camping behind the Magaliesberg while the commando was busy raiding, was one of the lucky ones, but his dreams of a maSetedi–Tswana alliance were finished. From this point, his interest in trade was confined to Bechuanaland.

Pilane also escaped with his life. Mzilikazi, who knew Pilane was involved in the raid, sent regiments to destroy his towns, conscript his men into the Ndebele army and take all his cattle. They also killed Morelle, his second wife. But Pilane, honed to anticipate disaster, had already fled into exile, this time heading northeast.[40] Pilane's trade connections again served as a lifeline. He made his way through and beyond the Waterberg to the people the Kgatla called 'BaLaka'.[41] They were the AmaNdebele of Langa, under inkosi Mapela, located in the Makapansberg near present Potgietersrus. The Langa were one of the small groups of trans-Vaal Ndebele whose ancestors migrated into the present-day Mpumalanga, Limpopo and Gauteng provinces beginning in the seventeenth century. In Pilane's time, Mapela's people were known as smelters of copper and tin, as well as iron, and involved in trade in tobacco and ivory.[42] While Pilane gained refuge at Mapela's, the other Kgatla who managed to escape made their way west, past the Madikwe (Marico) River to the headwaters of the Ngotwane River, where they and their cattle became prey of their old enemy, the Ngwaketse.[43] The Kgatla who remained behind were exempted from serving in the Ndebele military and looked after Mzilikazi's cattle. Pilane's uncle Molefi was recognised by Mzilikazi as their headman.[44]

Within a year after the Berends raid, the Ndebele left the Magaliesberg. Fearing another attack from Dingane in present-day KwaZulu-Natal and desiring contact with French and English missionaries, Mzilikazi moved his people west of the Madikwe River to Mosega in the North West province. In the months before the move, his regiments invaded this territory and cleared a large area for his occupation.[45] Their relocation reduced the Pilanesberg from a principal grazing suburb of Mzilikazi's Magaliesberg base to the Ndebele's most distant cattle outpost on the western periphery of the kingdom.[46] In the area between the Pilanesberg and Madikwe River, Tswana were used to herd cattle, collect ostrich and other bird feathers and raise tobacco.[47] No longer a threat to Mzilikazi, Pilane was permitted to return to his people.

Pilane was soon embroiled with Mzilikazi again. In Pilane's absence, his half-brother Kgotlamaswe made a bid for power, most likely with Mzilikazi's support. When Pilane returned, Kgotlamaswe declared himself the kgosi and refused to recognise Pilane. With Molefi's support, Pilane gained enough of a following to oust Kgotlamaswe, who went straight to Mosega.[48] Soon thereafter, Mzilikazi offered Pilane a herd of his cattle to oversee, but Pilane took it as a ruse to put him off guard and have him executed. Pilane bolted for the Makapansberg and gained refuge again at Mapela's.[49] Pilane's suspicions were well founded; when Andrew Smith passed through the Pilanesberg in 1835 he learned that two Ndebele regiments were on Pilane's trail.[50]

While he remained safe with the Langa, Pilane caught a glimpse of the trans-Vaal's future a few kilometres east of the Makapansberg. In about May 1836 a large party of *Bahibidu* ('red people') made their way north through the Strydpoortberg at Pienaarsnek. Led by Louis Tregardt, the group consisted of thirty wagons and drove large herds of cattle, sheep and horses. Several weeks later, Andries Hendrik Potgieter and eleven others on horseback traced Tregardt's route up to the Soutpansberg. The white colonisation of the trans-Vaal was about to get underway.[51] There is no way of knowing whether or not Pilane witnessed this contingent passing through, but given the active intersection of trade routes in this area with which he was long familiar, most likely he soon knew about it. The presence of the *trekkers* in present-day Limpopo province would have been important news, though not startling in quality. The Pedi of Sekwati were already in diplomatic contact with the Sotho of Moshoeshoe, and their messengers travelled the route the trekkers almost certainly adopted. And through old contacts with the maSetedi, many Tswana north of the Orange river understood that the Bahibidu coming out of the Cape were a different breed of *maKgoa* (foreigners, whites) than those who had been hunting or setting up mission stations.[52] Pilane may have assumed at that point that the appearance of Tregardt and Potgieter altered none of his prospects in the Pilanesberg. But within months, he knew they made all the difference. After finding Tregardt and reconnoitring the Soutpansberg, Potgieter took the route south to Thaba Nchu, met Gert Maritz's party, and in January 1837 formed a commando to raid Mosega. Nine months later Potgieter and Piet Uys's commando near the Madikwe River drove back Mzilikazi's forces again. Mzilikazi and his people then pulled out of the trans-Vaal and retreated north.[53] Word of these battles and the Ndebele exodus must have travelled quickly, because Pilane soon slipped back to the Pilanesberg.[54] And within a year, Bahibidu began to appear.

Apart from their reddish skin, bushy beards and long straight hair, the Bahibidu or maBuru as they soon were known, were similar to earlier visitors. They and the maSetedi came from the same direction, spoke the same language, rode horses, had guns and raided for cattle, sheep and servants. They also both fought on horseback in groups and were interested in hunting and trading. Such was probably the similarity that struck Pilane first. After all, Louis Tregardt passed through Limpopo province asking the way to Delagoa Bay.[55]

However, already significant differences must have been apparent. The maBuru coming into the area arrived with women and children, whereas only maSetedi men came that way and took African wives. The maSetedi returned to their homes after raiding or trading, but maBuru seemed bent on securing a place to settle, having no home in the south. Compared to the Ndebele, who also came as a group to make these prime grazing areas their permanent homeland, the maBuru looked a mere handful, but they demonstrated at Mosega and the Madikwe that they were mightier than Pilane's last overlords. They had many more wagons than the few maKgoa hunters, travellers and missionaries already seen in these parts, and the maBuru circled them to fight, with powerful effect. The questions on Pilane's mind must have included the following: What do they want from me and what do they want from my neighbours? Can I submit to them and still get something? Will they allow me to collect my followers and rule them? Will I be able to trade? Will they let me have cattle? Land?

Potgieter's trekkers entered Rustenburg and Pretoria districts gradually, fanned out into the good grazing areas and close to the springs. From the Swartruggens in the west to the Magaliesberg in the east, they divided up land for themselves, and let Africans know they were their subjects. The trekkers met little resistance. Perhaps because the trekkers were spread out and relatively few were north of the Magaliesberg, many like Pilane felt safe re-entering the area now that the Ndebele were gone. But all understood that they would have to submit. Mokgatle, kgosi of the Fokeng, welcomed Potgieter as a new conqueror, offered him support and received land in return (Kookfontein 265, where the present Phokeng stands).[56] Nearby, Potgieter selected two farms for himself, Magathashoek 270 and Buffelshoek 325. Other *dikgosi* followed Mokgatle's example by recognising Potgieter and asking him for land.[57] Pilane was among them.[58] About this time, Pilane acknowledged the coming of the new order in a more personal, symbolic way. His fourth wife Mmakgabo bore him a son, who was named Mantirisi ('Andries').[59]

There is every reason to believe that Potgieter came to know Pilane just as Berends had known him – a man with useful connections. It is likely, too, that from discussions with Berends in Thaba Nchu, Potgieter knew about Pilane before he led his trekkers into the Magaliesberg.[60] Pilane had parlayed his trading savvy with Berends and others to gain privileges from Mzilikazi, and he was soon to enjoy under the maBuru the freedom to pursue commerce. Before he could become of service to Potgieter, however, Pilane had first to deal with the Ndebele, who wanted him to fill the same role, and then move closer to the maBuru to gain their protection. In 1841, Mzilikazi sent a large force to attack Pilane at Bogopana and to force him to return with them to Matabeleland.[61] About 800 Kgatla died and most of Pilane's cattle were taken, along with three of Pilane's sons as hostages: Kgamanyane, Mantirisi and Moselekatse.[62] Pilane promised to follow them to Mzilikazi's but reneged.[63] The purpose of this raid remains somewhat unclear, but it appears to have been intended to gain Pilane's cooperation in opening up trade connections. The reason for supposing so is in the successful negotiation of the children's release, and for the cordial trade relations between the Kgatla and the Ndebele that can be documented at a later stage.[64] After raiding the Kgatla, the Ndebele attacked the Po, then living under kgosi Mogale on Mogale's River east of the *dorp* Magaliesberg (later Rustenburg). But Mogale and his people were aided by the Boers, who drove away the attackers.[65] Not long after the raids, Pilane moved his capital to the southeastern slopes of the Pilanesberg, because he wanted, in his words, to 'live closer to the whites.'[66] In addition to security, Pilane probably also had trade in mind; he built his new capital at Mmasebudule, north of Magaliesberg, on the Potchefstroom–Limpopo road.[67]

As they drove the Ndebele out of the trans-Vaal and ended the threat of Ndebele raids from their new base in present-day Zimbabwe, the ma-Buru introduced their own harsh form of law and order. As with the Ndebele, the maBuru could be ruthless with their enemies, exploitative of those they conquered, and generous towards those whose talents or skills they needed. They conscripted the defeated into their service. They took captive women and children and taught them their language. And like the Ndebele, maBuru readily took the lives and property of Africans. Yet, important differences would have been apparent to Pilane and other sharp observers in the Magaliesberg soon after the changeover in rule. The Kgatla and other African communities of the trans-Vaal knew that as the Nde-

MMADINALE ('THE CLAWER'): PILANE PHETO

bele had conquered territory, they took direct control of the survivors. Young women captives became wives, young men, military recruits, and most survivors, part of the Ndebele nation. The maBuru, on the other hand, wanted territory but seemed to have no ambitions for the conquered people on it, no roles available to swell their communities. Those conquered by the Ndebele had little choice but to become Ndebele, and even the maSetedi and maKgoa, such as Bloem and Buys, took wives from the places they resided rather than import them. But the maBuru married only maBuru, and multiplied from within. MaBuru were made up of family groups bent on acquiring wealth in various ways; the most powerful pursued hunting, raiding and trading; the others, cattle-keeping and farming. The hunting type needed young men to help them, as mercenaries. Women and youngsters were used by the farmers, but only as servants, not to become their wives or children. Under the maBuru the conquered could choose to render labour for free or in some way hire themselves out.

The leaders of conquered people faced similar dilemmas. The Ndebele had either killed these leaders, driven them away or made them vassals overseeing cattle or paying tribute in trade items. Leaders of adjoining territories had been expected to render tribute as well, failing which they were subject to attack. Disobedience and defiance had been grounds for quick execution. The maBuru, however, depended on conquered leaders to control their subjects and organise them to serve maBuru. They even gave them a title, *kapitein*, which made them responsible to maBuru on behalf of their people. Kapiteins were encouraged to increase their wealth and exercise power over their people, and if effective their lives were seldom at risk among maBuru. Strong kapiteins were no threat to maBuru authority, because kapiteins were ineligible to aspire to control over maBuru cattle, land or maBuru themselves. Of course, lest their power be converted into rebellion, kapiteins were forbidden to collect their people and required to scatter them about in small villages. Only if they failed to exercise influence over their people did the maBuru punish them or groom a replacement. A disgruntled kapitein could leave, but others of his group were sure to replace him. Conquered leaders under the Ndebele either lost their people to Mzilikazi or fled with them away from his authority; whereas under the maBuru, kapiteins could keep their people as a servile group or risk breaking them up in an attempt to flee maBuru authority.

Those who could or would not perform the kapitein's duties, did not remain. Mogale and his people, for example, were settled along Mogale's River on well-watered land, which attracted some of the first maBuru settlers.[68] Soon, they were forcing the kapitein to have his people dig irrigation channels. Then they learned from one of his people that Mogale had guns hidden in a cave. Under constant suspicion, Mogale was then betrayed again, this time by his own son, Maruatona, who organised auxiliaries to assist the maBuru in their attack on the Langa Ndebele. Mogale and a few followers then fled to Moshoeshoe, whereupon Maruatona succeeded him as kapitein.[69] Nearby to Mogale, the starving people of Mmamogale[70] had reason at first to be grateful for the arrival of Potgieter and his men, who gave them cattle as well as gifts to Mmamogale, the recognised kapitein. But Mmamogale had the misfortune of having *Kommandant* Gerrit Johannes Kruger settle next door, and soon the pressure to do Kruger's bidding was applied. When David Livingstone passed through in 1847, Mmamogale bared his back to Livingstone and displayed his whip scars. Within the year, he, too, had left for Basutoland, with only part of his people.[71]

Those kapiteins who cooperated with the maBuru tended to flourish in comparison. Mokgatle, next to whom Andries Potgieter settled for a time, was among the area's most wealthy kapiteins. During the 1840s, Mokgatle's followers steadily increased, having settled in fifteen villages by 1847.[72] He had many cattle, and was manufacturing copper ornaments, and iron and wood implements to sell.[73] Potgieter, who lacked interest in developing his agricultural land, placed few labour burdens on Mokgatle's people. He even permitted Mokgatle to have guns.[74] Potgieter, the leader of the maBuru's hunting and raiding faction, divided his time between Magaliesberg and the new settlement of Ohrigstad in Limpopo province, from which he hoped to develop trade with Delagoa Bay, especially in ivory and slaves.[75] In return for the privileges he extended to Mokgatle, Potgieter expected Mokgatle's men to assist in raiding Africans on the fringe of maBuru settlement. When precisely Mokgatle's regiments began joining Potgieter's men as auxiliaries is not clear, but the Fokeng were among those who helped invade Pediland in 1849.[76] Most likely they were part of the African contingent used to raid the Langa Ndebele in 1845 and Moletse Kwena in 1847.[77] Mokgatle's people also served as Potgieter's agents. In 1848 his men delivered ultimatums on Potgieter's behalf to Sechele, Potgieter's main enemy on the western frontier.[78] And by then Mokgatle's responsibilities included seeing that young runaway slaves (*inboekelinge*) were caught and returned to their maBuru owners.[79]

Potgieter's rule in the Magaliesberg was tied to his ambitions to establish a centre for hunting and raiding in Mpumalanga. Not interested in herding or farming, for which Magaliesberg was so well suited, he and his followers were inclined to use their central trans-Vaal farms for access to the *Adjunct Raad*[80] in Potchefstroom and as distribution points for supplying Boer farmers in the area with cattle, children and women stolen in their raids in present-day Mpumalanga and Limpopo provinces. These human captives, known as inboekelinge (literally 'apprentices'), were sold to Boer farmers, who in turned trained them as servants, artisans, herders and hunters.[81] In 1845 Potgieter and his followers began to transfer their residences to Ohrigstad, within a short distance of Delagoa Bay. Trading links were extended into central Mozambique and to the port of Inhambane. Until Potgieter moved his headquarters from Ohrigstad to Schoemansdal in Limpopo province in 1848, however, Potgieter remained *kommandant-generaal* and tried to keep all Boers in the trans-Vaal under his leadership.[82] Until at least 1849 he paid regular visits to Magaliesberg, which was receiving a steady stream of Boer immigrants.

He and Magaliesberg Kommandant Gert Kruger became the proponents, too, of excluding the English from the new Boer colony. Though himself in contact with English traders at Delagoa Bay and in the trans-Vaal, Potgieter raised the British bugbear among trans-Vaal colonists as a way of keeping out those in the Cape who were opposed to his scheme or keen to push him aside.[83] Of particular offence to Potgieter and the Magaliesberg Boers was the London Missionary Society (LMS), whose missions cum trade stations were located among the Tswana on the western frontier of Boer settlement. Of these, the Kwena of Sechele in particular opposed Boer expansion into their areas, acquired firearms from Cape-based traders and welcomed Africans emigrating from Boer territory. Sechele's LMS missionary David Livingstone also riled Potgieter by publishing reports of his slave raids in the Cape press. The last thing Potgieter desired was giving the Cape government an incentive to annex the trans-Vaal as they had Natal in 1842, incite Africans against Boers, and open the trans-Vaal to Cape interests. In 1848, when Livingstone visited the trans-Vaal and tried to set up a mission school at Mogkatle's, Potgieter and Kruger threatened Livingstone and wrote to the LMS demanding his recall.[84]

Others who accused Potgieter of oppressing Africans were threatened with libel suits. Potgieter and Kruger's anti-British campaign was effective in the trans-Vaal. As the traveller Baines discovered when passing through the Potchefstroom district, the Boers 'talk of nothing but the *Vervlugte* English-man'.[85]

Pilane was Potgieter and Kruger's African counterpart. He was the first leader of the area to be approached by the LMS, in 1844, and he rejected their approaches.[86] Among all the African leaders in the trans-Vaal, Pilane was most unfriendly to missionaries, to the point of being contemptuous. In 1845, when Pilane visited Mosielele of the Mmanaana Kgatla at Mabotsa, he was introduced to Rogers Edwards who headed the nearby LMS station. Pilane chided Edwards, calling him Mosielele's 'child'.[87] He regarded the missionary, in other words, as dependent on the chief, as unable to live on his own or command others. Pilane's insult shows that he believed in force as governing relations and determining one's position, a conviction that would have been reinforced by his having become Potgieter's most powerful African ally.

Pilane's military presence was felt all over the Magaliesberg and beyond. After Mokgatle had trouble maintaining his authority and was overthrown, Pilane's regiment marched in and reinstalled him.[88] And when cattle raiders in the area were mistaken for Ramokoka's Phalane, Pilane drove Ramokoka's people out of their settlements at Mooi River.[89] Sometime during the 1840s he also attacked the Mfatlha Ndebele and made their leader, 'Zwaartbooi' as the maBuru called him, a vassal.[90] In 1848 one of his regiments (maNoga, under Molatlhegi Dikobe) travelled to the present North West Province and helped install Montshiwa as kgosi of the Tshidi Rolong.[91] His ability to threaten force even outside his domain was probably rooted in authoritarianism within. In an act reminiscent of the powerful Mzilikazi's feelings of insecurity, Pilane accused two of his military officers of wanting to bewitch him, and had them executed.[92]

Along with might, Pilane had freedom of movement. From Mmasebudule, Pilane maintained contacts over a wide area. In 1843, when the naturalist Adulphe d'Elegorgue encountered him, Pilane was connected by trade to Sofala. The Kgatla obtained brass from there, and used it to manufacture earrings and bracelets. Pilane also told him of 'Mandrisse' (Inhambane?), a Portuguese town east-northeast of the Soutpansberg.[93] He had heard about it from 'Maschlapire' (Matlapeng, his brother-in-law), who had travelled there, taking a month each way.[94] He traded two small tusks of ivory with d'Elegorgue in return for a gun. Pilane was also known in the west, where Cape-based traders were active. In 1844 hunter-traveller George Methuen learned that Mosielele was negotiating for the marriage of Pilane's daughter.[95] Apart from being an LMS station, Mabotsa was a Tswana trading centre and stop on the wagon trade into Bechuanaland.[96] Before the end of the 1840s J.W. Wilson, a trader in Bechuanaland, regarded Mmasebudule as a place to sell guns.[97]

Pilane became a prosperous man under Potgieter, and widely known. In 1847 when he passed through the Rustenburg district en route to the Waterberg, David Livingstone reckoned Pilane's people to be 'more numerous than those we visited', comparing them favourably in this respect to the people under Mokgatle.[98] Livingstone did not refer to the adjacent mountains as Pilanesberg, but they were known as such by the Dutch speakers who named them in Pilane's honour; they were soon to be known as far as the Cape through the published letters of hunter Joseph McCabe.[99] Pilane's stature and wealth was attested by his thirteen wives, more than twice the number of his father Pheto Molefe.[100] All but two he married from Kgatla wards and only Mankube had he brought in from the outside.[101] His choices had the effect of distributing cattle among his people, because of the bogadi he provided his Kgatla in-laws.[102]

Pilane's success reflected his great value to Potgeiter, for his knowledge of and connections in the region and for his willingness to police other Africans and procure men for military service. As with Mokgatle's, Pilane's regiments are first mentioned assisting the maBuru in the 1849 attack on the Pedi.[103] Yet, the extended military involvement of the Kgatla with the Boers into the 1850s and 1860s, and Pilane's ability to move his regiments around the Magaliesberg in the 1840s, strongly suggest that the Kgatla, like the Fokeng, supported Potgieter's earlier military campaigns, which began in 1845. Pilane probably forced the least respected Kgatla to provide military conscripts. This would explain Pilane's boast of having executed two of his military officers, whom he accused of wanting to bewitch him. These men, Ramotshedisi and Mabine, were of the Masiana ward, which was made up of commoners descended from lowly Kgalagadi stock:

> Pilane is a rock of ironstone,
> He is a slippery rock, Pilane;

Those who touch it will lose their fingers;
Mabine touched it and lost his fingers.
He's also a torch pointing out sorcerers;
should he point you out with it you can die;
it pointed out the induna Ramotshedisi,
of Masiana Masilo's ward,
and he died, he really died, the induna,
he failed to revive again, the induna,
Ramotshedisi of Masiana ward.[104]

Pilane Pheto died in April or May 1848 at the approximate age of 58 years.[105] Soon thereafter, Pilane and Mankube's son Kgamanyane was installed as the new kgosi. The moment of Kgatla succession occurred when Boer leadership was also changing. In 1849 Potgieter and his hunting faction left the Magaliesberg area, and the Boer farming and herding community assumed greater control. Potchefstroom was growing fast as a market for trans-Vaal goods to supply the Cape, and an increasing number of Boer farmers in Magaliesberg set their sites on supplying it. After 1850 they steadily increased their demands for agricultural labour, and the farmers expected Boer officials to make Africans supply it. The officers who dealt most directly with kapiteins were the *veldkornetten* (field-cornets). They were elected by the local Boers and could call them out to help impose law and order on kapiteins and their people. Pilane's veldkornet was a young man who belonged to Potgieter's group, but when Potgieter left for good, he chose to remain behind in the Magaliesberg and pursue his ambitions there. At the time Kgamanyane succeeded his father, this veldkornet was rising in importance as a military and political leader, and soon he would be appointed to his uncle Potgieter's old position as kommandant. The veldkornet's name was Stephanus Johannes Paulus Kruger. Just as Potgieter and Pilane's fortunes were tied closely together, the same proved to be the case with Kruger and Kgamanyane.

ENDNOTES

1 The history of Pilane's predecessors is preserved in the praise poems and other oral traditions recorded in Mochudi by Isaac Schapera in the 1930s, and to some degree by Paul-Lenert Breutz in the 1940s and 1950s. See Schapera (1942a: 1–4; 1965: 46–53) and Breutz (1953: 247–256; 1987: 339–340). Schapera and Breutz regard the Kgafela Kgatla

and the four other BaKgatla royal lineages (Mosetlha, Mmanaana, Mmakau and Mo-tsha) as having been originally a single group who separated from the BaHurutshe before subdividing (Schapera 1942a: 1; Breutz 1987: 329–331).

2   For the Transvaal prior to the *mfecane* or *difaqane*, see Bergh (1999: 105–109), Parsons (1995) and Hall (1995).

3   It has been fashionable to designate Africans in arms as 'warriors', but 'trained militia' would be more accurate for the BaKgatla mephato and many similar military units formed at this time in the trans-Vaal.

4   According to Schapera (1942a: 5; 1965: 54–55). This land grant seems to have been forgotten, if not dishonoured, when the BaKgatla claimed it in 1875 (see ch. 4), and may be a convenient Kgatla fiction. Interestingly, Linchwe's own account of this episode makes no mention of Pilane, but places Letsebe in the fray and states that he was wounded. Linchwe also claimed that the Kgatla returned home with half of the recaptured cattle (Petition to Selbourne (1906), as taken by B.L. Vickerman, Willoughby Papers W 733; I am grateful to Barry Morton for a copy of this petition).

5   Smith journals, SAM, s.v. Bakatla (p. 89) and Bapiri (p. 121); Delius (1984: 15). The Pedi may have been encouraged by the Mogopa Kwena to come to their assistance in a dispute with the Fokeng, who were also attacked by the Pedi. See Breutz (1953: 63, 87–88).

6   Schapera (1942a: 7), Ellenberger (1939).

7   Schapera (1942a: 7), Breutz (1953: 9–11) and Rasmussen (1978: 52). For more on the Kololo, see Smith (1956) and Omer-Cooper (1966: 115–117).

8   Schapera (1942a: 7–8); Breutz (1953: 256–257); Ellenberger minutes, 27 Mar. 1902, Isaac Schapera transcripts from the Mafeking Registry. The Kgatla used chromite in smelting iron ore (Boshier 1969: 31) (I am grateful to Neil Parsons for this reference). For copper mining, see Mason (1982).

9   The detailed Pilane genealogies collected by Isaac Schapera using BaTswana informants (Schapera Papers PP 1/3/9, BNA) link some of Pilane's sons to age-regiments and show that the first of Pilane's sons to undergo initiation (from which the Noga regiment was formed in about 1842), and therefore most likely his first-born, was Letsebe, son of Modie, Pilane's 5th wife by rank. Kgamanyane, son of his first wife Mankube, was not initiated until the Soswe regiment was formed approximately seven years after Noga. Though initiates could vary greatly in age, at the minimum they had to have reached puberty and be mature enough physically to withstand the extreme rigours of initiation. This means that Letsebe was born no later than 1826. For male initiation (*bogwera*), see Willoughby (1909), Brown (1926: 74–89) and Schapera (1978). See also the brief notes – very similar to the published information – gathered by Andrew Smith in 1834–1835 (Smith journals, SAM) with respect to the BaTlhaping (p. 5), BaRolong (pp. 9–10) and BaSotho (p. 29).

10 Breutz (1953: 270) estimates that this regiment was formed in about 1826. Kgotlamaswe was from the third lapa of Pheto.

11 Schapera (1942a: 9). See especially Pilane's self-authored praise, in which Mankube's role as his full partner is emphasised (Schapera 1965: 60).

12 A policy also followed by Kgamanyane, Pilane's heir (see ch. 2).

13 Parsons (1995: 344–349), Keegan (1996: 175–179).

14 Boshier (1969), Mason (1982).

15 Bergh (1999: 9, 103–105), Parsons (1995: 347), Eldredge (1994a), Marks and Gray (1975: 410–411).

16 D'Elegorgue (1847: 412). I am grateful to Barry Morton for drawing my attention to and translating this passage. Matlapeng, son of Bogatsu of the Tlokwa, was Pilane's brother-in-law. Pilane's mention of 'Mandrisse' led d'Elegorgue to think him misinformed, that 'He was wrong, it was Manica [Sofala hinterland] he ought to have said'. But Mandrisse is more likely to have been one of the many names by which Tsonga traders from Delagoa Bay, and by extension their place, were known. For these, see Parsons 1995.

17 D'Elegorgue (1847: 434).

18 For more on these hunters, traders and raiders on horseback, see Legassick (1969) and Ross (1976).

19 Kirby (1939: I, 382).

20 Parsons (1995: 344–347).

21 Legassick (1969: 402).

22 Rasmussen (1978: 45–53).

23 For the classic summary, see Omer-Cooper (1966: 129–155). For the historiography of Mzilikazi, and a balanced view, see Rasmussen 1975. Rasmussen takes little note of Mzilikazi's trade policy, however.

24 Breutz (1953: 64–65, 111–112, 127–148, 164), Schapera (1942a).

25 Rasmussen (1978: 61, 193n6) gives the impression that Pilane fled soon after Mzilikazi moved north of Magaliesberg in 1827, but such was not the case, as the events discussed below reveal.

26 Breutz (1953: 64–65). For Mokgatle, see below and ch. 2.

27 Ibid.: 77–78; 182, 219, 291; Sillery (1952: 162). Mzilikazi had other loyalists, including such dikgosi as Magala of the Hurutshe and Matlabe of the Rolong, whose men accompanied Mzilikazi's regiments in attacks on their neighbours (Rasmussen 1978: 66–67).

28 Lemue (1834: 271) reported that a chief 'Pilni has under him several villages of quite considerable size' (I am grateful to Barry Morton for this source and its translation). See also Schapera (1942a: 8) and Breutz (1953: 257). Mzilikazi 'taxed' some of his other subjects in similar kind (Rasmussen 1978: 61, 66). Bogopana and Mmamodimokwana were within close walking distance (less than 50 kilometres west) of Rooiberg, an end-point on several Delagoa Bay hinterland routes (Bergh 1999: 9, 103–105).

29 Kirby (1939: I, 279, 382; II, 122, 141, 220), Smith (1970: 285–286). The northern Tswana were obtaining beads from the BaKalanga of western Zimbabwe, who tapped the Zambezi trade routes, but these beads reached Mzilikazi only after he migrated to Mosega in the North West Province.

30 Rasmussen (1978: 43, 68). For recent discussions of the controversy interpreting this battle in the context of the mfecane, see Hamilton (1995). 'Mantatee' was a loose reference to any of the Sotho- or Tswana-speaking, mobile groups of the highveld.

31 Rasmussen (1978: 74).

32 Ibid.: 62–64.

33 In early 1829 (Legassick 1969: 403–404).

34 Rasmussen (1978: 65–67, 70–71).

35 Methuen (1846: 79), Kirby (I: 382–383). Rasmussen (1978: 73–75) summarises Berends' motives for mobilising this force, but he characterises Berends and his commando as bent on spoils in the Griqua tradition. Such incentives were present among some of those who joined Berends' commando, but Rasmussen greatly underestimates Mzilikazi's decision to block the Griqua north of the Vaal, especially in the Magaliesberg-Pilanesberg where Berends' people and Pilane had been actively trading, as a factor in the commando initiative. Mzilikazi's restriction threatened Berends' plan of establishing peaceful trading relations with Sotho-Tswana peoples and thereby extending Griqua political power, just as it threatened Pilane's accumulation of cattle and the influence that came with them. For a discussion of Berends' economic and political aims at the time of the commando, see Legassick (1969: 421–427).

36 Schapera (1965: 60). Ape refers to the vervet monkey (kgabo), the totem of Pilane and most of his Kgatla followers.

37 The best account of Berends' raid, richly supported by evidence, is in Rasmussen (1975: 73–81). See also Legassick (1969: 428–432).

38 None of the accounts of the commando raid have suggested that the commando's arrival at the time Mzilikazi was least able to defend himself was anything other than circumstantial. But why must it be assumed that Berends was trusting to luck? Why must it be assumed that Pilane, who was in the neighbourhood and who had invited Berends to attack Mzilikazi, was unable or unwilling to send word that the time was ripe?

39 Smith (1836: 27).

40 Kirby (1939: II, 165, 175), Schapera (1942a: 8), Rasmussen (1978: 84).

41 Smith journal (SAM: 96); Schapera (1942a: 8). Pilane also lived part of his exile with the BaBididi, located in the Waterberg. Kirby (1939: II, 179).

42 Livingstone (1961: 97), Jackson (1983), Parsons (1995: 331–335).

43 Kirby (1939: II, 154, 218).

44 Schapera (1942a: 8).

45 Rasmussen (1978: 83–91, 97–101).

46 In 1835, Andrew Smith passed through this area and marked Mzilikazi's 'most advanced post' as north of the Cashan Mountains (Magaliesberg) and 25 miles west of the Odi River, which would be on the eastern side of the Pilanesberg. Smith journal (SAM: 107).

47 Ibid., Kirby (1939: II, 102, 119, 148–149, 152, 154).

48 Kirby (1939: II, 165, 175). Schapera (1942a: 8) states that Kgotlamaswe resettled in Mabieskraal west of the Pilanesberg, but when is not clear. He was there in 1849, however, when David Livingstone visited the area (Livingston 1959: II, 12).

49 Smith journal (SAM: 96), Kirby (1939: II, 165, 175).

50 Kirby (1939: II, 186, 190).

51 Bergh (1999: 124–125).

52 For the Sekwati–Moshoeshoe connection, see Sanders (1975: 141, 282), Delius (1984: 75). Eldredge (1993: 23–25) shows that the Pedi and Sotho were likely to have been

trading partners even earlier. Also worth noting is that all the major *Voortrekker* routes passed through or near to Thaba Nchu, some 80 kilometres northwest of Moshoeshoe's capital of Thaba Bosiu. The significance of Moshoeshoe's satellite settlement to the Voortrekkers's understanding of the trans-Vaal has yet to be emphasised in the literature. Thaba Nchu was founded in 1833 by Tswana, Kora and Griqua refugees from the Vaal-Harts region following intense Ndebele raiding. Among them was Berends Berends, Pilane's trading partner. Andries Hendrik Potgieter and Gert Maritz launched their commando against Mzilikazi from this point and used Thaba Nchu residents as auxiliaries (Thompson 1975: 110–112).

53 Ibid.: 126–127; Rasmussen (1978: 116–132).

54 It was the Tswana of the Magaliesberg area who informed Potgieter that Mzilikazi had emigrated north. Bergh (1999: 126–127).

55 For views of the Great Trek as motivated at least in part by economic objectives, see Readers' Digest (1988: 110–113) and Etherington (1991).

56 Breutz (1953: 64–65). Potgieter claimed all of Mzilikazi's territory, and then some, by right of conquest. For a map of Potgieter's claim and a discussion of its extent, see Bergh (1999: 14 [inset], 127–128).

57 Bergh (1999: 129–130), Bloemhof (1871: 236).

58 Bloemhof (1871: 236) giving the testimony of Wilhelmus Petrus Grobbelaar, who accompanied Potgieter, states that when Potgieter was located at the Mooi River before moving into the Magaliesberg the following 'captains' came to Potgieter asking for land: Mgata (Mokgatle of the Fokeng), Managota (?), Macalie (Mogale of the Po), Mamagalie (Mmamogale of the Mogopa Kwena), Pilaan (Pilane of the Kgafela Kgatla), Chopa (Ntshaupe of the Mosetlha Kgatla), Maluck (Malok of the Motsha Kgatla); Rhama Kok (Ramokoka of the Phalane Kwena) and Mankopie (Magobye of a Lete offshoot). Traditions collected from the following Rustenburg and Pilansberg district groups by Breutz (1953) show that they did not resist the Trekkers and in some cases that they welcomed or accepted them, or returned to the area after Mzilikazi left: Fokeng (pp. 64–65), Mogopa Kwena (p. 91), Modimosana Mmatau Kwena (p. 112), Modimosana Matlhaku Kwena (p. 127), Modimosana Maake Kwena (p. 148), Sefanyetso Taung (p. 164), Po (p. 182), Bogatsu Tlokwa (p. 203), Kgafela Kgatla (pp. 257–258), Tlhako (p. 291).

59 Mantirisi was a young boy by 1842. See below.

60 See footnote 52 above.

61 From d'Elegorgue, who met Pilane in 1843 and saw the remains of the battle (d'Elegorgue 1847: II, 434). D'Elegorgue locates the battle at Sogoupana Hills (Bogopana) near to Pilane's settlement, from which Pilane led hunting expeditions.

62 Schapera (1942a: 9).

63 D'Elegorgue (1847: II, 434).

64 Pilane's half-brother Molefi Molefe, who had supported Pilane's legitimacy during his years in exile from Mzilikazi, negotiated the release of the boys. For Kgamanyane's trade with the Ndebele, see ch. 2. It is possible that Mzilikazi wished to remove Pilane and his people from the area for fear they might direct Zulu regiments wishing to attack

him in Matabeleland, but this presumes that Pilane was already familiar with the routes to western Zimbabwe. In either case, Pilane's knowledge was what attracted Mzilikazi, and so it was likely to have interested Potgieter.

65 Breutz (1987: 413).

66 D'Elegorgue (1847: II, 434). I am grateful to Barry Morton for his translation notes on this source.

67 Schapera (1942a: 8–9), Breutz (1953: 267). For the Potchefstroom–Limpopo route, which constituted the 'eastern branch' into the interior, see Tabler (1955: 17–18). This route was recommended in 1850 by Joseph McCabe in his letter to the *Cape Frontier Times* (Baines 1964: II, 311).

68 Mogale Masite was kgosi of the BaPo ba Mogale (Po).

69 Breutz (1953: 183).

70 Mmamogale Segwati was kgosi of the BaKwena bo Mogopa (Mogopa Kwena).

71 Ibid.: 91, Livingstone (1960: 303), Livingstone (1961: 96). Mmamogale had run afoul of Potgieter soon after the trekkers arrived, by inducing Potgieter's commando to tame one of his old adversaries with the story that they were Mzilikazi's forces (Kruger 1902: 10–11).

72 Livingstone (1961: 95).

73 Also Livingstone (1961: 95), d'Elegorgue (1847: II, 340–342).

74 D'Elegorgue (1847: II, 540). Mokgatle had his personal guns repaired by David Livingstone (Livingstone 1959: I, 254). By 1850 his people were walking to Colesberg in the Eastern Cape to work for guns (Baines 1964: II, 109). Mokgatle was prohibited from collecting his people in one place or allowing missionaries to build schools, and he had to get the *Hoofdkommandant*'s permission to graze cattle on his own land.

75 Erasmus (1995: 37ff.).

76 Livingstone (1959: II, 57; 1961: 99).

77 Breutz (1987: 413), Livingstone (1961: 98, 99), Delius (1984: 37, 86).

78 To Sechele of the Kwena, to give up his guns to Potgieter or suffer an attack (Livingstone 1974: 149).

79 Livingstone (1959: I, 236).

80 A subordinate council (1840–1843) of the *Volksraad* in Pietermartizburg.

81 Morton (1994c).

82 Erasmus (1995: 37–44).

83 Potgieter's anti-British rhetoric appears to have its origin in earlier Voortrekker politics. See for example his 1841 letter to Pretorius in Du Toit and Giliomee (1983: 217).

84 Livingstone (1960: 303), Du Toit (1983: 940–947).

85 Baines (1961: II, 69, 173). *Vervlugte* is a corruption of *vervloekte* (cursed).

86 Methuen (1846: 182), referring to LMS missionary Walter Inglis, just returned to Mabotsa from 'Poolani a Baquaine chief [who lived among Boers] "who had him so totally *under their thumbs* [original emphasis]", that he told Mr. Englis, he must even report the conversation which passed between them'. In 1848 Livingstone reached Pilane's and

'had large attentive audiences at two villages. Could not get them to discuss the subject [of accepting a missionary]' (Livingstone 1960: 303). Inglis was subsequently transferred to Mathebe, among Moilwa's BaHurutshe.

87 Livingstone (1959: I, 140). Most likely Pilane was visiting Mosielele on business. Mabotsa was situated, as was Tshonwane, capital of Sechele of the Kwena, 'at the nexus of the missionary, hunter, and Voortrekker frontiers' (Ramsay 1991: 76; see pp. 76–82 for a discussion of the trade with these settlements to the north).

88 Schapera (1942a: 9).

89 Breutz (1953: 328).

90 This was Mochela Mfatlha (Breutz 1987: 432; item 17, War Council, Rustenburg, 20 Nov. 1852, SAAR: II, 371; Schapera 1965: 64n3, 68n1). This Zwaartbooi is not to be confused with Mathibe Kgosi, also known as Swaartbooij or Zwaartbooi of the BaHwaduba, Pretoria district.

91 Hendrick Molefi's account of Kgatla history – see p. 15, PP 1/4/2, Schapera Papers (SP), BNA; Schapera (1942a: 9); Matthews (1945: 17, 28n39). Matthews thinks the Kgatla were attending the installation rather than installing Montshiwa, but even the attendance of the Kgatla regiments attests to Pilane's status in the region nonetheless.

92 Schapera (1965: 59n4 and 5).

93 D'Elegorgue 1844. Inhambane was an ivory port during the eighteenth and nineteenth centuries (Alpers 1975: 104, 174, 175, 258n88) and in the 1840s and 1850s, the traders of Inhambane were also interested in trade links with the trekkers (Erasmus 1995: 44 citing de Waal 1953: ch. 5).

94 D'Elegorgue (1847: II, 540).

95 Methuen (1846: 250).

96 Livingstone (1959: I, 140); Cummings (1904: 340; for more on Mabotsa, see footnote 86). LMS missionary at Mabotsa, Rogers Edwards, was the father of Sam Edwards, a leading trader in Bechuanaland.

97 Livingstone (1959: II, 27).

98 Livingstone (1961: 95–96).

99 McCabe's letter of 26 Feb. 1850 to the *Cape Frontier Times* contains the first published reference to 'Palansberg' the mountains named by the Dutch-speaking immigrants in honour of Pilane (Baines 1964: 314). John Sanderson, in the Magaliesberg in late 1851/ early 1852, wrote that the 'Pillan's Berg . . . derives from a native chief named Pillan inhabiting it' (Sanderson 1860: 250).

100 Schapera's detailed genealogies of the Pilane lineage based on oral traditions indicate that at least 45 children were born to his wives (SP: PP 1/3/9). Pheto Molefe is listed with five wives.

101 Mmakgabo, mother of Moselekatse, was Tlhako by origin, but Pilane acquired her as his uncle Senwelo's widow.

102 *Bogadi* (bridewealth), usually cattle, was given to the father of the bride, who shared it with his uncles and brothers, and often the brother of his wife.

103 Livingstone (1959: II, 57; 1961: 99).

104 Schapera (1965: 59, including notes 4 and 5). Another of Pilane's military leaders was

MMADINALE ('THE CLAWER'): PILANE PHETO

Tlagadi, also of Kgalagadi origin and founder of the Tlagadi ward (Schapera 1952: 114).

105 Livingstone (1960: 297). Schapera (1942a: 9) gives 1850 the year of death, before the author came across Livingstone's letter just cited. For several years afterwards, travellers in the area of Mmasebudule, including Livingstone himself, continued to refer to it as 'Pilane's'. The cause of Pilane's death is not known, but it was probably natural, given the rigours of his life.

Chapter two

KGAMANYANE PILANE AND
PAUL KRUGER

Myself I say, 'having seen, are you startled, you men of Mokopana Mapela, now that you've seen the Slasher fighting, the Slasher with the bloodstained horn?' Sekgetla *[the Slasher]* . . . *kills, he also quenches fires, the Slasher, son of the woman from Tlokwaland.* (Kgamanyane's praise, composed by himself)

* * *

My rifle exploded just where I held it with my left hand, and my left thumb . . . *lay before me on the ground* . . . *My hand was in a horrible state* . . . *The flesh was hanging in strips. I bled like a slaughtered calf. I called out to my wife* . . . *to fetch some turpentine* . . . *to stop the bleeding* . . . *The two joints of what was once my thumb had gone* . . . *I took my knife* . . . *and cut across the ball of the thumb, removing as much as necessary* . . . *I had no means of deadening the pain, so I tried to persuade myself that the hand on which I was performing this surgical operation belonged to somebody else.* (Kruger 1902: 32–33)

Kgamanyane Pilane ruled the BaKgatla during an unsettled and tumultuous time for trans-Vaal Africans. Life was as difficult then as it had been in the reign of his father. Wars and raiding were common, with guns ever present. Slaving on a large scale made its debut. Natural reverses in the form of droughts, floods, locusts and disease became routine. Trade expanded, but the hunt declined, and migrant labour got underway. Political conflict among and between Africans and Boers was endemic, and attempts to resolve it were usually carried out with force. A constant stream of disgruntled emigrants left the trans-Vaal with no intention of returning. Only a few persons in this troubled region achieved prominence and found ways to thrive. Kgamanyane was among them. Few Boers controlled as much property as he. Like all Zuid-Afrikaansche Republiek (ZAR) Africans, Kgamanyane owned no land, but he and his BaKgatla followers gained access to it on terms that allowed them to accumulate wealth in stock and grain, build large towns, construct fine homes and equip them with manufactured items. His reign was marked by a steady increase in people and cattle.

*Stephanus Johannes Paulus Kruger, 1877.
Sketch by Lemington Muzhingi.*

From the beginning Kgamanyane aligned his reign with the maBuru. It was easily his best option. Those dikgosi who had opposed maBuru demands were living in exile with a smidgin of followers under other dikgosi. And who could say where events in these territories beyond maBuru control would lead? The maBuru had made the trans-Vaal their base to attack African kingdoms on their borders, and their opponents' future looked bleak. Even attempts from within the trans-Vaal to make contact with missionaries associated with these people threatened to bring down the wrath of maBuru, as Mokgatle aThethe had recently learned.[1] In 1849 the maBuru broke up a Tlhaping settlement somewhere in the vicinity of the later Bloemhof, killed many adults and took their children away.[2] Those living nearby in the Marico district yet independent of the maBuru had the choice of helping the maBuru or moving away. In 1850 Sechele of the BaKwena shifted his capital from Tshonwane in the Potchefstroom district to Dimawe in Bechuanaland for fear of an attack.[3] He was later joined by Mosielele from Mabotsa. Even so, rumours persisted that commandos were being mounted against the BaKwena, and Sechele stayed prepared for war.[4] The showdown came in August 1852, when a large commando under Kommandant P.E. Scholtz attacked Dimawe. A two-day battle ended in a standoff. The maBuru counted it a failure, because they had not dispersed the BaKwena, but they returned to the trans-Vaal with thousands of cattle and as many as 600 women and children, including one of Sechele's sons.[5] Only months before, a commando had moved into the Waterberg, attacked the Langa AmaNdebele and returned with children.[6] And within a month after Dimawe, Potgieter went into battle again against Sekwati's BaPedi, taking away 5,000 cattle, 6,000 sheep and goats, and a number of captured children.[7]

No matter how the maBuru were regarded as persons, they deserved their due as raiders. And in the present state of affairs, they were better joined than opposed. Other leaders than Kgamanyane had reached this conclusion. The maBuru had no shortage of allies in battle regardless of where their commandos fought, inside or out of the trans-Vaal. Coerced or willing, Africans went nevertheless, whether against Sechele's BaKwena, Moletse's BaKwena, Mzilikazi's AmaNdebele, Mapela's AmaNdebele or Sekwati's BaPedi. By the time Kgamanyane became kgosi, those who had already taken up arms in support of the maBuru included the BaTlhaping, BaRolong, BaHurutshe, BaPedi, AmaSwati, Langa AmaNdebele, BaFokeng and BaPo. So why not the BaKgatla? There was always the risk that the maBuru would find a reason to turn an African ally quickly into their enemy, as they had done to the BaPedi and Langa AmaNdebele. But, for taking part in their commando raids, Kgamanyane might expect to share in the spoils and gain the privileges others had received: keeping guns, staying settled in one place and ruling one's own royals and commoners. His young men would fight on the chance of gaining stock and wives, and his half-brothers would have to lead them.

Kgamanyane's Succession

When Pilane died in 1848, Kgamanyane was by no means assured of taking over the position held by his father. There is no doubt that he wanted to succeed Pilane, but then so did others. Kgamanyane was only 25, had lots of brothers and was sure to be challenged by groups of men pushing their respective candidates. And the push and shove would all be done as a local affair. The BaKgatla chose their leaders, not the maBuru. The circumstances, however, favoured Kgamanyane. He was the eldest son of his father's soulmate and first wife Mankube and had been initiated into manhood as the leader of maSoswe regiment. Kgamanyane's eligibility was clear to all; therefore his claim to succeed Pilane had to be addressed without delay. He had to be installed straight away or pushed aside.

Dispute among heirs was common among Tswana people, though succession tended to be less disruptive in the trans-Vaal bushveld than in the Bechuanaland sandveld. After the AmaNdebele moved north, BaTswana on the edge of the Kalahari had grouped themselves around their *dikgosi* in large settlements for defence against AmaNdebele in Matabeleland and maBuru in the trans-Vaal, with the effect that when succession disputes arose, they were in the habit of breaking up these populations or rearranging them at considerable inconvenience to all concerned.[8] In highveld areas such as the Rustenburg district, however, BaTswana reverted to the pre-mfecane system whereby the kgosi lived in one of several scattered settlements under his authority. Their settlements helped the kgosi's followers take advantage of locations best suited for grazing, mining, trade and agriculture. Scattered settlements made it more difficult for aspirants outside the kgosi's town to mobilise sufficient followers at succession time. Even the *kgosing* sub-wards, headed by the descendants of previous dikgosi and their brothers, were often separated from one another, sometimes by ten or fifteen kilometres. At the time of succession, a successful challenge might shift power from one settlement to the other but without entailing significant resettlement. The maBuru favoured this system, of course, because they felt less threatened by Africans living in small settlements than in large ones and because the dikgosi/kapiteins could be dealt with more directly. To be certain, however, the kapitein's power was worth vying for, especially at the level built by Pilane, and the late kgosi's high-handedness had created an opposition that at his death sought its outlet through the candidacy of Tau, eldest son of Pilane's first Kgatla-born wife Morelle, or rather Mmantselana, her *seantlo* (substitute).[9] When Pilane died, Tau was a mere infant.

Tau was supported (or rather the notion of a regency on his behalf) by most of the Kgatla commoners. Since the days of Kgotlamaswe, Pilane's challenger, enough BaKgatla had supported rival claimants to bogosi to make for lively tension among the royal kin, and so Kgamanyane's first effort was devoted to gathering around him sufficient support to withstand the Tau camp. Though outnumbered by the Tauists in terms of commoner support, Kgamanyane had the advantage that he and his many half-brothers were much older than Tau.

When it came to ranking the sons of the kgosi (in this case the sons of the thirteen wives of the deceased Pilane), two principles and two ways of reckoning seniority were always at loggerheads: the two principles were designation of the great wife by the kgosi and designation by his subjects. Often, to solidify his position upon succession, the kgosi was inclined to go along with his subjects' preference. But Pilane, as we know, had declared Mankube to be his great wife, whereas many BaKgatla considered Morelle and her seantlo Mmantselana to have held that position.

The two ways of reckoning seniority of the other wives further complicated the royal order. Some believed that a wife's position, and that of her sons, was calculated from the time she was *betrothed* to the kgosi, whereas others reckoned the union to be official only at the point of marriage. The Betrothers tended to support the sons much younger than their other royal half-brothers, because their mothers had not lived at the royal compound as long. Naturally, this notion appealed strongly to the less respectable commoners, whose daughters had had to wait to be chosen for marriage by the kgosi; whereas the Marriers tended to support the older sons of the kgosi by virtue of their longer, closer proximity to the deceased kgosi and their desire to preserve with his successor the relatively higher status they had enjoyed. Kgamanyane was the eldest of Pilane's sons, years beyond the infant Tau. In 1850, a decade or more would have to pass before Tau could be *initiated*, much less succeed to the throne.

Also, if the Bethrothers had their way, not only would Kgamanyane occupy an inferior rank with Tau's succession, but so would Tau's older half-brothers. Of the first six Pilane *malwapa*, five had sons who were grown men by the time Tau was born. Between the time Pilane betrothed Morelle and formally married her, Pilane fathered Kgamanyane and at least four other sons. Because Morelle had not given birth prior to her death in 1831 or 1832, and the many years that had passed before her substitute Mmantselana could bear Tau, meant that before Tau was born Kgamanyane's half-brothers were on their way to being grown men and thinking of themselves as future leaders. Letsebe had in fact been initiated *before* Kgamanyane, and headed the *mophato* of maNoga. The grown royal half-brothers, each the eldest son of his respective lapa – Tshomankane (son of Mmadipitse), Mantirisi (son of Mmakgabo), Kgari (son of Basetsane) and Letsebe (son of Modie) – supported Kgamanyane. To have done otherwise would have helped to vault the much younger Tau over their heads and lower their position in the royal ranks. As if to underscore this point, Kgamanyane's half-brothers shifted their respective locations to surrounding villages, from which they could encircle Tau should the lad be installed. Thus Kgamanyane came to power without too much fuss, because his adult half-brothers united behind him.[10]

Luck, if not intrigue, has often been an important factor in any royal succession. Yet, given the many talents Kgamanyane demonstrated as a kgosi, it is hardly farfetched to think that he foresaw the problems that would come with his father's death and laid plans in his early twenties to influence the outcome. Kgamanyane is represented somewhat unfairly in twentieth-century traditions as a kgosi who quarrelled with his brothers, because it is alleged they could not abide his selfishness and hunger for their cattle.[11] However, as his succession demonstrates and latter events will bear out, Kgamanyane retained the support of nearly all his brothers, and his son and successor Linchwe was able to do the same, to the great advantage of their respective political and economic positions. Unity within the royal family, with the exception of one and sometimes two disgruntled malwapa, was a lesson learned from Pilane and became a means with which

Kgamanyane expanded his power. At their respective successions, Pilane, Kgamanyane and Linchwe rearranged status within the royal family by backing one of the two principles of rank – betrothal or marriage – depending on which gave the kgosi the greater political advantage. In other words, they used the strategy that maximised support from within the royal family.

Kgamanyane's BaKgatla

By one means or another, probably through steady consultation with his advisors, Kgamanyane understood how to rope in followers and tether them. Mere threats and violence would not work in this regard, as Motlotle's disastrous regency had proved; and being kind or gentle was not Pilane's way. Pilane gave his people a stake in seeing his power used. And so would Kgamanyane. The difficulty that Kgamanyane faced, however, was figuring out how he was to remain powerful with more maBuru around. How was he supposed to keep his followers content and supportive, while living with the maBuru's labour demands and their calls to war, in a land where rainfall was uncertain and people had to be ready at all times to spread out?

Cohesion among royal relatives was vital to a community under pressure to disassemble. Kgamanyane knew that marrying commoners was *not* well suited for this purpose because doing so was more likely to encourage rivalry among commoners than loyalty to the kgosi.[12] Like Pilane, however, Kgamanyane set about taking the daughters of commoner families as his wives, and he outdid his father fourfold in this respect. He was not trying to create *nouveau* royalists, but simply indulging himself and giving commoners marriage cattle that he could confiscate for bad behaviour. *Bogadi* (bridewealth) was Kgamanyane's way of shutting commoners up, by giving them the means to support themselves.[13] But Kgamanyane's carefree association with damsels of commoner origin created risks that his mother Mankube had to point out. Before Kgamanyane had been installed as kgosi, he had taken several lovers, and they were betrothed to him. None had suited Mankube, particularly Nkomeng, a MoTlhalerwa of low origins. Nkomeng's son Maganelo was certain to grow up thinking he was to be the next kgosi. Mankube did approve of Dikolo, a royal MoTlhako from Mabieskraal on the other side of the Pilanesberg, and probably at her urging Kgamanyane asked the BaKgatla to recognise Dikolo as his great wife. Thus, in contrast to his father Pilane, Kgamanyane gave commoners the decision to select the *mohumagadi* (mother of the future heir). However, the effect was the same. By agreeing to provide the cattle for Dikolo's marriage, which they did, the commoners assured that the future succession excluded the son of one of their own daughters. In this way, commoner rivalry was stifled and the succession of Dikolo's first son, Linchwe, who was born several years after Kgamanyane was installed as kgosi, was ensured.[14]

At the same time, Kgamanyane's father's brothers and his half-brothers, especially those of senior malwapa, needed roles of importance to reinforce their status and gain privileges. They needed to be involved in deliberations, sit alongside Kgamanyane at public gatherings and head mephato. In those positions, they could share in public displays of power, be seen to limit the kgosi's actions, and have some authority to exact personal tribute and spoils. When accorded such roles, ranking royals lived in scattered settlements away from the kgosi and yet remained part of his political domain. By the same token, Kgamanyane made their cattle part of his legal domain, by virtue of his being their father's eldest son. Under Kgamanyane, royal cattle were herded by the kgosi's half-brothers on sufferance.[15]

Another vital constituency that Kgamanyane utilised was young, marriageable men. With them lay the care and protection of Kgatla cattle and service in Kgatla mephato, with all the attendant dangers. In their hands was reposed the safekeeping of the people's resources and the defending of their lives. As the only armed element in the community, moreover, they had the means of fending for themselves. Such men, looking forward to respectable civic roles that only married men with cattle could occupy, were also on the lookout for opportunities in which their prowess could serve these ends. Cattle, after all, were difficult to accumulate quickly; cultivating a herd was an undertaking of years – requiring husbandry skills, much personal inconvenience and considerable good luck in overcoming drought and disease. Caring for one's cattle meant patience, a quality few young men possessed. For them the shortest way to cattle ownership was dispossession. For generations, cattle raiding had been practised in the trans-Vaal for this very reason, and the MaKololo, AmaNdebele, maSetedi and maBuru had simply introduced new weaponry, equipment and organisational methods to increase the take. To young men on the fast track, the opportunity to join the latest, most effective raiding system yet known on the highveld had strong appeal.

Kgamanyane's calculus in keeping commoners, royals and young men within his administration had also to factor in those forces beyond his control. Though young when he succeeded his father, Kgamanyane would have understood this challenge from the beginning of his reign. The years of the mfecane had made large settlements and concentrations of cattle too risky, and the droughts and diseases that came in its trail increased the need for people in the trans-Vaal to spread out. The maBuru dealt with Africans as they found them: grouped in small, scattered settlements associated with a kgosi, and it suited their purposes to keep them there. Thus, while African leaders such as Pilane and Kgamanyane were restricted in their movements by maBuru, at times they had to contend with less predictable, more formidable threats to their communities. These opposing forces were not man-made (though there was no shortage of religious specialists ready to blame each natural crisis on human mismanagement). In 1849 or 1850, soon after Kgamanyane's installation, the people of Pilanesberg were devastated by an epidemic. And in the following year, a severe drought hit the trans-Vaal.[16] What transpired during these crises can only be surmised, but using later, documented years in the Pilanesberg as a guide, Kgamanyane's Kgatla most likely responded by trying to disperse.[17] Shortage of water and grazing in drought years meant breaking up herds and moving them away in small batches with a few herders. Though it minimised losses through thirst or starvation, this strategy was extremely dangerous, because it exposed cattle and herder alike to wild predators and rustlers.[18]

Kgamanyane's young menfolk were also wanted by the maBuru. Within a year of Kgamanyane's installation, Potgieter was back at Schoemansdal planning another war. In 1846 he had engaged the Sekwati's BaPedi as his auxiliaries in a raid against Moletse's BaKwena, and in 1848 against Mzilikazi.[19] In 1849 it was Sekwati's turn. Potgieter raised a commando against the BaPedi, using regiments from the BaFokeng, BaPo and BaKgatla as auxiliaries.[20] The maNoga under Letsebe, and maSoswe under Kgamanyane's half-brother Kgari, were the most battle-ready at that time.

Kgamanyane's Alliance

The official who called up Kgamanyane's men was Stephanus Johannes Paulus (Paul) Kruger. Like Kgamanyane, Kruger had gained power as a young man. After Potgieter shifted his permanent residence to Schoemansdal, young Kruger rose quickly to become the military leader of the Magaliesberg district.[21] Raised by his father Caspar Jan Hendrik Kruger among Andries Hendrik Potgieter's trekkers, Kruger shared Potgieter's penchant for communicating through force. Brilliant and indifferent to danger, young Kruger inclined toward delusions and visions. This was the young official, it was said, who stood on his head atop a DRC (Dutch Reformed Church) church gable.[22] He was also quick and ambitious. Made a deputy veldkornet in 1842, he was among Kommandant-generaal Andries Pretorius's early supporters and joined Pretorius's delegation to the Sand River Convention in January 1852. In rapid succession, he became full veldkornet and then, at 26 years, he replaced his uncle Gert Kruger as kommandant of the Rustenburg district. In the following August, he fought under Scholtz at Dimawe.[23] Weeks later, he and his Rustenburg maBuru joined Pretorius's commando against the BaRolong of Montshiwa. The defeated Rolong fled north across the Molopo River, and the commando returned with Rolong cattle and children. The BaRolong were being punished because they had refused to join Scholtz's commando against Sechele.[24]

The following year, when word reached Rustenburg that the Langa Ama-Ndebele of Makapansberg (part of the Waterberg) were terrorising the local maBuru, Kruger immediately formed a commando, and Kgamanyane responded to the call. The Langa were old friends of Kgamanyane's father; twice in the 1830s they had given him refuge. As recently as 1847, when David and Mary Livingstone visited them, the Langa were rich in cattle and sheep, grew abundant crops, raised and spun cotton, and were smelting bronze from local deposits of tin and copper. Mankopane, the head of one of their three autonomous groups, had 48 wives.[25] Their area was especially rich in game.[26] But not long before the Livingstones arrived in the Makapansberg, the maBuru had begun their predations. Langa had been the target of local farmers, in league with one of the Buys brothers, who confiscated their cattle and used Langa auxiliaries as battle shields against Moletse's BaKwena, who were then robbed of thousands of sheep and several hundred children.[27] Then, in 1849, Langa children began showing up for sale in Rustenburg, and in 1851 a commando was launched from Rustenburg that brought even more captive youth into the local market.[28]

In retaliation, the Langa ignited a terror campaign to drive out the maBuru. It began in 1853 with the entrapment of Hermanus Potgieter, his son and several others. Potgieter was the brother of Kruger's mentor, Andries

Hendrik Potgieter, the kommandant-generaal of Soutpansberg and Lyden-burg. The Langa killed everyone but Potgieter and his servant. They skinned Potgieter alive, then released Potgieter's servant so that he could broad-cast the event. Soon after, when a convoy of maBuru women and children were being shuttled out of the Soutpansberg, the Langa set an ambush and killed them all, and then attacked other whites in the area.[29] Mokopane's Kekana were also involved. When word arrived in Rustenburg, Kruger formed a commando, met up with Pretorius at his encampment (not yet mapped out as Pretoria), and then together the joint commando moved north to the Waterberg. It consisted of 200 maBuru and an unreported num-ber of African auxiliaries. Kgamanyane and his mophato were among them.

Kruger and Kgamanyane held strong memories of the battle that ensued, and both young men, still in their twenties, came out of it with a sense of personal glory. In his *Memoirs*, Kruger recalled the desire to avenge the 'foul murder' and 'butchery' of Potgieter ('a splendid shot and great elephant-hunter'), and he interspersed references to the 'Kaffirs' and underlined their 'outrages' – blood-stained clothes of white women and children, body parts 'roasted on the spit', and cattle stolen from Potgieter and other Boers. In Kruger's account the followers of Makapan (Mokopane) retreated on the approach of the commandos by going up into the mountains near their settlements and hiding in large caves, whereupon the maBuru laid siege. Kruger related how, under the cover of darkness, he entered one of these caves, disguised himself by speaking 'in their own language' and tried to lure the Langa into surrender. His ruse succeeded in getting close to 200 women and children into Boer hands, but it failed to induce the men to come out. The siege continued, though with continued drama, Kruger ever at the centre of action. In the end, most of those in the cave starved to death rather than come out, though a few managed to escape. A hand-ful were captured, and, as Kruger explained, 'it was absolutely necessary to shoot these cannibals, especially as none of the culprits were delivered up and the chief had disappeared'. As for the children, they were '*inge-boekt*, that is ... portioned out among Boer families and kept under strict legal supervision until they came of age'.[30] Kruger made no mention of the African auxiliaries who were present at the scene. It was as if they were not there.

Kgamanyane made certain the BaKgatla knew. After his return from the Makapansberg, he composed a praise song (*leboko*) for himself about the event. Kgamanyane's leboko was still remembered when Isaac Schapera recorded it in the 1930s, and many of its allusions were interpreted for him by BaKgatla who had heard it recited in the previous seventy or eighty years.[31] Its two main themes are Kgamanyane's violent deeds against Mokopane's people and his service to the Boers. It begins by placing him and his mophato – rather his (di)thaka (age-mates) – at the battle in the status of Boer auxiliaries:

> Warrior brother of Mantirisi, smeared with ashes;
> he was purposely made old,
> the Slasher of those who were arguing.
> Though his age-mates had not yet grown old,
> They eagerly smeared him with ashes;
> They smeared ashes over his head.

Schapera was told that the ashes refer to the point prior to the battle, when the maBuru made the BaKgatla smear white clay on their heads so that the maBuru could distinguish them from the Langa.[32] The leboko then portrays Kgamanyane's forces as taking the lead in the battle by driving the Langa up the mountain and into the caves, razing the countryside and leaving only a few stragglers.

> Lightning, brother of Nthwalwe and Seole,
> Lightning of Nthwalwe, strike the fallow fields
> Strike the caves of the BagaMokopana,
> Then someone will flee alone.

Kgamanyane then alludes to others than the Langa he had previously vanquished, on his own, to remind the listener that his reputation as *Segaketla* ('Slasher', or 'one who cuts down indiscriminately') and *Kgalemi* ('Rebuker') had already been earned.

> Circle round and round with Keledi's man, with the man of Mfatlha Maila.[33]
> We chased each other round an anthill;
> When he left he ran to a cave, and when he got to the cave he said
> 'Cave, split and let me hide.'

It is not clear at this point whether Kgamanyane's leboko refers to the raid against the Mfatlha Ndebele or the Langa Ndebele, but capturing cattle and slaves was part of the plan.

> We who are outside flee from the Rebuker;
> We've fled from the Rebuker, Pilane's son.
> He seizes cattle, he seizes people too, the Famed One also seizes young children.
> He seizes infants still at the breast.
> But the infants he seizes he does not keep – he gives them to the baHibidu.

Kgamanyane regards such deeds as a form of valour, that is, a daring exercise of power over the AmaNdebele, signifying so by naming himself in battle as *Kgatlapi* ('The Brave One'); it is his way of demonstrating his care for his own people.

> Myself I say, 'having seen are you startled, you men of Mokopana Mapela,
> now that you have seen the Slasher fighting,
> the Slasher with the bloodstained horn?'
> The Brave One pokes and pokes again, then
> he draws out the victim's entrails and says
> 'Weep and take comfort, MaMoagabo, take comfort, woman of Matabele;[34]
> Your child is not dead, he still lives;
> He's being nursed by the nurser of people,
> the nurser of Kgafela's orphans,
> who nursed Kgari and Mantirisi,
> and put Letsebe on his shoulders.'

Kgamanyane's message was clear: whether fighting in league with maBuru or going into combat on his own, the young kgosi of the Kgatla looked up to no other. His opponents could count on him to be ruthless. Of course, it should be no surprise to the reader that trans-Vaal leaders such as Kgamanyane were in vogue. For Kgamanyane to display any form of weakness would have invited his own destruction, at the hands of blacks, if not, whites. And who among the BaKgatla would have wanted to be under such a leader?

By reading Kruger's account of the same conflict, and keeping a close eye on what he includes and does not, we can easily see that Kgamanyane was not the only tyrant present at Makapansberg. Kruger's cold-heartedness toward his black allies and enemies alike is unmistakable, as is his indifference to the fate of black non-combatants. Starving to death in the caves of Makapansberg was the price hundreds of Langa paid for not handing over their leader. Kruger's commando was not there for hand-to-hand combat with the Langa military; Kgamanyane's auxiliaries took care of that. The Boers were there to see that black leaders and civilians alike were punished with death for offences to whites.

Wealth and Authority in Rustenburg District

The military alliance between Kgamanyane and Kruger was typical in the 1850s and the early 1860s. Other Rustenburg kapiteins such as Kgamanyane, including Mokgatle Thethe and Moatshe Ramokoka, were part of this raiding nexus, and strengthened themselves as a result. The cattle and other stock confiscated by their mephato on commando raids bolstered their powers of distribution and rewarded elders who backed them in council. And Boer leaders the likes of Paul Kruger supplemented their paltry official salaries with booty, all of it tradable.

Good profits could be got from selling inboekelinge. Those familiar with the trans-Vaal reported that trading in children was common.[35] In 1850 Thomas Baines was told by an ex-soldier at Potchefstroom, who had witnessed conditions in the trans-Vaal, that the Boers 'take and sell children and cattle from the Cafirs round about wherever they find themselves in sufficient force to do so'.[36] Rustenburg had its own slave dealer in 1851, and the *landdrost* of Potchefstroom was booking children he sold.[37] John Sanderson, who travelled through the southern trans-Vaal in 1852, wrote that children were a common sight on Boer farms.[38] And J.M. Orpen, ex-landdrost of Winburg, wrote in 1857 that 'the capture of children is a matter of common occurrence beyond the Vaal River.'[39] The same year, the *Natal Mercury* reported Moshoeshoe as saying that in 'Pretorius's country' (ZAR), Africans are 'publicly bought and sold as slaves'.[40]

Enslaving children was a good business for those too impatient for the slow accumulation of farming or herding; and a perfect sideline for the type who liked hunting game trophies and raiding cattle to build themselves up. As a young man, when Paul Kruger hunted elephants in Swaziland, he supplemented his earnings by purchasing children captured by the AmaSwati from the BaTonga to their north.[41] But petty slave trading was of minor consequence for a man with ambitions on such a large scale as Kruger's. His role model was Andries Hendrik Potgieter. When Potgieter converted Schoemansdal into a slave-raiding base and began to export children out of the Soutpansberg, his most important market became Rustenburg and Potchefstroom, where Boer settlers were the most numerous. With ivory becoming harder to obtain as elephants retreated well to the north, Kruger spent less time hunting and more joining in raids on people for their stock and children. Starting in about 1845, he was in the saddle on a routine basis. As an assistant veldkornet, Kruger and other Rustenburgers are known to have taken part in three raids – against Sekwati's BaPedi (1849), Mamoanwana's Mmakau BaKgatla (1850) and Mokopane's Langa AmaNdebele (1851).[42] Information about the latter two is sketchy, but both appear to have been much like the raid on the BaPedi, which resulted in the capture of children.[43] In the 1850s as Kommandant Kruger either led or participated with the kommandant-generaal in seven *documented* raids that produced children captives – against Mosielele's Mmanaana BaKgatla (1852),[44] Sechele's BaKwena (1852), Montshiwa's BaRolong (1852), Mokopane and Mapela's Langa AmaNdebele (1853), Mokopane's Langa Ama-Ndebele (1857),[45] and Gasebonwe's and Mahura's BaTlhaping (1857).[46]

In 1855 Kruger had enough capital to start buying farms in the Rustenburg district.[47] Then only thirty years old, Kruger had spent the previous decade on the move, either hunting or on commando. And from 1855, he involved himself deeply in trans-Vaal Boer politics as a backer of Marthinus W. Pretorius (son of Andries), as a participant in constitutional talks (1855, 1858), as the leader of the commando to the Orange Free State (1857), as a member of the first ZAR *Volksraad* (1858) and as part of the delegation to Moshoeshoe (1858). How Kruger generated capital to subsidise his mobile existence, when officers' salaries were low, and accumulated enough to launch himself in 1855 as a major property owner has not been accounted for, but the proceeds of raiding could not have failed to increase his purchasing power. Some of the farms he acquired were gifts for service, but most of them he bought, and in rapid succession. In 1858 he gained titles to Kleindoornspruit 108, in 1859 Kookfontein 265 and Boschfontein (?), and in 1860 seven more: Bierkraal 120, Welgevonden (?), Modderkuil 39, Middelkuil 8, Losperfontein 405, Koedoesspruit 33 and Beerfontein 263. He added other farms, including Saulspoort 38, soon after.[48]

Kruger's acquaintance with new ZAR laws, his authority as kommandant and his desire to have fuller access to the big kapiteins fed his land hunger. The four largest African groups in the Rustenburg district – the BaKgatla, BaFokeng, Mogopa BaKwena and BaPo – either lived on Kruger's newly-acquired farms or were settled nearby. Kruger gained these farms after the new ZAR Volksraad had declared that land was to be owned by ZAR citizens only and excluding kleurlingen ('coloured people').[49] The kommandant was then in a position to confiscate land occupied by Africans and previously not subject to Boer claims or neglected by their deed holders. Two of Kruger's first acquisitions were Kookfontein 265 and Beerfontein 263, farms which Andries Hendrik Potgieter had given to Mokgatle.[50] Other of his purchases, such as Modderkuil and Middelkuil, were occupied by the BaKgatla but had not been allocated to white owners. With effect from the 1858 Constitution, such farms became Government property, which only citizens could purchase after inspection (i.e. valuation for tax purposes). Kruger bought these properties, apparently at nominal sums, inspected them in his capacity as kommandant, and then obtained the title deeds in his own name in Pretoria.[51] In the case of Saulspoort, where some of Kgamanyane's BaKgatla were living, Kruger did not even have to do that: the ZAR gave it to him for his services. Thus at relatively low cost, Kruger acquired farms on which a large, permanent African labour force was resident, and on other farms nearby.

What did Kruger have in mind for these farms and the people on them? Kruger later stated that he bought these farms 'nearly seventh hand so as not to have the kaffers oppressed', in other words to exempt them from incessant labour demands imposed by their previous owners.[52] But his answer, as we shall see, seems rather too self-congratulatory in light of his later conduct, and somewhat misleading about the situation prior to the late 1850s. Until Kruger began to purchase them, these farms and others north of the Magaliesberg range had attracted little interest among Boer grain or crop farmers. The farms were part of an area suitable for grazing, but even cattle and sheep were lightly grazed there, apart from those owned by Africans. If Kruger bought these farms 'seventh-hand' as he claims, it was probably because they could be had cheaply, and the high turnover would have reflected their declining purchase value. Whites owned all the farms in the Rustenburg district, but they were having problems turning them to profit. They were raising some food crops and distilling *mampoer*, but mainly for their own consumption.[53] Rather than agriculture, it was game trophies – especially ivory – that made up by far the most exports from the Rustenburg district and other parts of the trans-Vaal, a pattern that persisted into the mid-1860s.[54] Of course, ivory was procured well to the north, and brought in through the trans-Vaal en route to the Cape.

By depending on Kgamanyane and Mokgatle, Kruger was able to retain his old sources of revenue while developing new methods of generating capital. These kapiteins dutifully sent their regiments on Boer commandos, which as kommandant (and from 1863 as kommandant-generaal) Kruger continued to lead into the late 1860s. From their active support of

Kruger's commandos already mentioned, Kgatla and Fokeng auxiliaries were present with him on Boer cattle and slave raids against Moshoeshoe (1858 and 1865), Langa (1858), and the Kekana AmaNdebele (1868).[55] The BaKgatla and BaFokeng were also trusted to procure ivory for Kruger from distant northern sources. Mokgatle obtained ivory, possibly by leading expeditions, but more likely by sending out the black Dutch-speaking elephant hunters who lived at his capital.[56] Kgamanyane's trade connections to the north were particularly valuable to Kruger. Since spending nearly a year in captivity as a boy at Mzilikazi's in 1842/3, Kgamanyane's familiarity with the Ndebele ruler and the road leading to him paid off when he rose to power. In Kgamanyane's reign, the major route connecting Magaliesberg to the north passed just to the east of the Pilanesberg, near to where the Kgatla lived. It crossed the Limpopo and went on to Shoshong, capital of the BaNgwato of Sekgoma, winding its way northeast to Mzilikazi's.[57] In the early 1860s, and probably before, Kgamanyane was taking his wagons on this route to hunt and trade for ivory.[58] In the process, Kgamanyane also put himself on good terms with Sekgoma.[59] In 1861 Kgamanyane's value was apparent as Kgamanyane shifted his capital from Mmasebudule to Kruger's farm Saulspoort 269 on the north-northeastern slopes of the Pilanesberg and astride the Rustenburg–Shoshong road.

Kapiteins with large followings also had the means of leasing land from Kruger. Farms unsuited to cash cropping were desired by the BaKgatla and BaFokeng for food crops and grazing. To retain use of this land, they were also willing to enter into contracts to provide seasonal labour on Kruger's adjacent farms. Such obligations included sowing crops, making water furrows, carrying dung and harvesting crops.[60] Such labour, however, was provided mainly by women. In 1862 one observer remarked that 'sometimes you see from 50 to 100 women on his [Kruger's] farm, to weed his garden and perform other domestic work'.[61] 'Often young women are called up for work [on Kruger's farm]', testified Christof Penzhorn, missionary of the Hermannsburg Missionary Society (HMS) at Beerfontein 263 [Saron], '[and] they often have to walk on foot for four hours to carry [in] the harvest. Even the kapitein's womenfolk are compelled to do this.'[62] The menfolk of these kapiteins, on the other hand, were free to tend cattle and hunt, and if choosing to work for other Boers, do so for remuneration. Africans had enough land to raise crops, and some had large herds. As one visitor to Rustenburg learned, whites in this district had problems getting Africans to work for them. Boer farmers were paying their male African labourers one heifer per year, while traders in Rustenburg offered between five and ten shillings per month in wages.[63]

Living standards of the larger kapiteins and some of their fellow town dwellers far exceeded those of the average Boer farmer. In the decade after John Sanderson visited Mokgatle in 1852, his town of Phokeng more than doubled in size and its orderliness and the fine quality of its structures had made it the local tourist attraction. In 1866, when a white visitor from Natal arrived at Rustenburg with only a day to spend, his host, a local British storekeeper, took him straight to see the town of 'the famous Macattee Chief named Magahlta' and view the spectacle. The visitor's impression was 'one of wonder'. He saw wide streets intersecting the town, many of its 600–700 round homes were encircled by walls that were plastered much better than the 'ordinary Dutch house', and the houses thatched so well that they had a 'better appearance than any thatching I have seen in this country'.[64] He was struck especially by the elaborate, decorative plastering of walls of houses, courtyards and even courtyard floors, which were 'swept scrupulously clean, so that breakfast might have been laid on it'. He remarked as well on the 'tasteful contrast' of polished, coloured abutments of the houses and the smooth surfaces above. As to 'order and cleanliness', the Fokeng were far above the 'Dutch Boers'.

> Many of the doorways were supplied with good plank doors on hinges, secured by lock, padlock, or bolt . . . but the door was made by themselves from [sawn] planks . . . The floors were carefully cemented . . . Some of the superior houses had an inner circle wall, for a bedroom, with a small doorway, also polished to imitate a door frame. One large house belonging to one of the principal wives of the Chief, had a number of compartments beautifully moulded and polished, with great taste, and furnished among other utensils with Basins, Cups, and Saucers, Pots and Pans, and even Foot pans, bought at Rustenburg. There was also a Box of Tools, which were turned to good account, for they sat us down upon chairs made after European models . . . and Tables [were made] the same. (A Visitor to Mokgatle's [Phokeng] 1866)

The kapiteins were particularly wealthy by the standards of the day. Mokgatle's compound was full of items displaying his purchasing power. He owned guns, carpenters' and metal-working tools, ploughs, grindstones, wagons and European clothing. Nearby stood his wagon house and a stone cattle kraal one and a half acres in area. The white doctor from Rustenburg paid house calls, often staying overnight in the guestroom featherbed, and a white tutor was employed to instruct Mokgatle's children in English.[65] Less is known of Kgamanyane's wealth, but enough to be assured it was substantial. He possessed wagons and a wagon house, many cattle and guns, and he married more wives than any kapitein in the ZAR, by far. In the trans-Vaal beyond ZAR control, only Sekhukhuni, with a reputed 48, had as many.[66] Both kapiteins exercised considerable authority, given the size of their respective towns and surrounding villages. Mokgatle's town of Phokeng had up to 600 houses in 1862, and Kgamanyane's people outside his capital lived in ten-to-twelve villages of 3,000 people. Their combined populations were estimated in 1862 at 11,000.[67] What is clear, then, is that in only a few years as Kruger's kapiteins, Mokgatle and Kgamanyane had increased their wealth and authority dramatically.

Slaves in the Early Republic

An additional ingredient in this profitable relationship was the small group of black artisans who worked for Kruger. 'He has his sawyers, tanners, limeburners, masons, thatchers, ploughmen, wagon-drivers, etc.' remarked one observer in 1862, 'and moreover his "shots" [who carry] on hunting expeditions'.[68] After years of slave raiding and domestic servitude, this new sort of African had begun to emerge in the Rustenburg district. Kruger was among the Boers who raised inboekelinge, trained them in various skills and put them to work as young adults. In the early years of Boer expansion, these *oorlamse* had been used mainly as personal servants, herders, ox drivers and hunters. But in the Rustenburg district of the late 1850s, where the economy was diversifying, skills were needed for processing leather goods, fruit and cash crops. The same held true for training 'Magaliesberg' oxen to trek and plough, tending to transport wagons and harness, building wagon and equipment houses, and assisting in the entertainment of guests. For those who had slaves, the advantages were many, and controlling them was not too difficult, because they had no land of their own or easy means of returning to their original homes. For the most part they were dependent on their owners for a place to live, though because of their skills some became attached to nearby African communities through marriage.

Such was the case for Matlhodi Kekana, also known as Paulina, as related by her descendants to her grandson, Naboth Mokgatle.[69] In or around

1853, while young, Matlhodi was captured in the Pietersburg area of the northern trans-Vaal during a raid on the Langa AmaNdebele followers of chief Mokopane. She became the inboekeling of a prominent Boer, remembered by Mokgatle's family as 'KaMongoele'. Mokgatle does not mention the Boer's given name, but the evidence – his Tswana nickname, which played on his intense religious piety (*Kamangole*, 'on the knees'), the Christian name he gave to Matlhodi, and the close ties he had with kgosi Mokgatle – points to him as none other than Paul Kruger, one of the leaders of the raid on Mokopane.

Paulina's responsibilities as Kruger's slave included working in the house, where as a young woman she was trained as a cook for his large family and its many visitors. She gained a reputation for her 'European' style cooking, which together with her attractive features caught the attention of Mokgatle, who visited Kruger often. Kgosi Mokgatle wanted Paulina as one of his wives and as his cook. It is revealing of Kruger, known as much for his intense religious conservatism as for his avarice and ambition, that he demanded bridewealth in cattle from Mokgatle. A 'number of cattle' then changed hands, at which point Paulina transferred her residence to Mokgatle's capital (Phokeng) and began her life as Mokgatle's wife. She bore him four children, of whom two survived.[70]

African kapiteins and their senior relatives were also interested in having oorlamse around, because like Paulina, they had a good command of spoken Dutch and were usually literate. Oorlamse enabled the BaFokeng and BaKgatla, among others, to adopt new technologies into their midst and communicate with the Rustenburg Boers and the ZAR government. Oorlamse were permitted to live among Africans, in order to encourage European ways and spread literacy and Christianity without, of course, challenging the temporal authority of the ZAR. Oorlamse, whether conscious of their role or not, were Boer agents of conservative change among their kaffer subjects.

Oorlamse and westernising kapiteins such as Mokgatle were showcases that helped Kruger and other ZAR leaders counter a notion popular in the British press that the ZAR Boers were half-civilised bumpkins running a predatory operation. The ZAR leadership, which was very sensitive to its image beyond its borders, put much effort into appearing to be morally upstanding. While silently condoning tens of commando raids that captured hundreds of inboekelinge and killed thousands of men and women, the ZAR Volksraad legislated against slavery and ZAR President Pretorius issued more than one proclamation banning the practice. Officially, commandos were conducted only against Africans who had taken the lives or property of whites, and the 'orphans' who were the unfortunate by-product of commando attacks were placed in the care of Boer families for proper upbringing. They were to be treated well, raised in the knowledge of Christ, and to be given their freedom when young adults. Africans in their midst required religious and moral education, too. Once civic order was established, the ZAR encouraged missionaries to establish mission churches near law-abiding kapiteins. In other words, the ZAR broadcast that it was doing its civic and religious duty, at one and the same time, by spreading 'civilisation' among the kaffers.

In their civic mode as upstanding slave-owners, the trans-Vaal Boers held that the kaffer children they had captured and registered as *inboekelinge* (lit. registerees) were being rescued from savagery and raised to be civilised (*oorlamse kaffers*). Once removed far from their homes, these children would become attached to their Boer owners, forget their African languages, and grow up as Dutch-speakers. Some did become Christians and learned how to read the Dutch Bible. Officially, enslavement was a merciful, uplifting act, one that bestowed comfort and privilege. The training that *inboekelinge* received in various skills, such as masonry, sewing, blacksmithing, thatching, wagon-making and gun repair also made them useful within the Boer community. They were simply a good investment. For the cost of a bit of food and shelter, they could be put to work on any day or as readily be sold for cash, given as gifts to friends, or bequeathed to one's heirs. Being young, impressionable and a long way from home, *inboekelinge* were easier to control than local kaffers, and by the time they became adults, *oorlamse* were easy to keep close by. Oorlamse men had no ready means of getting married except to *oorlamse* women, and the latter did not have to be married in order to be tied down with children. Yes, *oorlamse* women, especially the young attractive ones, had their value near to the men of Boer families.

The story of the oorlamse named 'Vieland' illustrates how deeply Boers in high places believed they were meeting their religious obligations. His story is based on what Vieland himself, at an advanced age, related about his past to the son of the man who had baptised him. As a boy of nine, Vieland was among the captives taken by Potgieter's forces when they attacked Mzilikazi's Ndebele at Mosega. The boy then became the property, or legally the apprentice, of Jacobus Venter, a man who later became highly respected in the Boer community. Venter was elected a church elder in the 'Dopper' community at Bloemfontein and rose to become Vice President of the Orange Free State. Venter, who named his black slave Vieland ('safe arrival'?), had the boy learn to read Dutch and know the catechism. Later, when Venter became blind, it was Vieland who read to him from the Bible.[71] Some time before he died, Venter gave Vieland into the care of old friend and fellow Dopper Paul Kruger. Vieland lived on Kruger's farm Saulspoort 38 and became 'one of Kgamanyane's people'.[72]

Thus, the Christian slave of the kommandant became the subject of the kapitein, and at a time when Kgamanyane was sensing that the ground under him was shifting. Though his authority had been suitably joined with Kruger's, Kgamanyane had resisted the idea that he could be controlled, even by the kommandant himself In the 1860s, however, his power and authority were confronted with a new threat for which he was unprepared.

ENDNOTES

1 Livingstone (1960: 301–302). Mokgatle had invited the LMS to send him a teacher.

2 Baines (1964: II, 170n36, 171, 172, 172n41), Freeman (1851: 260–261).

3 *Graham's Town Journal*, 10 Aug. 1850.

4 Ramsay (1991: 78, 80, 94–95); *Graham's Town Journal*, 19 Oct. 1850; Livingstone (1961: 95–96); Baines (1964: II, 73–74); Meintjes (1974: 25).

5 Ramsay (1991: 93–109), F. Morton (1994a: 170, 182n18).

6 *Graham's Town Journal*, 5 Jul. 1851; Sanderson (1860: 242).

7 Delius (1984: 38).

8 Tswana historical literature is replete with succession dispute accounts. For studies of this phenomenon, see Schapera (1963), J.L. Comaroff (1978), Crowder (1990).

9 Morelle, betrothed to Pilane before he met and married Mankube, was supported by many Kgatla because they claimed they had provided her bridewealth, as was customary for a kgosi's 'great wife' (i.e. mother of the future kgosi). Morelle was killed in 1831 or 1832 by Mzilikazi's regiments retaliating for Pilane's collusion in the Berends raid. Pilane had left Morelle behind, having absconded to the Langa (see ch. 1). On Pilane's return, he was given Mmantselana by Morelle's people as Morelle's substitute. Thus Tau, Mmantselana's eldest son, was regarded by Morelle's supporters as most entitled to succeed Pilane. Pilane, of course, had declared Mankube as his great wife, thereby marking Kgamanyane as his successor.

10 Interview with Selogwe Pilane (Ramaselwana), grandson of Mantirisi, Mochudi, 26 Jun. 1985 (Schapera 1942a: 9, 11). Schapera suggests that Tshomankane's claims to the rank below Kgamanyane also became the basis of another controversy, but this appears to be construed from Tshomankane's later alleged dispute with Kgamanyane and his migration to Bopitiko (Doornhoek 910). His move to Bopitiko, however, was caused not by a tiff with Kgamanyane but by Boer demands for Kgatla labour. See below. Breutz (DSAB: IV, 177) claims that Kgamanyane's uncles Kgotlamaswe and Molefi served as regents before he was old enough to be installed, but there is no evidence for this. In fact, Livingstone met Kgamanyane in January 1849 seven months after Livingstone had reported Pilane's death, and he referred to him as Pilane's son and who 'has a large tribe'. Livingstone then visited Kgotlamaswe on the opposite side of the Pilanesberg (Livingstone 1959: II, 12).

11 Schapera (1942a: 9), Breutz (1953: 259) and Selogwe Pilane's interview, which alone of these sources states which brothers supported Kgamanyane. Selogwe, like many Kgatla in recent times, is familiar with Schapera and Breutz's publications, and he has adopted their version that Kgamanyane's brothers broke with him by migrating, even though it contradicts traditions that have come directly to him.

12 In Bechuanaland, commoners often played a much different role; following a succession dispute, a new kgosi could move his residence to an open area in which his commoner supporters could collect, be elevated in social importance and insulate him from his royal opponents. And as Landau has shown, Christianising commoners under a kgosi-led mission church could be used for the same purpose (Landau 1995).

13 As opposed to giving loan cattle (*mafisa*), the usual devise used by royals in Bechuanaland, Basutoland and the old Northern Cape to attach commoners to their cause.

14 Interview with Seikgokgoni Pilane, Kgosing, Mochudi, 21 Dec. 1981.

15 For a summary of the law governing royal Kgatla inheritance, see 'Report of the Commission Appointed to Enquiring into the Estate of the Late Chief Linchwe Pilane', s. 343/25: 4–5, BNA. For more on royal cattle, see the testimony of Isang Pilane before the Linchwe Estate Commission, s. 343/24: 8, BNA. Isang asserted that Kgamanyane's claim of Pilane's cattle drove his brothers away, a version that surfaces in subsequent Kgatla oral traditions but one that is contradicted by nineteenth-century evidence. See below and chs. 4 and 5.

16 Sanderson (1860: 250), Ramsay (1991: 96). Sanderson did not suggest the cause of the epidemic, but it is not likely to have been smallpox. Sanderson observed that the Fokeng were marked with smallpox and that the disease was 'not now prevalent but formerly common and fatal'. It is possible that malaria, or what was known north of the Limpopo in the mid-1830s as 'Delagonian fever', spread into the Pilanesberg at the same time and had sufficient hosts by the late 1840s to make an epidemic possible (Wallis 1945: I, 54, 59, 74, 81, 137). In the 1860s and 1870s there are written references to 'fever' during wet years in the trans-Vaal and Bechuanaland.

17 See the events of 1869 below, and other examples in chs. 3, 4 and 5.

18 Lions were still plentiful north of the Magaliesberg.

19 See Delius (1984: 37) for more on Moletse. Delius places the battle a year later in 1847,

but it had been fought the year prior to Livingstone's visit in early 1847; see Livingstone (1961: 98–99). For Mzilikazi see Livingstone (1959: II, 57), Omer-Cooper (1966: 152), Wallis (1945: II, 225, 367). Delius refers to Moletse as a 'Kgatla' leader. For Moletse's *Kwena*, see Van Warmelo (1935: 44). In 1848 word reached Sechele that Potgieter had attacked the Langa Ndebele (Livingstone 1959: I, 236; 1974: 57n., 150). This may be connected to the 1848 report published by the *Commercial Advertiser* referred to by Freeman (1851: 274), in which the Boers were said to have besieged 'a native tribe' of some 4,000, trapped them in a cave, and burned them alive. I am grateful to Barry Morton for this reference.

20 Livingstone (1959: II: 57–58).

21 The town of Magaliesberg was renamed Rustenburg in 1850, and the Rustenburg district was created in 1851. For the early Boer districts, see Bergh (1999: 17).

22 Struben (1920: 110).

23 Kruger made it to full veldkornet the month before his election as kommandant (Kruger 1902: 41–42).

24 Testimony of S.J.P. Kruger (Bloemhof 1871: 258–259, 261; Matthews 1945: 17–18; Sillery 1952: 173). In his *Memoirs*, Kruger mistakenly places this battle in December 1853 (Kruger 1902: 50–52).

25 Livingstone (1961: 97–99). Mankopane was the leader of one of the Ndebele groups of the Makapansberg and is often confused with Mokopane (Mughombane) of the Kekana Ndebele. Adding to the confusion are Boer references to Mankopane as Mapela, the name of the Langa leader whom Mankopane succeeded. Also, ZAR documents often refer to Mokopane as 'Makapan'. I am grateful to Jan Boeyens for explaining the differences. On the Langa Ndebele, see Jackson (1983).

26 Struben (1920: 47, 52–53). I am grateful to Barry Morton for this reference.

27 Livingstone (1961: 97–98), Agar-Hamilton (1928: 190–191). Delius mistakes the year of this battle as 1847 (Delius 1984: 37). For Moletse's Kwena see Van Warmelo (1935: 44). For the Buys brothers, see Boeyens (1994: 196, 200–201, 210n52), Wagner (1980).

28 Livingstone (1974: 57n, 150); Livingstone (1959: I, 236); Sanderson (1860: 242); *Graham's Town Journal*, 5 Jul. 1851; *Natal Mercury* 9 Jun. 1853. I am grateful to Barry Morton for the latter two references.

29 Kruger (1902: 42–44).

30 Ibid.: 47.

31 'Ntwa Yakwagamokopana' in Schapera (1965: 65–69).

32 The ashes made the hair appear to be white or grey, thus the allusion to old age in contrast to the youthful mophato. Kgamanyane was in his late twenties at the time.

33 Mfatlha Maila appears to have been the leader of a faction of trans-Vaal AmaNdebele whose main group under Bohosi was conquered by Pilane, and whose subsequent leader Mochela Mfatlha (also known as Zwaartbooi) was a vassal of Pilane and Kgamanyane. Kgamanyane then brought Mfatlha's group under his authority. According to Schapera, the Mfatlha were known as BaBididi and BaTlhalerwa, the latter with reference to their totem (wild dog) (Schapera 1965: 68n1). However, Breutz distinguishes the Mfatlha of AmaNdebele origin from the BaBididi and BaTlhalerwa of

Karanga origin (Breutz 1987: 432, 473–474). Thanks to Jan Boeyens for noting this discrepancy.

34 Ndebele, i.e., Langa.

35 For more extended discussions, see F. Morton (1994a, 1994c), Boeyens (1994), Erasmus (1995: 37–39).

36 Baines (1964: II, 69).

37 Holden (1963: 388).

38 Sanderson (1860: 242).

39 Orpen (1979: 151). I am grateful to Betsy Eldredge for this reference.

40 *Natal Mercury*, 16 Apr. 1857.

41 Bonner (1983: 80–81).

42 On the Pedi, see Livingstone (1959: II: 57–58) and Baines (1964: II, 113–114, 123, 131); on the Mmakau Kgatla, see Baines (1964: II, 170n36, 171, 172, 172n41) and Bergh (1999: 156); on the Langa, see *Graham's Town Journal*, 5 Jul. 1851.

43 Two of Baines's independent sources confirmed that men and women were killed in the attack on Mamoanwana ('Sjambok'), which fits the standard pattern of raids that produced captive children as 'orphans'. In Mokopane's case, all later known raids against the Langa (1854, 1858, 1868) yielded captive children, so the 1851 attack is not likely to have been an exception. It appears to have been a raid, also, to follow up on Sjambok, who took refuge at Mokopane's. The raids on Mamoanwana and Mokopane also followed another in 1849, around June or July, when an unnamed group living somewhere in the vicinity of Potchefstroom was attacked, many of their adults killed and their children carried away – this according to one of the survivors (Freeman 1851: 260–261). I am grateful to Dan Galbraith for this reference.

44 This prior to Mosielele's flight to Sechele's Kwena at Dimawe. Moffat reported that Mosielele's people had 'many more' of their children taken by the Boers than did the Kwena (Wallis 1945: I, 154–155).

45 Theal (1969: I, 434).

46 Massa testimony in Bloemhof (1871: 62, 64); Collins (1965: 155–156); *Graham's Town Journal*, 26 Mar. 1859; August (Moloe) statement, 18 May 1874, COCP 879/7/61, 153–155 (I am grateful to Barry Morton for this reference).

47 Trapido (1980: 357).

48 Trapido (1980: 366n26). Trapido does not provide farm numbers and his 'Beeskraal' is certainly the modern Beestkraal and 'Modderkind' the farm Modderkuil. His list of farms has been compared with Breutz (1953: 27–39 and map), ALFTP, and Topo-Cadastral 2526 (Rustenburg) to determine their location and modern numbers.

49 Resolution 181 of 18 Jun. 1855 (Eybers 1969: 362).

50 Breutz (1953: 65); Bergh and Morton 2003: Declaration No. 25, Mokgatle Thethe. In his declaration, Mokgatle claimed that Potgieter had also allocated to him Boekenhout-fontein 260 and Turffontein 262, which came into Kruger's possession in the 1860s, but in all cases 'the [white] people took the land from me'. Mokgatle was probably asked to vacate Kookfontein by Kruger's predecessor. In 1847, when Paul Kruger's uncle Gerrit was the district kommandant, Mokgatle was complaining that he was no longer

master of his 'paternal territory' (i.e. Kookfontein), and in early 1852, before Kruger şucceeded his uncle as kommandant, Mokgatle had been living at Phokeng (Beerfontein) for some time (Livingstone 1961: 95; Sanderson 1860: 248).

51 Eybers (1969: 364, 405). The Registrar of Deeds testified in 1871 that it was customary before issuing a title deed for the *Government Gazette* to publish the Executive Council's intention to transfer ownership of a farm and for the Registrar to then wait three months for anyone to object (Bergh and Morton 2003: Declaration No. 7 [J.J. Meintjies]; see also Declaration No. 6 (P.J. van Staden).

52 Bergh and Morton 2003: Volksraad minutes, 13 Nov. 1871.

53 John Sanderson, who spent a month in the Rustenburg area in 1852, observed fruit orchards that produced low-grade brandy ('Cape Smoke'), and some tobacco and grain, but they were grown for local consumption only. Sanderson saw much more agricultural development in the southern trans-Vaal in the area of Potchefstroom (Mooi River Dorp). On Boer farms there and generally between the River and the Magaliesberg range, fruit trees were abundant, and tobacco was grown (Sanderson 1860: 241, 243, 245–247).

54 The *Natal Mercury* of 4 Dec. 1863 reported that 'A large quantity of ivory has been received from the Transvaal, and other large packets may be expected. There appears to be an indefinite supply of this article at the hunting depots of the interior. During the past season hunters have been unusually successful'. By 1866, Pretoria had become Transvaal's principal ivory market (ibid., 9 Oct. 1866). I am grateful to Barry Morton for these references.

55 Schapera (1942a: 10; 1965: 69ff.); Breutz (1987: 275); *Transvaal Argus*, 5 Feb. 1868.

56 Gonin to DRC, 13 May 1862, 15/7/2 (A), DRCA.

57 Baines (1964: II, 311); Wallis (1945: 187ff.; 1946: I, 30–32); Gonin to DRC, 12 Aug. 1869, 15/7/2 (A), DRCA.

58 Gonin to DRC, 13 May, 4 Jul. and 9 Aug. 1862, 15/7/2 (A) and (E), DRCA. In 1858, Kgamanyane's vassal, Zwaartbooi, was part of a Boer embassy to Mzilikazi. It was led by Kruger's political ally, T.J. Snyman, and Kruger's son-in-law, veldkornet Sarel Eloff (*Graham's Town Journal*, 9 Nov. 1858). According to the late Amos Kgamanyane Pilane of Mochudi, Kgamanyane employed his Bididi vassals, of whom Zwaartbooi was the leader, to collect ivory in the Thabazimbi area, and Kgamanyane conducted elephant hunts in the area near present Warmbaths (Interview, 20 Jul. 1980).

59 In 1867 after being overthrown, Sekgoma and 75 of his followers turned up at Kgamanyane's, and Paul Kruger gave them a place to settle northeast of Mabieskraal (*Natal Mercury*, 25 Jun. 1867, reprinting a report from the *Transvaal Argus* of 6 Jun. 1 867; P.J. van Staden to M.W. Pretorius, 7 Aug. 1867, SS90, R818/67, TA). They eventually resettled at Sechele's.

60 Bergh and Morton 2003: Declaration No. 18 (Christof Penzhorn) and No. 20 (Hercules Phillipus Malan), and statement of J.R. Lys in Volksraad Minutes, 11 Nov. 1871.

61 'Natives of the Transvaal', *Graham's Town Journal*, 11 Oct. 1862 as reprinted from *Zuid Afrikaan*. This lengthy, detailed commentary shows unusual gifts of observation. I am grateful to Barry Morton for this source.

62 Bergh and Morton 2003: Declaration No. 18. Penzhorn added: 'They bring along their own food and are, as far as I know, not paid. They must thresh the corn of the Commandant-General [Kruger was appointed to this position in 1863] on the farm where they may prepare the soil with hoes. This was stipulated under contract.' See also Declaration No. 17 (H.L. Gonin).

63 'Natives of the Transvaal', *Graham's Town Journal*, 11 Oct. 1862 as reprinted from *Zuid Afrikaan*.

64 *Natal Mercury*, 11 Dec. 1866.

65 Ibid.; *Natal Mercury*, 11 Dec. 1866.

66 Breutz (1953: 260–263) lists 25 wives, whereas I. Schapera ('Kgamanayane – Agnatic Male Descendants', in SP, PP 1/3/8, BNA) shows 44. In the 1930s Hendrik Molefi claimed that Kgamanyane had had 'about seventy' wives. 'History of the BaKgatla Tribe', ibid., PP 1/4/2. Breutz lists none of Mokgatle's wives, but he was said during his lifetime to have 26 wives and 70 sons (*Natal Mercury*, 11 Dec. 1866). One of Mokgatle's grandsons tried to find out, but was given answers varying between more than 40 and less than 40 (Mokgatle 1971: 40). For references to Kgamanyane's wagons, and so on, see Gonin to DRC, 13 May 1862 and 15 Apr. 1866, 15/7/2 (E) and Gonin to DRC, 13 Jun. and 9 Aug. 1862, 22 Sep. 1870, 15/7/2 (A), DRCA.

67 *Natal Mercury*, 7 Jan. 1862; note references to 'Bakahla' and 'Bamogale'. Also Gonin to DRC, 13 May 1862, 15/7/2 (E), and 22 Sep. 1870, 15/7/2 (A), DRCA.

68 'Natives of the Transvaal', *Graham's Town Journal*, 11 Oct. 1862 as reprinted from *Zuid Afrikaan*.

69 Mokgatle (1971: 39–40).

70 For a fuller discussion of Paulina and other female slaves, see Morton (2005, 2007).

71 Story of Stephanus Moloto, as told to the son of H.L. Gonin in 1938, written in the margin of Gonin to DRC, 23 Sep. 1867 (see also 12 Jun. 1867), 15/7/2 (E), DRCA. Breutz (1987: 345) ascribes the Moloto name as derived from Chief Moletsi (of the Bakwena baga Moletse of Soutpansberg) (Ramono's genealogy). Moloto was in fact the name of a chief and chiefdom of the Moletse BaKwena, Rhenosterpoort. (I am grateful to Jan Boeyens for this information). On the Moletse Kwena, see Van Warmelo (1935: 44). In 1982, before I was aware of slaving in the trans-Vaal, I interviewed the grandson of Stephanus, Dr. Ernest Sedumedi Moloto, then Professor of African Languages at the University of Botswana. 'E.S.' did not mention the name Vieland, or much of the history of Stephanus, telling me only that his grandfather had come from 'BoPedi' (Gaborone, 22 Feb. 1982). More recently, the historical novel *People of Welgeval* written by Stephanus' great-great granddaughter Botlhale Tema and based on family traditions, explains that her ancestor *adopted* the Moloto clan name of a close friend, an oorlamse who originated from the 'Moletji' (Bakwena baga Moletse) (Tema 2005: 3–9).

72 The DRC missionary Henri Gonin found Vieland there in 1865 and baptised him Stephanus (Gonin to DRC, Jan. 1865 and 12 Jun. 1867, ibid.). On Venter, see Dictionary of South African Biography: I, 845.

Chapter three

SAULSPOORT 38[1]

The fool puts out the fires of others,
He puts out those of the gun-brandishers,
And says, 'let the fires go out and mine burn,
May that burn of the foolish Nimble One,
Brother of Rakitla the Kgatla . . .'

The Slasher does not kill, yet he kills,
He also quenches fires, the Slasher,
Son of the woman from Tlokwaland.
(Kgamanyane's praise, composed by himself)

* * *

In our state there are easily 1,000 kleurlingen against one white. We
cannot but regard them as the archenemies of the whites. If we our-
selves help to prepare our enemies to get the opportunity to beat us,
it would be better to hand over our country to them and go away . . .
for their entire nature is such that as soon as they get that opportuni-
ty, they will not allow the whites to stay a day longer in the country.
(Paul Kruger)

In 1861 when he transferred his capital from Mmasebudule (Rhenosterfontein 86) to Kruger's farm (Saulspoort 38), Kgamanyane was making
a sensible move. Mmasebudule, located on the southeastern corner of the
Pilanesberg, was served by the Kgetleng (Elands) river and had good soil,
but it was hemmed in by Boer farms and situated far from the winter grazing areas needed for the Kgatla's herds, which had been expanding from
the booty earned in support of *seBuru* commandos. Saulspoort, a very large
farm by trans-Vaal standards, at 3,925 morgen (33.63 square kilometres),
was twice the size of Rhenosterfontein and with ample space, good soil
and year-round water to accommodate Kgamanyane's growing population
of followers. Also, Saulspoort was situated at the base of the northern slopes
of the Pilanesberg and faced the extensive winter grazing and hunting areas
stretching north to the Oodi (Krokodil) and Madikwe (Marico) rivers.
The plains below Saulspoort were open. When Kgamanyane moved there,

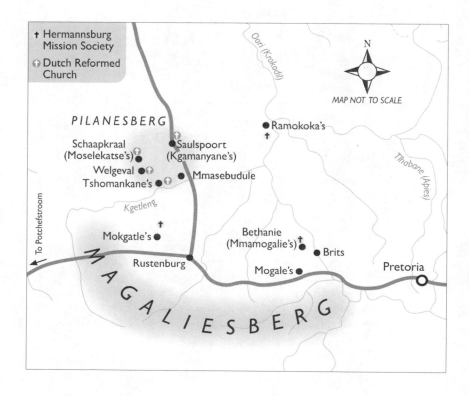

none of the surrounding farms were occupied by white farmers. Some Kgatla were already living on Kruger's adjacent farms of Modderkuil 39 and Middelkuil 8. Saulspoort itself was also familiar ground. The BaKgatla had long known it as Mmamitlwe or Moruleng, as well as Maremapoong after the old Kgatla settlement nearby. Forty years earlier, the area near Mmamitlwe had been occupied during the brief reign of Kgamanyane's uncle Letsebe, who settled next to the hill Mabule at Middelkuil 8, which a century before had been the site of the capital of the legendary Kgatla kgosi Masellano.[2] Saulspoort is identified with the storied Ntshole (Saul), whose people lived there under Pilane when the first Boers arrived in the area.

Kruger also had good reasons for wanting Kgamanyane at Saulspoort. Apart from using this gift farm as a base for winter hunting, Kruger had not developed it. With Kgamanyane's people on site, a dam could be constructed and the soil brought into production. Moreover, the partnership Kruger had formed with Kgamanyane in channelling ivory into the trans-Vaal and on to Durban and the Cape would be strengthened by having Kgamanyane at Saulspoort, which stood closer to the northern sources and lay astride the Rustenburg–Shoshong road. Increasing the ivory take was probably the major initial motive, because within months of resettling at Saulspoort, Kgamanyane departed on an ivory expedition to Shoshong and Matabeleland.[3] Certainly, Kruger was already thinking beyond profiting from game trophies and imagining better returns from his properties. With Kgamanyane's large kaffer concentration at Saulspoort, farms in this remote area of the Rustenburg district were more likely to attract white buyers, anticipating ready labour. The dried fruit and cash-cropping methods introduced in the Rustenburg area in the late 1850s were catching on, making the early 1860s a good time for Kruger's real estate ventures. And with Kgamanyane waxing wealthy from the commando raids that continued to involve the chief with the kommandant, Kruger could think of leasing, if not selling, the farm to the *hoofdkapitein* for a handsome sum.

Whatever Kruger's intention, or Kgamanyane's, in converting Saulspoort into a large Kgatla settlement, the farm quickly assumed central importance in their relationship, which began to deteriorate. Change for the worse between these erstwhile partners occurred because the trans-Vaal was being transformed by forces beyond their control. Until 1861, they had been accustomed to exerting their influence over others and suffering no opposition. After 1861, however, they were beset by troubles brought on them by peaceful men who undermined their authority and provoked them to act rashly. Kgamanyane's nemesis was the young Swiss missionary Henri Gonin, Kruger's, the dutiful Rustenburg landdrost P.J. van Staden. Gonin and Van Staden were anything but threats personally to the hoofdkapitein and the kommandant. They stood rather as proponents, respectively, of the supremacy of Christianity and civil law over the violent Kgatla and *Voortrekker* military culture of Kgamanyane and Kruger. The two represented a sentiment growing among trans-Vaal whites wishing to reduce the use of force and institute in its place regulations, laws, taxes and orderly relations between white and black. Kruger and Kgamanyane did not submit readily to such notions or willingly yield their powers. Instead, as might be expected of bullies, they made threats and indulged in displays of force. And, as their relative positions slipped, Kruger and Kgamanyane turned on one another, taking poor measure of the other's will or strength while exaggerating their own.

The New Order

Soon after Kruger built up his farm holdings north of Rustenburg, this area began to become an important source of home-grown exports. In 1860, for example, 'Magaliesberg' oxen suddenly began to appear in Cape trade figures. At Grahamstown, 62 were sold in February 1860, 70 in October and in February 1861, another 56 at prices ranging between £7.10 to £10.60 per head. Then in February 1862, 130 head sold at £8.16 on average, with 14 fetching £15.50. A month later, 642 head of Magaliesberg oxen and slaughter cattle were auctioned in Grahamstown, and in May 170 oxen and 22 cows.[4] Magaliesberg oxen had become a major drawcard. In 1863 the *Graham's Town Journal* announced the 'finest lot of oxen ever brought to the market', referring to 'large, fat Magaliesberg trek oxen . . . twelve spans'. Another 59 were announced for sale at the next market. By the mid-1860s, 'thousands of head of cattle yearly' from the trans-Vaal were reaching Natal and the Cape.[5] Also beginning in the late 1850s, British farmers from the Cape and Orange Free State made their way into the trans-Vaal, purchased farms and began cash-cropping in the Rustenburg area. They cultivated coffee, sugar cane, bananas, oranges and wheat.[6] By the mid-1860s cash crops were being planted north of Rustenburg, and coffee, sugar cane, dried fruit, tobacco and cotton were being produced for the market.[7] From the very areas Kruger was acquiring farms came the

Rustenburg district's first important cash earnings since the days of the ivory market.

This economic boom was accompanied by political and religious turbulence. For years unstable, the ZAR entered its final sequence of internal rebellions, while Kruger's Rustenburg was whirling with the religiosity of the four active rival theological groups in the trans-Vaal represented there: from right to left, the Jerusalem Pilgrims, the Christelijke-Gereformeerde Kerk (CGK) the Nederduitsch Hervormde Kerk (NHK), and the Nedersduitse Gereformeerde Kerk (Dutch Reformed Church – DRC).[8] Rustenburg was home to two of these factions: the breakaway NHK and its offshoot, the CGK, better known as the 'Dopper Church'. The NHK spread through the trans-Vaal as a reaction against Cape-based DRC, unpopular in the ZAR because it had opposed the movement of the Voortrekkers out of the Cape, gave allegiance to the Queen, adhered to British laws and had come under the influence of Scottish predicants. The first NHK minister in the ZAR was Hollander Dirk van der Hoff, who was installed by the United Volksraad at Rustenburg in 1853. Several years later, the ultra-conservative NHK members in Rustenburg led a breakaway movement from the young state church.[9] The 'Doppers', as the schismatic group was called, rejected the NHK practice of singing 'man-made hymns' (as opposed to psalms). In 1857, the Rustenburg Doppers established their own separatist anti-singing movement and, in 1859, with the arrival of Reverend Dirk Postma from the Netherlands, they formed their own church, the CGK. The lay leader of the Doppers was Rustenburg Kommandant Paul Kruger. The kommandant had undergone a religious calling at a time propitious for a political rise.

Kruger gained influence with the trans-Vaal maBuru because he could act decisively in chaotic moments and project cold religious certainty amidst competing fervours. Although the Doppers remained a religious minority, Kruger's commitment to the preservation of Boer outposts under threat from African resistance (sparked in part as we know by the very commando raids Kruger had led) and in defence of what Dunbar Moodie calls 'radical democratic liberalism', made him a popular figure in the 1860s. Kruger's faith was voiced in the belief long in circulation that the 'Volk' (i.e., the Voortrekkers and their descendants) were God's 'chosen people' and that the ZAR Volksraad was the 'voice of God'.[10] Kruger led commandos not only against recalcitrant kaffers on ZAR's borders but against Boer rebels who defied elected ZAR officials and Volksraad laws. His intense brand of religious politics made him the type who never doubted himself or hesitated to act once he had his mind made up. It was uncanny, though, how often what he decided needed doing for the good of the 'Volk', or anybody else for that matter, proved to be especially good for Paul Kruger.

Kruger got the backing of the Rustenburgers, in spite of Boer divisions typical of the day. In the political battles in the ZAR at large that often erupted in violence, the Rustenburgers showed a united front when Kruger stepped forward. They followed him against Schoeman when the latter attempted to scuttle Pretorius and Van Rensburg's presidencies. Kruger's service gained him state-wide popularity and full military leadership of the ZAR as kommandant-generaal, and in 1864 it kept the Rustenburgers behind him when he fought the rebel Piet Joubert at Zwartkoppies, northeast of Brits.[11] After this point, however, the Volksraad worked to calm the political waters and increase the authority of civil officials over that of the military. In the process Kruger became hard of hearing when listening to the 'voice of God' and showed reluctance in allowing his authority as military commander in chief to be relegated.

In spite of Kruger's popularity as a republican, the farmers in his own area were unhappy with him about the difficulties in getting kaffer labour. Rapid farm expansion was partly to blame, but Kruger was having no difficulty supplying workers to himself or his religious followers. Or at least it seemed so to vocal Rustenburg Boers, who knew that Kruger had plenty of kaffer labour and they had almost none. 'In this privilege', one 1862 report stated, 'in a more or less degree, the favourites of Baas Paul also participate, especially those belonging to his church (that of Postma). The Rev. Mr. Smits [of the NHK] can hardly get any Kafirs . . . This was openly complained of at Rustenburg.'[12] As labour shortages continued in the Rustenburg district, Boer resentment towards Kruger as the cause of these problems was constantly simmering. So too was their feeling that kaffers living on his farms were getting out of hand. Kgamanyane in particular was gaining a reputation in the district for being 'gruff' and 'surly'.[13]

The Arrival of Rev. Gonin

When missionaries appeared in the Rustenburg district, Kruger saw an opportunity of attaching men of the cloth to the likes of Kgamanyane, Ramokoka and other kapiteins as a way of cooling them down without involving other ZAR authorities in district affairs.[14] In May 1862, during a lull in the Schoeman affair, Kruger was the first to meet Henri Louis Gonin, the first missionary in the district since Livingstone's controversial visit in 1849. Gonin, a Swiss minister recruited by Rev. William Robertson of Swellendam, was part of the Synodale Mission of the DRC, which was created in 1857 to revive missionary efforts in South Africa and establish new stations among Africans north of the Vaal River.[15] He was escorted by Andrew Murray, DRC minister of the Bloemfontein congregation and popular figure among the Boers. From the beginning, Gonin got help from Kruger and several key Rustenburgers in meeting his everyday needs and gaining access to the surrounding African populations. But for the most part, Gonin thought himself a 'stranger in a strange land in the midst of a population for the most part if not hostile at least indifferent towards [me]'.[16] He knew no Dutch or *SeTswana*, lived in an area where the DRC congregation was a small minority and where the Boer population held suspicions of missionaries that since Livingstone's day had run deep.

In a real sense Gonin was rescued in his first months by three oorlamse with connections to Kgamanyane and *Baas* Paul. They helped Gonin get around, learn the local languages and make sense of the social landscape. The most valuable was 'Brother David', who served as Gonin's interpreter, language instructor and church attendant during the missionary's first year in Rustenburg. David spoke and read the testaments in SeSotho and SeTswana, understood kaffer language (IsiXhosa), Dutch and 'a little English'. He had been converted by the Grahamstown Wesleyans.[17] Also helpful to Gonin was his wagon-driver 'September', who read Dutch 'rather well'. September's brother 'January' followed McKidd to the Soutpansberg to work as his servant. January also knew Dutch and could read SeSotho. Gonin does not mention the brothers' origins, but subsequent events show they belonged to the BaRokologadi, a group who were then vassals of the BaKgatla.[18] When David left Gonin in 1863, January, just returned from the Soutpansberg, took his place as interpreter. Together, David, September and January helped Gonin to conduct church services in Rustenburg among the oorlamse, learn the local languages, meet Africans in the countryside and get his bearings while quietly cultivating the good will of local Boers and gaining acceptance for a DRC mission in the area.

In the meantime, Kruger's backing was proving to be of mixed value. He was more than willing to place Gonin in touch with the kapiteins near his farms, but Gonin realised Kruger was an unpopular figure with other near-

Henri Gonin and family, 1875. Clockwise from top: Henri Gonin, Fanny (1866–194?), Elisa (1870–194?), Amedeir (1868–1929), Henri-Theodore (1887–1932), Jenny (1838–1932). Sketch by Lemington Muzhingi, based on a photograph supplied to the author by Elizabeth Viljoen, Pretoria.

by farmers who were competing with the kommandant for each kapitein's ear. His problem was made the more difficult by a ZAR law that required a missionary to have an invitation from a *kafferkapitein* before being permitted to establish a mission station.[19] In May 1862 when Kruger accompanied Gonin to Mokgatle's, the Fokeng kapitein convened a public assembly and the vote was overwhelmingly against accepting Gonin. On Gonin's behalf, the kommandant approached kapitein Moatshe Ramokoka of the Kwena Phalane, and he flatly refused. 'As soon as [I] receive the book', he told Kruger, '[I] will die'. Kruger told Gonin that he suspected local Boer farmers of threatening the kapiteins.[20]

Kruger then escorted Gonin to Kgamanyane at his main residence on Kruger's farm Saulspoort. Kruger assured Gonin that 'many of the tribe of Gamjan had come to him and asked that [I] should remain to teach [them].' As it turned out Kgamanyane was away on an ivory trading expedition and not expected back until the end of the winter.[21] Though Kruger's acquaintance was proving to be something of a liability, the kommandant was the only Boer farmer in the area willing to introduce Gonin to the kapiteins, and as the principal supporter of newly-elected President van Rensburg, his friendship could prove to be invaluable. Gonin had no way of knowing, however, which political direction the ZAR was taking. In the year following Gonin's arrival in Rustenburg, the ZAR was in political turmoil with Kruger in the thick of things. While Kruger remained distracted by political matters, Gonin confined himself pretty much to Rustenburg, where he worked on his Dutch and SeTswana, held occasional services for the few local DRC church members, and taught the oorlamse who lived in the town.[22] He paid two visits to President van Rensburg in Pretoria and waited for the return of Kgamanyane, who was reportedly coming back to Saulspoort by December 1862.[23]

By mid-1863, when elections restored calm in the ZAR, Gonin decided to approach Kgamanyane on his own. He was encouraged to do so by January and September. These two brothers had recently been living among and teaching their fellow BaRokologadi of Sentswe, one of Kgamanyane's vassals in the western Pilanesberg. Before reaching Kgamanyane's, Gonin visited Sentswe's people, and Gonin got a 'good reception [from] . . . a good number who want to be taught and asked me to come and settle among them'.[24] All he felt he could do, however, was tell Sentswe to issue an invitation through Paul Kruger. Gonin went on to Kgamanyane's, with January in tow, and faced a cold reception. 'Many would like to read but they are afraid of the chief', wrote Gonin, 'and some are afraid of the whites'.[25] Again, Kruger's backing was insufficient to overcome the objections of neighbouring Boer farm owners. Several months later Gonin returned to Sentswe's and Kgamanyane's, and this time found Kgamanyane's younger brother Bogatsu eager to send a delegation to Kruger requesting that Gonin set up a mission at Saulspoort. Kgamanyane was not opposed to this. Before reaching Kgamanyane, though, Gonin had spotted a farm for sale near Sentswe's and had been taking some advice on real estate.

> In general, people advise us if we want to settle in this country, rather to buy farms for there is scarcely any ground left to the Government and even in the least favorable spots and then we should be always more dependent and every political revolution in the Republic would again bring our position into uncertainty.[26]

Gonin reasoned, in other words, that pinning his hopes on Kgamanyane and Kruger was too risky. Rather than wait to be invited to live at Saulspoort, Gonin decided to buy his own farm near Sentswe's and lure prospective converts there. By the middle of 1864 he was the owner of Welgeval 171 and had built a small church, with a Swiss cowbell on top.[27]

Gonin got a friendly response. In the first months, January and three other oorlamse at Sentswe's – Niklaas, April and Jakob – built Gonin a house, and people from the surrounding farms paid him visits. Among them was Vieland, who had made the 18-kilometre trek through the Pilanesberg from Saulspoort.[28] The local white farmers seemed content to have Gonin in the neighbourhood. When Veldkornet Sarel Eloff dropped by, Gonin made it a point to tell him that he intended to 'behave himself as a quiet citizen and . . . act according to the laws of the state'. But Gonin need not have; Eloff's reply shows that the missionary had already passed muster: 'Sure, we know you now and we know that you won't incite the blacks against the whites as others did.'

It began to dawn on Gonin, however, that being a farm owner limited his effectiveness as a missionary, no matter how acceptable his behaviour was to the Boer farmers and officials. Gonin was free to hold services and evangelise, but he had no means of starting a mission. Because no kapitein was living on Welgeval, he was entitled to have only four African heads of family living on his farm. Perhaps it hit him when Eloff rode by one day and reminded Gonin about having 'four kaffers . . . and that I had only to choose those I wanted'.[29] Gonin was also waking up to the fact that his Gospel message no longer held a monopoly in the Rustenburg district. In August 1864, HMS missionaries appeared on the scene, and in October two paid him a visit at Wegelval to chart a strategy. Gonin asked them 'to leave us the two tribes of Magata [Mokgatle] and Gamijan [Kgamanyane]',[30] Gonin's DRC was being swiftly overtaken, though. By December, the Hermannsburgers had established stations at Moatshe Ramokoka's (Phalane) and Mmamogale's (Bethanie), and in January 1865 he learned that Mokgatle wanted a German missionary (i.e., HMS) 'like those at Mohela's [Moilwa] and Secheli's'. It hardly improved matters when Gonin heard that Paul Kruger had promised the HMS could buy his farm at Mokgatle's. Gonin was soon brooding.

> In general strange to say these missionaries are less mistrusted than ourselves, by all parties here. The State church here considers us with suspicion, thinking that we are but spies sent to intervene against them and the members of the dissenting churches don't trust us either.[31]

Gonin had to find a way out of Welgeval. He was quickly losing ground to the HMS and creating doubts about his effectiveness. Just two years in his job, Gonin was already running the risk of losing his credibility in Cape Town. He had convinced his home office to bankroll Welgeval, and now he was going to have to tell them it was a wasted investment. His correspondence to his superiors runs pretty thin in 1865, and the little news that reached them could not have inspired their confidence. That year Gonin gained only a few candidates for baptism and ended up baptising no one; then his principal source of candidates, Sentswe's people, suddenly dried up. Rather than put up with the labour demands of their farm owner, the Rokologadi, including Niklaas, Jacob and April, migrated to Sechele's in Botswana.[32] The only residents at Welgeval were January plus September and Khoomane (September's brother-in-law), and their wives and children.

Kgamanyane Defiant

Meanwhile, Kgamanyane's profile as a threat in the district was growing. In fact ever since moving onto Baas Paul's Saulspoort farm, the hoofdkapitein had kept the local maBuru nervous. He was known to be too fond of mampoer, often drunk and violent. One story floated about that he had disembowelled a woman who came too near the male initiation camp.[33] Worse still, Kgamanyane had a reputation for unruliness with whites. Veld-kornet P.J. van der Walt (from the Marico district) stated that Kgamanyane had 'always been a disobedient kapitein' and Hercules Malan admitted that he could not control him. He alleged that Kommandant-generaal Kruger had suspended the kapitein at least once for drunkenness and that Kgamanyane had absented himself from the area often rather than submit to any discipline from ZAR officials.[34] In 1864 a rumour whizzed through the district that he was in revolt.[35] Thus Kgamanyane – regarded as the hoofd-kapitein, with more kaffers than any kapitein in the Rustenburg district, one whom the Rustenburg veldkornet called 'a big power', the man living on Paul Kruger's own farm and under his ultimate authority as kommandant-generaal – was the least controlled and the most dangerous.

In truth, Kgamanyane had come to despise the maBuru as weak, ignorant and dependent on kapiteins like him. He sensed the maBuru's fear of strong African leaders. His contempt is palpable in his self-composed leboko, which trumpets his role in leading the BaKgatla auxiliaries alongside Baas Paul's commando in 1865 to fight Moshoeshoe. In it he revels his duplicity towards the maBuru and laughs at their naïveté:

> I was on their side, then I joined that;
> I used to be a red-skinned Boer, [now]
> I've become a man of the Sotho, the Famed one,
> Son-in-law in Basutoland
> and eater of the people's gifts.
> On one leg I wear a trouser,
> On the other leg I wear a lion skin.[36]

In battle, he feigns loyalty to the maBuru while taking satisfaction in their injuries.

> Famed One, leader of troops attacking at night;
> the troops attacked in the early dawn . . .
> And I shot into the black darkness,
> the strong one, Pilane Pheto's son.
> I do not know if I hit, nor do I know if I missed.
> But, on seeing, I say I hit . . .
> I heard it whispered to Paul by Seabe's men and Tatlhagana's,
> They were saying 'A white man is wounded,

> A Boer from Masetlhana is wounded,
> Rakunetsa's son has been wounded.'
> I scoffed inwardly, as I laughed,
> I said, 'Whom did they want to be wounded?'

Kgamanyane's presence at the battle, which Kruger's commandos lost, was strictly for appearances.

> The fool puts out the fires of others,
> He puts out those of the gun-brandishers,
> And says, 'let the fires go out and mine burn,
> may that burn of the foolish Nimble One,
> brother of Rakitla the Kgatla.'
> The Slasher does not kill, yet he kills,
> He also quenches fires, the Slasher,
> Son of the woman from Tlokwaland.[37]

Kgamanyane played the fool, or so Kruger's forces thought, by killing other Africans on their behalf, whereas Kgamanyane thought of himself as the Nimble One, helping to weaken the maBuru's chances.

Kgamanyane's arrogance was underscored by the substantial arms his men had acquired in recent years. In spite of the 1852 Sand River Convention, the fact is that guns and powder had been seeping into the ZAR from its borderlands, especially from Shoshong and Ntsweng (Molepolole) in Botswana, and from white-controlled markets in Delagoa Bay, Natal, the Cape and the Orange Free State. Africans on foot were trekking to these areas for work or trade and returning with arms, and traders were penetrating the trans-Vaal market. The ZAR could not prevent even its own subjects from trafficking.[38] In the 1860s, commando leaders were ordering Kgamanyane and other kapiteins to call up auxiliaries *with their* guns.

The DRC Comes to Saulspoort

In spite of Kgamanyane's notoriety, when the hoofdkapitein invited Gonin to move to Saulspoort, the missionary jumped at the chance. His standing obligations were put aside. 'I would feel bad leaving behind the kaffirs who stay with us [at Welgeval]', Gonin declared, 'but we will have more influence if we stay with a big kapitein. If Paul Kruger agrees, we will go'.[39] Gonin did not speculate as to the reasons behind Kgamanyane's new attitude. His was a mission of faith; for a man who gainsaid any kaffir's belief, except in Gonin's version of Christianity, any reason for this timely invitation would do. Gonin's future depended on the encounter.

Kgamanyane's decision to have a DRC mission at Saulspoort was reached at a time when Baas Paul was promising HMS missionary Christof Penzhorn that he could buy from him the farm near kapitein Mokgatle's town.[40] Penzhorn, based in Rustenburg, established his mission station (Saron) near Mokgatle's town several months later, at about the same time as Gonin moved onto Saulspoort. Penzhorn then began negotiations for the purchase of portions of Kruger's farms, Beerfontein 263 and Turffontein 262. Mokgatle put up the cattle to purchase the land, for which Kruger demanded a whopping £900.[41] Kruger, always ahead of the game, was on to yet another way of extorting kaffer wealth. He had confiscated Beerfontein from Mokgatle in the 1850s, it being the farm Voortrekker leader Andries Hendrik Potgieter had granted Mokgatle for his people's use; and in 1869, months after Penzhorn used Mokgatle's cattle to purchase part of Beerfontein, Kruger purchased Turffontein for a trifling £7.10, then resold it to Penzhorn in 1871 for £900.[42] No matter that the price was exorbitant, Kruger knew that the kapiteins would pay it. Once the missionary purchased the land in his own name, the kapitein and his subjects could remain there, cultivate the land and not have to contract their labour to the surrounding maBuru – for the time being.

In late 1865 or early 1866, at the time Kgamanyane invited Gonin to relocate to Saulspoort, Paul Kruger informed Kgamanyane that the hoofdkapitein had to buy this very farm.[43] The amount demanded – £900 – shows that Kruger at least was consistent in his standard of banditry. Goods and cash would suffice. Kruger knew full well that African ownership of land was prohibited by the ZAR constitution and was probably expecting Kgamanyane to turn to the HMS or DRC.[44] In the coming weeks, Kgamanyane and his people came up with cattle, sorghum, leopard skins, riems and money to the sum of £400, and Kruger gave him three additional months to deliver the balance. In April, when Gonin asked Kruger for permission to move onto Saulspoort, the £400 had already been paid in. As Gonin put it, 'seeing that the transaction had gone that far already, and having faith in Kruger, I started building a house'.[45]

The prospect of having a legal purchaser living on the property appealed to Kruger, then in negotiation with Penzhorn and Mogkatle over Beerfontein and Turffontein. Up to this time, Kgamanyane had not yet delivered to Kruger the balance of the payment on the £900 asking price, but Kruger was not in a position to go to Saulspoort and demand it. The kommandant-generaal had broken his leg, which Kruger recalled 'compelled me to nine months of inactivity, during which time I only managed to crawl about on crutches'.[46] From Rustenburg, Kruger helped Gonin by sending orders for bricks to be made and grass cut; his oorlams Vieland also helped construct the building. Sometime between August and October 1866, Gonin moved to Saulspoort and entered his 'large, one-room house' with a large kitchen house under construction next to it.[47]

Kruger's Troubles

Gonin arrived when Kruger's economic and political stars were in bad alignment. For one thing, his properties and the farms around them were losing value due to a collapse in the market for trans-Vaal products. By the mid-1860s, white farmers producing for the market had ceased enjoying ups and had begun to suffer steep downs. Until the early 1860s, optimism had been high: the cattle trade was doing well, and sheep were brought in to develop the wool market. By 1864 wool and cattle exports were lucrative businesses, and yet other means had appeared to replace the declining ivory trade. In 1866, however, the roof caved in. After good exports in early 1866, a harsh drought crumpled agricultural earnings. Ten thousand sheep perished in the Swartruggens alone. Africans dispersed with their cattle and labour or migrated to Natal for work, leaving severe labour shortages. Trade went into a severe slump for the rest of the decade.[48]

Meanwhile the Rustenburg farmers complained that, apart from using his authority to gain a disproportionate share of local labour, Kruger had deprived the district of labour at crucial times with his call-ups of auxiliaries to go on commando against Moshoeshoe (1865), Mapela's Langa Ndebele and Mogemi's Kekana Ndebele (1867) and Mokopane's Kekana Ndebele (1868). Allegations began to circulate that these commando raids were unprovoked, that they were orchestrated to avail commando higher-ups of children. After the Volksraad re-enacted its prohibition against slave raiding and introduced fines for officials found to be involved, the Rustenburgers assembled in September 1868 and called on the Volksraad to deal with reports that Kruger and Malan had been killing adults in the Soutpansberg and coming back with their children.[49]

To add to their woes, President Pretorius and Kommandant-generaal

Kruger were getting bad press outside the ZAR. In the 1860s English newspapers in the Cape and Natal carried reports of slave raiding in violation of the Sand River Convention and of the ZAR's failings to take action.[50] In late 1865 Cape Governor P.E. Wodehouse started sending complaints to Pretoria. SeBuru blood boiled, because they knew British officials took no action against the British merchants raking in cash from the illegal gun trade. But the ZAR ran real risks if their international image was tarnished. That is why suddenly, in early 1866, Pretorius instructed town magistrates (landdrosten), of all people, to enforce the law. At the same time the Volksraad called for a review of slave trading laws and in July it enacted a statute once again prohibiting the traffic 'to avoid the appearance of the slave trade'.[51] The Volksraad had been trying to put an end to slave raiding while improving the supply of labour from sources nearby to Boer farms in the Pretoria and Rustenburg districts. Beginning with the Ordinance of 1864, which entitled any Boer farmer to have up to five African families reside on each of their farms, the Volksraad passed in 1866 the *Kafferwet*, which introduced passes and made black men liable to pay tax.

By the time Kruger had fully recovered from his fracture, he was delayed in forcing the Saulspoort deal. In 1867, the kommandant-generaal was called away from the Rustenburg district to mobilise a commando for Soutpansberg, which finally got underway mid-year. Kruger's military campaign ended in disaster. As a result he had to attend the Volksraad to defend himself, and at the same time Boer farmers in the Rustenburg district were embarrassing him with their petitions about labour shortages. Kruger used this moment to raise with the Volksraad the question of Africans 'wishing to purchase land', but the Volksraad took no decision.[52]

In early 1868, Kruger came to the Pilanesberg for the first time since early 1866 and declared that the Volksraad had refused to allow him to sell Saulspoort to Kgamanyane. He then tore up the written agreement of the original transaction, pronounced the £400 already paid in as rent and demanded the remaining £500 as part of a twenty-year lease, commencing from the original transaction in early 1866. He then drew up a rental contract and got one of Kgamanyane's brothers to sign it.

Gonin's Plan

Up to this point, Gonin had made no mention of any of these developments to his superiors in Cape Town. We must remember that Gonin was under great pressure from the DRC to produce results, and that his purchase of Welgeval had yielded only a handful of converts, whereas the HMS were moving broadly into the Rustenburg district and setting up missions on or near the other major kapiteins. As recently as 1865 a DRC inspection team had found Gonin wanting in his ability to speak SeTswana and being too concerned about his personal comforts and needs, while the mission suffered as a result. He was asked to resign.[53] Gonin talked the DRC out of it by forecasting good prospects with Kgamanyane's BaKgatla. In order to continue his missionary work, to which he was committed unquestionably, Gonin needed desperately to gain acceptance among the BaKgatla and use his power, such as it was, to keep them on Saulspoort and the surrounding farms. Gonin's late-1866 to early-1867 reports of steady Kgatla interest in the Gospel, including from the sons of Kgamanyane himself, was sufficiently reassuring to the DRC that in mid-1867 they sent young Pieter Brink to assist him in mission work.[54] Let us here recall that in April 1866, when he got Kruger's permission to move to Saulspoort, Gonin stressed in the two May letters reporting this meeting that he would *not* have to purchase the farm. Thus, any hint later to the DRC that the kommandant-generaal had drawn the BaKgatla into a land deal would have jeopardised Gonin's standing with his superiors and risked his recall.

Gonin continued to keep the DRC ignorant of his moves. Not until well after the fact did Gonin report to his superiors that he had allowed himself to become the BaKgatla's legal representative. After Kruger confronted the BaKgatla with a rental contract, Kgamanyane and the BaKgatla refused to recognise the document signed by Kgamanyane's brother – they knew that a contract meant a call on their labour without compensation. Gonin claims that at this point Kgamanyane approached him for assistance. The BaKgatla were aware that other white persons had been acting as 'agents' on behalf of Africans in challenging maBuru in court.[55] And, at the time, Mokgatle and HMS missionary Christof Penzhorn were still in the process of buying Beerfontein and Turffontein from Kruger.[56]

Gonin, though outwardly passive and quiet in his demeanour and one who encouraged other whites to think that he was detached from all but religious matters, could be quickly resolute, especially when his future hung in the balance.[57] Gonin 'agreed to handle the case on condition that [Kgamanyane] leave things entirely to me'. He approached 'some people' in Rustenburg and was appointed by 'those [BaKgatla who were] against hiring the place . . . as their agent to take the matter to court, if necessary'. When word of Gonin's appointment reached Kruger, the kommandant-generaal went straight to Saulspoort, summoned Kgamanyane and had him sign a paper that 'removed from me any right to represent his people'. He forced the kapitein as well to sign the contract, then went to the mission and presented Gonin with an ultimatum: either Gonin pay the remaining £500, in which case he would have full title to the farm; otherwise Kruger would withdraw his guarantee that the BaKgatla could remain on Saulspoort.

Gonin decided to pay. Again, without informing Cape Town, Gonin looked for the necessary cash. He borrowed part of the money in Rustenburg, but nearly half of the £500 was drawn from the Swiss savings of his wife Jenny neé de Watteville Gonin.[58] Only after he had paid the first of four cash transfers to Kruger did Gonin, for the first time, inform his superiors about the entire episode. Gonin's report, penned in January 1869, was written in such a convoluted way that events described over the previous three years and leading up to the purchase, at first glance, appear to have transpired in the previous few months. Also hidden from view is the anxiety Gonin suffered over this extended period, when he faced the prospect of losing another DRC mission and with it most likely his missionary post. He acted entirely on his own, knowing that the DRC would question his judgment and block proceedings. He had waited, therefore, until he could present the DRC with a *fait accompli*. The closing lines of his January 1869 report sugared the pill:

> The Saulspoort mission is going well. The people trust me more, because we supported them and because they have a place to stay. Brink is now preaching in Setswana. I hope I did the right thing in buying Saulspoort, because in this country coloureds dare not own property. They all live on places that belong to Boers, on whom they are dependent. *Other missions have bought property* (my emphasis).

The DRC in Cape Town was not impressed. His superiors saw Gonin's purchase as a unilateral move on his part and decided not to reimburse him. Up to this point, though he had laboured in the mission field for six years, Gonin had yet to earn their trust or full support. Even his request to have his salary *reduced* seemed hardly to have stirred them into sympathy (they did comply with the request, however, shaving £50 off his yearly stipend). Gonin was probably as much a mystery to the DRC as he was to the Doppers of the Rustenburg district (and no doubt to Kruger and the BaKgatla). His delay in informing them shows that he believed they would scotch the deal. It is easy to imagine him grousing that the DRC had sent him to Rustenburg on a shoestring, let him compete with the well-supported HMS workers in the area, and then had criticised him for slow results. With his wife's support, Gonin simply decided to purchase Saulspoort on his own.[59]

Thus, the DRC mission acquired its foothold in the Pilanesberg because this rather quiet, enigmatic young couple took a gamble. Henri (aged 32) and Jenny (31), with a growing family, risked their futures owning Saulspoort.[60] They did so even though Kruger was making a handsome profit at their expense, as well as from other missionaries.[61]

Gonin versus Kgamanyane

Perhaps because of the personal risks involved in acquiring Saulspoort, Henri Gonin felt immediately a surge of self-importance. In August 1869, the month he got the title deed, Gonin declared something of a miniature war against Kgamanyane by publicly obstructing his exercise of authority over several of his subjects. The incident arose during *bogwera* when five initiates, who were being rounded up for the circumcision camp, bolted for safety by running to Gonin's house. All were his catechism students. Among them was Tau, pretender to Kgamanyane's throne.[62] In the months leading up to this incident, Gonin had written off Kgamanyane as a mission supporter. No longer obliged to serve the hoofdkapitein's interests, he now regarded Kgamanyane as a heathen drunkard ('a slave of drink') who wanted a missionary around just to teach his own children how to read and write, to the exclusion of others. Gonin had not seen the 'hand of God' in Kgamanyane's request to start a mission; the hoofdkapitein was too 'afraid he might have to give up his numerous wives and drinking'.[63] Gonin was banking his future on attracting converts from young Kgatla men and oorlamse. These were the very people Kgamanyane had begun persecuting in the months leading up to Gonin's purchase of Saulspoort.[64] With Saulspoort now his own, Gonin could gather around him a Christian core that Kgamanyane could not touch. So, when Tau and the four other frightened youths burst into his mission house, Gonin decided to give them refuge.

> Khamajane became extremely angry and ordered them to be beaten, yes even killed if they renounced their old customs ... The other heathen kaffers made a lot of noise and wanted me to hand them over, but I stood hold of them and sent those annoying people away ... Khamajane was very angry with me for daring to deny him of his people ... He uttered strong words to me; yes he even uttered threats [against] me and my students. As far as I was concerned, I did not worry much about it, because there is little he can do.[65]

Gonin had been persuaded, probably by Tau himself, that the young man was 'actually the legal chief'.[66] He was probably misinformed, too, about Tau's motivation for wanting to escape. Gonin believed Tau and the others refused initiation because 'their conscience illuminated by God's Word did not allow something like that'. Closer to the truth is that Tau wanted to save his skin; during bogwera youth with political futures had a habit of disappearing.

As for the missionary who two years later would assert that 'I have never concerned myself with kaffer affairs', now Gonin was backing a political faction against Kgamanyane.[67] And as Saulspoort's owner, Gonin had the upper hand in this confrontation. After years of struggling to get his mission under way, he was full of confidence.

> I am very pleased about the loyalty and the courage of those five youngsters. I could not have expected this; they had only just begun their studies, only two of them are able to spell but are not yet candidates for baptism; it does show that God's Word changes the heart and that it does not return to him without effect. His name is believed, I am full of faith for the future. The gates of hell will be powerless against the church, which is founded on the rock of centuries.[68]

Gonin looked on the drought that hit the Pilanesberg in the second half of 1869 as another divine signal. After locusts descended on the 1869 harvest and drought persisted until December, cattle perished by the thousands and black people in the Pilanesberg began to starve. The BaKgatla dispersed with their remaining cattle to find grazing and lived off the land by digging for roots. Kgamanyane's town was almost empty.[69]

> If there is no rain very soon, I fear there will be a famine, because the kaffers are presently unable to sow ... The hand of the Lord has been

upon this land quite severely in these last few years in order to visit the sins of the people. But alas! There are not many who acknowledge this or take it really seriously.[70]

Kgamanyane may very well have contemplated this latest disaster as evidence of Gonin's handiwork. Gonin once reported, half in jest, that in his first months at Saulspoort he had chastised Kgamanyane for persecuting the BaKgatla who, in Gonin's words, 'are serious about embracing the Gospel'. Gonin told Kgamanyane that the Lord 'would come upon him if he was to dispute with God'. Ten days later, a thunderstorm hit the area, which 'entirely ravaged' Kgamanyane's own sorghum fields while all the other fields 'remained untouched'. Gonin told Kgamanyane the destruction of his fields 'was the Lord's doing', noted the strong impression it made on 'the other kaffers who ascribed it to magic' and took satisfaction in reporting a surge of attendance at the following Sunday services.[71] In the drought of 1869, Kgamanyane was expected on behalf of his people to beseech the ancestors (*badimo*) that they might approach the supreme *Modimo*, who sent rain. The absence of rain could be interpreted as a failure on the part of the kgosi to carry out his duties, or that the badimo were dissatisfied with his conduct or with the behaviour of the people generally.[72] In November, as famine set in, Kgamanyane's disposition towards the Christians softened, or, as Gonin put it, he 'is again better disposed towards us', even though as recently as August they had disputed over Tau.[73] And in December, the rains that promised salvation began to fall.

From this point, Kgamanyane resigned himself to Gonin's presence, and the Christian group began to grow. By 1870, Gonin had attracted an assortment of students and baptismal candidates, from near and far. They included January, now baptised as Petrus, and his brother September, whom Gonin christened Abraham. Kruger's Vieland was among them; he became Stephanus (Moloto) and married a woman (Hannah Malau) from 'Makooskraal' (Ramokoka's kraal?) who 'was brought up among the Boers and knows Dutch'. Gonin performed the marriage ritual. Gonin also baptised a man he does not name but describes as 'from Sechele's, a black Dutch-speaker, taken as a child by the Boers'. In November 1869, Gonin baptised another man who had been with him three years. And in January 1870 a stranger who had come to live at Saulspoort nine months earlier was baptised as Franz (Phiri). By then, Gonin had received twelve adults into the church.[74] By mid-1870 he was drawing between fifty and sixty to his Sunday services, and between twenty and twenty-five pupils to his evening school. His students included members of Kgamanyane's family.[75] At Welgeval, Abraham was there with his wife Abrahama (Ndebele origin) and their children Fatima, Joanna, Isaak and Simon, together with several others, probably oorlamse: Abrahama's sister, Abrahama's brother-in-law Phoomane, as well as Andreas, Moses and Jacob.[76] Pieter Brink, who had been at Moselekatse's in the western Pilanesberg since February 1868, appears to have spent more time in Rustenburg courting the postmaster's daughter than at Moselekatse's pushing the Gospel. Elsewhere in the district, the HMS was gaining plenty of converts at Bethanie (Losperfontein 405) – where Gonin's ex-translator David had settled near kapitein Mmamogale – and at Saron (Beerfontein 263) near Mokgatle's.[77] Like Saulspoort, Losperfontein and Beerfontein were once Kruger's properties and had been purchased by HMS missionaries. Christianity was certainly taking hold in Kruger's district, and as a paying proposition.

Swart Gewaar

During the surge in kaffer Christianisation and mission land purchases in the Rustenburg district, white farmers and officials were stepping over one another in dragooning able-bodied blacks onto their farms. When Veldkornet Malan demanded labour from Mokgatle, so did Kommandant J.A. Esterhuyse, insisting his senior rank required Mokgatle to supply him first – leaving the kapitein to deal with Malan on his own. At the time Kommandant-generaal Kruger, as Mokgatle's farm owner, was exacting his own labour, presumably as rent.[78] East of the Pilanesberg, kapitein Magobye was pressed by the kommandant-generaal, the local veldkornet (J.L.J van Rensburg) and Rustenburg Veldkornet D.J. van der Merwe, as well as by the surrounding farmers.[79] Conveniently, the labour shortages were blamed on the Government. In late 1867 chatter buzzed that the President was going to be suspended, and the following year a string of petitions calling for action on the labour question began to reach Pretoria. Most of them came from the Rustenburg and Pretoria districts.[80]

As with the grumbling, so with fears of a black eruption. Until recently the maBuru had felt almost invincible, their commandos every year or so providing regular harvests of cattle and children. But it had become clear that there were some Africans the Boers could not defeat, and some who were gaining strength. The ZAR was no longer expanding and doubts about defending its boundaries were growing. Rumours circulated that Sechele's BaKwena, Sekwati's BaPedi, and Moshoeshoe's BaSotho were planning to invade the trans-Vaal. Meanwhile, Schoemansdal, the white outpost in the Soutpansberg planted by Potgieter, was collapsing under regular raids by surrounding VhaVenda.[81]

Kruger posed as the voice of the disgruntled, feeding their insecurity.

> In our state there are easily 1,000 kleurlingen against one white. We cannot but regard them as the archenemies of the whites. If we ourselves help to prepare our enemies to get the opportunity to beat us, it would be better to hand over our country to them and go away ... for their entire nature is such that as soon as they get that opportunity, they will not allow the whites to stay a day longer in the country.[82]

Kruger established his public image as the citizen toughest on kaffers. In one well-known case, a man named 'Rasubaas' or 'December' whom Kruger had ordered to work for farmer A. Smit in 1866, came to Kruger in 1869 to complain that he had not yet been paid. Kruger ordered him back. After another payless stretch, Rasubaas absconded, whereupon Smit complained to Kruger. The kommandant-generaal summoned Rasubaas and had him flogged. He then wrote Rasubaas a pass to proceed to landdrost P.J. van Staden for the purpose of registering his complaint! Rasubaas was bold enough to do it. But after Van Staden put him in the hands of the agent S.J. van Kervel du Toit, who wrote up his complaint for the Public Prosecutor in Pretoria, the kommandant-generaal entered Du Toit's premises, dragged Rasubaas out on the street, gave him a 'solid beating' and ordered him back to Smit. Rasubaas lingered awhile in Rustenburg awaiting the outcome of the complaint, then left for Sechele's.[83] Other, similar incidents were reported.

P.J. van Staden

Pretorius's unwillingness or inability to reign in Kruger and other officials administering the *sjambok* policy was cause for growing concern among Boer farm and town dwellers alike. They, too, feared a black revolt but believed that the heavy hand of Kruger and his ilk was more likely to spark than to stifle one. They were as worried that blacks might leave the ZAR altogether, taking their labour with them.[84] They were willing to entertain the likelihood that kleurlingen had real grievances, were entitled to government by law and deserved protection from those veldkornetten and kommandants who, like the kommandant-generaal, took the law into their own hands, particularly in the remote farm areas.

Petrus Johannes van Staden, the popularly elected, long-standing landdrost of Rustenburg, was among the civil authorities who favoured regularising labour relations on district farms. Since the 1864 Ordinance, entitling whites to domicile five African families on each of their farms, and the 1866 Kafferwet, which introduced passes and taxes on black men, Van Staden had assumed principal authority in the Rustenburg district in carrying out the letter of these laws, only to be challenged by the kommandant-generaal's actions and of those kommandante and veldkornetten tied to him, demonstrated so clearly in the Rasubaas affair on Van Staden's doorstep in Rustenburg and in the wholesale pressure Kruger's group put on kafferkapiteins in the rural areas. Nevertheless, Van Staden persisted in following the lead of the Volksraad and communicated with kapiteins in this regard. He gained in many cases a welcome reception and compliance, representing as he did a relief from Kruger's regime.

In Saulspoort, where Kruger so often had had his way, Kgamanyane gave the landdrost a cordial reception. Upset by Kruger's extorting of his cash and stock in a fake sale of Saulspoort and then dealing with Gonin instead, Kgamanyane was open to the well-mannered Van Staden. By this time, it should be mentioned, Kgatla groups under his brothers had left Saulspoort and settled in the western and southern Pilanesberg. Most, if not all, of these farms were owned by Kruger's son-in-law, Veldkornet Sarel Eloff. By designating Kgamanyane's brothers as kapiteins, Eloff enabled large numbers of kaffers to live on his farms and avoid the five-family limit otherwise required by law.[85] Several of the farms near Kgamanyane's kapiteins were owned by another of Kruger's sons-in-law, Veldkornet Hercules (Harklaas) Phillipus Malan. The BaKgatla knew him as *Makopye* ('fat forehead'). Like Kruger, Malan and his mother were originally Voortrekkers who came with Potgieter. He was named after his grandfather, who had been staked and posted alongside Piet Retief at Mgungundlovu, and the son of Jacobus, who had been killed at Italeni (1838).[86] As in Saulspoort, so too on the other side of the Pilanesberg: Kruger's in-laws pressed Kgamanyane's people into service on neighbouring farms.

Van Staden led Kgamanyane to believe that by living on mission property and paying the new 'hut tax', he and his followers would be exempt from providing free (i.e. forced) labour to the maBuru. The Kafferwet of 1866 provided for annual taxation, but in the Rustenburg district no systematic attempt was made to collect it until early 1869. In March of that year, P.J. van Staden instructed Kgamanyane to collect the tax and turn it over in the form of cash in due course, which he did. Van Staden assured Kgamanyane that payment meant he and his people were exempt from labour contracts and 'free' to hire out their labour to whomever they wished. This was in accordance with the new law.[87] The effect of the tax was extortionate in that the amount required was based on hut estimates provided by veldkornetten and that the payment was due in cash. The BaKgatla had to sell their stock on quick notice, and the surrounding white farmers took advantage by buying it at rock-bottom prices.[88] However, the prospect of gaining a labour exemption was sufficient inducement to cooperate. In April Kgamanyane handed over between £1000 and £1200, and a year later, the same. The proceeds Van Staden collected from the hoofdkapitein amounted to half of the annual total returns from the Rustenburg district in 1869 and 1870.[89]

Like Rasubaas, so Kgamanyane; Van Staden's ruling notwithstanding, Baas Paul had his own interpretation of the law. As kommandant-generaal he regarded the kommandant and the veldkornetten of the Rustenburg district as his subordinates in the carrying out the task of delivering labour to white-owned farms. They were particularly concerned about labour shortages on their own farms and on properties they had sold that were being leased to nearby kaffer settlements. And being accustomed as they were to ordering kapiteins to deliver up labourers on demand, they were particularly upset with Van Staden for promising labour exemptions. In 1869 Baas Paul and Van Staden had heated words.[90] If Van Staden and his veldkornetten had told black tax-payers they were free to hire out their labour when and to whom they wished, Baas Paul would beat it into them that they were not.

Kruger decided to make hoofdkapitein Kgamanyane his next example. Since 1869, after paying his tax, Kgamanyane had refused to respond to requests from three veldkornetten (P.J. van der Walt, N.J. Smit and G.S. Botha) to deliver labourers. Kgamanyane later told Gonin that he had been asked by Van Staden to keep his people together for the purpose of tax collection, which agrees with Van Staden's statement before the 1871 Commission on Native Affairs.[91] When Smit and Botha complained to Kruger, the kommandant-generaal sent word to veldkornet Hercules Malan to discipline Kgamanyane. Malan went to Saulspoort and administered a public beating to the hoofdkapitein, using a sjambok.[92] At this very time, Kruger had been forcing Kgamanyane to provide labour to build a dam on Saulspoort itself, Kruger claiming that the BaKgatla had moved to Saulspoort on the understanding that they would build it. The humiliation the BaKgatla labourers endured is still recalled by their descendants.[93] It is also likely that Baas Paul himself gave Kgamanyane a beating at Modderkuil 39, a farm near Saulspoort, in front of owner Nicolaas Roets. Kgamanyane claimed as much, and BaKgatla later stated that Kruger had Kgamanyane tied to an oxcart wheel for the purpose.[94] When Van Staden returned to collect tax in June or July 1870, Kgamanyane angrily displayed his scarred back. 'I am ashamed to appear before you like a *vaalpens*', Kgamanyane said. 'I have received a beating, unlike other kapiteins'.[95]

The tussle for authority over kapiteins found its resolution in the June 1870 Kafferwet. Unable to withstand the pressure from Kruger and his supporters, the Volksraad backtracked on its 1866 law placing civil authorities in charge and granted Kruger the authority to govern kapiteins over and against the rulings of landdrosten. The law retained in principle the authority of landdrosten and veldkornetten with regard to tax collection and issuing passes, but Art. 26 contained the zinger: 'The Kommandant-generaal shall ensure, together with his subordinate officers, that this Act is strictly carried out and shall punish those who disobey'.[96] At Saulspoort, this was interpreted as the Volksraad's way, in Gonin's words, of giving 'black people to the complete authority of Kruger'.[97] It was probably explained that way to Kgamanyane by Veldkornet Malan, who announced the new Kafferwet in Saulspoort.[98] Kruger himself did the rounds with Veldkornet Johannes van Rensburg for the purpose of acquainting kapiteins Mokgatle, Moatshe Ramokoka, Mmamogale and Mogale with the act. Then, on 6 September the kommandant-generaal gave Kgamanyane notice that Kruger was calling 'a meeting with all the whites there and that Kgamanyane and his chiefs should be present'. A local *leBuru* then put out the rumour that 'during the meeting the whites would take the guns from [the BaKgatla] and their children [from them]'.[99]

Kgamanyane had had enough. He convened a kgotla and put to his people his wish to emigrate. All agreed, and that night thousands of Ba-

Kgatla from Saulspoort and the surrounding towns gathered up their belongings and began to move. The exodus continued through the next day and into the night. The following morning – Sunday, 11 September – Kgamanyane left with the last of his people. Altogether an estimated 10,000 to 15,000 had vanished.[100] Gonin described the scene:

> In the night, from Friday to Saturday, the flight began. On Saturday, the field-cornet and our white neighbours heard about it and went after them the whole night and on Sunday, to try to bring them back if possible. But quite soon they experienced difficulties in getting them to turn back. Everywhere they saw families, men, women, and children, running away with cattle, sheep and goats. They told me it was a sad and horrible thing to watch them. The whole Sunday we were afraid the Boers would force them to return, and that it might come to bloodshed, but it didn't.

The few who remained behind were the baptised Christians and students at the mission, mainly oorlamse, and some very old people.[101]

ENDNOTES

1   Before the 1930s, Saulspoort was known by its old number: 269.
2   Schapera (1942a); Maganello Pilane, Jul. 1931, SP, PP 1/1/2, BNA. Maganello claims that the Kgatla were living at Mabule during Pilane's rule, confusing his reign with that of Letsebe (1815–1820). See ch. 1.
3   Gonin to DRC, 9 Aug. 1862, 15/7/2 (A), DRCA.
4   *Graham's Town Journal*, 27 Feb. 1861, 8 Feb., 15 Mar. and 31 May 1862; *Natal Mercury*, 30 May 1863; *Transvaal Argus*, 29 May 1866. I am grateful to Barry Morton for these references.
5   Ibid., 24 Mar. 1863.
6   *Graham's Town Journal*, 8 Nov. 1859; *Natal Mercury*, 11 Dec. 1866.
7   *Graham's Town Journal*, 27 Feb., 2 Mar. and 19 Nov. 1861; 8 Feb., 15 Mar. and 31 May 1862; and 24 and 27 Mar, 2 Jun. and 24 Nov. 1863; *Transvaal Argus*, 29 May, 12 and 26 Jun. and 17 Jul. 1866; *Natal Mercury*, 11 Dec. 1866 and 30 Apr. 1867. See also Child (1979: 76–77).
8   Smith (1952: 205–206). The Jerusalem Pilgrims were the followers of J.A. Enslin of the Marico district, who planned to lead his people on a trek across Africa to Jerusalem (Templin 1984: 135–136).
9   Kruger (1969: 74–75), Templin (1984: 125–152), Moodie (1975: 52–61), McCarter (1869: 94–95).
10 Moodie (1975: 26–28, 30–31).

11 Kruger (1969: 98–99); Theal (1964: IV, 451).

12 'The Natives in the Transvaal', *Graham's Town Journal*, 11 Oct. 1862, reprint from the *Zuid Afrikaan*. See also *Natal Mercury*, 11 Dec. 1866.

13 Gonin to DRC, 12 Dec. 1862, 15/7/2 (E), DRCA.

14 In the late 1850s, ZAR officials began to allow select missionaries to work among Africans. In 1856, the old ZAR nemesis, Sechele, asked President Pretorius to send him a 'teacher and bricklayer' as a 'symbol of peace'. Marico district veldkornet Jan Viljoen urged asking the Hermannsburg Mission Society (HMS). In 1857 Heinrich Schröder arrived at Dithubaruba, Sechele's capital, and the HMS also set up missions at Dinokana (Moilwa's BaHurutshe) and Shoshong (Sekgoma's BaNgwato). The ZAR liked the HMS because they promoted friendly relations between Africans and Boers, and encouraged mission activity with gifts of gunpowder and shot to Sechele and Sekgoma. The Berlin Mission Society then entered the ZAR, and the DRC followed. In 1862 Henri Gonin and Alexander McKidd arrived at Rustenburg, the latter going on to the Soutpansberg. See Grobler (1997: 249–252); Mignon (1996: 4–9); Smith (1957: 162–169); Chirenje (1977: 70–85); Ramsay (1990: 113–114); *Hermannsburger Missionsblatt* Apr. 1866.

15 Gonin to State Secretary, 13 Feb. 1875, SS 185, R458/75, TA; Gonin's reminiscences, 29 Aug. 1899, 15/7/2 (D), DRCA; Du Plessis (1911: 284–285).

16 Gonin to DRC, 10 Jan. 1863, 15/7/2 (A), DRCA.

17 Gonin to DRC, 13 May 1862, 15/7/2 (E), DRCA. Hereafter, the relevant files of Gonin's correspondence will be indicated by (A) through (E). Gonin understood David to be of 'Matalete' origin, which Maree (1967: 30, 34) mistakenly ascribes to 'Malete'. David was likely a member of the BaFokeng. When Gonin visited 'Magato's' (town of Mokgatle, kgosi of the BaFokeng), David was there to help him translate, and Gonin referred to David '[who] . . . lives here and preaches among his own tribe' (ibid.). See chs. 4 and 6 of Volz (2006) for 'David Modibane Mokgatle' and his possible Mogopa Kwena origins. I am grateful to Stephen Volz for drawing my attention to his dissertation material on David.

18 September, who was in his late twenties when Gonin first met him, had been a 'servant' in the Colony and 'amongst other masters, he served Mr. Joubert of Murraysburg, where at first he heard a little of the Lord Jesus' (Gonin to DRC, 6 Mar. 1866 and 18 Dec. 1875, [A]).

19 Gonin to DRC, 9 Aug. 1862 (A).

20 Gonin to DRC, 13 May 1862 (E).

21 Gonin to DRC, 9 Aug. 1862 (A).

22 Gonin to DRC, 4 Jul. and 2 Aug. 1862 (A).

23 Gonin to DRC, 17 Dec. 1862 (E).

24 Gonin to DRC, 19 Jun. 1863 (E).

25 Gonin to DRC, 14 Aug. 1863 (E).

26 Gonin to DRC, 30 Jan. 1864 (A).

27 Gonin to DRC, 2 Feb. and 15 Jul. 1864 (E). Welgeval is situated inside the Pilanesberg Game Reserve and 10 kilometres northwest of the pleasure resort, Sun City.

28 Gonin to DRC, 15 Jul. and 18 Oct. 1864, Jan. 1865 (E).

29 Gonin to DRC, 15 Jul. 1864 (E) and 11 Oct. 1864 (A).

30 Ibid.

31 Gonin to DRC, 9 Jan. 1865 (A).

32 Gonin to DRC, Nov. 1865 (E); Ramsay (1991: 112); Breutz (1987: 450).

33 Gonin to DRC, 16 Dec. 1864 (E).

34 Bergh and Morton 2003: Declaration No. 17 (H.L. Gonin), No. 19 (P.J. van der Walt) and 20 (H.P. Malan); see also Gonin to DRC, 17 Dec. 1862 (E).

35 Gonin to DRC, 17 Dec. 1862 and 15 Jul. 1864 (E), DRCA.

36 Schapera (1965: 71–72). Schapera mistakes as 1858 the year Kruger fought Moshoeshoe, whereas Kruger paid a diplomatic visit to Moshoeshoe in that year and led a commando against him in 1865 (Thompson 1975: 237, 283; Sanders 1975: 272–273, 277, 290; Meintjes 1974: 45, 62). Kgamanyane calls himself 'Son-in-law' in reference to his marriage to two of Moshoeshoe's daughters. In the 1850s, Kgamanyane married Peete as his twenty-first wife, and in the early to mid-1860s, Mokgechane (no. 31). Kgamanyane's neighbour Mokgatle was also in contact with Moshoeshoe. In 1858, when Kruger and Schoeman were sent by Pretorius to Moshoeshoe's, they found Mokgatle at Thaba Bosiu on a visit, and the Fokeng kapitein did the introductions. In 1866, Mokgatle appears also to have entered into a marriage alliance with Moshoeshoe, as did Mapela of the Langa Ndebele. See Kgamanyane's malwapa, SP, PP 1/3/9, BNA [approximate marriage date estimated from number of progeny and the fact that 40 wives were married by 1866: Gonin to DRC, 6 Jan. 1866 (E)]; Nathan (1941: 62–63); *Natal Mercury*, 11 Dec. 1866; Sanders (1975: 273).

37 Ibid. The fire refers to both the kgotla fire of a family and the fire of the entire group, around which a kgosi and his ranking royals and advisors sit. It is used here to refer as well to the maBuru's (gun-brandishers) defeat.

38 Bergh and Morton 2003: Declaration No. 6 (P.J. van Staden), No. 17 (H.L. Gonin), No. 18 (C. Penzhorn), No. 19 (P.J. van der Walt), No. 20 (H.P. Malan), No. 21 (D.J. van der Merwe) and No. 22 (J.L.J. van Rensburg). On 21 February 1867 the *Transvaal Argus* (Potchefstroom) reported that 'the number of firearms imported yearly into Kaffirland is enormous . . . Many of our Boers who live far from town are supplied at Sechomo's [Sekgoma at Shoshong] with ammunition at a rate so low, that our storekeepers cannot compete with it.' On the eastern side of the ZAR, guns arrived mainly from Natal overland to the Transvaal or through Delagoa Bay. Figures from Natal several years later suggest how large the gun trade had become:

Natal Gun Exports from Durban and Pietermaritzburg (1872–1877)

To the Transvaal	12,358
To Delagoa Bay	19,608
Total:	31,966
Annual average:	5,327

(J.W. Hawthorne to H. Bulwer, 11 Jan. 1878, encl. 3 in Bulwer to M. Hicks Beach, 29 Apr. 1878, 4b, A. 596, TA).

39 Gonin to DRC, 6 Jan. 1866 (E). See also 6 Mar. 1866 (A).

40 Gonin to DRC, 9 Jan. 1865 (A).

41 Bergh and Morton 2003: Declaration No. 18 (Penzhorn) and No. 25 (Mokgatle Thethe);

42 For more on Beerfontein see Bergh and Morton 2003: Declaration No. 25 (Mokgatle Thethe). For more on Turffontein, see RAK 3017, Turffontein 297 (now 262), TA. The £900 purchase price for Turffontein, listed in the land register (RAK) and dated 28 Jun. 1871, is likely the purchase price of the portions of Beerfontein and Turffontein. Penzhorn claims that he purchased it on Mokgatle's behalf (Bergh and Morton 2003: Declaration No. 18 [Penzhorn]).

43 The approximate date of Kruger's initial demand on Kgamanyane to buy Saulspoort has been reckoned from Gonin's lengthy, contorted account of his purchase of the farm in Gonin to DRC, 12 Jan. 1869 (A), together with evidence provided by Gonin between 1866 and 1868. The reader should be aware that (a) Gonin' January 1869 letter is disjointed, sometimes contradictory and devoid of certain vital information; and (b) the history of the selling of Saulspoort has been interpreted differently elsewhere (see Maree 1966: 54–56; Mbenga and Morton 1997), largely because of uncritical evaluation of Gonin's January 1869 letter. I believe that when he wrote his January 1869 letter, Gonin had concealed from the DRC for months his efforts to buy the farm, for reasons that will be spelled out later in this chapter. Events leading up to the purchase demonstrate that Gonin was closely involved in the negotiations long before he notified his superiors.

44 Maree (1966: 54) states that on or before 1868 the Volksraad allowed chiefs to buy land for transfer to the name of the government, but the earliest resolution in this regard is Art. 346, 14 Nov. 1871 (Bergh and Morton 2003: Proceedings of the Volksraad, 14 Nov. 1871).

45 Gonin to DRC, 12 Jan. 1869 (A). In his 1866 letters reporting his meeting with Kruger (Gonin to DRC, 2 May 1866 [A] and 13 May 1866 [E]), Gonin did not refer to a transaction. Instead he stressed that he did not have to buy Saulspoort, that Kruger 'has given [the farm] over *so to say* to Gamajan for use, and even in his Testament he has expressed it as his will that the Kaffirs should not be driven away from there' (my italics).

46 Kruger (1969: 98). Kruger broke his leg on return from the 1866 Volksraad in Potchefstroom, which was held in February (Meintjes 1974: 41), meaning that he broke it sometime in late February or early March. In early March, Gonin looked for Kruger in Rustenburg, but failed (Gonin to DRC, 5 Mar. 1866 [E]). Kruger reported his fracture on 17 March (Kruger to Pretorius, 17 Mar. 1866 in Engelbrecht 1925: 113).

47 Gonin to DRC, 2 May 1866 (A), Gonin to DRC, n.d. (between letters 17 Jun. and 6 Dec. 1866) (E).

48 *Natal Mercury*, 25 Jan. and 11 Dec. 1866, 9 and 30 Apr. 1867, 6 Oct. 1868; *Graham's Town Journal*, 15 Mar. 1870; *Transvaal Argus*, 12 Jun. 1866, 19 Jan. 1869.

49 *Natal Mercury*, 13 Oct. and 24 Nov. 1868, reprinting reports from the *Transvaal Argus*.

50 *Natal Mercury*, 13 Mar. and 26 May 1859, 12 Sep. 1861, quoting *Oude Emigrant* of 27 Aug. 1861, 18 Jul. 1862, 6 Dec. 1864, 24 Feb., 23 Oct. and 6 Nov. 1866, 14 Mar. 1867; *Graham's Town Journal*, 12 Apr. 1859, 3 Jun. and 11 Oct. 1862; extract from *Die Republikein*, Dec. 1865 in *Parliamentary Papers*, c. 4141: 2–3.

SAULSPOORT 38

51 *Government Gazette* Extract, 23 Jul. 1866 in *Parliamentary Papers*, c. 4141: 10; Cory (1940: VI, 179); for correspondence between Wodehouse and Pretorius, see *Parliamentary Papers*, c. 4141: 4, 6–11. See also Kistner (1952: 240–243, 253–255).

52 *Report* 1904: 21. It is not clear from this source as to whether or not Kruger identified himself as the prospective seller of the properties in question. The matter of African 'locations' was referred to the Executive Council, but no action was taken until the 1870s, following the recommendations of the 1871 Native Land Commission; see Bergh and Morton 2003.

53 Maree (1966: 47–49).

54 Gonin to DRC, 20 Aug. 1867 (E).

55 S.J. van Kervel du Toit, for example, was a well-known Rustenburg agent who, beginning in the 1860s, wrote prolifically on behalf of Africans in their dealings with officials, especially with regard to land issues (Bergh and Morton 2003).

56 Beerfontein 263 and Turffontein 262. The purchase agreement was signed in November 1868. Ibid.: Declaration No. 18 (C. Penzhorn) and 25 (Mokgatle Thethe).

57 Even to his own superiors he had cultivated an image of passivity. 'It is not in my character', he wrote to the mission secretary, 'to take the bull by the horns, my way is rather to labour quietly and in patience, without much ado' (Gonin to DRC, 1 Jul. 1866 [A]). And in front of an 1871 Volksraad commission he declared that 'I have never concerned myself with kaffir affairs and also not between them and white people' (Bergh and Morton 2003: Declaration No. 17 [H. Gonin]).

58 Gonin to DRC, 8 May 1869 and 26 Sep. 1876 (A) and 20 Nov. 1888 (C).

59 DRC Secretary C. Murray did send £60 as a personal contribution toward the purchase (Gonin to DRC, 8 May 1869 [A]). The farm remained in the Gonin family until after Gonin's death (see Mbenga and Morton 1997).

60 In 1869 Henri and Jenny had had four children: Auguste (six), Anna (four), Fanny (three) and Amedei (one) – and four more were soon to come (from a genealogical chart supplied by a great-granddaughter of Henri and Jenny, Elisabeth Viljoen of Pretoria, to whom I am deeply grateful).

61 Saulspoort was a grant farm, for which Kruger had paid nothing.

62 For Tau, see ch. 2 and note 65 below. The regiment being formed was maFatlha, headed by Kgamanyane's eldest son Maganelo, of the second house of Nkomeng. Some wanted Maganelo to succeed his father, as we shall see in the next chapter.

63 Gonin to DRC, 6 Jan. 1866 (E) and 25 Sep. 1867 (A). See also Bergh and Morton 2003: Declaration No. 17 (Gonin).

64 Gonin to DRC, 7 Apr. and 6 Oct. 1868 (A).

65 *Die Gereformeerde Kerkbode* (1869: 302). Translation by Linda van Jersel, Gaborone.

66 Gonin referred to him only as 'Khamajane's brother' (Gonin to DRC, 12 Aug. 1869 [A]). For the controversy surrounding Tau, see ch. 2. Tau is regarded as a member of maFatlha regiment initiated that year, though Gonin's actions suggest Tau was not formally initiated. The initiation dates of Tau's *younger* brothers Komane and Mainole in 1873 and 1878, respectively, suggest that Tau's brothers resulted most likely from one of Pilane's junior brothers 'raising seed' in Tau's mother (the seantlo Mmantselana) after

Pilane's death. See Pilane: agnatic male descendants, SP, PP 1/3/9, BNA. For more on Tau's mophato, see Klass Segogowane, 'The Kwena War', Aug. 1932, PP 1/1/2, SP, BNA.

67   Gonin made this statement before the 1871 Commission for Native Affairs (Bergh and Morton 2003: Declaration No. 17 [Gonin]).

68   *Die Gereformeerde Kerkbode* (1869: 302).

69   Gonin to DRC, 24 Nov. and 13 Dec. 1869 and 18 Jan. 1870 (A).

70   Ibid., 1870: 16.

71   Ibid. 1867: 127–128.

72   For a discussion of Kgatla rain-making beliefs, see Schapera (1971: 17ff.).

73   Gonin to DRC, 24 Nov. 1869 (A).

74   Gonin to DRC, 16 Jun. 1866, 12 Jun. and 23 Sep. 1867 (E); 6 Oct. 1868, 24 Nov. 1869, 18 Jan. 1870 (A).

75   *Die Gereformeerde Kerdbode* (1870: 403–404).

76   Gonin to DRC, 25 Sep. 1867 (A).

77   *Hermannsburger Missionsblatt* Apr. 1866: 60; Du Plessis (1904: 376–377); Gonin to DRC, 25 Sep. 1867 and 24 Nov. 1869 (A). Gonin thought the Lutherans 'baptise too soon'.

78   Ibid., Declaration No. 18 (C. Penzhorn).

79   Ibid., Declaration No. 21 (D.J. van der Merwe).

80   Ibid., Section II (Petitions to the Volksraad re Native Affairs); Gonin to DRC, 2 Dec. 1867 (A).

81   Boeyens (1994: 193ff.).

82   Bergh and Morton 2003: Declaration No. 28 (S.P.J. Kruger).

83   *NatalMercury*, 31 May 1870, reprint from the *Transvaal Advocate*; Bergh and Morton 2003: Declaration No. 21 (D.J. van der Merwe). Kruger would have known the Public Prosecutor, O.C. Weeber, who later went on record as saying that 'in civil cases a native, as soon as he falls under a Landdrost and Field-Cornets, should be treated the same as a white man' (ibid., Declaration No. 2 [O.C. Weeber]).

84   In the late 1860s, a minor exodus to Bechuanaland of small groups in the Pilanesberg was already underway. Among them were the people of Bottman (Tlhako ba Leema) who left for Sechele's in November 1867 after what Gonin heard was a 'threatening letter from the veldkornet [to Bottman]' (Gonin to DRC, 2 Dec. 1867, DRC [A]). At about the same time and under similar circumstances, Mabe and Sentshu left with their followers; see Gonin to DRC, 1 Jul. 1866 (A); Gonin to DRC, Nov. 1865 (E); Ramsay (1991: 112); Breutz (1953: 291, 420).

85   Only farms with kapiteins could have more than five families in residence. Kgamanyane's groups on Eloff's farms were overseen by his brothers Moselekatse at Driefontein 48(?), and Tshomankane (England) at Doornhoek 910 and Uitvalgrond 105. Kgamanyane also had two vassal groups, the BaTlhako ba Leema under Tlogwane (Bothman or Bottman) at Ruighoek 169 and the BaRokologadi under Sentswe (Sentshu) at Schaapkraal 170(?); see D.J. van der Merwe and P. Brink to M.W. Pretorius, 10 Jul. 1869, SS 112, R741/69, TA; P.J. van Staden to B.C.E. Proes, 3 Sep. 1869, SS 113, R999/69, TA. Topocadastral April 1994: 2526, Rustenburg. Maree (1966: 44) places January (of Sentswe) at Ruighoek, but this is not certain. For more on Tlogwane, see H. Gonin to

H. Shepstone, 13 Aug. 1879, SN 1, N181/79, TA; Breutz (1953: 312–313). Many state[?]
presented as fact in Maree's work are never referenced and are difficult to att[?]
appears to have used a blend of missionary correspondence (Breutz 1953) and interviews conducted in Saulspoort and Mochudi among elders. Maree's book, though
valuable, contains many inaccuracies and should be used very cautiously.

86 DSAB IV: 339–340; Schapera (1965: 99, 99n1).

87 Bergh and Morton 2003: Declaration No. 6 (P.J. van Staden), No. 17 (Gonin) and No.
20 (Malan); Gonin to DRC, 6 Mar. 1869 (A).

88 Gonin to DRC, 6 Mar. 1869 (A).

89 Bergh and Morton 2003: Declaration No. 6 (P.J. van Staden); *NatalMercury* 31 May
1870, reprinting from the *Transvaal Advocate* the total returns for the Rustenburg district reported in 1869 (£2,022) and 1870 (£1,968). The latter figure is confirmed in U.S.
Dunbar Duncan to B.C.E. Proes, 1 Feb. 1871, SS 131, R. 135/71, TA.

90 Bergh and Morton 2003: Declaration No. 20 (H.P. Malan).

91 Ibid.: Declaration No. 6 (P.J. van Staden) and No. 17 (H.L. Gonin).

92 Ibid.: Declaration No. 17 (H.L. Gonin) and No. 20 (H.P. Malan).

93 BaKgatla oral tradition gives the forced building of the dam and Kruger's flogging of
Kgamanyane as the *raison d'être* for Kgamanyane's exodus from Saulspoort to Bechuanaland. On 4 January 1982 at the Moruleng dam site itself, Chief Tidimane Pilane
gave me a detailed oral account of how old men were yoked for the purpose. For a
version based on similar traditions, see Mbenga (1997). The Kgatla recall that because
oxen were scarce, men young and old were harnessed to oxcarts and forced to haul
loads of stones. These accounts are consistent with other evidence for the period: the
drought, reported cattle losses, labour shortages and the recent opening of the diamond fields which drew young men from all over the region. What is necessary to
account for, however, is that the dam site was on Saulspoort, which in 1870 was *Gonin's*
farm, not Kruger's. Moreover Gonin, who wrote letters and appeared before the 1871
Commission on Native Affairs all in connection with the causes behind Kgamanyane's
departure from the Pilanesberg, makes no mention of the dam or its construction.
Before the same Commission, H.P. Malan referred to the supposed accord between
the BaKgatla and Kruger regarding the dam, but no other contemporary source refers
to it. Gonin gave the Commission three other reasons for Kgamanyane's flight (including Malan's flogging), but he acknowledged a fourth that, astoundingly, he then claimed
he could not remember (Bergh and Morton 2003: Declaration No. 17 [H.L. Gonin],
and No. 20 [H.P. Malan]). It may be that the passage of time has embellished the dam-
building episode in Kgatla traditions, but not likely. For nearly a century, Kgatla have
been consistent in their recounting. They brought it up in their 1903 address to the
Lieutenant Governor of the Transvaal Colony (SNA 116, NA 672/03, TA), and in 1923
Deborah Retief, a DRC missionary who started working with the BaKgatla in 1889,
remarked that 'They still tell in Mochudi how *Oom* Paul handled them like oxen. One
old man still shows the scars on his body where he was beaten with a whip used to drive
oxen'(*De Koningsbode Kerstnummer*, Dec. 1923: 41). What appears most probable is
that Gonin sat quietly while Kruger forced the BaKgatla to build the dam on the mis-

sionary's property, perhaps fearing to mention this unpleasantness lest Kruger retaliate, perhaps rationalising the dam as contributing to the development of the mission. In 1871 Gonin's DRC superior J.H. Neethling of Cape Town, after visiting Saulspoort, reported that he understood the 'real reason for [Kgamanyane's] departure, [but] we choose not to mention [it] for the sake of those involved' (*De Gereformeerde Kerkbode* 1871: 409).

94 Bergh and Morton 2003: Declaration No. 6 (P.J. van Staden) and No. 17 (H.L. Gonin); H. Gonin to M.W. Pretorius, 20 Oct. 1870, SS 128, R1330/70, TA; Segale Pilane for Lentsoe Pilane to A. Lawley, n.d. (1903), SNA 116, NA 672/03, TA. Roets, whom the Kgatla dubbed *Tauyadiphala* (lion among the impala), was known as the 'despoiler of people' (Schapera 1965: 95n2).

95 Bergh and Morton 2003: Declaration No. 6 (P.J. van Staden) and No. 23 (J.L.R. van Rensburg). A vaalpens refers to a lowly person, usually a Kgalagadi or Bushman. They were despised and often badly treated by BaTswana (see ch. 5).

96 Bergh and Morton 2003: Appendix I (Wet No. 9 [1870]).

97 Gonin to DRC, 22 Sep. 1870 (A).

98 Bergh and Morton 2003: Declaration No. 20 (H.P. Malan). Malan stated before the 1871 Commission on Native Affairs, 'My idea is that the Landdrost has to deal with matters in the office and the Commandant General with matters outside'.

99 Ibid.: Declaration No. 23 (J.L.R. van Rensburg); Gonin to DRC, 22 Sep. 1870 (A). Gonin states the meeting was called to take place in Pilanesberg, but later Kgamanyane informed Pretorius that he had been summoned to Paardekraal, in Rustenburg (Gonin to Pretorius, 20 Oct. 1870, SS 128, R1330/70, TA). This agrees with Kruger, who stated that he had ordered Kgamanyane and his sub-chiefs to come to him for a meeting on the 20 September, for the purpose of explaining the Kafferwet. Kruger to Pretorius, 1 Feb. 1871, SS 131, R166/71, TA. See also Engelbrecht (1925: 202–203). It seems likely, therefore, that the rumour carried a great deal of force; were they to respond to Kruger's summons, the leaders of the BaKgatla and the usual armed male escort (standard procedure when a kgosi and his entourage journey outside their area) would necessarily have been far away from Saulspoort.

100 Gonin to DRC, 22 Sep. 1870 (A) and Kruger to M. Viljoen, 12 Sep. 1870 in Engelbrecht (1925: 196); the figure is taken from Roger Price's letter of 30 Nov. 1870, in Smith (1957: 201), in which Price estimated the number of Kgamanyane's BaKgatla seeking entry into Sechele's territory. Gonin did not estimate the number of emigrants, but Price's figure could not be far off, given the tax revenues generated by Kgamanyane the same year. At 10 shillings hut tax per adult male not in service to a white farmer, and 5 shillings for those in service, an average of £1,000 for tax years 1869 and 1870 (see note 20 above) would have meant at least 2,400 adult male taxpayers. Assuming gender balance, the presence of a small, but non-productive segment of elderly men, less than 100 percent tax collection, and children constituting up to 50 percent of the population, a figure of at least 10,000 BaKgatla under Kgamanyane's authority seems reasonable.

101 Gonin to DRC, 20 Sep. 1870 (A); Bergh and Morton 2003: Declaration No. 17 (H.L. Gonin); *De Gereformeerde Kerkbode* (1870: 403–404).

Chapter four

EMIGRATION

The stronghold of the tribe of Kaffirs called Kaminyani is on a coppy [kopje], or hill, about eight hundred [sic] feet high, and probably a mile and a half in circumference at the base. Although it is an immense jumble of rocks, the inhabitants have managed to construct their huts in regular tiers up to the summit, on which stands their chief's residence. A river runs round two sides of the base, but a spring is reported to exist higher up among the rocks.

The Kaminyane ... have waxed fat, obtained immense herds of cattle, and become bumptious. (Gillmore 1876: 244)

Kgamanyane's emigration from Pilanesberg to Bechuanaland in 1870 led to the establishment of the Kgatla capital of Mochudi, on Phuthadikobo Hill, where it has remained ever since. The incident that supposedly sparked the exodus – Paul Kruger's beating of Kgamanyane – has become the central myth of modern Kgatla history.[1] It portrays Kgamanyane as a symbol of African resistance, a man who refused to submit to Boer oppression, sought freedom for himself and his people and led them to safety and opportunity beyond the boundaries of Boer-controlled territory. In this telling, the territory Kgamanyane and his people colonised, known as '*Kgatleng*', became the base from which BaKgatla joined other Africans in the Bechuanaland Protectorate and across the border in opposing white domination in the Zuid-Afrikaansche Republiek (ZAR), the Union of South Africa, and the Republic of South Africa. Likewise, Kgamanyane's successors became voices of black liberation, not the least among them his great-great-grandson Linchwe Kgafela Pilane, kgosi of the BaKgatla baga Kgafela from 1958 to 2007. When I entered kgosi Linchwe's office for the first time in 1979, a Black Panther poster hung prominently on the wall.

Yet, it seems hardly fitting to trumpet Kgamanyane as a Moses. Over the prior two decades, other African leaders had been leaving the trans-Vaal to get their people away from Boer rule. Kgamanyane's decision was certainly significant for future generations of Botswanan BaKgatla, but it was hardly divinely inspired. Moreover, in modern South Africa the general rule is

89

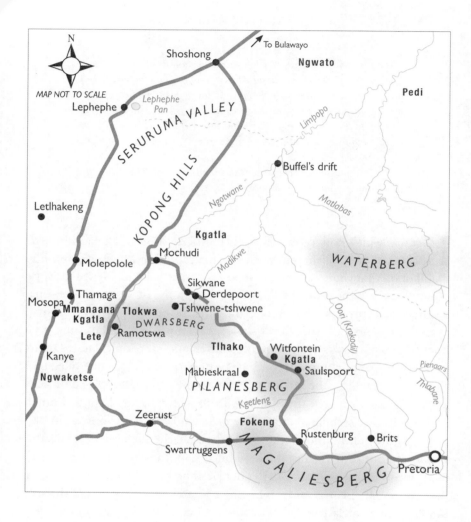

that those who flee oppression deserve to be admired less than those who stay, resist and deal with the consequences. The Africans who remained in South Africa developed the organisations, ideas and methods that posed the truly heroic challenges to white minority rule. And most importantly, the fixation on Kgamanyane's flogging and sudden flight has obscured the nature of Kgamanyane's rupture with Kruger, which had more to do with a struggle for status and power than Africanist resistance to racist rule.

What distinguishes Kgamanyane from other leaders of his time is that he and his people did not flee the Boers; rather, they migrated slowly westward through Boer territory, en masse, with their cattle. They spent nearly a year *inside* the ZAR, staying within easy riding distance of Paul Kruger and other ZAR officials. And the final destination they selected, northwest across the present Botswana–South Africa border, was not much further away. Kgamanyane took his time, simply because he and his people were not pursued and they were not harassed. The fact is that Kgamanyane, though unable to prevent himself from being flogged at Saulspoort, was, together with his followers, more than of a match for ZAR officials. His Ba-Kgatla were many, and they were armed. Kgamanyane led a methodical emigration because, as a ZAR hoofdkapitein, he had the military and political clout to pull it off. In more than twenty years of service to the ZAR, he had accumulated the means with which to establish his own authority elsewhere if necessary. And before he left, he made certain that many Kgatla would follow him.

Kgamanyane departed from Saulspoort as a way of preserving his authority over the BaKgatla and his relative power in the region. It relieved him from dealing with Kruger and provided him leverage in appealing directly to President Pretorius. Kgamanyane had no desire to leave the ZAR. He intended his departure to be a sojourn, rather than an exodus, a ploy to gain the ZAR's intercession. For months after leaving Saulspoort he communicated with President Pretorius and P.J. van Staden, wanting to return to Saulspoort and offering to provide labour to the ZAR once back. Only when it became clear to him that no one could guarantee him protection from Kruger did Kgamanyane decide to relocate his followers into the territory of Sechele Motswasele, kgosi of the BaKwena. And even after settling at Mochudi and laying plans to capture Kwena cattle, Kgamanyane kept open the possibility of a return.

Though he left suddenly, Kgamanyane knew exactly where he was headed.

His grandmother and his mother were BaTlokwa, and his maternal kin were living in what was then the northern Potchefstroom District, soon to become Marico District, below the slopes of Tshwene-tshwene in the Tweedepoort Hills.[2] The trek to Tshwene-tshwene (Kalkftontein 111, near Vleeschfontein) took only a few days. En route they passed through the Swartruggens ward of veldkornet Petrus J. van der Walt, who did not bother them. As Van der Walt put it curtly, 'they were armed with guns'.[3] By then, no efforts were being made to stop, much less attack, the BaKgatla. The only measure Kruger took was to issue Kgamanyane with a fine for having left Saulspoort without a pass.[4] At Tshwene-tshwene, Kgamanyane was greeted by the BaTlokwa kgosi Matlapeng, his *malome*.

There Kgamanyane weighed his options. He could travel a few more days into Bechuanaland and seek asylum among Sechele's BaKwena. From Tshwene-tshwene stretching out to the west from the Tweedepoort, he could easily see the eastern part of Sechele's kingdom. Several times in the past decade, Sechele had sent messengers to Saulspoort encouraging Kgamanyane to give up living with the maBuru and relocate to his kingdom.[5] Two of Kgamanyane's kapiteins in the western Pilanesberg, one his brother Letsebe, had already accepted Sechele's offer. But Kgamanyane also wanted to see if it was possible to arrange a return to Saulspoort. Thus, while his emissaries went to Ntsweng to inform Sechele that the BaKgatla had arrived at the border of his Kwena kingdom, Kgamanyane sent his brother Bogatsu to Henri Gonin asking the missionary to entreat M.W. Pretorius on Kgamanyane's behalf. Kgamanyane had had his troubles with Gonin, but he had perhaps already learned that Gonin was sorry to have lost Kgamanyane's BaKgatla. Kgamanyane was also discovering the value of staying on good terms with the man who was so popular among oorlamse. Bogatsu arrived with Kgamanyane's translator, oorlams Andries Maomogwe, so that Bogatsu's SeTswana could be translated correctly into Dutch. Gonin was a willing messenger. Through him Kgamanyane wrote to Pretorius giving his reasons for leaving the Pilanesberg (the previous beatings and fear of being beaten again at the meeting Kruger called), stating his desire to 'live in peace with the whites', pledging his willingness to allow his people to work for whites and declaring that, if he sees 'that people treat him and his people well, he will consider moving back'. He also asked that Kruger's fine be lifted.[6]

The result proved disappointing. After receiving Gonin's letter, Pretorius instructed P.J. van Staden 'to attempt to get Gamajan back, and if he returned he would be placed under the landdrost and would be absolved of the fine imposed by the Kommandant-generaal'.[7] Van Staden immediately wrote to Kgamanyane requesting he come to Rustenburg for a meeting, but Kgamanyane begged off, fearing he would be beaten again by Kruger. 'His heart [stated Kgamanyane] was in his home farm, [but] the Government did not give him enough land . . . and he did not want to come and live on the land of the [Commandant] General'. Van Staden answered that as landdrost he still 'held him responsible for the tax', whereupon Kgamanyane 'let me know that I should spare myself further trouble in getting them [the Kgatla] back before some other provision had been made'. Van Staden broke off communication and turned the matter over to the Executive Council.[8]

So, it was clear. No one in the ZAR hierarchy was yet ready to stand up to Kruger and rein him in. By the same token, the kommandant-generaal and the veldkornetten were not ready to take on Kgamanyane. So be it. It was time to see what arrangement could be worked out with Sechele. The Kwena kgosi would like the BaKgatla to stay near to him, no doubt to build up his personal strength, but the BaKgatla might be better off settling at a distance from Ntsweng and, if possible, within easy reach of the Pilanesberg. Some scouting around was in order. There was no hurry. Matlapeng's people would not mind the BaKgatla settling at Tshwene-tshwene for the time being. The grazing was good and there was water nearby. At Tshwene-tshwene the rains were on time, and once the seeds were put in the ground, several quiet months could pass until the harvest.

View from Tshwene-tshwene: The BaKwena

At the time Kgamanyane arrived on the fringes of Kwena territory, the BaKwena baga Kgabo of Sechele I (ruled from about 1829 to 1892) had for some time been the largest territorial power west of the Madikwe river.[9] After the upheavals of the 1820s and 1830s the BaKwena recovered and were the most successful of the peoples bordering the Kalahari sandveld at withstanding domination by the Voortrekkers and the ZAR. In 1852, when based at Dimawe, they were attacked by a large commando under P.E. Scholtz. Sechele's forces were defeated at Dimawe, but Scholtz failed to dislodge them from the area. Thereafter the maBuru refrained from confronting the BaKwena, and friendly diplomatic relations between Sechele and ZAR officials began to develop, even though African groups from the ZAR continued to relocate to his kingdom and settled there as *bafaladi* (refugees).[10]

The BaKwena were a coalition of many SeTswana-speaking groups scattered over a vast area known as the *Kweneng*, which was loosely administered from Sechele's capital (after 1864) at Ntsweng (the hill above the attached settlement of Molepolole). In the rainy months, they grazed their cattle deep into the Kalahari sandveld and, during dry periods, in the eastern Kweneng adjacent to the trans-Vaal. Molepolole stood astride the major trade route connecting the Cape with the interior (the 'Road to the North' or 'Missionary Road') and was the starting point for trade routes leading west to the Kalahari, northwest to Ngamiland and many points beyond. Moving back and forth over much of present-day central and eastern Botswana, Sechele's people developed large reserves of cattle and dominated the supply of ivory, skins, ostrich feathers and other trade items exported from the Kalahari region. Until the 1870s, Sechele's capital was the most important trade centre north of the Cape, the scene of early missionary activity and the haven of SeTswana-speaking groups of bafaladi or *meratswane* fleeing the ZAR and neighbouring African states. The Ba-Kwena were estimated to number 35,000, and their bafaladi another 18,000 to 20,000. Molepolole itself had approximately 10,000 residents.[11]

Sechele's prestige and personal connections in the region, rather than his exercise of military power, gave the BaKwena their sense of unity. Sechele's territory was a quietly growing zone in which men of the leading families husbanded cattle and traded; it was not an expanding empire controlled from the centre. The BaKwena had access to firearms and Sechele could mobilise a military force and stockpile ammunition and powder, but guns were owned by civilians who were dispersed throughout the Kweneng and liable for military duty only when called. There was no standing army with which to control the BaKwena or strengthen their claims against neighbouring states. Sechele held his people together by arbitrating amongst them and their far-flung interests, continuing personally to attract traders and other useful outsiders into his territory and holding in check the greediness of royal households. Sechele kept neighbouring states at bay through diplomatic means. He avoided confrontation with the ZAR by working with Marico veldkornet Jan Viljoen in calming difficulties with the Marico maBuru and corresponding regularly with the President M.W.

Pretorius. Through the LMS missionaries, who counted him among their most prestigious converts, Sechele received recognition from the British and maintained friendly relations with the AmaNdebele. With less adroitness, he embroiled himself in the affairs of the royal family of the BaNgwato, his immediate neighbours to the north and alienating the party that emerged victorious in a dynastic dispute – at a time when the BaNgwato were beginning to eclipse the BaKwena as the dominant economic and political power in the region.[12]

By the mid-1860s, Sechele's statecraft had begun to slip. The exercise of military strength assumed greater importance in binding people together, whereas the inability to use force encouraged disloyalty. These trends surfaced as Sechele attempted to increase control over the bafaladi elements within his state. His territory was too large, however, and his loyal military wing too weak for him to succeed. For some time Sechele had welcomed bafaladi to settle at his capital, only to see the larger bafaladi groups resettle at a distance. There was something about Sechele that attracted people, then repelled them. Perhaps it was not so much Sechele as his BaKwena, who resented Sechele's generosity and his unorthodox interests and personal habits. The kgosi's mind was too active and unconventional. He loved nothing better than conversing with outsiders – missionaries, explorers, traders, hunters – or demonstrating his great familiarity with the Bible or hosting visitors for tea at his European-style house, all to the exasperation of his people, who wanted nothing to do with western ways. They were also impatient of the refugees Sechele allowed to settle next to Ntsweng at Molepolole, and who used up scarce grazing and farm land, which bordered the Kalahari Desert. Bafaladi were a nuisance and deserving of contempt. To satisfy his people's grumblings, Sechele gradually distanced himself from the refugees by demanding that they pay him tribute, thereby submitting to an inferior position. After a few years, most refugee groups grew tired of the insults and moved away. This was true particularly from the mid-1860s on. The BaLete had fled the trans-Vaal maBuru in the early 1850s and joined Sechele at Dithejwane, but in 1863 they left him rather than submit to his demands for tribute, settling at Mankodi 40 kilometres southwest of Ntsweng, then further still in 1865 to Ramotswa. In 1865 the BaLete were joined by Sentswe's BaRokologadi, Kgamanyane's one-time vassal who had been living near Gonin's first mission at Welgeval. Other bafaladi living near Sechele eventually found conditions unbearable. The BaKgatla baga Mmanaana under Mosielele who left Mabotsa to join Sechele in 1850, refused to pay him tribute and moved to Mosopa in 1863. In 1870 Tlogwane (Bothman) came back from Molepolole with his BaTlhako ba Leema to live at Ruighoek 169 not far from Gonin's farm Welgeval. Mabe's BaTlhako, who had been with Sechele since 1860, left him after Mabe died in 1874 and returned to Mabieskraal, west of the Pilanesberg.[13] As of 1870, only a few bafaladi wards were to be found at Molepolole, located at the northern foot of Ntsweng Hill. Among them were the BaKaa of Mosenyi and the followers of Kgamanyane's brothers Letsebe and Kgabotshwene, who had settled next to the LMS mission station.

The View from Tshwene-tshwene: Phuthadikobo

In November 1870, two months after arriving at Tshwene-tshwene, Kgamanyane led a large delegation to Sechele's and made a formal request to settle in the Kweneng, as the BaKwena territory was known. Two reports of what transpired between these two dikgosi show that the meeting was amiable. LMS missionary Roger Price wrote:

> [From their encampment] on the border of Sechele's country, the chief Kgamanyane with a large escort came here about a week ago to arrange with Sechele about a place to build upon. It is improbable that they may come and settle down at this place. Anyway they will not be more than twenty or thirty miles from here. They have now returned to their encampment and some of Sechele's people have gone to show them various places where a town could be made. Apparently the tribe numbers from ten to fifteen thousand, possibly more.[14]

According to Kgamanyane's great-nephew Maganelo, Sechele initially wanted the BaKgatla to settle at Semarule Hill, near Molepolole.

> But Kgamanyane refused, saying to him: 'Mokwena, you have children and I have children, and it may happen if they are too close together that they may fight at the grazing-grounds and afterwards cause us to fight as well.' And Kgamanyane said 'I think it would be better for me to settle here at the grave of the old man Mothsodi.'[15]

Kgamanyane knew of Sechele's difficulty in keeping immigrants under his control. His mention of children quarrelling was an obvious reference to Matlapeng, his maternal uncle and host at Tshwene-tshwene. Only a year or two before, Matlapeng had been living next to Sechele at Molepolole. He had been there since the 1850s, following a run-in with the maBuru, and moved his people from the trans-Vaal to Sechele's capital at Dithejwane and followed him to Ntsweng in 1864. Then in 1868 or 1869, fights broke out at the cattle posts between young BaKwena and BaTlokwa men, resulting in Matlapeng's decision to preserve peace by breaking up his settlement and moving away from Ntsweng to Tshwene-tshwene, which the BaTlokwa regarded as part of Sechele's territory. To them, the Dwarsberg immediately to the south and southeast marked the line.[16] No doubt Kgamanyane had also heard of Matlapeng's neighbours immediately to the south – the BaLete – and of their choice to live at the fringe of Sechele's territory at Ramotswa.

Kgamanyane's request to settle away from Molepolole was approved by Sechele, and so was Kgamanyane's choice of Motshodi's grave, next to Phuthadikobo Hill. If he could not keep his bafaladi close to Molepolole, Sechele could use them in areas adjoining the trans-Vaal to bolster his chances in resolving an old boundary dispute with the ZAR government. Neither the BaKwena nor the maBuru had effectively occupied the area in which Kgamanyane asked to settle, but both claimed it. Since the 1850s, the ZAR had held that its own western boundary extended into southeastern Bechuanaland, though they did not survey it or attempt to get it recognised as such by any other party. In 1868, after word of the Tati gold discoveries had spread, President Pretorius went much further, proclaiming that the territory extending northwest all the way to the Okavango Delta was part of the ZAR.[17] The gold discoveries and the ZAR's outlandish land claims quickly got the attention of the British colonial administrators at the Cape and Natal. Known for their smug indifference to matters in the interior, suddenly the Crown's officials became excitable in their concern for the inhabitants of these distance parts. They now professed deep concern about Boer slave raiding, even though this issue had failed to get a rise out of British officialdom since the 1852 Sand River Convention. Just as quickly, English press reports of Boer rapacity multiplied. The anxious Cape Governor Wodehouse and Natal Lieutenant-Governor Keate wrote to London about their fears for the future of 'natives', 'native tribes' and 'native races' on ZAR borders. (Finding gold in the interior meant that the time had arrived for kaffers to be promoted to 'natives'.) Naturally the pleas forwarded by Wodehouse and Keate on behalf of 'native Chiefs' were for British 'protection'.[18] Macheng of the BaNgwato, near to the Tati, was among the first to send such a request, by the hand of LMS missionary John Mackenzie, while the *Natal Mercury* reported that a passing trader heard Sechele say he was ready to do the same.[19] White passion for British intervention just as suddenly cooled, however, when London announced that the colonists themselves would have to foot the bill. Disappointing reports about the amount of gold at Tati may have also had something to do with the drop in enthusiasm. By the end of the year, Sechele had lost any illusion of Englishmen coming to his rescue and chose instead to approach the ZAR Volksraad to join him in settling the border dividing his kingdom and their republic.[20] The border issue languished until early 1871, when the ZAR submitted its entire western boundary to arbitration.[21] Sechele was pleased, therefore, to see Kgamanyane select Phuthadikobo, because by settling there with his permission, Kgamanyane could strengthen the BaKwena's claim to the plains between Phuthadikobo and Tshwene-tshwene.

The area had been empty for generations. No major settlement had been built since the days of Sechele's great-great-great-great grandfather Motshodi, whose grave near Phuthadikobo Hill marked the environs with his name. The BaKwena and other Bechuanaland BaTswana had long regarded the plains around Phuthadikobo and extending southwest as off limits. When Kgamanyane stood on Tshwene-tshwene Hill looking north across the plain below he was surveying an historic buffer zone. The area was particularly dangerous in the nineteenth century, as one group after another, from maKololo to maBuru, came out of the trans-Vaal hills to trouble the occupants below. Each invader was a reminder to the BaNgwaketse, BaKwena and BaNgwato that they best keep the Kalahari tight to their backs and their settlements away from the foothills of the trans-Vaal bushveld plateau. In 1871, the only occupants of the plains between Tshwene-tshwene and Sechele's capital of Ntsweng were the Mmanaana Kgatla of Pilane at Kgabadukwe and Thamaga, south of Molepolole, and scattered Kwena cattle posts under the care of their Vaalpens, BaKgalagadi slaves. Phuthadikobo and the area around it was infested with lions.[22]

When Kgamanyane received permission to settle at Phuthadikobo, few BaKgatla were willing to follow him. 'Many among Gamjan's people are hesitant to go there', wrote Henri Gonin after visiting Tshwene-tshwene in

April 1871, and, at Kgamanyane's urging, going to see the site of the future capital. When he reached 'Mochuli', Gonin was disappointed. 'It does not appeal to me very much – a lot of sand and little water: I fear the poor people will suffer a lot of want by drought. It does not appear very healthy either'.[23] Rains in this area were certainly scant, in contrast to Tshwene-tshwene's green surroundings, which Gonin 'quite liked'. But Kgamanyane's mind was made up. In this matter he would simply leave his people behind with the choice of following or not. No pleading, cajoling or threats were used. Events rather than words would persuade them. While they were accustomed to expressing their opinions in public, and to disagreeing with him, Kgamanyane made the decision to leave Tshwene-tshwene on his own.

Kgamanyane could see what Gonin and the others could not – that Phuthadikobo Hill, and the plains around it, would prove the perfect spot for his people. The area had excellent physical qualities in abundance. The Ngotwane River, which flowed along Phuthadikobo's base, extended northeast towards the Limpopo. Thirty-eight kilometres southeast of Mochudi, the Madikwe River flowed out of the ZAR's Marico District, turned northeast and ran parallel to the Ngotwane. The Madikwe was joined by the Oodi (Krokodil) River to form the Limpopo and was fed in turn by the Ngotwane at Buffel's Drift. The triangle of 1,900 square kilometres formed by these rivers amounted to an extensive grazing territory bordered by water on two sides for a distance of 100 kilometres. Prospects for agriculture near to Phuthadikobo were also excellent. Good soil stretched southeast in a wide band for more than 30 kilometres.[24] Maize, or mealies, the new crop catching on in the trans-Vaal, would grow there in abundance. Phuthadikobo Hill and the adjacent hills and kloofs had their own special attractions. Their rocky slopes provided clear views of the surrounding plains and protection for the rondavels nestled against them. Building the new capital would be relatively quick work, too, as the nearby Ngotwane and its feeder streams made available the water, mud, clay, grass and wattle needed for house construction. Stones, gathered at one's feet, made sturdy compound walls and kraals.

Kgamanyane recognised that this territory, though perceived by others as a no-man's land, would give the BaKgatla the security they needed and a base from which to expand. This old danger zone was now located just off the centre of important new developments in the region; Phuthadikobo was within easy reach of the two main roads connected to northern Bechuanaland and Matabeleland, in between which lay the Tati, where a 'gold rush' had recently got underway.[25] One road came up from the ZAR through Saulspoort; the latter through the new diamond fields of Griqualand West to Sechele's and Shoshong, capital of the BaNgwato. This was the historic 'Road to the North', or the 'Missionary Road'. As well as sitting adjacent to these major arteries of trade and communication, Phuthadikobo straddled three uncharted but clearly emerging boundaries in the region: (1) between Sechele's BaKwena territory and that of the ZAR, (2) between white expansion in the south and black expansion in the north and (3) between the trans-Vaal/northern Cape bushveld and the Bechuanaland sandveld, known as the Kalahari. After moving to Phuthadikobo, Kgamanyane's people would become part of each side of these three divisions in a peripheral yet integral way: the BaKgatla at Phuthadikobo would be far enough away to avoid being dominated by more powerful groups on either side, but close enough to their resources to gain ready access. Since the days of Pilane and before, Kgamanyane's people had flourished by raiding other people's cattle, and settling at Phuthadikobo would allow them the perfect location to build up their herds and, if possible, take cattle from the BaKwena.

From Tshwene-tshwene to Phuthadikobo Hill

About harvest time, in May 1871, Kgamanyane decided to begin the process of moving the BaKgatla to Phuthadikobo Hill. About a third of his people followed him to Mochudi. Some returned to Saulspoort, and the rest, approximately half of those who had left with him from Saulspoort the previous September, remained at Tshwene-tshwene. Others had died from the hardships entailed in shifting homes.[26] Among the rocks and slopes around the western and northern base of Phuthadikobo Hill, clusters of rondavels and courtyards were constructed close together, with the Kgosing section and the main kgotla occupying the central position. At least six wards were established: Malebye, Mabodisa, Makgophana, Manamakgothe, Masiana and lastly, built well up the slopes of Phuthadikobo Hill was the royal Kgosing ward, where Kgamanyane and his brother Bogatsu lived with their families.[27]

Kgamanyane was still holding out the chance for a return to the trans-Vaal. In September 1871 he contacted landdrost Van Staden asking permission to return to Saulspoort.[28] No reasons were given, but they are not difficult to guess. Apart from Bogatsu, none of Kgamanyane's adult brothers had followed him. Tshomankane remained at Bopitikwe with his small group of followers, and Mantirisi, Kgari and Moselekatse remained anchored on farms not far from Saulspoort.[29] As long as Kgamanyane stayed at Mochudi he ran the risk of being usurped or, more likely, losing the succession for his adolescent son and designated heir, Linchwe. Though only in his late forties, Kgamanyane was in failing health. He also had reason to hope that Baas Paul's power was slipping in the ZAR. Kgamanyane's departure with his followers had caused quite a stir in the Rustenburg District. The shocking notion that thousands of kaffers could just up and leave the ZAR, when labour was in short supply and the government was just figuring out how to get its coloured subjects to pay taxes, became a major talking point in the Volksraad. In response to complaints on other related problems from white petitioners mainly in the Rustenburg and Pretoria districts, the Volksraad appointed a commission to look into kaffer administration. Kgamanyane could not have failed to hear from Saulspoort that the *Kaffercommissie* appointed was gathering evidence from Gonin, Penzhorn and Mokgatle along with other missionaries and kapiteins, as well as landdrosten, veldkornetten, kommandante and the kommandant-generaal himself.[30]

It remained to be seen whether anything of value to Kgamanyane would come of the ZAR's sudden concern. There was at least some promise. Evidence from the Kaffercommissie, replete with accounts of beatings inflicted on chiefs and commoners alike, incessant and arbitrary demands for labour, and extortion of goods and money over land exposed the heavy-handedness particularly with regard to the ZAR's kommandante, the kommandant-generaal and the veldkornetten who did their bidding. In November 1871 the Volksraad, though it fell short of reprimanding Kruger, accepted the commission's recommendations that would reduce his authority. It resolved to enact legislation permitting kaffers to choose their contract employers, placing kaffers under civilian authority during peace-time, prohibiting the beating of kapiteins and permitting kaffers to lodge complaints with the landdrosten against veldkornetten. The Volksraad also agreed to 'instruct the government to reserve land or attempt to procure same, suitable for kaffer locations . . . or for the purchase by kaffer tribes'.[31] The majority in the Volksraad had also lost patience with the already unpopular President M.W. Pretorius. Many voting maBuru blamed Pretorius for losing ZAR territory after he submitted the ZAR's disputed boundary to arbitration, and the resulting Keate Award, announced also in November 1871, fixed the ZAR southwestern border at the Makwassie stream. When elections were held in 1872, T.F. Burgers became the new ZAR President by a landslide. Gonin expected Burgers to liberalise ZAR rule and grant locations to the kaffers. In December 1872, Kgamanyane contacted a veldkornet to relay his message to Burgers that he desired to return to Saulspoort, and he also sent one of his daughters to be taught by Gonin.[32]

The Burgers administration, though friendlier than Pretorius's, was largely unresponsive. They were taking measures that promised to ease the burden of white rule on their black subjects, but were not putting the details into place. The major obstacle to Kgamanyane's return, Paul Kruger, was removed in 1873, when the kommandant-generaal resigned his post out of dissatisfaction, in part due to Burgers' elevation of the civil administration in African affairs. But the only indication of Burgers' interest in Kgamanyane, per se, was the November 1873 letter from Burgers' State Secretary to Pieter Brink of the DRC Pilanesberg, requesting information on 'Khameyane'. Gonin was then on leave in Switzerland. Brink replied that Kgamanyane was willing to return to Saulspoort, that he was intending to travel to Pretoria early in 1874 to meet Burgers and that he had in fact ploughed his fields at Saulspoort.[33] In March 1874 Gonin, while still in Switzerland, got word from HMS missionary Christof Penzhorn at Mokgatle's that Kgamanyane was expected to return.[34] However, the matter seems to have ended there, and Kgamanyane stayed put. When Gonin returned to Saulspoort in early 1875, Kgamanyane was still in Mochudi.[35] Even if the ZAR was under Burgers, returning to Saulspoort without firm government guarantees was riskier than securing his rule in Sechele's territory – not that Mochudi was risk-free.

In 1873 signs began to appear that Kgamanyane was expecting to stay in Mochudi. Early in the year, male initiation got underway. One of Kgamanyane's brothers returned to Saulspoort rather than take part.[36] MaTlakana (the 'Vultures') was the name of the regiment being formed, and it was to be led by Linchwe. Bogwera meant that teenagers had been clamouring for promotion to manhood, and that once Kgamanyane gave them the go-ahead, the youngest regiment, maFatlha, had to guide them through the ritual. It meant that their mothers and fathers must stay nearby, in order to provide them with food during the three-month ordeal.[37] All this could happen only if most of the BaKgatla were willing to gather at Kgamanyane's place. Mochudi rather than Saulspoort had become the sacred location for circumcision camp. By consenting to bogwera, Kgamanyane was also behaving as though he were independent of Sechele's authority. Calling for initiation was a kgosi's prerogative, not that of a bafaladi leader. And Kgamanyane had declared, even put his mark on a paper, that the BaKgatla regarded Mochudi and its surroundings as Sechele's territory.[38] Rather than wait on Sechele to declare bogwera open and invite his youth to be initiated into one of Sechele's regiments, Kgamanyane made the maTlakana his own, and they were to be led by his heir apparent. Moreover, all trainees were recruits for Kgamanyane's army. If Kgamanyane was Sechele's subject, serious doubts that such was the case were raised with the initiation of maTlakana. The matter was not necessarily resolved when, in May, after the harvest, Kgamanyane sent tribute (*dikgafela*) to Molepolole. To clear up this and related matters, Sechele decided that a visit to Kgamanyane was in order.[39]

Approach of War

By 1874, Sechele had convinced himself that the BaKgatla were helping themselves to his people's cattle. 'From the time Khamajan came to live in my country', he later declared, 'many of my cattle got lost and could never be recovered'.[40] Word had reached him that Kgamanyane's young men were driving them into the trans-Vaal. In about 1873, most likely during his visit to Mochudi, Sechele confronted Kgamanyane on the issue and some thirty beasts miraculously appeared. But at least fifty more remained unaccounted for. The time had come for Sechele to show Kgamanyane that the BaKwena had the power to enter the trans-Vaal and bring cattle back to the Kweneng. The surest demonstration of force required a scapegoat, of course, and a herd of unprotected cattle.

In 1874, a minor succession dispute gave Sechele his opening. Sechele loved to embroil himself in other people's affairs, to show that he was a big man, and this dispute would allow him to throw his weight around and serve up an example for Kgamanyane's instruction. The succession dispute concerned the BaTlhako of Mabieskraal, situated immediately west of the Pilanesberg, not far from Gonin's old farm, Welgeval 171. Recently BaTlhako had moved back to the trans-Vaal after living for more than a decade at Molepolole. In 1860 Mabe and his people had joined Sechele after Mabe had been flogged by a leBuru, probably the Elandsrivier ward veldkornet Sarel Eloff. Mabe died at Molepolole in 1874, and Moetlho, his eldest son of the first *lelwapa*, was challenged by Lekwakwe of the second lelwapa for the succession. Moetlho settled the issue by rounding up Mabe's cattle and taking them back to the ZAR, where he got permission from veldkornet H.P. Malan to settle with his followers at his father's old place, the farm Mabieskraal 161.[41] He was soon in contact with the DRC missionary Pieter Brink at Bopitikwe, whereupon Brink began visiting Mabieskraal as a mission outstation. Brink reported that Lekwakwe then complained to Sechele about being cut out of the inheritance, though Sechele later stated that Lekwakwe *and* Moetlho 'came to me to divide [their patrimony] between them'. Regardless, Sechele seized the opportunity to intervene. In Sechele's words, 'I sent my son Sebele to fetch their cattle'. By that he meant a regiment under Sebele entered the ZAR and rounded up Moetlho's herds.[42] Brink estimated that 600 head of cattle and 400 sheep and goats were taken back to Sechele's country.[43] There Sebele divided the stock in three equal herds, one each for the disputants and the third for himself 'for his trouble in acting as arbitrator'![44] Sebele placed his and Lekwakwe's shares near Mochudi – for the obvious purpose of advertising Sebele's prowess. Sechele must have been chuckling, too, when the ZAR remained dead silent about the raid. In spite of reports from Malan to the Rustenburg landdrost and Brink's appeal to Pretoria on behalf of Moetlho, the word came back to Brink from ZAR acting President Piet J. Joubert that 'the Government is not in a position to commence [war] with Sechele'.[45] With his extensive information network, Sechele had reason to believe that Sebele's regiment was not likely to arouse much excitement among the maBuru, because it passed through territory unoccupied by whites and was directed against the insignificant Moetlho at a time when Pretoria faced much graver threats from African forces in the north and east.

Kgamanyane was himself taking little notice of Sechele's breast-beating or of the fact that his own followers were readying themselves for the confrontation to come. He was dying, from what Linchwe and the other BaKgatla believed to be the effects of the thrashings Malan and Kruger had administered five years earlier in Saulspoort.[46] Sometime in May 1875 Kgamanyane, then little more than fifty years old, expired at Mochudi.[47] By then, preparations for a conflict with the BaKwena had already been put into place. Kgamanyane's corpse was whisked away to Rhenosterfontein 86, the farm where he had been installed as kgosi in 1849, and buried there in the old *kraal*. Their choice of Rhenosterfontein for his gravesite shows that Kgamanyane's people had embraced him as they had Pilane, and that they also faced a simple fact. In war, their enemies must not know where a kgosi's remains are interred, lest they dig them up for the medicine that would destroy the BaKgatla. The manure kraal floors at Saulspoort and Mochudi were too new, too shallow, to disguise a fresh grave underneath.[48] The BaKgatla, too, had decided to refuse tribute to Sechele. Dikgafela had not been rendered up after the previous year's harvest, and within weeks of being informed of Kgamanyane's death, when Sechele sent his collectors to Mochudi, the BaKgatla took the timing as well as the request itself as an insult. According to Charles Williams of the LMS mission in Molepolole, Sechele's demand for tribute was 'a blind to cover his real design, which was to expel the [BaKgatla]'.[49] The wagons were sent back empty.

Then Sechele and his son Sebele got their comeuppance. Lekwakwe, whom Sechele had anointed as Mabe's co-heir, died in June or July at Molepolole. When word reached Moetlho, he came with his men and snatched away Lekwakwe's herd *and* Sebele's share of 'arbitration' cattle, which were being grazed south of Mochudi near the Madikwe River. Moetlho's men passed through the territory occupied by the BaKgatla and the BaLete of Mokgosi, without so much as a murmur of protest from either group. Sechele appealed to the ZAR for assistance, and the cattle were returned.[50] Sebele was convinced that Linchwe assisted Moetlho, while Sechele accused Linchwe to his face of abetting Moetlho's raid with Mokgosi.[51] The BaKwena and BaKgatla were now trading insults and threats:

> SECHELE: You supported the BaTlhako when they stole the cattle.
> LINCHWE: I don't deny it; but you're accusing me because I'm strong enough to oppose you.
> SECHELE: If that's the case, you should have sent an army instead of a pack of thieves.
> LINCHWE: I am not your shepherd!
> SECHELE: Now I'm going to throw a snake, whose head will strike you, just as its tail will strike Makgosi.[52]

Linchwe is remembered in Kgatla tradition to have replied:

> If you send a snake, I will send a Lion; a snake can be killed by a woman, but not a lion. Only men can shoot it.[53]

Sechele was determined on war. According to Charles Williams and Heinrich C. Schulenberg, two missionaries who knew Sechele and were in the area at the time, the kgosi of the BaKwena chose to provoke the BaKgatla and the BaLete because he was convinced the BaKwena could drive them both out of the area and confiscate their cattle at the same time. Cooler heads in Molepolole tried to restrain Sechele from embarking on a war, but Sechele ignored their advice. For some time he had been building up his supply of Winchesters, horses and lead. In early August Sechele ordered all his able-bodied men to assemble at Molepolole and prepare for battle. On 9 August 1875, a force of 2,000 men and 120 horses and riders left the capital and marched in the direction of Mochudi.[54]

ENDNOTES

1   See Mbenga (1997) for the most recent evidence of the persistence of this myth. This seriously flawed article, which purports to explain the context of the flogging incident, relies heavily on twentieth-century secondary sources and oral traditions collected in the 1990s.

2   Remains of the site were briefly surveyed in 1996 (Huffmann et al. 1996).

3   Bergh and Morton 2003: Declaration No. 19 (P.J. van der Walt).

4   Ibid.: Declaration No. 6 (P.J. van Staden); Gonin to Pretorius, 20 Oct. 1870, SS 128, R1330/70, TA.

5   'Petition from the Bahgatla raad to the English Government' (Linchwe et al., November 1894, HC 108, BNA). An incomplete version appears in Schapera (1942a: 39–40).

6   Gonin to Pretorius, 20 Oct. 1870, SS 128, R1330/70, TA, translation by Ria Groenewald.

7   Bergh and Morton 2003: Declaration No. 6 (P.J. van Staden).

8   Ibid. One gets the feeling that van Staden was afraid to go to Tshwene-tshwene.

9   Ramsay (1991: esp. 50–166); Sillery (1952: 104–114; 1964); Okihiro (1976); Smith (1957).

10 Ramsay (1991: 113–116); Grobler (1997).

11 (B. Morton 1993: 91); Undated Map (1868?), Bolton Papers, ADD MS. 46, 152, BM.

12 Ramsay (1991: 69–84, 117–145). See also Grobler (1997).

13 Ellenberger (1937: 45–46); Sillery (1952: 136); Schapera (1942a [ii]: 12); Breutz (1953: 291, 450). H. Gonin to DRC, 29 Jul. 1872 (A), DRCA; Schulenburg report, 9 Jul. 1875, box 2H, HMSR, BNA; Holub (1976: 30–31). Sometime in the early 1870s, the BaTlhako ba Leema moved from Ruighoek to resettle at Tshwene-tshwene (J.S. Moffat to T. Shepstone, 16 Dec. 1880, SN4, unnumbered, TA). Ramsay (1991) argues that bafaladi groups, which BaKwena termed meratswane, retained the status of 'first among equals' in Sechele's kingdom (p. 112), 'were autonomous' (p. 119) and their leaders were 'loci of autonomous authority' (p. 133) and were 'free of tributary obligations' (p. 119). The bafaladi who moved away from Molepolole saw it differently. The BaLete told Schulenburg in

EMIGRATION

1865 that after living eight years under Sechele they had left him because they had been treated as 'inferiors' and that their leader Makgosi was not 'treated as a chief' (Schulenburg report, 3 Jan. 1876, box 2H, HMSR, BNA).

14   Price to Mullens, 30 Nov. 1870, LMS, box 36 (1870).

15   Maganelo Dikeme Pilane, 'The Kgatla-Kwena War', Jul. 1931, SP, PP 1/1/2, BNA. Maganelo's grandfather Mantirisi was Kgamanyane's younger half-brother (Smith 1957: 202).

16   Ellenberger (1939: 280); J.S. Moffat to H.C. Shepstone, 16 Dec. 1880, SN4, unnumbered item, TA. The BaKgatla also understood Tshwene-tshwene to be outside the ZAR (Linchwe testimony, 17 Oct. 1894, BPBC: 23).

17   Proclamation of 29 Apr. 1868, *Parliamentary Papers*. C. 4141: 18.

18   *Parliamentary Papers*, C. 4141.

19   Ibid.: 14–15 (Macheng to Wodehouse, 29 Mar. 1868 and Wodehouse to Macheng, 2 Jun. 1868); *Natal Mercury*, 21 May 1868.

20   *Natal Mercury*, 8 Dec. 1868.

21   Bloemhof (1871).

22   In 1876, following a dispute with Sechele, Pilane and his followers moved to Mosopa to join his father Mosielele (Ramsay 1991: 153–154).

23   Gonin to DRC, 24 May 1871, in *De Gereformeerde Kerkbode* (1871: 204–205). Translation by Linda van Jersel, Gaborone.

24   For an agro-pastoral sketch of the area, see Schapera (1943a: 128 opp.).

25   In the 1860s, the Tati (now the Northeast District of Botswana) was located between the territories of the BaNgwato and AmaNdebele. In 1867 German explorer Karl Mauch announced the presence of gold near present-day Francistown, and a gold rush ensued. Two hundred Europeans were camped there by 1868. The rush began to sputter in 1870.

26   Gonin to DRC, 7 May and 29 Jul. 1872, 17 Apr. 1873 (B), DRCA; P. Brink to N.J.R. Swart, 16 Dec. 1873, SS 164 R2091/73, TA; interview with Ratsegana Sebeke, Marapo Lands, Kgatleng, 26 Jul. 1982.

27   Corroborated references from I. Schapera notes of interview with Maganelo D. Pilane, Jul. 1931, Schapera's transcript of T.L. Phiri 'The War with the Kwena', from *Lesedi la Sechaba* (Jun. 1932–Jul.1933), and Schapera notes of interview with Klaas Segogoane, Aug. 1932, PP 1/1/2, SP, BNA. Single references to other wards (Phuting, Moganetsi, Huma, Mapotsane) are made in these sources and in more recent, but suspect, oral traditions. Interviews with Ratsegane Sebeke, Marapo Lands, Kgatleng, 26 Jul. 1982 and Harris Thulari, 28 Jul. 1982, Modisane ward, Mochudi.

28   Bergh and Morton 2003: Declaration No. 6 (P.J. van Staden).

29   Morton (1998a: 84–88).

30   Bergh and Morton 2003: Sections I, II and III.

31   Volksraad minutes of 14 Nov. 1871, in ibid., Section VII.

32   Gonin to DRC, 7 May, 29 Jul. and 6 Dec. 1872 (A).

33   Brink to N.J.R. Swart, 16 Dec. 1873, SS 164, R2091/73, TA.

34   Gonin to DRC, 19 Mar. 1874 (A), DRCA.

35   Gonin to N.J.R. Swart, 13 Feb. 1875, SS 185, R458/75, TA.

36 Gonin to DRC, 17 Apr. 1873 (A), DRCA. Gonin mentions no name, but he could have been referring to Komane, Tau's younger brother, or to Kobedi, eldest son of Pilane's twelfth lelwapa. See Pilane agnatic male descendants, PP 1/3/9, SP, BNA.

37 For the best discussions of initiation, see Schapera (1978) and Willoughby (1909).

38 Two documents, one in SeTswana with Kgamanyane's mark and the other in English, were shown to Samuel Melvill in 1880 (Melvill report, 9 Apr. 1880 in Schapera 1943a: 35). Melvill and P.J. van Staden did not mention these documents in their Transvaal Commission report of 30 Nov. 1878. Cf. draft report with annexures in SN 2, N287/79 and report with attached correspondence in SS 454, R3773/80, 209–305, both TA. Sechele claimed that Kgamanyane had given him 'a written understanding that I should always be regarded as the sole owner of the soil' (Sechele to Sir Garnet Wolesely, 3 Oct. 1879, SS 454, R3773/80, 235, TA). For the Melvilll/Van Staden Commission, see ch. 5.

39 J. Mackenzie to J.S. Moffat, 1 May 1874, box 37 (1874), LMS. In October 1878 Sechele told S. Melvill and P.J. Van Staden that Kgamanyane had paid him tribute 'as a token of the country being his [Sechele's]' for the first two years, namely the 1872 and 1873 harvests (Melvill and Van Staden report, SS 454, R3773/80, para. 12, TA).

40 Sechele statement, 30 Oct. 1878, before Melvill and Van Staden, SN 2, N287/79, Annex. A, TA.

41 P. Brink to H. Shepstone, 25 May 1880, translation. SN 3, R192/80, TA.

42 Sechele statement to Melvill and Van Staden, 30 Oct. 1878, SN 2, N287/79, Annex. A, TA. Before leading a regiment into Moetlho's area, Sebele may also have first attempted to get the ZAR to intervene on Sechele's behalf. According to HMS missionary Heinrich Schulenburg, Sebele and Taylor, an English trader at Molepolole serving as Sebele's interpreter, traveled to Pretoria in an effort to get the ZAR to return the cattle. Schulenburg report, 3 Jan. 1876, box 2H, HMSR, BNA.

43 P. Brink to H. Shepstone, 25 May 1880, translation. SN 3, R192/80, TA.

44 Sechele statement to Melvill and Van Staden, 30 Oct. 1878, SN 2, N287/79, Annex. A, TA.

45 P. Brink to H. Shepstone, 25 May 1880, translation, SN 3, R192/80, TA. Burgers' ZAR government was becoming increasingly concerned about the security of its northern and eastern borders and the possible loss of the Lydenburg gold fields. An open conflict with the BaPedi was months away (Delius 1984: 192–205). When Sechele's troops entered the trans-Vaal, Burgers was in Europe.

46 Address to Sir Arthur Lawley, n.d. (1903), SNA 116, 672/03, TA.

47 Gonin to DRC, 15 Jun. 1875 (B), DRCA.

48 Schapera (1943a: 11).

49 C. Williams to Secretary. LMS, 17 Jan. 1876, LMS. Williams uses 'Bakgaghela' (BaKgafela), by which the BaKgatla sometimes represented themselves (BaKgatla baga Kgafela).

50 Sechele to Osborne, 21 Jun. 1878, c. 2220: 132, PP.

51 Sechele statement to Melvill and Van Staden, 30 Oct. 1878, SN 2, N287/79, Annex. A, TA; C. Williams to Sec. LMS, 17 Jan. 1876, LMS; Ramsay (1991: 149). See also H. Goold-Adams report of 5 Mar. 1888 in Schapera (1943a: 37), but Goold-Adams's information is muddled.

52 This exchange was reported to Heinrich Schulenburg, then missionary to Mokgosi's

BaLete at Pata Lekwapa (Ramotswa) (Schulenberg report, 3 Jan. 1876, box 2H, HMSR, BNA). Translation from the German by Jens Werner.

53 T.L. Phiri statement, Jul. 1931, PP 1/1/2, SP, BNA.

54 Williams to LMS, 17 Jan. 1876, LMS; Schulenburg reports, 14 Dec. 1875 and 3 Jan. 1876, box 2H, HMSR. Williams was the LMS missionary in Molepolole (1874?–May 1877). Schulenberg was the HMS missionary in Shoshong (1859–1863), capital of the BaNgwato, and worked among the BaLete at Mankodi (1864–1875) and Ramotswa (1875–1876). For the HMS in eastern Botswana see Mignon (1996: 7–19).

Chapter five

WAR

Stakes pierce the Kwena.
They pierced Sechele Motswasele
And pointed his legs to the sky . . .

Eat and eat quickly, Madingwana of Kwenaland,
You comrades of Raditsebe;
Whoever has a wife, enjoy her right now.
Whoever has a sheep, kill it for her;
You see, I am darkness, I'm coming,
I am Misery, and I'm already close by,
I am plodding up to the streets and to the gateways of Mosenyi's village.
(Linchwe's praise, composed by himself)

* * *

We bought this country with the blood and lives of our fellow-men. (Petition of Linchwe and his advisors, 1894)

So commonly is bloodletting associated with the meaning of war that anyone writing military history is obliged to serve it up in detail. Life away from the battlefield, if mentioned, is for dramatic emphasis: the calm surrounding the fatal clash. Military history is often taken as history itself, as primeval subject-matter for the essential male. Since prehistoric times it would seem that combat constitutes manhood's ultimate test. Africa's past too is as vital to this notion as any other; for what else may explain that African history's best selling work is *Washing of the Spears?*[1] For certain the Kgatla–Kwena War had its bloody confrontations, and the Battle of Mochudi – fought on 11 August 1875 – was vivid enough. For several hours, in and around the rocks of Phuthadikobo Hill, an intense struggle took place, resulting in many deaths and casualties. Memory of the battle has survived in BaKgatla oral traditions, which describe in rich detail and in an entertaining manner the experiences and reactions of combatants on both sides. Yet, in military terms, the Battle of Mochudi was pronouncedly anti-climatic. The battle merely began the Kgatla–Kwena War and played at best a minor role in determining the outcome. For another eight long years, an unspectacular, intermittent series of small-scale raids dragged on and gradually sputtered to a stop. When a final truce was reached, the BaKgatla and BaKwena had limped to a stalemate. This was not a war of defining moments or turning points.

Though thousands died during the Kgatla–Kwena war, the BaKgatla were concerned less with winning militarily than defending Mochudi and stealing BaKwena cattle. Building up herds protected the future of the people. War was an excuse to divest the enemy of their means of survival while fattening themselves. Also, the BaKgatla were the better cattle raiders because of their connections with the trans-Vaal. They had African allies in the Rustenburg District who wanted BaKwena cattle, too, and who would help the BaKgatla hide the takings. The BaKgatla appealed to Pretoria for help against the BaKwena and got permission to keep their booty safe in the Saulspoort area. Sechele was forced thereby to try and get his claims to the disputed territory recognised by the ZAR and, as the war dragged on, by the English who ran the Transvaal as an Annexed Territory from 1877 to 1881. If Sechele could claim that the land occupied by the BaKgatla belonged to Sechele, though, then the BaKgatla could claim it belonged to the ZAR or to the Annexation Government, and ask for white 'protection'. The BaKgatla, who for long had lost the notion of an autonomous BaKgatla state and most definitely disliked being ruled by Sechele, simply claimed to be ZAR subjects. As long as Boer and Briton proved sympathetic to the BaKgatla, and until 1881 they were, the BaKgatla need only dig in around Phuthadikobo and wait for Sechele to give in.

Keeping the BaKwena at bay proved relatively easy. The BaKwena were saddled with disadvantages. Though numerically superior to the BaKgatla, the BaKwena had no recourse but to attack the BaKgatla when they were concentrated at the easily defended Phuthadikobo. Laying siege was not an alternative for a civilian army on call-up with heavy obligations back home. Moreover, Sechele's ranking officer, his eldest son and heir Sebele, was incompetent. Sebele showed a lack of courage in his first battle against the BaKgatla and failed to assemble an effective force thereafter. Sechele's meddling in the political affairs of the BaNgwato and BaNgwaketse also deprived the BaKwena of the support of these two powerful groups in his war against the BaKgatla, just as his treatment of bafaladi turned many of them into the allies of his enemy. During the war, the BaKgatla were joined at different times by the BaLete and BaTlokwa and all had spies inside Sechele's territory. Apart from the support he received from the BaKaa of Mosenyi and the BaKgatla baga Mmanaana of Pilane (that but for one year), Sechele faced the BaKgatla alone. Sechele's herds in the Mochudi neighbourhood became easy pickings for Kgatla raiders. As the war dragged on and as a prolonged drought set in (1876–1880), many of the cattle that Sechele's people held onto died of thirst, and the BaKwena began to starve. These droughts caused suffering among the BaKgatla, too, and in part they explain the low rate of military activity, but they and their cattle had access to the Ngotwane and Madikwe rivers and sand beds. The BaKwena, who were confined to the parched areas adjoining the Kalahari thirstlands, had access to no water whatsoever. They were devastated.

The Battle of Mochudi (Wednesday, 11 August 1875)

As we followed the events leading up to the war in the last chapter, Sechele had taken the decision to send a large force under the command of Sebele to attack the BaKgatla at their capital, Mochudi, some 60 kilometres due west of Molepolole. Sebele and his men left Molepolole on 9 August 1875. This contingent of more than 2,000 men hoped to take the BaKgatla by surprise. On the first day, a Monday, they moved due east, passing the Kopong Hills on the way. En route, they were met by four messengers from Mochudi and headed for Molepolole. They carried the report from Linchwe that, after the entreaties of Williams and Kgosidintsi, he was prepared to offer Sechele tribute as demanded. Sebele had the messengers seized and then proceeded with the march as planned. The contingent camped that night near the Tshele and Seleme kopjies. Then, the next afternoon, they circled north of Mochudi and camped Tuesday night in the rolling plains not far from where the BaKgatla of Mabodisa ward were settled beneath Phuthadikobo Hill. In the meantime, one of the messengers had escaped and made his way back to Mochudi and informed Linchwe of the approaching force. However, Linchwe and his uncles assumed that the BaKwena would approach Mochudi in the usual way, namely, from the south, and so they were not prepared for the attack that came at dawn on Wednesday.

Regrettably little is known of the battle, because only one eye-witness account appears to have been written, that being very brief and anonymous.[2] In addition, in the 1980s when I collected oral traditions, few men were alive who could recall in any detail what they had been told about the event. One tradition that has survived, however, is worth reproducing here, because it says a great deal about the battle and gives the BaKgatla's own interpretation of Sechele's reasons for dispatching his forces at that particular time and for placing them under the command of Sebele. Its interpretation is open to dispute, and its several dramatic flourishes show it has been embroidered for effect, but many of the details of the tradition can be corroborated with contemporaneous sources. The tradition was recorded in the winter of 1982, more than a hundred years after the Battle of Mochudi. It is drawn from a transcription of a recorded interview with an elderly Kgatla historian who patiently answered many questions in the presence of two other knowledgeable men and thereby bequeathed this account of the battle and the war that followed.[3] Where the tradition is confirmed, contradicted or supplemented by the eye-witness account printed in *De Volksstem*, and other, contemporary, second-hand reports of the battle, mention will be made in the footnotes.

The tradition begins not at Mochudi, but in Molepolole, at the point when Sechele realised that the BaKgatla would have to be dealt with after Linchwe refused to pay tribute. It argues that the moment was a difficult one for Sechele and that the manner in which he mobilised the BaKwena was influenced by his political insecurity. Sechele emerges here as a calculating schemer, a characteristic in keeping with his political life at other times. According to this tradition, Sechele regarded Linchwe's refusal to pay tribute as an opportunity to get rid of two persons who challenged his authority: one was, not surprisingly, Linchwe. The other, however, was Sebele, Sechele's ambitious son.

> In the Kweneng, Sebele was planning to fight his father Sechele at the same time the BaKgatla and the BaKwena were already preparing for battle against each other ... [After] Sebele was lashed [by Sechele, for serious misconduct], he ran away to Khama [the recent usurper of the BaNgwato throne, in Shoshong; in 1872 Sebele and his regiment had assisted Khama in overthrowing Macheng] with whom he planned to come and beat Sechele. Feeling threatened, Sechele went to Linchwe and asked for help. He said to him, 'uncle, there is the lion, help me. Provide me with strong lads to ward off the danger of this lion. Help me, provide them to kill him.' Then when he returned [to Molepolole], Sechele called his people together and told them that the ma-Koni [lit. 'northerners', often used in reference to outsiders, in this case, referring to the BaKgatla] were coming to attack them. 'MaKoni

say this land's totem is kgabo [vervet monkey, the Kgatla totem]. Is not this land for *kwena* [crocodile, the Kwena totem]?' The people retorted, 'Is that so? Therefore summon Sebele.'[4] Sebele was then called home and on his arrival he was told that the maKoni were coming to attack. Sechele is said to have told him, 'You see the maKoni are coming to invade this land yet you stay away!'

Immediately Sebele was put in a fighting spirit and began to prepare for war. He went to buy *dipathusi* [cloth] and paper with which he wrapped his legs. With this sort of attire he now resembled an army lieutenant and began to march about shouting 'What can the maKoni do to us?!'

This passage, which portrays Sebele as vain and given to public display, corresponds with what is remembered of Sechele's son by the BaKwena themselves, who accorded him little respect.[5] The story is not explicit as to why Sebele should be placed at the head of an army on the chance of his becoming a hero should the BaKwena come away with a victory, but as events related in the tradition imply, Sebele was expected to humiliate himself.

The Kwena regiments then set forth on their march and made camp at the foothills of the Tshele and Seleme kopjies [west of present-day Rasesa, eight kilometres west of Mochudi]. From here some men were sent out as scouts to go and espy the Kgatla regiments' movements and determine the distance of their 'reach' from the Kwena camp. They brought back the information that the BaKgatla were still at a distance so that a move to attack them would be exposed in daylight. The contingent instead left again and moved nearer [to Mochudi]. On the second night they established their camp at Ngwaritshi, or ga Makakatlelo. Here they lit their fires to keep themselves warm in the night breeze. But the flames from their fires revealed to the BaKgatla where the BaKwena were camping.[6]

There was no tingling of fear or uneasiness [among the BaKgatla] whatsoever. They believed the BaKwena were mere people against whom they could just drive away by whipping them. So they slept.

On the next day, early at dawn, they [the BaKgatla] woke. They shouted their war-cry: 'Come out BaKwena! Come out, black sons of *Mma Seadingwe*. Stand stalwart Sebele, stand like the tamboti tree.'[7]

Sebele's BaKwena stood up. He gave out a command to the different regiments to take their battle positions (in such commands usually is embedded a praise for the regiment).

At this point the story makes clear that the regiments under Sebele included two bafaladi groups still under Sechele's sovereignty, the BaKaa of Mosenyi and BaKgatla baga Mmanaana of Pilane.[8]

Sebele shouted: 'BaKaa of Suwe Lebelwane, don't look askance like strangers not allowed to eat, come and sit here.'[9]

Turning around he pointed his eyes at the Mmanaana regiment and said: 'Mokhikhitshwane the Beast eaters, the cannibals who would eat human flesh instead of beef. Come out, Hee!'[10]

In the command to the Mmanaana Sebele also called on a *moruti* [Christian priest] to come forward and pray to God to give them strength and vigour in their war.[11]

The priest stepped forward and started to pray: 'Oh Lord our God, please help us to kill and destroy these people. But Lord also give to them the strength and power to kill us in turn.'

A voice called forth: 'Hey! Where do you get such bad words?! Hey, say 'Amen'!'

Sebele went on to give orders to his regiments. Mothakola[12] was ordered to head for the Mabodisa *kgoro*, while the BaKaa were ordered to pass by some wells situated near Nkwalle's homestead (It is here that my grandfather Ramonthle died later, during the battle).[13]

When the Kwena regiments assembled in Makakatlelo and were assigned their strategic positions, the leader of the Mmanaana regiments gave special orders to his men. He did this by first spreading out the fingers of his hand. Then he cautioned his men that the BaKgatla were their brothers and that they were not to kill their own brothers.[14] Giving out orders he pointed out the significance of his spread out fingers and the intent of each finger when he pointed to it. This is what he is supposed to have said: 'Look here when I point like this [Sebeke illustrates] don't look at this finger but look at this one. When the BaKwena and the BaKaa attack our brothers, we must stay in the background and then retreat.' And they did as they were told. When the Mmanaana men attacked, they came via the spur between the hills where the railway line now passes through.[15]

115

The Kwena regiments attacked at Mapotsana ward because the Mabodisa regiment had not arrived yet.[16] They invaded Mapotsana with gusto and actually besieged the place and set the valley on fire.[17] Meanwhile my fathers, I mean the men of Mochudi, were still occupied with drinking *bojalwa* (millet beer). Suddenly a man galloped up to them and announced the presence of the BaKwena, crying out, 'You sit here smoking dagga [and] here are the BaKwena coming!' The BaKgatla immediately swung into action and, because of the influence of the dagga they were ruthless with their spears. They ran into the BaKwena mercilessly stabbing them. They were also using guns.[18]

At this point the story begins to elaborate on the conduct of Sebele, who earned much notoriety among the BaKwena for his cowardice at the Battle of Mochudi.[19]

Sebele apparently was chilled and frightened by the horror of the scene because he slipped from his saddle. The BaKwena retreated. While in his fright Sebele's saddle girth broke and the saddle fell on the ground. He struggled to cling to the horse's mane. When he finally gripped it he bowed on his horses' back (Its name was 'Bronc') and made away on it, the horse galloping at high speed. He ran away past Rantsikwe and stopped at a cluster of trees near Rabikimane's shop. That is where he cut away the leather case on which he carried rifle balls and threw them on the ground. Sebele was able to get away from the battle because of the custom that prohibited the killing of a kgosi on the battlefield. If the commander or leader of the regiment is the son of a chief he is not killed.[20]

While Sebele was running away, the action on the battlefield was intense. In the middle of the battle, the moruti with the Mmanaana Kgatla regiment had his horse shot dead out from under him and when it collapsed the moruti was already on his heels running away to save his life. And they immediately retorted: 'Let them do so, it has served you right! This is the fate you looked for this morning!' The Kwena regiments were repelled by the BaKgatla and went for good.

When the BaKwena were escaping, the Mmanaana men ... arrived at Borejane and caught sight of the cattle trails and so went after them immediately. It was at Seboeng that the Mmanaana men captured the cattle of the Sebeke [Ratshegana's] kinsmen. These were the first group of cattle to be seized by the BaKwena.[21]

When the BaKwena arrived home they waited outside [Molepolole] first because the custom is that they must wait first before entering. A message was sent to Sechele that they were back. Sechele then put on a shirt and hat made from baboon's skin. Thereafter he led the procession of the Kwena regiments into the village, singing a mocking song:

'Are you running away, are you running away?! Hee a hee! Are you running away, BaKwena, from Mochudi? Are you running from ma-Koni, the black ones, are you running away?'

By this he was ridiculing them and particularly Sebele. 'Was it not you who conspired against me and went to Gamangwato in an attempt to gather all strength against me? I also have been to my mother's people. Go and seek help from your mother's people as well.'[22]

It may be that this Kgatla tradition, passed on by Ratsegana Sebeke and which purports that Sechele launched the battle of Mochudi in an indifferent military manner primarily to undercut Sebele's political base, has survived because of its entertainment value rather than its historical interpretation. Yet, the tradition does demonstrate that the BaKwena, for whatever reason, misjudged seriously the amount of force necessary for taking Mochudi and driving the BaKgatla out of their territory. If not wishing for Sebele's defeat, Sechele was responsible for making his weak-minded son responsible for such an important task. Whatever number of armed men the BaKwena could put into the field, they lacked experience as the aggressors against a determined foe. Their most recent encounter of any note was fought long ago in 1852, when they defended their old capital at Dimawe against an attack by P.E. Scholtz's commando.[23] None of the four regiments formed since Dimawe was battle-tested, except under Sebele three years previously (August 1872), when they fought the followers of Macheng at Shoshong. In a dawn attack, Sebele's forces torched the town and then drove Macheng's group from the capital. Shoshong was hardly a glorious victory, though. The BaNgwato were deeply divided, and Sebele's regiments merely joined the rebel group headed by the future Ngwato kgosi, Khama III.[24] At Mochudi, Sebele appears to have assumed that he was in for another easy victory if he simply used the tactics that had worked so effectively at Shoshong, but this time his forces were up against armed veterans who many times had seen combat as Boer auxiliaries.[25] When the Battle of Mochudi was over, the BaKwena left behind as many as 100 dead, whereas the BaKgatla lost fewer than 20.[26]

The First Phase: September 1875 to April 1877

The BaKgatla assumed that the conflict between themselves and Sechele's people would not end with the Battle of Mochudi. They wasted no time in putting into place the means by which they could defend themselves for the long haul. Immediately, all the men and women went to work building a stone wall around Mochudi, complete with shooting holes. It took them three days.[27] Then they looked for the enemy's cattle, before the BaKwena could drive them to safety. Sebele's retreating army had left the BaKgatla free to take thousands. The major posts were located west of Molepolole at Letlhakeng and north of Mochudi in the Seruruma Valley, bordering on Ngwato territory. Each post was in the care of a few BaKgalagadi and Bushmen slaves. The BaKgatla swept into these areas and rounded up the lot, BaKgalagadi and Bushmen included.[28] The spoils, however, presented their own problem. They could neither be kept where they had been seized nor moved near Mochudi, because the BaKwena could simply retake them; the men required to protect thousands of cattle were needed to protect Mochudi itself. In order to defend their settlement and keep Kwena cattle, slaves and territory, the BaKgatla had to have a rearguard. The trans-Vaal was nearby, but using it meant first getting the permission of the ZAR. Also, before the ZAR could be approached, the BaKgatla needed to determine who would represent them.

Since Kgamanyane's death in May, there had been too little time to see to the choice and installation of their new kgosi. The natural choice was Linchwe, son of Kgamanyane's great wife Dikolo Ramontsana Tlou from Mabieskraal. However, when his father died, Linchwe had not completed the 'white' phase of *bogwera* that admitted him to manhood. That was possible only in July, by which time the BaKgatla were preparing for Sechele to strike.[29] Linchwe also had a rival. He was Maganelo, older half-brother, initiated in Saulspoort before Kgamanyane left for Tshwene-tshwene, and leader of the maFatlha regiment. As son of Nkomeng, whom Kgamanyane had betrothed before Dikolo, Maganelo could claim seniority. He was also publicly declaring his entitlement.[30] To deal with this challenge and avert division among the BaKgatla, time was needed to assemble the decision-makers, especially Kgamanyane's brothers and his uncle Molefi (Pilane's loyal brother and sometime regent), to discuss the succession. In the meantime, the leadership was taken up by the regent Bogatsu, Kgamanyane's full brother. Though Kgamanyane or Linchwe are always referred to in the reports at the time as leading the BaKgatla, it was Bogatsu who commanded them in the Battle of Mochudi and who set Kgatla strategy in the months that followed. While Bogatsu was the effective leader, the BaKgatla needed a kgosi in order to deal with Pretoria. The maBuru dealt only with kapiteins.

Thus, when the Battle of Mochudi was concluded, Bogatsu quickly brought over from Pilanesberg his ranking brothers. By late August or early September, all but one of the senior uncles of the future kgosi had arrived – Tshomankane, Tau, Moselekatse, Mantirisi, Kgari and Bafshwe. The ancient Molefi Molefe, who stood in for Pilane during his years of exile, was also present. Only Letsebe was absent. He and his younger brother Kgabotshwene, who had been in Molepolole when the BaKwena attacked Mochudi, were suspected by Sechele of aiding the BaKgatla. They escaped from Molepolole with their lives and fled to the Transvaal.[31] The uncles deliberated, briefly. They put aside Maganelo's claim, ignored the old dispute between Tau and Kgamanyane and chose Linchwe as Kgamanyane's successor.[32] This was not the time for a quarrel over leadership.

Their haste to resolve the succession put on the kgosi's chair a youngster unknown to the uncles who chose him. Linchwe aKgamanyane[33] had no experience of leadership apart from his role as head of the recently formed maTlakana regiment. Only seventeen or eighteen years old, Linchwe was, like most lads then, required to spend his youth at the cattle post. His father had also discouraged him from attending the DRC school at Saulspoort, though he had managed secretly to gain enough knowledge of the alphabet to begin to read the Bible.[34] Unlike several of his brothers (including Maganelo) and his uncle Tau, however, he could not write. Perhaps his inexperience favoured his selection. His uncles might have assumed they would gain influence with Linchwe, because the lad would have to depend on them for advice.

On the other hand, the BaKgatla were engaged in a war, the end of which could not be predicted, and the uncles were not going to fight it. In the past, the BaKgatla had endured many tests in battle and followed leaders who, apart from their particular political or social skills, liked to celebrate taking lives. Kgamanyane and Pilane held the BaKgatla together and fostered their emergence as a regional power not just by being clever, but by spilling blood. The uncles were going to be important to Linchwe in offering their insights and sanctioning his actions, but the men who armed his regiments wanted to know if Linchwe could fight. The last thing they wanted was a coward like Sebele; they needed a man who would bring cattle their way. Their future as men, as family heads, depended on it. The BaKgatla had made their mark in the past by raiding other people's wealth, and their future together now depended on a kgosi who was as eager as they to take what belonged to the BaKwena.

The young Linchwe also had to be recognised as a hoofdkapitein by the Zuid-Afrikaansche Republiek. It would be of little advantage to the BaKgatla if their cattle remained around Mochudi – the BaKwena would simply come over from Molepolole and take them. They had to be run into the trans-Vaal for safekeeping, which meant convincing the ZAR that it was in their interest to assist the BaKgatla in their fight against the Ba-Kwena. Linchwe was too young to know how to approach Boer officials. Such matters were understood by the uncles, who had years of experience of dealing with the maBuru, but Linchwe was the kgosi, and he would have to do it.

Within a week or so of his installation, Linchwe was in Saulspoort. There he was introduced to Henri Gonin, who had served as Kgamanyane's correspondent with Burgers' government over the previous five years. Gonin was particularly keen to keep the BaKgatla in the DRC fold and was worried that the LMS might somehow lay hands on the people he had been cultivating for Christianity for the past decade.[35] Since Kgamanyane's death, Gonin had hoped Linchwe would become the successor. 'I think', anticipated Gonin, 'he is willing to favour us; he reads the Bible, but he is really still meeting a lot of temptations.'[36] Gonin received the new kgosi and his entourage cordially, and then agreed to write to Acting President Joubert and officials in the Rustenburg District on Linchwe's behalf, as he had done in the past for his father. The letter, the first penned in Linchwe's name, reveals that the BaKgatla had put together a diplomatic war strategy that would encourage the ZAR to back Linchwe against Sechele. They would get Joubert's attention by raising the spectre of a kaffir league on the ZAR border. Not by coincidence, it consisted of the ZAR's major adversaries.

> Leincheu, Son and heir of Khamayane (Gamjan) *opperhoofd van de Bakhatlas*, at the moment here present, asked me to inform you that Secheli, after he attacked him (Leinschue) without reason, is presently looking all over for allies, and the *kaffir kapteinen* Gasesiwe [Gaseitsiwe of the BaNgwaketse], Montxioe [Montshiwa of the Tshidi BaRalong], Khame [Khama III of the BaNgwato] and Mapela [Mankopane Mapela of the Langa AmaNdebele] seem to be pulling together to eradicate the BaKgatla. He, Leinchue, fears that although he is strong enough to defend his people against only Secheli, the BaKhatla will be overpowered by the greater numbers. And I humbly ask the Government of the Republic to help him, in case these above mentioned *kapteinen* would attack him.[37]

> He wishes, with his people to be considered *completely as an ally of the State* [emphasis added], and if it is necessary and he is in the position to do so, to be of service to the State. Furthermore Leinchue has the honour to inform Your Honour that he has sent his own cattle and the cattle he had taken from Secheli, to the area of this State which is situated on the Crocodile River and that he has already informed P.J. van Staden, Landdrost of Rustenburg, as well as H. Malan, Field-Cornet of the Elands River Ward about this.[38]

Whether Linchwe and his advisors were aware or not, Van Staden had already informed Joubert of the Kwena attack on Mochudi and put his anti-Sechele feelings on record. 'I ordered that a watchful eye be kept on Secheli's actions', he wrote to Joubert, 'because he must not infringe on my District, and if he wants to, I will stop him'.[39] As Van Staden explained it three years later, the Kgatla defeat of Kwena forces at Mochudi greatly eased matters for the ZAR, then preoccupied with an impending war against the BaPedi and fearful that Sechele would choose this time to mobilise the border kaffirs against them. To their relief, the BaKgatla had become the ZAR's 'barrier against Sechieli'.[40] Linchwe's letter was well received in Pretoria. Many months passed before Pretoria formally acknowledged Linchwe's existence, but it would contain the news that Pretoria regarded Linchwe's BaKgatla in Mochudi as ZAR subjects residing on ZAR soil.

In the meantime, the BaKgatla took the initiative in the fighting. Moreover, it was the BaKgatla, not the BaKwena, who put together an alliance. The Kgatla success in withstanding Kwena military force encouraged the BaTlokwa and BaLete to break away from the BaKwena. The BaLete, whom

Sebele's forces had also attacked on 11 August, were the first to join forces with the BaKgatla. In October a combined Kgatla–Lete force invaded the Kweneng. Bogatsu took command of the Kgatla regiments, with Linchwe remaining in Mochudi. In the classical style, it was more a cattle raid than a military venture, and it ended in disaster. After taking large numbers of cattle south and west of Molepolole, the returning forces stopped near Thamaga (seat of Pilane's Mmanaana Kgatla who had joined Sebele's attack on Mochudi), where they camped without regard to defence. The Mmanaana Kgatla shot their way into Bogatsu's encampment, giving much better than they got, and taking back all the cattle. Among the tens of dead left in the battlefield lay Maganelo. The survivors returned home empty-handed.[41] The defeat at Thamaga ended Bogatsu's military leadership. Thereafter Linchwe took command. Because the time had come to plough, however, organised fighting subsided for the coming growing season. People on both sides scattered to the lands to look after their crops, but left themselves unprotected. Thus began the time of *bonokwane* (villainy), in which armed marauders, Kgatla and Kwena alike, moved about on horseback terrorising isolated families; hacking off limbs, burning rondavels with people trapped inside, and slaughtering small stock.[42] The purpose was simply to keep civilians off the land and their crops unattended. The drought, which set in that year, compounded the misery.

Meanwhile, Linchwe assumed greater control over the war effort and Kgatla affairs. Immediately he understood the importance of gaining support from the Saulspoort BaKgatla. He got in touch with Tshomankane and his other trans-Vaal uncles, and coordinated with them the moving of stolen Kwena cattle into the Pilanesberg for safekeeping near the Crocodile River. In early 1876 he visited the area north of the Pilanesberg where a cluster of BaKgatla of the Mabodisa kgoro were living, levied cattle from the adult males, and used them, with Gonin's help, to purchase from a Mr Louis the nearby farm Holfontein 361 for the Mabodisa to live on. Some of the funds came from a levy on BaKgatla men returning from the Kimberley diamond fields.[43] With the trans-Vaal BaKgatla backing him, Linchwe was able to control an area extending from the Mochudi environs all the way to the Pilanesberg. Fortunately for Linchwe, this territory was being vacated by the Boers (who had been lightly scattered there), as the ZAR lost ground against its African adversaries along its borders. A group of Doppers influenced by the teachings of Jan Lion Cachet, a disciple of Dirk

Postma, became disillusioned with Burgers, abandoned their farms and trekked northwest. Forming three parties, they passed through Khama's Ngwato kingdom into the Kalahari in search of a new settlement area. Known as the *Dorslanders* ('Thirstlanders'), they assembled first in the Pilanesberg on Witfontein and Holfontein, the farms where BaKgatla were residing under Mantirisi Pilane, and then laagered on the Limpopo River headwaters, located on the edge of Khama and Linchwe's territories, before traversing the Kalahari.[44]

The unsettled state of ZAR affairs and the arrival of the Dorslanders placed Linchwe in the awkward position of having to negotiate with Burgers's government while keeping on good terms with the anti-Burgers Dorslanders laagered at his *stoep*. Sechele, aware of Linchwe's dilemma, tried to exploit it to his advantage. The Kwena kgosi also assumed that the ZAR and the Boers of the western trans-Vaal recognised him as the sovereign of the territory occupied by Linchwe. In January 1876, when the second group of Dorslanders were awaiting permission from Khama to cross his territory to Ngamiland, Sechele wrote to them that Linchwe and Khama had allied with another group (*Malkander*[45]) to attack the Boers. Sechele declared his own peaceful intentions and stated that the BaKwena were at war with the BaKgatla 'so I will be glad if he is defeated by you'.[46] In the months to come, the Dorslanders committed a series of crimes in Khama's territory and insulted him, behaviour that Sechele seems to have encouraged. Sechele collaborated with the Dorslanders, who kept in touch with him by travelling through Mochudi, to encourage Khamane, Khama's brother living in exile in Molepolole, in his desire to overthrow Khama.[47]

Linchwe dealt cautiously with the Dorslanders. He had Fred J. Lewis, one of the few maKgoa in Mochudi, handle his diplomatic correspondence. In 1874–1875, Lewis had been the Rustenburg landdrost's clerk and translator, as well as a private agent, and sometime in early 1876 he arrived in Mochudi most likely as the ears and eyes of Rustenburg landdrost P.J. van Staden, who was worried that Sechele would intrude into the ZAR on the pretext of chasing Linchwe.[48] Lewis may have met Linchwe for the first time in January 1876 when the kgosi was in the trans-Vaal acquiring Holfontein 361.[49] Like other single white men in the region, Lewis also traded on the side – at a time when Mochudi was emerging as a through-point on the commercial road from the trans-Vaal to Shoshong.[50] Lewis served as Linchwe's secretary for most of 1876, having his letters and documents that bear Linchwe's mark witnessed by other traders passing through. His first letter on Linchwe's behalf was sent to Louw du Plessis, head of the Dorslanders. It shows that Linchwe was afraid to confront the Dorslanders, who were commandeering some of his stock, and that he had to dispute Sechele's allegations that he and Khama were conspiring against the Dorslanders, while at the same time acknowledging that Mochudi and Shoshong were in contact:

> I have the honour to thank you for all the trouble you took with regards to Mr. Krieling's horse. Referring to the report that I would help Khama, I have to inform you that it is a blatant lie. I already have my hands full with Secheli and have no desire to be attacked from both sides. I will have the bull that is still with you fetched at a later stage. If it should die I would be very indebted to you if you could get me another one. Brenger (?) is going to Bamangwato with cattle, I am informing you, so that you should not become suspicious about his mission.
>
> With greetings to you, Lichue, Chief of the Bakhalta.[51]

The Dorslanders nevertheless continued to support Sechele. In March, several weeks after Lewis wrote to Du Plessis on Linchwe's behalf, Sechele used the Dorslander area as a corridor to outflank the BaKgatla. He ordered his commanders Ramodibe and Rantseo to lead their respective regiments into the trans-Vaal via the Limpopo and Matlabas rivers, head for Witfontein (immediately north of the Pilanesberg), where the stolen cattle were kept, and drive them back to the Kweneng by the same route. Pursuing BaKgatla intercepted some cattle inside the Transvaal near Buffel's Drift and overtook Rantseo, who unwisely elected to pass south of the Dorslanders and head due west toward Molepolole – north of Mochudi. The bulk of the cattle ('several hundred'), however, returned with the men of Ramodibe, who had followed Sechele's instructions and made it back to Molepolole.[52] A spate of atrocities on both sides followed this raid, and once again the BaKgatla began preparations for a retaliatory assault on Molepolole.

Before the attack was launched, both Linchwe and Sechele appealed to Burgers to restrain the other. In late April, on Linchwe's behalf, Lewis reported from Holfontein that Sechele's men had raided 'far within the acknowledged boundary of this State' and asked Burgers 'to do your utmost to put an end to this state of affairs'.[53] A week later, back in Mochudi, Lewis and (H.A.?) Smith as 'Agents for Linchwe of the Bakhatlas' wrote again to Burgers reporting another of Sechele's raids on Linchwe, in which four BaKgatla had been killed. They appealed to Burgers 'not to allow men to be ruthlessly murdered when depending on the protection of the government of your honor's country, without punishing the offenders'.[54] Meanwhile, Sechele was using LMS missionary Charles Williams to write to Burgers claiming that Pilanesberg BaKgatla were about to assist Linchwe in an offensive against the BaKwena and asking that Burgers prevent them 'from leaving your territory'.[55] Lewis, Smith and Williams received no replies. Burgers then was preoccupied with the war against the BaPedi, the President himself preparing to lead a large force against Sekhukhuni in the coming weeks. Burgers' silence might also have had something to do with the fact that he needed Kgatla auxiliaries for his imminent campaign.[56] When Burgers formally wrote to Linchwe in July, though, it was obvious that Linchwe and Sechele's correspondence with Pretoria had created the impression that Linchwe's people were located inside the ZAR. Burgers informed Linchwe that Mochudi lay within the ZAR boundary and that the kapitein and his people were subjects of his government. Linchwe was quick to register his surprise, and express his willingness to accept ZAR status.

> My late father Gajaman used to reside near Pilanesberg in the Rustenburg District, but about six years ago the Transvaal officials made things so difficult for him that he moved away from there to here. Everybody I know has regarded this as his departure from the Republic and considered him to be outside the boundaries of the State once he had crossed the Marico River. Until his death he never knew that he was to remain a Transvaal subject forever, and I, although I was in the company of Transvaal officials more than once, never heard of such a thing until this day. The issue between Secheli and myself is merely that he is laying claims to this place, so if it belongs to Your Most Honourable's government, it means I have been fighting for you all this time. I am satisfied to be a Transvaal subject, but I must strongly insist for powerful assistance, for I am unable to comprehend why I am left by myself to protect the borders. I have not managed to find out where the border of the Republic is exactly situated, but if Your Most Honourable will have this shown to me, I will thereafter conduct myself as a loyal subject and do my best to protect it.[57]

Linchwe had pronounced himself a ZAR ally. Within days, Linchwe had volunteered 200 of his men into ZAR service by posting them along bank of the Crocodile River, 'which should be sufficient to guard that border. In case of an attack from any side, my people will do their utmost to defend the border'.[58]

Linchwe had need of Burgers in July 1876; his forces had just suffered a defeat at Molepolole. In June, after bringing regiments over from Saulspoort and getting the BaTlokwa to join him, Linchwe marched on Sechele's capital.[59] It is difficult to believe that Linchwe, then no older than eighteen, assembled and led this army against the BaKwena, but such was the case. Men close to Linchwe described the central role he played in all events leading up to and including the Molepolole attack and credit him as well with introducing a new method of deploying his regiments.[60] Before Linchwe took command of the Kgatla troops in early 1876, only his uncle Bogatsu had led them in battle, with disastrous results at Thamaga the previous October.

> Linchwe felt very bitter about the defeat the BaKwena had inflicted on the BaKgatla. He strongly criticised the method of organising and commanding the troops. He planned to invade again, with himself alone in command . . . [First] he sent all the cattle without exception to the Crocodile River, with the Makoba [maKoba] age-set as herd-boys . . .[61] The chief separated the people who were to remain with the cattle and those who were going to war. The army set out . . . scouts went ahead and kept sending back reports. When they were near, Linchwe arrayed them. The Maganelwa [maFatlha] were the rearguard waiting to receive the booty, the Matuku [maThukwi][62] were to be given the cattle and pass them on to the rearguard.[63]

> [As the BaKgatla approached Molepolole] the BaKwena, rejoicing over their earlier victory, were full of confidence, and jeered at the 'children of the maFiri'[64]
> They tried hard, but the BaKgatla, refusing to be daunted, captured cattle, goats and sheep, which they gave to the rearguard, who brought them to Mochudi.[65]

Yet, once again, those who initiated the attack returned the losers. As Linchwe's force approached Molepolole, his men killed herders, captured cattle and repelled a makeshift troop sent from the town. Facing certain defeat, the BaKwena got the support of the town's white traders, who issued Sechele's men with breech-loading rifles and ammunition. The battle then quickly swung against the BaKgatla and their allies who, after losing a number of men in a matter of seconds, fled east beyond the town with BaKwena chasing them and slaying all stragglers. Fifty BaKgatla died, and Linchwe nearly lost his life.[66] Though driven back from Molepolole, the retreating BaKgatla at least held on to the booty. In addition, Linchwe's deployment of troops from front to rear, primarily to remove stock from the enemy, gave the BaKgatla the upper hand in the months to come. Now that Burgers regarded all BaKgatla as ZAR subjects, Linchwe could use the Pilanesberg openly as a rear base of operation and Sechele could not re-enter the trans-Vaal or attack even Mochudi, without upsetting Pretoria.

Sechele and his people were feeling the pinch. In September Williams wrote to his superiors in London that Sechele 'has suffered very heavy losses in cattle, the people are unable to go hunting, the harvest was a failure, and worse of all, many lives have been sacrificed and most revolting murders have been practised . . . The war and hunger are having a bad effect on the Congregation.'[67] A month later, when Griqualand West labour recruiter Alexander C. Bailie arrived in Molepolole, he learned that the last two harvests had been lost and that water and grazing around the Kwena capital were nearly exhausted. Bailie predicted a 'very severe famine'.[68]

Sechele turned to Bailie for help. According to Bailie he 'offered his country to the British Government . . . [and] deputed me to settle a peace between himself and Leucini [Linchwe], which I undertook'.[69] Bailie, whom Griqualand West Lieutenant Governor Nicholas Southey had sent in a 'northerly direction' to promote labour migrancy, hoped that peace in the area would increase the flow of Kwena and Kgatla workers, and make it easier for men from Ngwato to Ndebele territory, to make the journey to the diamond fields.[70] Bailie went directly to Mochudi, where he was met by Linchwe's uncles Bogatsu and Tau together with a 'number of councilors'. Bailie claimed that the BaKgatla agreed to stop fighting until 'a meeting be held', presumably between Sechele and Linchwe. A treaty was drawn up in the meantime, later signed by Sechele, but Linchwe put it aside. Two months later, DRC missionary Pieter Brink arrived in Mochudi after being invited to start a mission and discovered that peace was still not at hand. No fighting had taken place recently, and Sechele still wanted to make peace, but 'Leincwe does not trust him'. Brink and LMS missionary John S. Moffat, who had recently replaced Williams in Molepolole, visited back and forth trying to reconcile the two sides. Linchwe, however, remained suspicious and no agreement resulted, while an undeclared truce continued.[71]

Linchwe was reluctant to settle because Burgers's government was slipping into the abyss. Burgers' campaign against Sekhukhuni was a fiasco, and keeping the semblance of a military force on the northern border was draining the ZAR coffers empty. In bankrupt Pretoria, any request from Linchwe to come to his rescue against Sechele was a sure guarantee for a laugh. Linchwe distrusted Bailie as much as he distrusted Sechele. To the BaKgatla, Bailie's visit was evidence of a growing English presence from the south, and as mediator between Sechele and Linchwe he was unconvincing. Through Bailie, Sechele had offered his territory to Britain; his long-standing friendship with English traders and LMS missionaries made him a promising ally for promoting British interests. Moreover, Bailie was happy to support Sechele's wish to be regarded as sovereign of the territory that Linchwe's people had taken. The 'articles of agreement' proposed by Bailie as the basis of peace negotiations had, as article 2, that Linchwe 'hereby acknowledges . . . that the ground [the BaKgatla] at present occupy is part of the territory of the Chief Sechele'.[72] This Linchwe could not concede, but with only a weak ZAR behind him, the only thing Linchwe had to bargain with was time.

Annexation of the Transvaal

In January 1877, Natal Secretary of Native Affairs Theophilus Shepstone marched with a police escort into Pretoria with instructions to annex the Transvaal. By April he completed the formal transfer of authority from an acquiescent Burgers to himself. Under Shepstone as its Administrator, the Transvaal became part of an envisaged British South African federation that was to include Griqualand West and the territory north to the Zambezi.[73] Boer protest was apparent, but no resistance materialised. Kruger, who headed the anti-British party, left the country.[74] Linchwe and his advisors had now the problem of determining how long the British were likely to stay in charge and how friendly they were likely to be toward the BaKgatla in their dispute with Sechele.

The British were scarcely more than a vague image to the BaKgatla. Linchwe and his people had had their share of contact with English and

Scottish traders and missionaries since the days of Pilane, and in the 1870s, white English-speakers were speculating in land in the Rustenburg and Marico districts, swelling the population of such small towns as Zeerust and Rustenburg, dominating Kimberley and the diamond fields, and trading all the way north to Barotseland. Some, like Fred Lewis, were making a coin or two on the side as agents of Boers, English and Africans alike.[75] Before 1877, however, Linchwe had no direct knowledge of British government, apart from that experienced briefly by his men while working as miners in Griqualand West. The same could be said of the two DRC missionaries then in contact with Linchwe, Henri Gonin and Pieter Brink. Gonin was Swiss and had spent his entire career at Saulspoort under ZAR rule. Brink, a Cape-born Afrikaner, became a missionary in the ZAR at the age of 21 and married Annie Groep, daughter of the Rustenburg Postmaster.[76] Gonin welcomed British rule because he thought it 'desirable for mission work', but Brink expressed nothing in writing on the subject.[77]

The BaKgatla knew that maBuru disliked the maKgoa because they favoured certain Africans against them and because the Cape British had ambitions to encroach on Boer territory. Before Kgamanyane emigrated from Saulspoort, his father-in-law Moshoeshoe had asked that his people be made British subjects, a request that was honoured in 1868 when Basutoland was annexed as a Crown Colony. When Britain annexed the Transvaal, however, no African leader, Sekhukhuni included, had asked to be protected from Boer rule. In the Transvaal the point had been reached where the maBuru could no longer expand and were coming to terms with their independent, and sometimes stronger, African neighbours. Armed blacks were becoming a threat to white hegemony north of the Vaal River, and Linchwe may have suspected that Shepstone had arrived for this reason. The British had displaced the Boers without encountering resistance, and throughout 1877 and into 1878 had ruled unchallenged. On the fringes of the western trans-Vaal, at any rate, Britain was perceived as a new power in the region.

Linchwe's fear of annexation was reinforced by developments in the diamond fields. Since the establishment of Griqualand West in 1871, the Cape takeover of the diamond fields had resulted in a great deal of BaTlhaping land being divided up into farms and offered for sale to whites.[78] These events were tied to increased animosities between the trans-Vaal maBuru and the British, who claimed that they offered Africans 'protection' from the Boers. There is little doubt that Linchwe and his advisors were aware of this growing white rivalry. At least since 1875 and likely before, Kgatla men had been walking down to the diamond fields to work, and like other Africans had been harassed by maBuru in retaliation.[79] Another source of intelligence on the BaTlhaping and their relations with the Griqualand West whites was Linchwe's in-law in Kuruman, David Matsau, assistant to the Tutor at the Moffat Institution, John Mackenzie. Matsau had acted as one of Linchwe's spies since the Kgatla–Kwena War broke out.[80] Matsau belonged to Letsebe's group in Molepolole, where he had been converted by the LMS, and entered the Moffat Institution in 1872, to which he remained attached until the late 1870s. While at Kuruman, Matsau and Mackenzie became friends of Mankurwane Molehabangwe, one of the principal Tlhaping dikgosi under pressure by land speculators in Griqualand West.[81] Soon after the Transvaal was annexed, Mankurwane declared himself a British subject, in the manner of Sechele. Khama had followed suit.[82] Linchwe thus faced the prospect of being isolated by his stronger neighbours, who were so quick to align their interests with Britain. With Bailie in support of Sechele's claim to the territory in dispute, the question remained whether or not Shepstone in Pretoria would adhere to Burgers' acceptance of Linchwe as a Transvaal subject and offer him 'protection' from Sechele.

Rather than take a chance, Linchwe kept out of sight of Pretoria. Having lost Fred Lewis as his correspondent,[83] he also needed a little time to take the measure of young Pieter Brink, the new DRC missionary in Mochudi. It did not take long. Brink – impulsive, goggle-eyed, and indiscreet – had grand visions that required constant delusion and exaggeration. Brink trumpeted each pregnancy of his wife to Cape Town, and took as a badge of honour Linchwe's sobriquet for his missionary – 'big strong bull'. Dreaming of converts by the legion in Mochudi, Brink saw 'thousands' of kaffers in the kraal, which was 'as big as Cape Town', and getting 'larger and larger'. To ingratiate himself with Linchwe, he declared his sympathies with the kgosi against his superior Henri Gonin over the problems arising with the Holfontein purchase, and eagerly accepted his role as Linchwe's messenger to Sechele for the purpose of negotiating 'peace'.[84] What Sechele thought of this leBuru nincompoop, not to mention Linchwe's talent of picking representatives, is not difficult to imagine, but Linchwe had use for a Dutch-speaking missionary who stood no chance of gaining acceptance among the anti-Boer BaKwena and who feared to cross Linchwe lest his conversion rate in Mochudi fall off. Moreover, when the time came, Brink could be used to communicate with the Annexation Government. He was also familiar with Rustenburg officials who had been friendly with Linchwe and were carry-overs from the defunct ZAR, such as P.J. van Staden.[85]

War Resumes

In May 1878 Brink wrote to Theophilus Shepstone that Sechele had declared war on the BaKgatla.[86] This letter, the first penned by Brink on Linchwe's behalf, drew Shepstone's attention for the first time to the Kgatla–Kwena controversy and initiated a long history in Kgatla–British relations. It proved to be a fateful step. In the letter, Linchwe gave a heavily slanted account of the conflict and claimed that Sechele, having now once again declared war, gave Linchwe no choice but to defend himself. The communication disguised its intended purpose. Linchwe calculated that he stood a better chance thereby of pre-empting Sechele's claim to the disputed territory than by allowing Sechele first to raise the issue. There was a chance, by then, that the Kwena kgosi had already done so. Sechele's missionary John Moffat had been in the Transvaal since January.[87]

Initially, Linchwe's ploy gained him the upper hand. Shepstone got the impression that the BaKgatla resided in the Transvaal and were therefore entitled to British protection. With only an outdated map to guide him, Shepstone assumed that Linchwe's people were Transvaal subjects. He therefore had his Secretary for Native Affairs Henrique Charles Shepstone write to Linchwe to say he was entitled to defend himself 'but in so doing you must consider that you are defending the Govt under which you live and that you are not fighting on your own account'.[88] Shepstone's Colonial Secretary Melmouth Osborn then informed Sechele that Pretoria had received report of his war declaration and to be warned that by 'making war on any tribe living within this Territory, [Sechele] makes war upon the Supreme Govt'.[89] Pleased with this outcome, Linchwe soon sent Shepstone another letter complaining about Sechele. It is doubtful, however, that Linchwe was aware that he and the Transvaal government were already working at cross-purposes. For Osborn's letter to Sechele prompted a reply that startled the Transvaal Government and made the BaKgatla, rather than the BaKwena, the centre of controversy. Sechele informed

Osborn that the BaKgatla resided in Sechele's country, outside the Transvaal. As for the Transvaal boundary, Sechele had provided the previous Transvaal government with a submission to help clarify the issue.[90] Thus, Linchwe's attempts to avert an Anglo–Kwena alliance had given Sechele the opportunity to open diplomatic relations with the Transvaal as a neighbouring authority. By raising the border issue, Linchwe had made the BaKgatla the disputed possession of the English and the BaKwena. Within weeks, Shepstone decided to form a commission to find out where the Transvaal's jurisdiction ended and Sechele's began.[91]

The Melvill–Van Staden Commission

Before the commissioners could begin their task, Linchwe and the BaKgatla had drawn the BaKwena back into open fighting. Linchwe ignored H.C. Shepstone's appeal to allow Kwena cattle access to the Madikwe River until the commissioners arrived. In early August the BaKgatla killed several BaKgalagadi moving Sechele's cattle towards the Madikwe, and on the 19th of that month, Sechele's regiments launched an unsuccessful attack on Mochudi.[92] Sechele had everything to gain by Pretoria's recognition of his claim and was ready to cooperate with Shepstone, but when Shepstone learned of the attack on Mochudi, he doubted Sechele's sincerity and hesitated in sending the commissioners. Shepstone feared embroiling his administration in a squabble that might prove to be outside the Transvaal. His attitude in the matter was also influenced by Brink, who visited Shepstone in late August and told him that 'any Commission now to Secheli will be useless'.[93] Like the administrations of Burgers and Pretorius before him, Theophilus Shepstone's was finding that the BaKgatla of Pilanesberg were willing supporters of Pretoria's military campaigns against other Africans. Shepstone had made it his business to establish credibility among the maBuru by whipping the BaPedi, and the BaKgatla were among those who stepped forward to help him do just that. While Shepstone was finding reasons not to get involved with Sechele's problems, Tshomankane Pilane, Linchwe's uncle and supporter against the BaKwena, was helping Shepstone's officials round up a 'contingent' of an estimated 550 auxiliaries for the impending campaign against Sekhukhuni.[94]

At this juncture, the intervention of the other missionary, John Moffat, proved decisive in reviving Shepstone's interest in the commission. Since

June, when Sechele had been warned by Pretoria, Moffat had written letters that supported the BaKwena and undercut the Kgatla position. Moffat portrayed the BaKgatla as 'exceedingly lawless' and 'not thoroughly under [Linchwe's] command'.[95] As Kwena advocate, Moffat's eye was already focused on a future British Africa. He was not, as one LMS historian has argued, 'the stuff of which missionaries are made' but rather a restless man easily discouraged with the trials of ordinary mission work.[96] In this respect he belongs to that category of LMS missionaries who sought other outlets and who, like Livingstone and Mackenzie, believed that the salvation of Africa depended as much, if not more, on the extension of British influence than the spread of Christianity. In the Kgatla–Kwena War, Moffat believed the answer to Sechele's desperate position was the intervention of the new Transvaal Government. The way to get it was by raising the bugbear of a black alliance forming against the Transvaal over Linchwe's misdeeds:

> Lencwe, half in the Transvaal and half out, and using the Transvaal as a basis of operation is coming to be looked upon as really an ally of the Government, and I quite foresee in a short time this wretched dispute arming against the Government the whole of the Bakhalagadi tribes, by which I mean the Bamangwato, the Bakwena and the Bañwaketse. It would be useless to tell them that it is madness; they are mad on the subject of white encroachment.[97]

Secretary for Native Affairs H.C. Shepstone seriously questioned Sechele's integrity after the attack on Mochudi, but Moffat wrote on Sechele's behalf that it 'was in reality a measure of self-defence.'[98] H.C. Shepstone's misgivings about Sechele remained, and he and Theophilus Shepstone doubted that a commission would succeed, but they gave way, and the commission was appointed on 11 October. Consisting of Surveyor General Samuel Melvill and Rustenburg landdrost P.J. van Staden, it was instructed to 'inquire into the causes of the dispute with a view if possible of getting it amicably settled' and if Sechele's allegations proved true that the BaKgatla were using the Transvaal to keep Kwena cattle and launch attacks, to 'cause the chief Lencue to be distinctly informed that such a state of affairs cannot be allowed to continue'. As for the issue of the Transvaal boundary, Melvill and Van Staden were told 'His Excellency is not desirous of now entering into or discussing it'.[99]

The commission failed to bring Linchwe and Sechele together. Melvill and Van Staden summoned Linchwe and Sechele to Zeerust, but only Linchwe came. He left before Melvill and Van Staden arrived, though, leaving behind the message that he was interested only in meeting Sechele, whereas he understood that Kgosidintsi, Sechele's brother, had been sent in his place.[100] Word was then sent to Sechele and Linchwe to meet the commissioners in Ngwaketse country on the Kolobeng River, but on 29 October, the day appointed, only Sechele made an appearance, arriving with a large armed party. Linchwe sent instead a letter promising that his uncle Bogatsu would soon represent him, but by the 30th Bogatsu had not come. Linchwe's erstwhile allies against Sechele – Matlapeng of the Ba-Tlokwa and Mokgosi of the BaLete – were also invited, but they also stayed away. After taking Sechele's statement[101] the commissioners sent Linchwe an invitation to meet them on the Madikwe River, alone. They then journeyed east, through Mokgosi's town of Ramotswa on the Ngotwane River, where Mokgosi's son gave Melvill and Van Staden a statement.[102] Linchwe did not turn up. Thus Melvill and Van Staden returned to the Transvaal having failed to end the Kgatla–Kwena War or even begin negotiations.

Linchwe's standoffishness is not difficult to explain. Not expecting the commission and preparing to launch another attack on Molepolole, Linchwe had called the formation of another mophato, and initiation was underway when the commissioners summoned him to Zeerust.[103] Furthermore, the commission had been appointed following the appeal of Moffat and against the advice of Brink, suggesting that its agenda was pro-Sechele.

The commissioners' recommendations, which supported Sechele's claims, would have confirmed the BaKgatla's worst fears. Melvill and Van Staden proposed a line along the Madikwe separating Sechele and the Transvaal and recommended that Linchwe either resettle to the east of the river or, if remaining in Sechele's territory, abandon his claims over the Pilanesberg BaKgatla and with their BaTlokwa and BaLete allies cease using the Transvaal as a base of operations.[104]

The commission report then languished in Pretoria. For more than a year, no action resulted. In January 1879, Cape Governor Sir Bartle Frere approved the recommendations, but the matter was then either lost in an administrative shuffle, relegated to low-priority status, or probably both. The BaKgatla–BaKwena War had gone silent in the interim, and T. Shepstone had more important things on his mind than to reopen the issue – such as resignation. He stepped down as Administrator in March and was replaced by Sir Owen Lanyon, at which point the Kgatla–Kwena file appears to have been passed back to H.C. Shepstone's office, where it was shelved. More important matters had come to Pretoria's attention. Since late 1878 the Transvaal Government was at pains to demonstrate its strength against African powers on its borders. In December, the BaPedi turned back the British force led by Col. Rowlands, and in January 1879 Cetshwayo's forces shattered the illusion of a British South Africa at Isandlhwana. For the rest of 1879 the British were preoccupied with putting down Pedi and Zulu resistance, and in simply figuring out which Africans and how many the Annexation Government actually had under its jurisdiction.[105] Interest in the Kgatla–Kwena War lapsed utterly. The only concern with the western border was preventing the smuggling of gunpowder into the Transvaal, and suspicions in this matter were directed at Sechele, not Linchwe.[106] By then the Kgatla image in Pretoria had also begun to improve. In the Pedi campaigns of 1878 and 1879, Linchwe's regiments, under Tshomankane 'England' Pilane, served on the side of the British and, in the words of Brink, 'placed a plume on the head of the BaKgatla'.[107]

For most of 1879, the BaKgatla and BaKwena upheld a truce. Too little strength was available on either side to continue the war. Previous fighting, drought, poor harvests, deaths from malaria and loss of cattle had exhausted Sechele's people and brought famine to the Kweneng.[108] When Roger Price arrived in Molepolole in June to take the place of Moffat, the BaKwena had had another bad harvest and had lost thousands of cattle. By the end of the year, in spite of rain, the 'people, through their sunken cheeks and eyes still tell of great want'.[109] In the dry months that followed, competition between Kgatla and Kwena herders for the waters of the Madikwe and Ngotwane rivers led to renewed clashes and stock theft. By October Sechele had lost complete access to these rivers, and once again stolen Kwena cattle were being shuttled across to the Pilanesberg. Sechele, who had been waiting since February for a response to his enquiry on the Melvill–Van Staden report, complained to the new Governor of the Transvaal, Sir Garnet Wolseley, Sir Owen Lanyon's superior.[110]

The Melvill–Ferreira Commission

Finally, in April 1880, the Transvaal Government intervened. By then Transvaal officials were feeling more confident of the future. The BaPedi and AmaZulu had been defeated under Wolseley's command. Financial problems remained, but new efforts were directed in a 'search for solvency'. The principal method was a hut tax of 10/- collected from all Africans residing within the Transvaal boundaries.[111] H.C. Shepstone was also giving Africans a sympathetic ear in their complaints about their mistreatment by local maBuru and the shortage of land for their own use. Therefore, in response to Sechele's request, Wolseley had Lanyon appoint a two-man commission to demarcate the boundary between the Transvaal and Sechele's territory. Samuel Melvill, assisted by Ignatius Phillip Ferreira, late Commander of Ferreira's Horse, was instructed to inform Linchwe that 'once the boundary has been determined, Lenchwe and his followers will be required to choose finally between remaining either in the one country or the other'.

> If they remain in Secheli's country they will be Secheli's people and will not be allowed to use Tranvaal territory as a base of operations against Secheli or as a place of refuge for stock secured in their depredations. Should they attempt to do so, their stock will be taken from them and they will incure the displeasure of this government ... If on the other hand they choose to remain in Transvaal territory, they will be protected as our subjects and will be required, in return for such protection and the other advantages they will gain, to pay taxes.[112]

The commission's hearings, which also involved the BaNgwaketse, BaTlokwa and BaLete, resulted in the beaconing of the Transvaal boundary. Following the advice of the Melvill/Van Staden Commission, Melvill and Ferreira placed the Transvaal border along the Madikwe River to the Crocodile River, thereby leaving Linchwe's BaKgatla in Sechele's territory. Melvill informed Linchwe of the decision he would now have to take.[113] At once, Linchwe travelled to Pretoria and met Wolseley, who confirmed Melvill's ultimatum. Linchwe then contemplated relocating his Mochudi followers back in the Transvaal.[114]

Linchwe was labouring under the assumption that the maKgoa were able and prepared to divide his people. He could not maintain his authority by swearing loyalty to the Queen any more than he could by continuing to defy Sechele.[115] To make matters worse for Linchwe, the Transvaal then created a new Commissioner, with headquarters in Zeerust, who would be responsible for the Transvaal's western border. The man appointed was John S. Moffat, ex-missionary from Molepolole and friend of Sechele. In early October, within a month of taking up his appointment, Moffat was in Mochudi to deliver another ultimatum to Linchwe:

> I told him that if he still holds to his present location he must withdraw his Cattle from the Transvaal and must not come to the Bakhatla of Magliesburg [sic] in the capacity of chief any more, and that if they still hold to him, they can only do so by emigrating from the Transvaal.[116]

Moffat was enjoying this moment of triumph. Only two years before, he had entered Mochudi on a 'peace mission from Sechele', and the BaKgatla had run him out of town. Now, with the Transvaal Government at his back, Moffat was imposing the very conditions that Sechele had demanded prior to the outbreak of the war. Moffat addressed Linchwe condescendingly and wanted the BaKgatla to respect his newfound authority. Instead, Linchwe 'protested loudly against the position taken by the government', reported Moffat, 'and considers himself badly used'. Moffat then rejected Linchwe's request that Mochudi be placed inside the Transvaal boundary, and as soon as he returned to Zeerust Moffat recommended that Pretoria take immediate action.

> If a single cattle-post, or perhaps two, were taken possession of, it would be quite sufficient . . . If Lencwi be once convinced that we are in earnest, it will have a certain and good effect. If he really thinks of moving, which I doubt, it will bring matters to a head . . . I am sorry to have no better result to my visit. I had been hopeful that Lencwi and his people would have been open to moral influence, but they are wrong-headed, and will listen to nothing but their own view of the matter and what is worse persist in misunderstanding and misconstruing all that is said to them.[117]

Certain that Sechele would renew the war now that the English backed him, the BaKgatla expected the BaKwena to attack and Linchwe prepared to return to the Transvaal.[118]

Linchwe's predicament was much closer to a favourable solution than he could have suspected. The young kgosi, still in his early twenties, had no way of knowing that the Transvaal Government, so confidently represented by Moffat, their 'Native Commissioner, Western Border', would cease to function within twelve months, whereas Linchwe had another forty years as ruler of the BaKgatla on both sides of the border. The Transvaal Government, then under review by the Gladstone cabinet and discredited by the costs of dealing with African resistance over the previous year, was not looking for new worlds to conquer. Moffat's report was, in fact, referred up to the New High Commissioner, Sir George Colley, with Wolseley's recommendation that nothing be done. 'The policy should be at the present time to avoid as much as possible getting into any conflict with the natives. It will be unwise to put the foot down unless we are prepared to accept the consequences.'[119] This late October minute was the last correspondence to be enclosed in the administration's file on the Kgatla–Kwena dispute. Within weeks, the attention of the Government was being directed elsewhere. In December 1880 Boer resistance to English rule was underway, and overthrow followed in a matter of months. In Zeerust, Moffat was himself beaten by the Boers and imprisoned.[120] After a series of defeats, the British formally handed back the Transvaal to the Boers in August 1881 with the signing of the Pretoria Convention.

ENDNOTES

1 London: Jonathan Cape, 1966, first edition.

2 This private letter, dated 12 Aug. 1875 at 'Kamyani' [Kgamanyane, i.e., Mochudi], was printed in the 28 Sep. 1875 edition of *De Volksstem*. I am grateful to Barry Morton for a copy of this source.

3 The name of this gentleman is Ratsegana Sebeke of Marapo lands, south of Mochudi. Present at the interview of 4 August 1882 was Harris Thulari, of Madibana ward, Mochudi, my interpreter, Edwin Gare and myself. Rre Gare, an historian in his own right, died in 1984 at the age of 83. *Borra* Sebeke *le* Thulari have also since passed away. The English and SeTswana versions of the interview were transcribed and translated by William Sentshebeng, then a University of Botswana student and now a member of the UB Faculty of Education. Copies are reposed at the Botswana National Archives, Gaborone.

4 As head of the ranking, able-bodied maThubantlwa regiment, Sebele would have been expected to take part in any general military operation. In 1875, Sechele was well into his 60s and too old to lead his regiments in battle.

5 See, for example, the leboko composed by them for Sebele, the 'noxious herb' in Schapera (1965: 136–143). Sebele was known for his drunkenness and public disturbances (Smith 1957: 296). At the 4 Aug. 1982 interview *Rre* Sebeke related several obscene stories about the man.

6   Although the description is unclear, the Kwena army appears to have moved from its first camp to the second in the early evening of the second day. The mention of fires giving away their position is contradicted by Schulenburg's second-hand account, which claims that the BaKgatla were caught by surprise, though one of Linchwe's messengers had arrived back in Mochudi with word of Sebele's army shortly before the attack (H. Schulenburg to HMS, 3 Jan. 1876, box 2H, HMSR, BNA). It is also contradicted by the events early in the battle, when it is clear the BaKgatla were not prepared.

7   'Ntwsang BaKwena! Mothakola o monthso baga Mma Seadingwane, Tswelang kwa! K re bu! Bu! O eme jaaka mokopha Sebele, jaaka Kwata ya Morikuru'. I am grateful to Wazha Morapedi for this translation. The meaning of this phrase is uncertain, though it is likely a Kgatla rendition of a Kwena praise for themselves, '*Makgakga mantsho agaMmaseotisanaga*' ('bold black ones of him who desolates the country') (Schapera 1965: 125n1). The tamboti (*Spirostachys africana*), a tall, straight tree found in the bushveld, where the norm is low-lying, spreading acacia trees of many varieties.

8   Sebeke's tradition tallies with the January 1876 account of Heinrich Schulenburg, who stated that the army consisted of 'original' BaKwena and the BaKaa and Mmanaana Kgatla (under Pilane) (Schulenburg to HMS, 3 Jan. 1876, box 2H, HMSR, BNA). Linchwe's praise song about the war also contains passages that tie Kaa leader Mosenyi of Suwe Lebelwana to the battle scene (Schapera 1965: 78–92, especially 90).

9   'Bakaa [BaKaa] baga Suwe aLebelwane, bu ga dijo di latolelwa moeng empa moeng ka mathlo a dibona, tswang le nneng fa'. Suwe, the father of Mosenyi, died before 1863 (Schapera 1945: 116).

10   The reference to cannibalism was symbolic. 'Man eating' was a common euphemism for a politically dominant person or group, one that 'eats' the power of the other, thereby making the other subordinate.

11   The LMS gained most of its early adherents from bafaladi groups settled around its mission at Molepolole. The BaKwena proper lived above Molepolole atop Ntsweng Hill. The LMS also maintained a mission at Mosopa, where another Mmanaana–Kgatla group was settled under Mosielele.

12   Mothakola is not a name used by the BaKwena for any of their regiments, and the third person singular prefix form suggests it refers to the regimental leader. Possibly it is an incorrect rendition of maTlolakang, a regiment formed in the decade prior to the battle, or of Tumagole, the leader of maTlolakang. Tumagole was Sebele's younger brother. Sebele was the leader of maThubantlwa (Schapera 1977: 312).

13   According to Sebeke and Thulari, Mabodisa consisted only of Mapotsana, Malebye and Phuting wards at the time of the battle.

14   The Mmanaana Kgatla were distant relatives of the Linchwe's Kgafela Kgatla.

15   Meaning that the BaKaa circled to the west of Mochudi and entered through Phaphane, the same direction they retreated during the battle. This conforms with Linchwe's references in his praise to the path of retreat taken by the BaKaa (Schapera 1965: 90).

16   Mapotsana is part of Mabodisa kgoro and is located at the north-northeastern foot of Phuthadikobo Hill. 'Mabodisa regiment' refers to the men of Mabodisa who were members of various regiments.

17 This agrees with *De Volksstem*'s account: 'On the morning of the 11th, Sechele's commando attacked the town on the north side, most of Kamyani's men being out to the south expecting the enemy from that side. This enabled Sechele's men to penetrate a considerable distance into town, and destroy about a hundred huts by fire.' Schulenburg heard that the BaKwena entered Mochudi and 'lit parts of it', but only after both sides had begun fighting (Schulenburg report, 3 Jan. 1876, box 2H, HMSR, BNA).

18 *De Volksstem*: 'Kamyani's men rushed from different points, and when both sides had been firing at each other for about one hour and a quarter, the latter charged in good old style (I was quite surprised) and drove the enemy – to use an old simile – like chaff before the wind.' Schulenburg heard that the BaKgatla allowed the BaKwena to attack their town because they were low on ammunition and needed the BaKwena close to shoot effectively. 'The Bakuene then forced their way into the town and set fire to a part of it. At this point Leincue gave orders for an attack with assegais and Sechele's army was repelled' (Schulenburg report, 3 Jan. 1876, box 2H, HMSR, BNA). The tradition's reference to dagga is not necessarily apocryphal. Cannabis was commonly used then and after. From the gist of the story, it appears that the BaKgatla were drinking beer and smoking cannabis deliberately as a stimulant for battle.

19 Schapera (1942a: 12); Sillery (1964: 143); A. Bailie report, 6 Nov. 1876, C2220: 53, PP.

20 Sebele's royal immunity from attack underlines his cowardice. For other references to this practice among BaTswana, see Schapera (1965: 129n), Ellenberger (1937: 37). It was not always honoured, though, as we shall see below, with reference to Maganelo.

21 Part of the Kwena force moved south and raided cattle from the BaLete (Schulenburg report, 3 Jan. 1876, box 2H, HMSR, BNA).

22 Sebele's mother was Selemeng Kgorwe, a MoKwena, and thus Sechele is mocking Sebele's unpopularity among the BaKwena and his attempts to conspire with the BaNgwato to unseat him. Sechele's mother was Sejelo, daughter of Ramodisa, junior son of Kwena kgosi Motswasele I (1770–1885) and therefore an uncle to his son-in-law (Ramsay 1990: 55).

23 The most extensive account of this battle is by Ramsay (1991: 97–109).

24 Ramsay (1991: 143–145), Parsons (1973: 29).

25 The men at Mochudi included those who had been in pitched battles four times in the previous ten years: against Moshoeshoe (1865), Mapela's Langa Ndebele and Mogemi's Kekana Ndebele (1867) and Mokapane's Kekana Ndebele (1868). See ch. 2.

26 Schulenburg heard 120 BaKwena, 18 BaKgatla (report 3 Jan. 1876, box 2H, HMSR, BNA); *De Volksstem*: '75 [of Sechele's men] are lying dead by the huts, how many out on the flats I do not know' and 10 BaKgatla (28 Sep. 1875); a 4 Oct. 1875 letter to *De Volksstem* written by three Molepolole traders (S. Boyne, J.M. Wright and D. Brooke) was published on 23 Oct. 1875 criticising the previous anonymous report on grounds largely unrelated to the battle, but asserting that only 58 BaKwena died and that 'Linchne's [*sic*] had lost at least as many as Sechele'. However, Charles Williams, LMS missionary at Molepolole, who treated the wounded, said the BaKwena 'left from 60 to 80 dead on the field' (C. Williams to LMS, 17 Jan. 1876, PP 1/5/15, SP, BNA). On 18 Sep. 1875, Henri Gonin reported to ZAR President Burgers after hearing from Linchwe that the

BaKwena had left 67 dead on the battlefield, and the BaKgatla lost 17; then, three days later, he wrote to Burgers that the number of confirmed dead had reached 80 (H. Gonin to T.F. Burgers, SS 192 R1759/75 and R2201/75, TA).

27 Schulenburg report, 3 Jan. 1876, box 2H, HMSR, BNA.

28 *De Volksstem*, 23 Oct. and 13 Nov. 1875; testimony of Khama, Barwinye, Sebele, Mopi, Linchwe, Rakabane, and Ramonnye, BPBC: 6, 7, 13, 19–20, 23–25; S.G.A. Shippard to H. Loch, 26 May 1894, HC 108, BNA. 'When one Bechuana tribe attacks another, the Bushmen and Bakalahari belonging to both are placed in the same category with cattle and sheep – they are to be "lifted" or killed as opportunity offers' (Mackenzie 1971: 132–133). I am grateful to Barry Morton for this reference. BaKgalagadi were the original Tswana-speaking occupants of the Kalahari region and were conquered and subjugated by later immigrants, such as the BaTlhaping, BaRolong, BaNgwaketse, BaKwena and the later Kwena offshoots, the BaNgwato and BaTswana. They, together with other subjugated elements, such as Bushmen, BaTlaro and BaYeyi, were widely used by wealthy BaTswana as domestic servants, herders, hunters, serfs, porters and concubines. Referred to, depending on the region, also as Basarwa, Bathlanka, Malata, Balala and Makoba, they were inherited, exchanged or pawned among the wealthy and sometimes sold to the Boers. A full study of this social and economic phenomenon is long overdue. See B. Morton (1994b) for the most recent, detailed discussion.

29 Klaas Segogwane interview, Aug. 1832, PP 1/1/2, SP, BNA.

30 For Maganelo and Nkomeng, see ch. 3.

31 Klaas Segogwane interview, Aug. 1932, PP 1/1/2, SP and Isang Pilane statement, 26 May 1931, PP 1/3/6, SP, BNA. Charles Williams wrote from Molepolole that soon after the Battle of Mochudi, 'spies from the Bakgagahila [Kgafela Kgatla] were continually being chased in our immediate vicinity, my house was for some days a refuge for poor Bakgagahilas who remained here when the others removed to Mochudi. Sechele was hunting high and low for one if not more of them, and that one [was] one of my best assistants. They all happily escaped and are now at Mochudi' (C. Williams to LMS, 17 Jan. 1876, PP 1/5/15, SP, BNA). See also 4 Oct. 1875 letter from S, Boyne, J.M. Wright and D. Brooks in *De Volksstem*, 23 Oct. 1875. According to Isang, Letsebe did not go to Mochudi but resettled near Zeerust, and Kgabotshwene in Mabieskraal. Letsebe soon joined Linchwe's war against Sechele and he and Kgabotshwene eventually resettled in the Kgatleng (Linchwe's territory). See below and chapter 6.

32 It is possible that Linchwe was not formally installed until several months later. Two of Isaac Schapera's informants in the 1930s asserted that the installation came after the battle of Thamaga, which was fought in October or November 1875 (see below). See also T.L. Phiri article in *Lesedi la Sechaba*, June 1932–July 1933, and Klaas Segogwane statement Aug. 1932, PP 1/1/2, SP, BNA.

33 Son of Khamanyane.

34 Gonin to DRC, 15 Jun. 1875 (B), DRCA.

35 He had been worried about this at least since 1872. 'If we don't [send a missionary to Kgamanyane's] other missionaries from other missions will settle there and harvest what we have sown' (Gonin to DRC, 29 Jul. 1872 [A]).

36 Gonin to DRC, 15 Jun. 1875 (B).

37 Apart from the BaNgwaketse, who assisted the BaKwena indirectly in the war, none of the other groups mentioned played any role in the Kgatla–Kwena conflict. In fact, before Linchwe had Gonin write the letter to Joubert, he knew that Khama III had informed LMS Andrew Mackenzie that he intended to remain neutral. This knowledge was conveyed to Linchwe by Mackenzie's catechist Matsau Motsisi, who was present when Khama spoke to Mackenzie. According to Khama, Linchwe saw this as a green light to raid Kwena cattle on the southern border of Ngwato territory (Khama testimony, 15 Oct. 1894, BPBC: 6–7). Linchwe testified (17 Oct. 1894, BPBC: 23–24): 'When I fought I only had to deal with the Bakwena.'

38 Gonin to Burgers, 21 Sep. 1875, SS 195, R2201/75, TA. Translation by Ria Groenewald.

39 Van Staden to Burgers, 18 Aug. 1895, SS 192, R1758/75, TA. Translation by Ria Groenewald.

40 H.C. Shepstone to M. Osborn, 10 Jul. 1878, SS 291, R2389/78, TA.

41 Gonin to DRC, 18 Dec. 1875 (B); Maganelo Pilane statement, Jul. 1931, PP 1/1/2, SP, BNA. The Mmanaana Kgatla were led in this particular battle by Gobuamang (Ramsay 1991: 153). Judging from Schulenburg's account of the battle (Schulenburg 3 Jan. 1876, box 2H, HMSR, BNA), which does not mention him by name, Maganelo appears to be the 'one of the royal house [who] fell' (*einer vam Köningsgeschlecte dabei gefallen ist*) and whose corpse rather than be buried or left for the vultures (as was the custom for commoner dead), was taken into the town by the victors, skinned, the femur cut out of the body and converted into a war trumpet, for the purpose of intimidating the BaKgatla in future battles.

42 C. Williams to J. Mullens, 8 May 1876, box 38, LMS; Holub (1976: 421, 423). Traditions on the Kgatla–Kwena war in Schapera's collection (PP 1/1/2, SP, BNA) contain many references to such atrocities.

43 After Gonin registered the farm on 26 Apr. 1876, Louis informed him that Linchwe had paid only part of the agreed-upon price and demanded that Gonin make up the difference of £600! Remarked Gonin, 'I am in big trouble.' Years passed until Gonin got Linchwe to reimburse him (Gonin to LMS, 16 Mar. 1877 [B]; Linchwe Estate Commission, p. 21 S 343/25, BNA and p. 83, S 343/24, BNA). See also minuted testimonies of Dikeme Pilane, Kefas Mogale, Moreri Phiri, John Molefe and Tshipe Frans Phiri, 6–7 Sep. 1934, NTS 3462, B128/308, SAA; S.J. K. du Toit to M. Osborn, 31 Aug. 1878 and H.C. Shepstone to T. Shepstone, 30 Oct. 1878, SS 302, R3129/78, TA; H.C. Shepstone to S.J.K. du Toit, 12 Nov. and 31 Dec. 1878, SN 102: 73–77, 118–121, TA.

44 Jordan 1881; DSAB II: 146–147; Templin (1984: 149–151); Gilmore (n.d.: 276–277); Gonin to DRC, 16 Mar. 1877 (B), DRCA; Parsons (1973: 42–43). Parsons, basing himself on Walker (1962: 371) and Thompson (1969: 435), portrays the Dorslanders as part of 'Transvaal Expansionism'. Yet, the ZAR under Burgers was contracting at the time, rather than expanding, and losing control of its borders in the north, northeast, and parts of the western trans-Vaal. The process of reversing Boer territorial gains began in the mid-1860s, with the deterioration and ultimate abandonment of Schoemansdal, and continued until the late 1870s, when the British annexation forces and later

the second ZAR government embarked on military campaigns that resulted ultimately in the defeat of the BaPedi and BaGananwa. However, these efforts strengthened ZAR presence in the northern and northeastern districts, whereas the western districts remained contested territory until 1902.

45 Probably refers to Malagas, an Ndebele Ndzundza subchief of Mabhogo Magodongo ('Mapoch') of the Soutpansberg, and at loggerheads with ZAR officials (Van Coller 1942: 120). I am grateful to Jan Boeyens for this reference. See also Bergh and Morton 2003: Declaration No. 10 (Holthausen).

46 Sechele to L.M. du Plessis, 5 Jan. 1876, A779, I, TA. 'I am with you at all times and want to live in peace and love . . . I stay your friend, Sechele.' Louw du Plessis and (?) Kreling were co-leaders of the second of three Dorsland trek parties (Jordan 1881: 149–160).

47 Khama to Du Plessis, 11 Mar. 1877, A779, vol. 2, TA.

48 In August 1875, Van Staden had reported to Burgers that he had ordered his veldkornetten 'that a watchful eye be kept on Secheli's actions, because he must not infringe on my District, and if he wants to, I will stop him' (P.J. van Staden to T.F. Burgers, 18 Aug. 1875, SS 192, R1785/75, TA).

49 F.J. Lewis to T.F. Burgers, 30 Apr. 1876, SS 208, R1054/76, TA, written on Linchwe's behalf from Holfontein.

50 Lewis spoke English and Dutch, the language known to most of the BaKgatla. See F.J. Lewis to N.J.R. Swart, 25 Jul. 1874, SS 173, R1031/74, TA. Emil Holub (1976: 424) discovered while in Mochudi in 1876 that 'nearly all of [the BaKgatla] speak Dutch'. For references to Lewis as a trader in Mochudi and Molepolole, see Bailie report, 17 May 1877 with annexure of 9 Oct. 1876, C2220: 76, 78, PP (reprinted in Schapera 1942a: 34).

51 Linchwe to L. du Plessis, 15 Feb. 1876, A779, vol. 1, TA. Translation by Ria Groenewald. 'Krieling' refers to Jan Christoffel Greyling, commandant of the second Dorsland Trek at that stage (before Du Plessis was elected). I am grateful to Nicol Stassen for this clarification. Brenger appears to be a trader based either in Mochudi or Shoshong.

52 Ramodibe returned through southern Ngwato territory via the Seruruma River valley. See F.J. Lewis to T.F. Burgers, 30 Apr. 1876, SS 208, R1054/76, TA; J.W.(?) Smith and F.J. Lewis to T.F. Burgers, 6 May 1876, SS 210, R1462/76, TA; Khama testimony, 15 Oct. 1894, BPBC: 7; C. Williams to J. Mullens, 8 May 1876, box 37, and idem, 25 Sep. 1876, box 38, LMS; T.L. Phiri article in *Lesedi le Sechaba*, June 1932–Jul. 1933, and Klaas Segogwane statement, Aug. 1932, PP 1/1/2, SP, BNA.

53 F.J. Lewis to T.F. Burgers, 30 Apr. 1876, SS 208, R1054/76, TA.

54 F.J. Lewis and (H.A.?) Smith to T.F. Burgers, 6 May 1876, SS 210, R1462/76, TA.

55 C. Williams to T.F. Burgers, 5 Jun. 1876, SS 210, R1463/76, TA. Sechele sent his 'hearty congratulations on your safe return [from Europe] and his best wishes for the success of all your enterprises'.

56 Burger's force was made up of 600 Transvaal Africans, 2,400 Swazi, and 2,000 Boers, 400 of whom came from the Rustenburg District. T.S. van Rooyen (1951: 248–249) gives the number of African soldiers and auxiliaries, by kapitein, most of whom are recognisable as dikgosi of the BaKwena, BaPhalane and Bapo. One name, 'Saul Compagna'

probably referred to Tshomankane, Linchwe's uncle who was then the ranking royal among the Pilanesberg BaKgatla.

57 Linchwe to Burgers, 10 Jul. 1876, SS 211, R1874/76, TA, witnessed by Fred J. Lewis, G. Bromely and P.G. Bodenstein. Translation from the Dutch by Linda van Jersel. See also [F.J.] Lewis and [J.W.?] Smith to Burgers, 10 Jul. 1876, SS 211, R1875/76, TA, in English, in which they stated that they 'never had the slightest idea that Linchue was a subject of the S.A. Republic' and that they had been writing on his behalf because 'we never heard of a law or custom being in existence according to which a Kafir chief, a subject of the government could be represented by another Kafir, but not by a white man'.

58 Linchwe to Burgers, 18 Jul. 1876, SS 223, R3851/76, witnessed by Fred J. Lewis and J.W. (?) Smith. Translation from the Dutch by Linda van Jersel. The reference to the Crocodile may be to the Limpopo – the river north of the junction of the Madikwe and Crocodile Rivers. In either case the location would have been well to the east-northeast of Mochudi.

59 S. Melvill and P.J. van Staden report, 30 Nov. 1878, SS 454, R3773/80, TA.

60 T.L. Phiri article in *Lesedi le Sechaba*, June 1932–Jul. 1933, and Klaas Segogwane statement, Aug. 1932, PP 1/1/2, SP, BNA. Thomas Phiri served as Linchwe's secretary and head of the Sikwane DRC congregation after 1890 (see ch. 7), and Klaas Segogwane, also of Sikwane, was one of Linchwe's messengers. They provided Schapera with extended traditions on the Kgatla–Kwena war and other phases of Kgatla history.

61 Initiated two years later in 1878 and led by Ramono, Linchwe's full younger brother.

62 Initiated in 1863 in Saulspoort and led by Bogatsu.

63 This means that Linchwe's regiment, maTlakana, would bear the brunt of the battle.

64 'Hyenas.' MaFiri was the name of Pilane's regiment.

65 T.L. Phiri article in *Lesedi le Sechaba*, June 1932–Jul. 1933, as well as Segogwane statement, Aug. 1932, PP 1/1/2, SP, BNA. Holub (1976: 423) and Ramsay (1991: 154) assert that the BaKgatla returned with no cattle, whereas Phiri and Segogwane credit the formation of Linchwe's Motsotsobyane cattle post to these takings. See also interview with Selogwe Pilane, Mochudi, 7 Aug. 1979.

66 Holub (1976: 421, 423), Ramsay (1991: 154–155). Emil Holub arrived in Molepolole the day following the battle. The BaKgatla traditions recorded by Schapera mention the battle but are mum about the defeat, though the battle is remembered by the BaTlokwa, perhaps because their leader Gaborone is said to have rescued Linchwe at a crucial point in the conflict (Ellenberger 1939: 281). The white traders who issued the rifles were probably acting in self-defence. The BaKgatla apparently had already threatened to come to Molepolole and 'settle the white men and particularly the teacher and one of the traders' after hearing Sechele's story that he had sent his men to attack Mochudi the previous year because the 'white men had pressed him to fight . . . against his will' (C. Williams report, 17 Jan. 1876, PP 1/5/15, SP, BNA).

67 C. Williams to J. Mullens, 25 Sep. 1876, box 38, LMS.

68 Bailie report, 6 Nov. 1876, C2220: 53 as reproduced in Schapera (1942a: 33).

69 Bailie report, 17 May 1877, C2220: 76, as reproduced in Schapera (1942a: 34).

WAR

70 Ramsay (1991: 161–163). Two months after Sechele met Bailie, word reached Saulspoort that Sechele had 'asked to become a citizen of England' (P. Brink to T.H. Neethling, 12 Dec. 1876, 15/4/3/2 [B], DRCA). Bailie's trip seems to have been inspired by an acute labour shortage in the diamond fields that began in July 1876 and lasted for the rest of the year. Apart from gaining 'expressions of chiefly good will', however, Bailie's and other recruiting missions met with little success (Worger 1987: 86, 92–95).

71 P. Brink to T.H. Neethling, 9 Mar. and 15 May 1877, 15/4/3/2 (B), DRCA; H. Gonin to DRC, 16 Mar. and 4 Dec. 1877, 15/2/1 (B), DRCA; P. Brink to T. Shepstone, 18 May 1878, SS 454, R3733/80, TA; Moffat (1969: 145).

72 Annexure of 9 Oct. 1876 to Bailie Report, 17 May 1877, C2220: 78, as reproduced in Schapera (1942a: 34).

73 Goodfellow (1966: ch. 7); Davenport (1981: 130). For a summary of political and economic motives behind the annexation, see Delius (1984: 217–225).

74 As part of a delegation to England protesting annexation (Meintjes 1974: 85–88).

75 Mysteriously, Lewis was present in Molepolole when Bailie first arrived in October and Lewis witnessed Sechele's signing of the Terms of Agreement before Bailie took it to Mochudi to present to Linchwe. See Lewis's name on the Annexure of 9 Oct. 1876, C2220: 78, as reproduced in Schapera (1942a: 34).

76 Gonin to DRC, n.d. [Aug. or Sep. 1870], 15/7/2 (B), DRCA. Widow of J.J. Malan [Brink's mother] to Murray, n.d. [1886], 15/4/3/2 (B), DRCA. According to his mother, Brink underwent a deep religious conversion at the age of 15, and thereafter was preoccupied with becoming a missionary. When the Transvaal was annexed, Brink was 33 years old.

77 Gonin to T.F. Neethling, 16 Mar. 1877, 15/7/2 (B). 'The choice between Kruger and Burgers [is difficult]. 'Hard to tell which would be [have been] the greater disaster for the country.'

78 Shillington (1985: 45–55).

79 Moodie (1878: 589), Worger (1987: 73–76). In July 1876 seventeen of Linchwe's men who had worked in Kimberley were stopped by the veldkornet in Christiana and forced to hand over their guns and ammunition in return for passes to continue north (Linchwe to Burgers, 8 Nov. 1876, SS 221, R3390/76, TA).

80 Matsau (Matsawi) was present when Khama told Mackenzie in Shoshong soon after the Kgatla–Kwena War erupted that the BaNgwato would not protect Kwena cattle along the Ngwato–Kwena border. According to Khama, Mackenzie and Matsawi passed through the Kwena cattle post area en route south and Matsawi diverted to Mochudi to inform Linchwe, who then sent a regiment to rob the cattle, knowing the BaNgwato would not interfere (BPPC: 7). See references to 'Matsawe' in Bechwana District Seminary Committee, 11 Apr. 1872, box 37, LMS. Sechele was convinced the BaKgatla of Molepolole had spied for their kin in Mochudi (C. Williams to LMS, 17 Jan. 1876, PP 1/5/15, SP, BNA).

81 Matsau's name appears as witness to a letter from Mankurwane to Sir Owen Lanyon, 1 Aug. 1878, and certified as a 'true translation' by John Mackenzie (A596, vol. 4b, TA). In the 1880s, Matsau become Mankurwane's personal secretary. His two daughters were married to Linchwe's brothers Ramono and Segale (see ch. 6). According to LMS

145

WHEN RUSTLING BECAME AN ART

missionary John T. Brown, who worked among the BaTlhaping, anti-British feeling among Tlhaping chiefs was increased by the diamond-field takeover (Brown 1875: 4).

82 Mackenzie (1969: 209–210); Khama to L. du Plessis, 11 Mar. 1877, A779, vol. 2, TA.

83 After writing a letter for Linchwe in November 1876, Lewis disappears from the written record.

84 P. Brink to T.H. Neethling, 9 Mar. and 5 May 1877, 15/4/3/2 (B), DRCA. For the 'big strong bull' title, see idem, 1 Nov. 1880.

85 Rustenburg Doppers the likes of H.P. Malan, Sarel Eloff and Paul Kruger opposed the annexation government and worked to get rid of it. Malan vacated his post as veld-kornet, which during the annexation period was filled initially by C. Phillip Minnaar and soon thereafter by Charles John Topper.

86 T. Brink to T. Shepstone, 18 May 1878, SS 454, R3773/80, TA.

87 Moffat and his family visited Pretoria and others parts of the Transvaal, to get away from the fever (probably malaria) in Molepolole. Moffat returned to Molepolole by June. See J.S. Moffat to J. Mullens, 17 Jan. 1878, box 39, LMS; Moffat (1969: 146–147). Judging from his later correspondence with Pretoria, Moffat made no representations to Shepstone's administration regarding the Kgatla–Kwena conflict.

88 T. Shepstone note, 29(?) May 1878 and H.C. Shepstone to Linchwe, 3 Jun. 1878 (draft), ibid. (in the printed correspondence, this letter is falsely attributed to M. Osborn. PP, C2220: 130–131).

89 M. Osborn to Sechele, 4 Jun. 1878, PP, C2220: 131.

90 Sechele to M. Osborn, 21 Jun. 1878, ibid.: 131–132. Sechele's claim was probably spurious, given Burgers' correspondence with Linchwe and Lewis in July 1876, though in the waning months of Burgers' administration, it is possible that Sechele was able to reopen the issue for discussion.

91 M. Osborn to Sechele, 29 Jul. 1878 and M. Osborn to P. Brink, 6 Aug. 1878, ibid.: 133–134.

92 J.S. Moffat to M. Osborn, 21 Aug. 1878, and H.C. Shepstone note, 3 Sep. 1878, SS 301, R3076/78, TA; Linchwe to M. Osborn, 23 Aug. 1878, C2220: 258; T. Shepstone to B. Frere, 2 Sep. 1878, vol. 3: 905, SPUP.

93 T. Shepstone to B. Frere, 2 Sep. 1878, vol. 3: 905, SPUP.

94 M. Osborn to T. Shepstone, 11 Sep. 1878, vol. 6: 1890, SPUP. Only 354 were mobilised, of whom a mere 23 came from Tshomankane, but P.J. van Staden in reporting these figures to H.C. Shepstone noted his concern over the problems of recruiting auxiliaries from Tshomankane's area because, according to a report Van Staden had received from Henri Gonin, Tshomankane did not understand himself to be the appointed chief in his ward (i.e., that Linchwe had this authority) (P.J. van Staden to H.C. Shepstone, 24 Sep. 1878, SS 306, R3405/78, TA). The 'Rustenburg Native Contingent' left for Pediland in early September and returned in early December (T. Shepstone to B. Frere, 16 Dec. 1878, vol. 3: 1017, SPUP).

95 J.S. Moffat to M. Osborn, 21 Jun. 1878, PP, C2220: 132–133; J.S. Moffat to M. Osborn, 21 Aug. 1878, SS 301, R3076/89, TA.

96 Smith (1957: 268–269).

146

97 J.S. Moffat to T. Shepstone, 11 Sep. 1878, SN 1a, N34a/78, TA.

98 J.S. Moffat to H.C. Shepstone, 12 Sep. 1878, ibid.

99 H.C. Shepstone to S. Melvill and P.J. van Staden, plus enclosures 11 Oct. 878, SN 102: 25–33, TA; see also H.C. Shepstone to J.S. Moffat, 1 Oct. 1878, SN 102: 4–6, TA; T. Shepstone to B. Frere, 5 Oct. 1878, PP, C2220: 312–313.

100 Linchwe to Van Staden, 25 Oct. 1878, Annexure C, SN 2, N287/79, TA.

101 Sechele statement, 30 Oct. 1878, Annexure A, ibid.

102 Ikaneng (or Gert) statement, 2 Nov. 1878, Annexure B, ibid.

103 H. Gonin to DRC, 27 Oct. 1878, 15/2/1 (B), DRCA. Gonin reported 'big festivities' in Mochudi and Saulspoort. The regiment formed was headed by Linchwe's brother Ramono and half-brother Segale. It was named maKoba (lit. 'those who drive away with contempt'). They were being initiated for preparation for war and to be sent to the mines to return with guns and ammunition (Schapera 1947: 26).

104 S. Mevill and P.J. van Staden Report, 30 Nov. 1878, SS 454, R3773/78, TA. (Annexures A–D are missing in this report. For those and the original draft see SN 2, N287/79, idem).

105 See Shepstone's 5 May 1879 circulars to landdrosten, commissioners and missionaries requesting names of 'tribes', 'chiefs' and numbers of adult males in their respective districts. SN 102: 322–324 and 329–332, TA

106 M. Osborn to Sechele, 7 Feb. 1879 and J.S. Moffat to Osborn, 18 and 19 Feb. 1879, SS 454, R3773/80, TA.

107 P. Brink to T.H. Neethling, 20 Mar. 1880, 15/4/3/2 (B), DRCA. On at least one occasion, Tshomankane was commended for his service to the Administration (H.C. Shepstone to P.J. van Staden, 21 Nov. 1878, SN 102: 156–157, TA. See also P.J. van Staden to H.C. Shepstone 27 Nov. 1878, SN 1a, 52/78, and S.J.K du Toit to O. Lanyon, 27 May 1879, SS 345, R1894/79, TA. For the Kgatla in the Pedi and Zulu campaigns, see note 94 above and Gonin to DRC 29 Jan., 29 May and 12 Nov. 1879, 15/7/2/1 (B), DRCA; Breutz (1953: 260). 'England' was a nickname Tshomankane had acquired long before annexation, for reasons that are obscure. Tshomankane personally disliked the name, considering it an insult (J.H. Neethling report, *Die Gereformeerde Kerkbode* 1871: 407–408).

108 J.S. Moffat to J. Mullens, 2 Jan. 1879, box 40, LMS; Moffat later reported that 'cattle died by thousands of poverty' (Memorandum, 29 Jun. 1885, PP, C4588: 105).

109 R. Price to J. Mullens, 2 Jul. 1879 and R. Price to W. Thompson, 18 Dec. 1879, box 40, LMS.

110 Sechele to G. Wolseley, 3 Oct. 1879, SS 454, R3773/80, TA.

111 Following H.C. Shepstone's Memorandum of 17 Oct. 1879 on 'laws regarding natives' (SN 102: 568–585, TA) a hut tax was enacted as law no. 6 of 1880. See also Shepstone's Memorandum of 21 May 1881, SN 103, TA; De Kiewet (1965: 252–254). According to Shepstone, the tax was 'paid cheerfully throughout the Province' (H.C. Shepstone to O. Lanyon, 31 Jan. 1881, A596, 5a, TA).

112 Wolseley to Lanyon, 1 Apr. 1880, S454, R3773/80, TA. See also Shepstone's instructions to Melvill and Ferreira, 9 Apr. 1880 in SN 102: 927–934 and his announcement of the commission to Sechele, 8 Apr. 1880, idem: 933.

113 Isaac Schapera located the original Melvill–Ferreira Report in the Mafeking registry (since destroyed by fire) and reproduced it in Schapera (1942a: 34–37). A copy of the boundary agreement between Melvill and Sechele may be found in RC 8/7, BNA. For the Melvill–Van Staden boundary recommendation, see para. 22 of 30 Nov. 1878, SS 454, R3773/80: 227–228, TA.

114 H.C. Shepstone minute to G. Wolseley, 20 Jul. 1880 and O. Lanyon to P.J. van Staden, 11 Aug. 1880, SS 454, R3773, TA.

115 H.C. Shepstone proposed renegotiating the boundary with Sechele so that Linchwe could be incorporated into the Transvaal without having to move from Mochudi, but Wolseley turned him down. See note 114 above, and Wolseley's undated minute (received 17 Aug. 180) in the same file.

116 J.S. Moffat to H.C. Shepstone, 11 Oct. 1880, SS 454, R3773/80, TA. Moffat resigned from the LMS in 1879 and applied immediately for government service. See J.S. Moffat to O. Lanyon (?), 15 Oct. 1879, idem.

117 J.S. Moffat to H.C. Shepstone, 11 Oct. 1880, SS 454, R3773/80, TA.

118 P. Brink to T.H. Neethling, 8 Oct. 1880 (postscript dated 15 Oct. 1880), 1 Nov. 1880 and 16 May 1881, 15/4/3/2 (B), DRCA. Brink wrote these letters from the Pilanesberg, where he had been living since mid-1880.

119 G. Wolseley minute of 25 Oct. 1880, SS 454, R3773/80, TA.

120 Moffat 1969: 164–165.

Chapter six

CONSOLIDATION

The kapitein [Linchwe] has recently removed many of the kaffirs from the state either to fight [against Sechele] or as guards. (H.P. Malan to P.J. Joubert, September 1881)

* * *

Linchwe looked after 40 women he enherited from his father and looked after them well, but he never took them. (Deborah Retief as quoted by Johan Reyneke, emphasis added)

When the maBuru rose against the Transvaal government, they did not attempt to conscript the Pilanesberg BaKgatla. The rebels were afraid that Linchwe's forces might retaliate. The Kgatla had carefully cultivated the British, though to little avail, while remaining aloof from a rebellion led by Kgamanyane's nemesis Paul Kruger, if not looking for their own opportunities to prey on the rebels. Rumours to the effect that Linchwe's regiments were attacking maBuru, or likely to do so, were rife at the time, as were fears of a general black rebellion.[1] The fact is that maBuru rarely bothered Transvaal Africans who were likely to fight back. This lesson was delivered most spectacularly by Mokgatle aThethe (also known as 'Magato') and his BaFokeng to rebel leader Paul Kruger.

> Then Paul went to Magato's kraal the following day and demanded from him two horses and men to help them, but he refused, therefore PK seized him calling upon the Boers who were with him (10 in number) for help. Magato's people then entered in, and there was a fight. One of Magato's men had PK on the floor by the throat and was about to dispatch him with a battle axe, when the missionary ran in and saved him. Magato's people wanted to send him to the camp but Magato said he must first ask the Govt. what he was to do. The Missionary is Mr. Penzhorn. PK then had a long talk with Magato reminding him that they had been children together, and after some time he was allowed to go. He got two horses from Magato. PK left Rustenburg on Thursday the 23rd for Heidelberg.

Thereafter the BaFokeng were left undisturbed by the rebels and they suffered no retaliation at the war's end.[2] Linchwe's BaKgatla also had the measure of the maBuru. They neither feared the maBuru nor wanted a fight. What Linchwe needed was a *quid pro quo*: let me alone and let me control my people in the Pilanesberg; I will let you alone and you shall have nothing to fear from Africans on your Bechuanaland border. ZAR president Paul Kruger understood, as his tattered state was being rebuilt, that the ZAR could not control the BaKgatla and dare not alienate them. Linchwe, on the other hand, poised to rule over his new territory, understood that the key to the BaKgatla's success against the BaKwena was friendly relations with Kruger.

Unsurprisingly, the collapse of Annexation hastened the resumption of conflict between the Kwena and the Kgatla. Now that Sechele had lost British backing, it was left to the Kwena alone to drive out the Kgatla. Moreover, with the ZAR inclined to allow Linchwe to have his way, it was all the more urgent for Linchwe to build up his followers, to colonise more territory, and to press for ultimate victory over Sechele's forces.

The Kgatla–Kwena War: The Final Phase, 1881–1883

In February 1881, when a Boer victory over British Annexation forces was imminent, Sechele sent out his regiments from Molepolole. No direct attack was mounted against Linchwe's stronghold at Mochudi; instead regiments were broken up into small raiding parties for the purpose of terrorising isolated BaKgatla cultivating in their fields and herding at cattle posts. Sechele's decision not to attack Mochudi, which during the rains was empty because its inhabitants were away farming in their distant and scattered fields, lost him the opportunity of destroying Linchwe's capital with little loss of life. Linchwe, whose spirits had been down in recent months to the point of contemplating a return to the Pilanesberg, would have been given another reason to go. Sechele's blunder was compounded by allowing his men to resort to the murder of women and children. Instead of dispiriting his enemy, as no doubt was the intention of these acts, he riled them up. The commitment of atrocities, which had the advantage of being difficult to prevent, merely incited the BaKgatla to retaliate in kind, so that innocent civilians on both sides met gruesome, meaningless deaths.

For two years, off and on, the BaKgatla and BaKwena murdered each other. Some women and children were captured and taken away as slaves, others herded into rondavels and the thatch set on fire. Others were speared or shot in fields, or grass tied round their heads and set alight. Women's breasts were cut off, their private parts knifed. The cruelty and sadism of the war is memorialised in Kgatla traditions by an incident that took place near the Madikwe River, when a group of Kwena *bonokwane* encountered a man and his wife walking from their field. 'They killed [the man], and then said to his wife, "show us how you used to sleep with your husband in the blankets", and the woman in fear of death did so with the corpse.'[3] Such atrocities, by both sides, which were reported in Molepolole and Mochudi at the time, were recalled in detail fifty years later, and were repeated to me a century after the fact.[4]

The war also became a struggle for cattle. With fields abandoned out of terror, meat became more important as a food source, particularly for men who bore arms and stayed on the move. Raids for cattle became increasingly more common than attacks on women and children, and adult men faced each other in combat more frequently. No pitched battles were fought, however, because stealth and surprise determined the number of cattle a raid could produce, and speed, the distance one could travel without being overtaken. It was a time when individuals took personal risks in hopes of acquiring cattle of their own. This was not a war between two armies, but a series of small private raids launched by temporary clutches of men moving across lines. Men ceased living at home. Those who were not fighting or protecting their herds worked in the diamond fields to obtain guns and powder.[5] The others, in pursuit of their stolen cattle or in search of cattle to steal, unsettled an area stretching from Molepolole to present-day Gaborone, east to the Madikwe River, north to Buffel's Drift, west to Lephepe and back to Molepolole – roughly equivalent to 14,000 square kilometres.

As insecurity grew and stock soared in value, old ties and loyalties felt the strain. Linchwe tried talking his Saulspoort people under Moselekatse into resettling near Mochudi and, when they refused, he sent his regiments from Mochudi on two occasions to confiscate their cattle. All this was done with the knowledge, and Gonin believed the connivance, of local Boer officials.[6] The BaKgatla also stole horses, at a premium for rustling cattle, from their old supporters, the BaLete.[7] Tension was widespread in the region, along with uncertainties as to which territory belonged to whom, and violence erupted where claims were the weakest. The Ba-Kwena picked a quarrel with their peaceable neighbours, the Mmanaana Kgatla at Mosopa and tried to involve the BaNgwaketse. The BaNgwaketse chose this time as well to invade Ramotswa in an unsuccessful attempt to drive the BaLete into the Transvaal.[8]

During the winter of 1882, hunger joined the ranks of the enemy. The previous year's harvest, reduced through drought and terror in the countryside, began to run out within months. By August, food had become scarce in Mochudi and Molepolole, with much attendant suffering.[9] In October the area's population was hit by smallpox, which had been carried up from the diamond fields.[10] By December, when Brink resumed his mission in Mochudi, famine had struck. The BaKgatla were scattered all over the country looking for food.[11] By then both sides were exhausted and the fighting had stopped.

A formal truce awaited only a neutral arbitrator. Sechele proposed kgosi Mokgosi of the BaLete, whom Linchwe rejected. Finally, by mid-1883, Montshiwa of the BaRolong managed to bring the two sides together and, after visiting both capitals, forge an agreement.[12] Montshiwa assumed the role of peacemaker because the spill-over effects of the war had divided the leaders of the region at a time when Boer filibusters and British land speculators in the south were threatening the survival of the BaTlhaping, BaRolong and their Tswana neighbours to the north. Montshiwa wished simply to bring the BaKgatla, BaKwena and others with him into an alliance.[13] His concern was bringing about a lasting truce, rather than resolving the disagreement that had caused the conflict. Montshiwa's peace pact, which ended the Kgatla–Kwena War, left open the question of territorial jurisdiction. The ZAR wanted nothing to do with the issue, or with Linchwe. In early 1882, Linchwe travelled to Transvaal in an attempt to get the new ZAR government to affirm Burgers' ruling that he was a ZAR subject and to redraw the Transvaal boundary in his favour, but President Paul Kruger simply referred the matter to the British Resident and offered Linchwe's people in Saulspoort passes to leave the ZAR.[14] Henceforth, Linchwe claimed the land from the Madikwe to Kopong, 30 kilometres west of Mochudi, as belonging to the BaKgatla, whereas Sechele continued to regard the BaKgatla as his subjects. These claims remained in dispute for the next sixteen years. The failure of Linchwe and Sechele to bury their differences stemmed, nevertheless, from the fact that the BaKgatla had occupied the eastern Kweneng and prevented the BaKwena from re-taking it.

Thus the BaKgatla secured a territory free from direct outside control and gained something approaching independence by default. Given the general turmoil and uncertainties affecting southern Africa at the time, laying claim to the sizeable niche known as Kgatleng ('where the BaKgatla are') was no mean accomplishment. For the first time since the reign of Pheto, the BaKgatla assumed a territorial identity. The new capital, Mochudi, was situated between 25 and 85 kilometres from each of its boundaries and was used to administer a land rich in grass and blessed with perennial water.

The River Villages

Once secure, the Kgatleng began to attract new settlers, became the site of new villages and took shape as a network of paths and roads connecting all of its parts to Linchwe's kgotla in Mochudi. Though many kin still remained separated in the Pilanesberg, the BaKgatla of Mochudi had found at least a partial solution to the problems of territorial and political fragmentation that perplexed all the BaTswana of the western trans-Vaal throughout the nineteenth century. Some, such as the BaLete, BaHurutshe and BaTlokwa, had adopted the same strategy of migrating west and claiming territory from the BaKwena and BaNgwaketse, but in terms of size and extent of resources none gained territory comparable to what, after 1883, the BaKgatla possessed.

Much of the growth and stabilisation of the Kgatleng was directed, if not initiated, from Mochudi. Too much was at stake to allow the peopling and ordering of the Bechuanaland Kgatla to chance. In 1882, before the outcome of the war was clear, Linchwe sent his regiments to Saulspoort, took their cattle, and succeeded in getting an important segment of the Saulspoort group to follow them. Three settlements soon sprang up along the Madikwe River: Sikwane, Mathubudukwane and Mabalane.[15] They were situated close to the drift at Derdepoort, through which passed the only direct wagon road between Mochudi and Pilanesberg. Linchwe used the 'river villages' to settle those of his uncles who were rejoining the main body of the BaKgatla after Kgamanyane's death in 1875. The river villages helped Linchwe establish his presence on the left bank of the Madikwe River and oversee the grazing of cattle on unoccupied Boer farms across the river.

All three were loyalist, royal enclaves. Sikwane, built directly opposite Derdepoort on the drift, was established by Kgari Pilane, Linchwe's uncle, who moved over from Saulspoort in 1882.[16] With its royal ward and four commoner wards, it was the largest of the three. The same year another uncle, Letsebe Pilane, settled five kilometres downstream at Mathubudu-kwane. Letsebe, who had left the Pilanesberg before Kgamanyane, had lived near the LMS station at Molepolole and left there following the outbreak of the Kgatla–Kwena War. Reluctant to settle in Mochudi, he and his few followers moved to near Zeerust. After the British left the Transvaal, he joined the Kgatla fight and approached his nephew Linchwe to be allowed to enter the Kgatleng. Settlement in Letsebe's village was restricted to his own immediate family, however, perhaps because of their attachment to the LMS.[17] Mabalane, two kilometres from Sikwane, was established by Rakgo-batana (Ntereke) Molefi Molefe. Ntereke was another leading Saulspoort figure, who came over in 1882 and resided first in Sikwane. Shortly there-after, he was placed at nearby Mabalane and built his own small village, consisting of the single Molefe ward. Ntereke's father had followed Kga-manyane to Mochudi and was revered by him and Bogatsu. Ntereke's sis-ter Mokgethi was Kgamanyane's third wife.[18]

Reordering the Royal Family

Establishing the river villages moved Linchwe closer to rearranging his extended family in a way that strengthened his authority. This process, underway since 1875, had been put into place by Kgamanyane himself and his brother Bogatsu before Linchwe's ascension to power. As Kgamanya-ne's death approached, divisions that remained within the Pilane group had to be addressed. At the time, five of Kgamanyane's brothers were still in Saulspoort: Tshomankane, Mantirisi, Kgari, Moselekatse and Bafshwe. Three others – Letsebe, Kgabotshwene and Diphotwe – had left the Ba-Kgatla altogether and taken their few followers with them. Only two of Pilane's older sons, Bogatsu and Tau, had followed Kgamanyane. Tau him-self, as we know, had ambitions to succeed Kgamanyane. We should also remember that Maganelo, Kgamanyane's first-born son of his first-wed wife, Nkomeng, had his supporters, too. Tau and Maganelo had made the journey to Mochudi with Kgamanyane not necessarily out of loyalty, but in order to keep alive their chance of ruling.

To avert a crisis following his death, Kgamanyane and Bogatsu forced a constitutional interpretation that would enable Linchwe to succeed Kgamanyane and enlarge his following at the expense of his opponents. The impending war made this easier to push through, as has already been indicated, but here it is worth pointing out that much longer-term strategies were in play. Tau's claim was the easier to deny, because Kgamanyane's succession at Pilane's death established the priority of Linchwe's claim. In order to exclude Maganelo, however, Linchwe's candidacy was based on the order of betrothal of Nkomeng and Dikolo (Linchwe's mother). Nkomeng had been married first, but Kgamanyane asserted that beforehand he had formally arranged to marry Dikolo, who was then a young girl.[19] The use of betrothal as the principal for giving seniority to Linchwe's mother over Maganelo's also had the effect of elevating the rank of several wives who were comparatively young and whose children were much younger than Linchwe or were yet to be born. Linchwe's succession therefore offered this group, on account of their age as well as the principal of their rank, the chance to overtake families in the royal Pilane lineage that heretofore had been senior. Naturally the newly vaulted were expected to look up to Linchwe and give him their support. The new kgosi, in other words, would be expected to assume the role, as well as the office, of his father. The manner in which he was supposed to accomplish this was explained to him by Kgamanyane:

> When Kgamanyane was dying, he was taken to Mopiping wa Mgatlapa, where a shelter was erected for him and [his attendants]. Linchwe was then summoned from Monametsana cattle post. When Linchwe arrived, Kgamanyane then ordered that all his wives, including the one he had married the day previous, be brought from the village. They were brought to him and they sat down around him. Kgamanyane then sat up straight and stared at them. Then he is supposed to have said these words of admonition to Linchwe:
>
> 'Linchwe, take care of these women. They have born and will bear many people who will help you. If you send them away, saying "my father is dead, why must you be here?" don't do it. Remain a patron of these people.'
>
> Kgamanyane died soon thereafter, and Linchwe obeyed the request of his father. He provided the guardianship to his father's wives. He strengthened his village and kept the royal households together. Many

> houses were built at Kgosing for them. Many children were born and
> were regarded as Kgamanyane's offspring. That's how it was.[20]

Kgamanyane left behind at least forty-six wives, many of whom were younger than Linchwe and his brothers. After 1875 they bore children who looked to Linchwe as their kgosi and helped to isolate their elder brothers who otherwise would look on Linchwe and Ramono as their age-mates and equals.[21] The self-respect of wives betrothed when young was also increased, as was the derision their children used against the offspring of wives betrothed when mature, even though it had no bearing on rank.[22]

Such a solution was risky in the short run. As long as Maganelo remained alive, his claim could be revived in the event of Linchwe's death. Such a possibility was real given the prevailing insecurity caused by the Kgatla–Kwena war immediately following Kgamanyane's death. Before the war quieted down long enough for Linchwe to be installed formally, though, Maganelo was killed in a battle near Thamaga, and the risk of Linchwe's group being unseated was eliminated.[23] Maganelo's claim survived through his brother Segale, who was, however, younger than Linchwe and more easily controlled. Segale was extremely bright and talented and in fact proved to be a valuable member of Linchwe's inner circle, but he was ranked in all formal occasions as second to Linchwe's younger full brother Ramono. Segale's case parallels that of Tau, who was given second position behind Kgamanyane's younger full brother Bogatsu. Bogatsu was the leading figure during the early years of Linchwe's reign, making key decisions and representing Linchwe on several occasions. After Bogatsu died sometime in or before 1885, Tau became the senior uncle, but his role was largely ceremonial. By then Linchwe represented himself, and his group was made up of men his own age.

Several of Kgamanyane's half-brothers joined Linchwe during the Kgatla–Kwena war, but he kept them from settling in Mochudi and delegated them peripheral administrative duties. In the early 1880s, when Linchwe insisted they relocate to the Kgatleng, they were placed along the Madikwe for the purpose of overseeing the river villages. These arrangements were acceptable to all parties. Apart from Tau, the only uncles to be found in Mochudi were Tau's brother Komane, who was Linchwe's age, and Kobedi and several others who were younger. They served as Linchwe's advisors and as his lieutenants in the maTlakana and maKoba regiments, and more than likely, they were the ones who performed the role of raising seed among Kgamanyane's wives and increasing the number of Linchwe's dependents.[24]

Among the BaKgatla who remained in the Transvaal, Linchwe used generosity to keep his authority intact. Through Henri Gonin he bought Holfontein 361 for Mantirisi and his followers.[25] Linchwe also married Tshomankane's daughter Mogaritse as his second wife and gave Tshomankane charge of the Pilanesberg Kgatla regiments. These new alliances were important in keeping the Transvaal Kgatla involved in fighting the war against the BaKwena. In the first three years of the war, Linchwe's cattle were kept near Holfontein, and Tshomankane brought needed reinforcements to the Kgatleng. Linchwe's father-in-law and another uncle, Bafshwe, also earned Linchwe's people the admiration of the British, who used Tshomankane's regiments in their campaigns against the BaPedi. Only Moselekatse, who assumed control over the people living on Saulspoort 38, remained aloof from Linchwe and began to set himself up independently of Mochudi. In 1881, therefore, Linchwe confiscated his cattle.

As the Kgatla–Kwena War drew to a close, Linchwe's close advisors and lieutenants in Mochudi had emerged increasingly as a Kgamanyane, and less a Pilane, group. Ramono and Segale assumed greater importance, as did Pone, Masibane and Kupakang. Linchwe's brothers also assumed the role of military leaders, as new regiments were initiated. In the years to come, all men of fighting ability would fall under their lead:

Regiment	Year Initiated	Commanders	Lieutenants[26]
maTlakana [Komane, Kobedi]	1873[27]	Linchwe	Pone
maKoba	1878[28]	Ramono	Segale
maJanko	1883[29]	Modise	Motshwane
maNtwane	1892	Mochele	?

Linchwe's circle was also related to other important figures in the BaKgatla community. Linchwe's great wife Motlapele was the daughter of Poonyane Ramasilo, head of the Makgophana sub-ward of Manamakgothe kgotla and his third wife Lekgwalo, came from the Molefe sub-ward of Kgosing. Molefe had the largest royal lineage outside of Pilane and Kgamanyane. Ramono and Segale also married daughters of the Molefe

Mantlu and Boikanyo, respectively. In addition, two of Kgamanyane s wives, Mosothwe and Selolweng, born in the Molefe and Malebye (Mabodisa) sub-wards, respectively, were elevated in rank on the principal of betrothal and their sons incorporated into Linchwe's circle. Motshwane, lieutenant of maJanko, was Selolweng's son. In turn, Malebye of Malebye sub-ward married Linchwe's sister Ntletleng and became one of Linchwe's councillors and his *Ntlahsi a Marumo* ('distributor of weapons').[30] Such marriages helped to make Linchwe's political circle into a family.

Spoils of War

At the war's end, the BaKgatla were wealthy in cattle once again. The BaKgatla had fought for this very objective, as well as to control the water and grazing of the Ngotwane and Madikwe rivers. Cattle brought status, but in these arid parts they were needed even more for survival. The soils in the Kgatleng that were suitable for agriculture were located mostly between Mochudi and the river villages and represented less than two percent of the total area of the Kgatleng, as later demarcated.[31] In years of good rainfall, this area was probably sufficient to feed the population. The BaKgatla were using ox-drawn ploughs as early as the 1870s and producing grain surpluses for sale.[32] Stored surpluses were nevertheless inadequate to cover the bad years. Extreme drought occurred in 1878 and 1882, and 1880 and 1884 were not much better. Even in the wet years, harvests were usually too small to reach the next harvest. 'During this time of the year', one missionary discovered in the 1880s, 'the people live almost entirely on milk sometimes for two or three months'.[33]

The manner in which cattle spoils were distributed reveals how Linchwe and his advisors understood that their followers needed cattle to stay alive. Raided stock were brought back to Mochudi and presented to the kgosi at the main kgotla, and the bulk were given to those who captured them. The remainder were placed under the kgosi's care and herded at his several Diphatsa and Motsotsobiane cattle posts. From these herds, which reached numbers well in excess of one thousand head, Linchwe gave them out in ones and twos to members of the *morafe*, including the poor. Eventually, the Diphatsa and Motsotsobiane herds dwindled to around two hundred and became the personal property of Linchwe and his family. Among these, some were given out permanently as loan cattle (*mafisa*) to poor relatives. During the war, as well, a number of small raids were conducted without Linchwe's direction and the returning raiders often hid stock for themselves on the way back and presented only one or two beasts at the kgotla. Thus, by the end of the war, virtually every family had acquired stock for draught purposes, as well as for milking.[34] In the 1880s the BaKgatla grazed their cattle almost entirely along the Ngotwane and Madikwe Rivers up to the Limpopo. No other dependable surface water was available.[35] During the rainy season, cows could be grazed somewhat further away, but the oxen were needed for ploughing in Talane, the name by which the agricultural belt between Mochudi and Sikwane was known. The posts had to be close enough to the permanent villages for men to visit them regularly and their herding sons to return home occasionally, and for soured and curdled milk to be brought in for family consumption. The BaKgatla had no servants to fulfil these functions that, for the BaTswana controlling the Kalahari, were commonly performed by Ba-Sarwa and BaKgalagadi.

Linchwe was the sole owner of the BaKgalagadi who had been captured during the war from the BaKwena, along with their cattle. They became his personal property and part of his inheritance.[36] These herders enabled Linchwe to establish cattle posts at considerable distances from Mochudi. Posts were maintained on the lower Ngotwane and inside the Transvaal south of Derdepoort and along the right-hand bank between the Madikwe and Oodi Rivers. In 1883 and 1885, when two thousand of his cattle were grazing between the Tweedepoort and Dwarsberg, a local ZAR official seized them in an effort to tax Linchwe for the use of the area; Linchwe then had to hire six farms from the ZAR in order to gain access to the Transvaal for his cattle.[37] At the time, much of the area between the Kgatleng and Zeerust was unoccupied by white settlers.[38]

Apart from Linchwe, who had the means to utilise the Transvaal, the BaKgatla lacked the space to expand economically. The Kgatleng was a land seldom productive enough to feed its people and became instead a base from which the men, at least, must venture out seasonally in search of food and additional income.[39] Labour migration, which began during the Kgatla–Kwena War, became an established pattern. In 1880 records in Kimberley refer to the presence of, among others, Kgatla miners, and Kgatla traditions mention that Linchwe ordered the newly formed maKoba to work in the diamond mines at about that time. Their task was to earn

£8 each for the purchase of arms and ammunition.[40] After the war, Ba-Kgatla made their journeys as individuals or as part of a small group, a pattern that held. The war veterans were the first of the four known generations of labour migrants from the Kgatleng.[41] As they moved back and forth, a system of tapping their income for the benefit of others came into being. In 1884 or thereabouts, Linchwe began to levy a £2 tax on every returning worker, the first Tswana kgosi to use this money-spinning device.[42]

The Emergence of Literacy in the Kgatleng

In Mochudi, the constant coming and going of people – migrant labourers, traders, missionaries, labour recruiters and officials, not to mention Linchwe's steady visits to the Transvaal – enhanced the ability of Linchwe and his inner circle to follow events in the region, discern new developments and plot strategies accordingly. What was clear to them, even as the war began, was that the BaKgatla leadership required new methods of communicating with, and representing themselves to, important persons who were other than maBuru. Their need to communicate in written Dutch and English – and present themselves as 'modern men' – was made all the more urgent, however, by having to compete with the BaKwena for the recognition of their territorial claims by the Annexation government, the ZAR and British expansionists moving north from the Cape.

Since 1876 the BaKgatla had resorted to using outsiders, such as Fred Lewis and Pieter Brink, as official correspondents and interpreters. Such persons, who appear to have been willing and sympathetic, were nevertheless often away. Lewis stayed less than a year in Mochudi before disappearing over the horizon, and DRC missionary Pieter Brink kept moving back and forth between Mochudi and the Transvaal until his death in Rustenburg in 1886. The only solution was using the few available BaKgatla for the task, while the royal family undertook the slow process of acquiring literacy. Brink was therefore encouraged to establish a school. In 1880, with Linchwe's support, Brink opened Mochudi's first school, and reported that lots of people visiting the school belonged to the 'most outstanding' BaKgatla. Linchwe was 'very good for us', wrote Brink, '[he] says he can't do without me'.[43]

Problems soon developed. Within months, Brink left Mochudi with his family because of the war, leaving Mochudi without a teacher. The gap was filled by Samuel Radipholo, baptised by the LMS before the war, when Radipholo was part of Letsebe's BaKgatla in Molepolole. By the time Brink returned to Mochudi in 1883, however, Radipholo had given the school a new direction. He put a premium on English, the region's new language of power. Brink's reinstatement of Dutch led his pupils to threaten his person and block him from entering the church, until 'Linchwe and his brothers sided with Brink and calmed things down'.[44] Linchwe was soon to realise, however, that as much as Mochudi needed a missionary to run a school and obtain the necessary textbooks, Brink's control over baptism and appointment of church elders posed real dangers. As he alone determined admissions and promotions, Brink was seen invariably as playing favourites. Not long after Brink dismissed Radipholo as an elder and appointed Jakob Rakgole in his place, tensions erupted after Brink refused to admit one of Radipholo's protégés into the church, 'because I thought him not humble enough and not wanting salvation enough'. Radipholo mounted a church 'revolt' that put Mochudi in an uproar. This time the rebellious pupils included Linchwe's own brother.[45] By then, Linchwe and his advisors had decided to look elsewhere to develop education in the Kgatleng.

Rather than rely on DRC missionaries, the Mochudi BaKgatla turned instead to the young DRC evangelists at Saulspoort to come to their service. These evangelists were drawn from the very Saulspoort Christians whom Kgamanyane had persecuted before departing for Bechuanaland. With Kgamanyane gone, mission work became more attractive. Christian training could also lead to income that sometimes was sufficient to free them from labouring in the fields or cattle posts. Teachers and evangelists employed in the larger missions, moreover, were usually *salaried*, and as such were virtually the only Africans who could live at home in the rural areas while earning steady cash. The DRC evangelists and teachers at Saulspoort were also catapulting themselves above those families who refused to intermarry with them, with or without their education. Many of the leading DRC converts were of inboekelinge origin, belonged to groups that the BaKgatla had subordinated by force in recent times, or had come to the Saulspoort mission expressly for instruction, some arriving from as far away as from Pediland. Apart from their learning, in other words, they lacked any standing among the BaKgatla, having no marital and historical ties to any of the established wards in and around Kgamanyane's old capital. It was typical for male evangelists to marry the daughters or sisters of other evangelists, suggesting they were unacceptable to established Ba-Kgatla families. (Female teachers of the same background, on the other hand, were more than acceptable among Christian men from established BaKgatla wards; men of the royal Pilane line certainly married their share, as we shall see.)[46]

Still, Linchwe needed these Saulspoort evangelists and teachers to build the religious and educational institutions in Bechuanaland. The earliest to have an impact was Leoke Mariri. This DRC evangelist originated from the lowly Tlhalerwa, the people attacked and taken captive by Kgama-nyane's regiments around 1850.[47] He joined Gonin's payroll as a teacher in 1875. Together with Joseph Madisa, of Pedi origin, he was sent in 1877 to the Morija Training School run by the Paris Evangelical Missionary Society.[48] In 1879, after successful completion, Mariri was stationed with Tshomankane at Bopitikwe. Madisa taught at Saulspoort and then at 'Rasai' near Ramokoka's BaPhalane.[49] Described by Gonin as 'a good man, but not very capable', Madisa gradually disappears from view in the record, though his son, Abel, later featured prominently. Leoke Mariri was thought too money-conscious by Gonin and Brink, but he proved popular among the BaKgatla loyal to Linchwe. In 1884, not long after Kgari Pilane and other Saulspoort Christians established Sikwane, Mariri was permitted by the DRC and Linchwe to settle in Sikwane and minister to Kgari's followers. Mariri built a 'decent new school' not long thereafter[50] In the years to come, Mariri and other Saulspoort- and Morija-trained teachers would enter the service of Linchwe, enlarging thereby his ability to interact with the world outside the Kgatleng and to regulate and control the mission-based institutions within.

The calculated process with which Linchwe and his circle consolidated the administration of the Kgatleng and transformed its inner workings was also becoming a hurried one. For, not long after the protracted war with the Kwena had ended in Linchwe's favour, the Kgatleng became his base to contend with the new power in the region. His people had gone to war with the BaKwena as a necessary means of acquiring cattle and territory and minimising the effects of maBuru rule. By 1884, however, a third enemy had established itself in Linchwe's world. The British, who had so easily been displaced in the Transvaal only three years before, were once again challenging the ZAR for supremacy, this time north of Griqualand

CONSOLIDATION

West in the land of the BaTlhaping and BaRolong. News of Stellaland, Goshen and the Bechuanaland Wars was carried to Mochudi by the miners returning from Kimberley, by Montshiwa himself, and by the most literate MoKgatla of that time, LMS catechist David Matsau. He lived in Taung and was the secretary to Tlhaping kgosi Mankurwane Molehabangwe, among the leaders resisting British expansion in the region. Vehemently anti-British, Matsau was stricken by the LMS from the catechist list for 'disturbing the peace in our churches' and 'making statements . . . which were a serious departure from the truth' in southern Bechuanaland. Matsau then visited the BaNgwaketse, BaKwena and BaKgatla to encourage them to reject the protection about to be offered by British officials.[51] Linchwe knew that maKgoa were no different than maBuru in that they liked to use Africans to fight other Africans on their behalf – his people had ingratiated themselves with the ZAR and the Transvaal Annexation government by that method – but he was also beginning to see that they shared a desire to possess African land. There was also little to suggest that maKgoa and maBuru were opposed to sharing spoils with one another. When the Boer flags went down in Stellaland and Goshen and the Union Jack went up, maBuru remained on the farms they had acquired as filibusters.[52] These developments, which occurred as the Cape government intervened in the affairs of Mankurwane, Montshiwa and other Tswana leaders in the south, could not have escaped the notice of Linchwe and his advisors. Nor could his people have failed to discern that the visible line of *seKgoa* advance beyond Kimberley was proceeding, not towards Pretoria, but along the Road to the North.

ENDNOTES

1   Lagden diaries, entries 20, 23 and 26 Feb. 1881, MSS Afr. S.147, RH; H. Gonin to DRC, 25 Apr. 1881, 15/7/2 (B) and P. Brink to J.H. Neethling, 16 May 1881, 15/4/3/2 (B), DRCA.

2   Lagden diaries, entry 3 Mar. 1881, Mss. Afr. S147, RH; H.C. Shepstone memo, 14 Apr. 1881, SN 4a, N10/81, and also in A596, 5b, TA; A. Ritter to Secretary Native Affairs, 8 Jun. 1881, SN 4a, N97/81, TA. Henri Gonin alleged that the altercation took place at Mabieskraal (Gonin to DRC, 29 Jun. 1981, 15/7/2 [B], DRCA).

3   Klaas Segogwane interview, PP 1/1/2, SP, BNA.

4   Price (1956: 459, 461–462, 464, 482–483); P. Brink to T.H. Neethling, 6 May 1881, 15/4/3/2 (B) [based on reports from Mochudi received in Saulspoort; Brink was away from Mochudi for the duration of the war]; Maganelo Pilane, Thomas Phiri and Klaas Se-

gogwane interviews, PP 1/1/2, SP, BNA; interview with Ratsegana Sebeke and Harris Thulari, August 1982.

5 Smith (1957: 297), Schapera (1933: 645).

6 H. Gonin to DRC, 28 Jun. 1882, 15/7/2/1 (B), DRCA; H.P. Malan to P.J. Joubert, 30 Sep. 1881, KG 1, CR 47/81, TA.

7 Thomas Phiri interview, PP 1/1/2, SP, BNA.

8 Smith (1957: 297); J. Good to W. Thompson, 3 Dec. 1882, box 41, LMS; Ellenberger (1937: 47).

9 Price (1956: 503); H. Gonin to DRC, 22 Aug. 1882, 15/7/2/1 (B), DRCA.

10 Price (1956: 505); Smith (1957: 290).

11 P. Brink to T.H. Neethling, 20 Feb. 1883, 15/4/3/2 (B), DRCA.

12 Statement of Isang Pilane, 29 Oct. 1932, PP 1/4/5, SP, BNA.

13 W. Price to W.E. Bok, 2 Apr. 1883, PP, C3841: 6; Molema (1966: 129); Smith (1957: 298); Shillington (1985: 136): Schapera (1942a: 13).

14 H.P. Malan to ? (Secretary for Native Affairs, ZAR, Pretoria), 4 Feb. 1882, SS 599, R84/82, TA. According to Malan, who had been appointed as Native Commissioner Rusten- burg, 'Kapitein Linsou came to my farm and asked me whether I could mark a bound- ary between him and Secheli, since Secheli bothers him everyday. The land where he now lives was given to his father by the old Republic [!], that his father died there and that he would like to die there as well . . . Also that Linsou was a subject of the old Republic and Sechele was not and that he, Linsou always obeys the laws.' See also W.E. Bok (?) to H.P. Malan, 16 Feb. 1882, SS 615, R906/82, TA.

15 P. Brink to J.H. Neethling, 2 Aug. 1883, 15/4/3/2 (B), DRCA.

16 For Kgari, see F. Morton (1998a: 88).

17 Statement of Isang Pilane, 26 May 1931, SP, PP 1/4/6, BNA.

18 Ibid.; P. Brink to J.H. Neethling, 2 Aug. 1883, 15/4/3/2 (B), DRCA. Brink refers to him as 'Hendrick', the name taken also by his second son. For Ntereke, see F. Morton (1998a: 94).

19 Schapera (1942a: 11); Interview with Seikgokgoni Pilane, Kgosing, Mochudi, 21 Dec. 1981.

20 Interview with Ratsegana Sebeke, Molapo lands, Mochudi, 4 Aug. 1982. Rre Sebeke heard this tradition from Ramfolo Kgamanyane (born about 1860), in whose house Sebeke spent most of his youth. For additional information on Rre Sebeke and this interview, see ch. 5.

21 The re-ranking of wives is apparent in Kgamanyane's detailed genealogy, as recorded by Isaac Schapera during the 1930s. The sons affected can be determined by compar- ing age, based on regimental initiation and/or baptism records, with their seniors or juniors. Some of Kgamanyane's sons were placed below brothers who by age were a generation their junior. Molomowatau, for example, was born in about 1860, but ranks behind Mokotedi, who was born in 1886, and Mongale, initiated with Molomo- watau, ranks behind Pheto Jona, who was born in about 1882. Regimental age has been estimated at 21.5 years, based on an average of 28 initiates for whom regimental membership was recorded by Schapera in his Kgamanyane genealogy and birth dates as recorded in the DRC baptism registers, 15/4/2/1 (A), DRCA. Dates of regimental

CONSOLIDATION

initiate have been confirmed from DRC correspondence used in connection with the regimental lists (which are not entirely accurate) provided in Schapera (1977: 317).

22 'The wives of my grandmother [MmaRamfolo] claimed they were senior to her because they had been chosen while they were young, unlike MmaRamfolo who was chosen after she had grown up. Ramfolo [born ca. 1860] was ridiculed by these children, and he died of a broken heart' (Interview of Seikgokgoni Ramfolo Pilane, Kgosing, Mochudi, 21 Dec. 1981). *Mma* Seikgokgoni, for many years deceased, gave me this information on the understanding that it would be confidential.

23 H. Gonin to DRC, 18 Dec. 1875, 15/7/2 (A), DRCA. It is altogether possible that Maganelo was murdered by Linchwe's supporters during the battle. Linchwe was designated successor probably several months before his formal installation after the battle of Thamaga. See ch. 5.

24 The levirate was practised among the BaTswana at least into the 1930s, and was employed by the BaKgatla within the chiefly line following the death of Kgafela, Linchwe's son, in 1916. The missionary Deborah Retief, who arrived in Mochudi in 1887, alleged that Linchwe 'looked after 40 women he enherited from his father and looked after them well, *but he never took them*' (Reyneke 1923: 43; emphasis added; translation by W. van den Akker); see also Schapera (1941: 316–323).

25 See ch. 5.

26 Commanders, in order of their rank by birth: Linchwe and Ramono were from the first Kgamanyane *lapa*, Modise and Mochele from the second. Lieutenants: Pone was from the seventh, ahead of Komane and Kobedi, 'sons' of Pilane; Segale from the second, and Motshwane from the eleventh.

27 H. Gonin to DRC, 17 Apr. 1873, 15/7/2 (B), DRCA. Schapera (1977: 317) places this incorrectly at 1874. The second stage (white bogwera) was not completed until 1875.

28 H. Gonin to DRC, 27 Oct. 1878, 15/7/2 (B), DRCA. Schapera (1977: 317) places this incorrectly at 1880.

29 P. Brink to J.H. Neethling, 2 Aug. 1883, 15/4/3/2 (B), DRCA. Schapera places this incorrectly at 1884.

30 Interviews with Selogwe Pilane, Mosanteng, Mochudi, 22 Jul. 1982, and Ratsegana Sebeke, Molapo lands, Mochudi, 26 Jul. 1982.

31 In 1899, when the Bakgatla Reserve was beaconed. See ch. 7. In 1940, the total arable land in the Kgatleng was estimated at 32,000 acres, or roughly 1.4 percent of the total land area of 3,200 square miles (Schapera 1943a: 128, 129 and map facing 128 showing arable and grazing areas).

32 Anderson (1974: 148–149); Interviews with T. Phiri (Jul. 1931) and K. Segogwane (Aug. 1932), SP, PP 1/1/2, BNA.

33 M.E. Murray, n.d. [between 1882 and 1884], 15/4/3/8 (B), DRCA.

34 Mochudi interviews with Gabriel Palai, Makgophana, 24 Jul. 1979; Galemone Monowe, 24 Jul. 1979; Rramaiba Moremi, Makwadi, 26 Jul. 1979; Selogwe Pilane, Masiana, 30 Jul. and 7 Aug. 1979; Leitshole Leitshole, Makgophana, 9 Aug. 1979; Bakgatlabatsile Pilane, Phaphane, 18 Dec. 1981; Ratsegana Sebeke, 4 Aug. 1982, Marapo lands; Linchwe Estate Enquiry (1935), S343/24, BNA.

165

35 Interview with Selogwe Pilane, Masiana, Mochudi, 7 Aug. 1979.

36 Mochudi interviews with Selogwe Pilane, Masiana, 30 Jul. 1979; Leitshole Leitshole, 9 Aug. 1979; Edwin Gare, Ramoswana, 5 Jan. 1983; Interview of T. Phiri (Aug. 1931), SP, PP 1/1/2, and Linchwe Estate Enquiry (1935), S343/24, BNA.

37 P. Brink to J.H. Neethling, 2 Aug., 4 Sep. and 30 Oct. 1883, 15/4/3/2 (B), DRCA; District of Marico Commission of Enquiry, 18 Mar. 1885, and S.G.A. Shippard to H. Robinson, 4 Feb. 1886, HC 4/13, BNA; Linchwe to R.C. Williams, 30 Jan. 1904, LTG 124, 110/41, TA.

38 G.J. Niekerk, Commissioner of the South West border, ZAR, informed Pretoria that 'a considerable number of farms have been bought, entirely with the intention of letting them to kaffirs' (Niekerk to E. Bok (copy), 19 Apr. 1887, HC 14/5, BNA). See also Tabler (1960: 19) and Gilmore (n.d.: 232–242).

39 In drought years, the BaKgatla were crossing into the ZAR to forage for food (P. Brink to J.H. Neethling, 3 Aug. 1883, 15/4/3/2 [B], DRCA).

40 Schapera (1933: 68, 90, 93; 1947: 26).

41 By 1889 BaKgatla were working in the Witwatersrand goldfields and by 1892 in those of Mashonaland, as well as on Transvaal farms. See Schapera (1947: 27); J. Moffat to S.G.A. Shippard, 23 Mar. 1889, HC 27/16, BNA; B. Beyer annual report, 6 Jun. 1890, 15/4/3/1 (B), DRCA; interview with Ratsegana Sebeke, Marapo lands, Mochudi, 4 Aug. 1982.

42 The levy was later reduced to £1 (Schapera 1943b: 68, 90, 93).

43 P. Brink to J.H. Neethling, 8 Oct. 1880, 15/4/3/2 (B), DRCA.

44 H. Gonin to DRC, 10 May 1883, 15/7/2 (B), DRCA. See also idem, 28 Jun. 1882.

45 P. Brink to J.H. Neethling, 21 Oct. 1885, 15/4/3/2 (B); H. Gonin to DRC, 15 Jun. 1886, 15/7/2 (B), DRCA.

46 Evangelist Matsau Motsisi alone is to be counted among BaKgatla of 'respectable' birth, but his somewhat tortured persona, and light brown skin, marked him as an outsider. Molefhe Motsisi, Matsau's grandson, saw his grandfather before Matsau's death in 1918. Matsau was also tall (Interview, Mochudi, 10 Jul. 1995).

47 Maree (1966: 473–474), Breutz (1953: 22, 400, 403). The Mariri totem was *phiri* (dui-ker), suggesting ultimately a non-Tlhalerwa origin, possibly Seleka or Pedi: interviews with Francis Phiri, Mochudi, 23 Dec. 1981; Rev. J. Phiri and England Kgamanyane Pi-lane, Saulspoort, 6 Jan. 1982; Prof. E.S. Moloto, Gaborone, 22 Feb. 1982.

48 H. Gonin to DRC, 23 Jul. 1877, 15/7/2 (B), DRCA; For Madisa's origins, interview with Prof. E.S. Moloto, Gaborone, 22 Feb. 1982.

49 H. Gonin to DRC, 4 May 1886, 15/7/2 (C), DRCA.

50 H. Gonin to DRC, 14 Aug. 1884, 15 Jun. 1886, 15/7/2 (C), DRCA. For Linchwe's permis-sion, see kgotla statement of Stephen Molotsi, DMC 3/8, BNA. Since 1880 Mariri had been complaining about his low wages: L. Mariri to P. Brink, 8 Oct. 1880 (letter in SeTswana, translation in Dutch in P. Brink to J.H. Neethling, 8 Oct. 1880), 15/4/3/2 (B), DRCA; H. Gonin to DRC, 9 Oct. 1880, 15/7/2 (B), DRCA.

51 Minutes, Bechuanaland District Committee, 9 Feb. 1886, box 44, LMS; W. Price to W. Thompson, 16 Jun. 1884, box 42, LMS; and J. Brown to W. Thompson, 4 Dec. 1885, box 43, LMS. Matsau's daughters were married to Linchwe's brothers and close advisors, Ramono and Segale. For Matsau, see also ch. 7.

52 Shillington (1985: 123–165).

Chapter seven

THREAT FROM THE SOUTH

Since the Protectorate was proclaimed in this country, we spoke nothing to the Government, simply because we wanted to study the Government. (Linchwe, November 1894)

* * *

All these events and historical patterns and parallels were known to all the Batswana and their chiefs, and they all read the signs of the times into them. (Molema, Montshiwa)

The past was an incomplete guide for Linchwe and his advisors now facing British officials. The men who ruled the BaKgatla had sharpened their survival skills by contending with AmaNdebele, maBuru and BaKwena – cattle-keepers and hunters at heart like themselves. BaKgatla were used to *thinking* like their enemies.[1] A man's worth came from the animals he could take, the land he could keep in crops and the inferiors he could control to look after both. Men went to war to increase their individual worth, not to sacrifice themselves for others. Power came as a concession of many to the few willing to help men organise to increase their worth, rather than just to help themselves. The maKgoa now coming from the south were different. Apart from the occasional missionary interpreting for them, none of these maKgoa knew seTswana or seBuru, his languages, and none had the time to learn. They were coming into the territory to camp, not settle, and moving about constantly on horseback or wagon. They made up their minds quickly about this kgosi or that, and passed on their impressions to the maKgoa making decisions.

'Studying the Government', as Linchwe put it, meant sorting out the differences among the maKgoa who rode into Mochudi with varying holds on his future. Dealing with maKgoa, no less than maBuru, over the years had also taught them that the deeds of white people, as opposed to their words, determined their true intent. This skill put them in good stead with the seemingly headless Bechuanaland Protectorate administration, which, after being informally declared in Linchwe's kgotla in April 1885, repeatedly altered policy in its first ten years. Linchwe and his advisors some

167

how managed to interpret correctly key, usually sudden, shifts in colonial behaviour and respond by choosing the safest path – and Linchwe changed the way he behaved. The wild intensity that characterised his success as a war leader now gave way to quieter arts. Like Kgamanyane and Pilane, Linchwe was equipped to run a predatory community – knowing when to be ruthless and violent, so as to raise the odds of success. However, in the 'Protectorate', as the maKgoa called it, Linchwe learned that appearance at times carried more force than deeds. His fate and that of the Kgatleng under seKgoa rule would depend on how he was perceived by white officials, none of whom knew him.

In the first decade of colonial rule, the BaKgatla presented themselves as the loyal subjects of England's Queen Victoria. Professing loyalty to a supreme, distant and unknown monarch provided advantages in dealing with white men in the neighbourhood impatient to seize land and fill their pockets. An added danger was the presence of British officials who promoted the extension of white Cape rule. The BaKgatla had already learned from Britain's annexation of the Transvaal that the British were not the kind-hearted souls they professed to be. It did not take the BaKgatla long to discover that some who wore the Queen's uniform and pronounced Protectorate policy were, at heart, pro-Cape men. Usually they proved to be the friends of Cecil Rhodes and, after 1889, favourable to the interests of Rhodes's British South Africa Company (BSA Company). In order to obstruct and divert these agents of Cape colonialism, the BaKgatla quietly formed alliances with other people, black and white, who likewise perceived the threat from the south. Linchwe was prepared to work with white men who had an interest in keeping his kingdom intact, and he soon buried differences with old enemies in order to pool valuable information.

After struggling for generations to survive and rebuild their little kingdom, Linchwe and his people lived with no illusions. They knew the balance of their fate could easily be tipped by the will of the Queen, who alone had enough power to control her white subjects. They were painfully aware, too, that the Queen's will was unreliable. As recently as August 1881, the British had formally handed the Transvaal back to the Boers over the protests of Africans gathered in Pretoria for the occasion, including Linchwe's own representatives, Bogatsu and Tshomankane.[2] In 1885, therefore, when they were told that the Queen had decided to 'protect' them from the maBuru, the BaKgatla did not bother to ask 'why?', 'in what manner?' or 'for how long?' No official arriving in Mochudi would, at any rate, have given honest, much less correct answers to such questions. For one thing, the British government they represented had itself no clear idea of what future was in store for the Protectorate, much less the BaKgatla. For another, the officials sent to announce its declaration had their own, private designs for committing the Crown to the direct administration of this vast territory. Thirdly, neither the Crown nor these self-appointed imperialist officials were strong enough to prevent officials with pro-Cape sentiments from determining in the short run which purposes the new Protectorate would serve. From the beginning the Protectorate never spoke with one voice, to Linchwe or to any other of the Bechuanaland dikgosi. The men who represented the Crown invariably represented other, more immediate interests. The Crown was both a symbol of their authority and a cover for their personal ambitions. The Queen's Men were obliged, therefore, to function at varying levels of deceit, not only in their dealings with dikgosi, but with each other.

The Warren Expedition

In April and May 1885, Major General Sir Charles Warren and his officers passed on horseback through Kanye, Molepolole, Mochudi and ultimately to Shoshong for the official purpose of informing the respective dikgosi that the British government had assumed jurisdiction over their countries.[3] In 1884 Warren had ended ZAR hopes for westward expansion by driving Boer freebooters out of Stellaland and Goshen and declaring a protectorate over the BaTlhaping and BaRolong. By ordering Warren yet further north in 1885, London was extending the British sphere in order, so it professed, to prevent the ZAR and the Germans in South West Africa from linking up across the Kalahari.[4]

In addition, Warren and his principal assistant, ex-LMS missionary Rev. John Mackenzie, were hoping to use the expedition to involve Britain in a much more direct, imperial commitment. They were convinced that Britain would have to set up its own administration in the Protectorate in order to safeguard the interests of Africans from the evils of all white colonials, especially those from the Cape. Though apprehensive about the intentions of the ZAR Boers, Warren and Mackenzie feared more the Cape men, who had been responsible for most of the land-grabbing in Griqualand West and Stellaland, and whose hand was also apparent in Goshen.

Wanting to prevent Cape expansion, Warren and Mackenzie envisaged a Protectorate in which settler-farmers sent out from Britain would increase productivity, stimulate fair commerce and promote the Christianisation of the African population. By using Mackenzie's influence with the 'LMS chiefs' (Gaseitsiwe, Sechele and Khama), they hoped to obtain land concessions with which to lure the Colonial Office into converting the Protectorate into a Crown Colony.

As the expedition passed through each of the capitals en route to Shoshong, Warren and Mackenzie kept quiet about their grand scheme and their fears regarding the Cape colonials. Publicising either would have exceeded their orders and incited opposition from the Cape Government – in short, have jeopardised their ulterior mission. So, instead, they confined themselves to justifying the declaration of the Protectorate in terms of the 'Boer Threat'. Though in Kanye, Gaseitsiwe begrudgingly accepted these reasons (the previous year filibusters from the ZAR had raided more than one thousand head of Ngwaketse cattle),[5] at Molepolole Warren and Mackenzie encountered real resistance. Sechele and Sebele rejected the notion that the BaKwena needed any protection from the Boers. Protection from the BaKgatla, perhaps, but not from the maBuru. Since the Boer attack on Dimawe in 1852, neither the ZAR nor any of its white residents had threatened to seize land from or attack the BaKwena or any other of the people Warren and Mackenzie had earmarked for protection. Sechele, no doubt rankling from Britain's abrupt abandonment of the Transvaal and their failure to restrain Linchwe, was content at this moment to tell Warren and Mackenzie that the BaKwena would protect themselves. Repeatedly he probed Warren for a more rational reason for the presence of his expedition.[6]

In Mochudi, Linchwe bypassed the Boer issue and went straight to the question that mattered. He wanted to know what the British were going to do about Sechele's long-standing claims to Kgatla territory.[7] Linchwe assumed that Warren and Mackenzie had come to revive Britain's interests west of the Madikwe River that, in 1881, Wolseley had abandoned along with his Transvaal administration. Linchwe, who since the days of John Moffat had associated LMS missionaries with the show of British power, also expected Mackenzie, like Moffat, to side with the BaKwena.[8] Mackenzie disclaimed any concern for the Kgatla–Kwena dispute and ignored the assumptions underlying Linchwe's question, but events were to prove Linchwe right. The expedition, which paused briefly in Mochudi, soon departed for Shoshong, where Warren and Mackenzie were pinning all their hopes for a major land concession.

Upon reaching Shoshong, Warren and Mackenzie were warmly received. In 1876 Khama had appealed to British High Commissioner at the Cape for protection against the Dorsland Trekkers and claimed to have formed an 'alliance' with Britain.[9] He was now willing to cooperate by making his 'magnificent offer' of a large territory for the settlement of British farmers. Its boundaries represented, in Neil Parsons's words, 'a great sweep through present-day western [Zimbabwe] to [the] Gwani-Zambezi confluence'.[10] Khama, who anticipated conflict with the AmaNdebele and the ZAR, sacrificed little to the British Protectorate, which in turn he could use to safeguard his eastern border; moreover the tract he offered to Britain he did not actually control, and the white farming settlement envisaged would stand conveniently outside Khama's territory and inside Lobengula's.[11]

On their return to Mafikeng, Warren and Mackenzie succeeded in gaining similar concessions from Sechele and Gaseitsiwe.[12] Like Khama, Sechele and Gaseitsiwe handed over territory to the east, where they exercised no effective authority. It was a free investment for showing loyalty to the Crown and one that promised substantial future returns. By accepting the concessions, Warren and Mackenzie were recognising Sechele and Gaseitsiwe's territorial claims that the BaKwena and BaNgwaketse would be in a position to revive if white settlement did not materialise (the maBuru, after all, had never regarded these areas as suitable for their settlements, so why should the maKgoa find them any different?). Thus, on the map accompanying Warren's report of the expedition, Sechele's grant to the British Queen consisted of all the land between the Ngotwane and Madikwe rivers. Having passed through that concession to and from Shoshong, both Warren and Mackenzie knew full well that it was controlled by Linchwe, but Warren made no mention of this fact in his report.[13]

Warren's report, which proposed using the concessions to make Bechuanaland a Crown Colony complete with an imperial administration and police force, was quickly rejected by the Colonial Office. The eclipse of Mackenzie-styled imperialism in mid-1885 by proponents of Cape expansionism is a well-known story. While Warren and Mackenzie moved through the new Protectorate, Gladstone's government fell with the loss of Khartoum, and was replaced by Salisbury's, which favoured enlarging the British Empire while opposing the extension of imperial authority. Salisbury regarded the former as necessary to prevent other European powers from gaining an upper hand in the quest for territory, the latter, to avoid unpopular costs of administration and military protection. Though itself short-lived, Salisbury's ministry set in motion a southern African policy that prevailed for the next ten years. After recalling the Warren Expedition, Salisbury turned to the Cape Government as its ally in preserving Britain's claims in the northern interior. He encouraged the Cape to annex British Bechuanaland and assume authority for the governing of the Bechuanaland Protectorate.[14]

Standing in the way of immediate Cape expansion was the financial obstacle that had occasioned the imperial retreat. The Cape Government wanted control over the new territories to the north but lacked the capital to fulfil its ambitions. Its recent failure to impose effective administration in Basutoland also increased restraint among the most ardent Cape expansionists. In time they would clamour for British Bechuanaland and the Bechuanaland Protectorate, but in 1885 Britain had no choice but to give birth to and care for the twin territories it had already put up for adoption.

The result – the Queen's proclamation of 30 September 1885, which brought into formal existence the Crown Colony of British Bechuanaland and the Bechuanaland Protectorate – was as could be expected. Both Colony and Protectorate were placed under the Governor of the Cape Colony, acting as High Commissioner. The Colony was to be administered by the handful of officers placed there in 1884, augmented by the single appointment of Administrator of British Bechuanaland, with his headquarters at Vryburg. In the Protectorate itself, no civil officers were stationed at all. This much larger addition to the British Empire was recognised simply by placing it under the Administrator at Vryburg, attaching to his title 'Deputy Commissioner for the Protectorate', and allowing him to use thirty or so mounted 'Bechuanaland Border Police' with which to exercise authority over an area equal in size to England, Wales and Scotland combined. Thus the Bechuanaland Protectorate, which was conceived by Warren and Mackenzie as a white settler colony, denied by Salisbury as an unwanted expense, and maintained by Britain as a charge for the Cape, became the neglected orphan of the Empire, with no party accepting full responsibility for its future.

The BaKgatla and the Early Protectorate

In Mochudi the new Protectorate was so inert as to be acceptable. In contrast to neighbouring dikgosi, Linchwe had anticipated no advantages from the coming of British rule and therefore welcomed its lifeless appearance. Khama was disappointed that his concession of land had been rejected by Salisbury, and it rankled with Sechele that, after cooperating with Warren and Mackenzie, the British did not reciprocate by supporting his claims over the BaKgatla. It is possible that the DRC missionary in Mochudi at the time, Reverend Pieter Brink, had read the newspaper reports about Warren's proposal and about Salisbury's acceptance instead of the much scaled-down administrative plan (upon which the 30 September proclamation was based) drawn up by Hercules Robinson, the Cape Governor and also the new High Commissioner for the Protectorate.[15] With some confidence, at any rate, the BaKgatla regarded the initial and infrequent comings and goings of the Bechuanaland Border Police (BBP) as posing no threat. In welcoming Col. Frederick Carrington, Commander of the BBP, on his first visit to Mochudi, Linchwe calmly walked up to Carrington and stroked the Commander's enormous moustache.[16]

For three years, Linchwe had neither a single grievance against the Protectorate nor a complaint against any one of its officials or police. Until November 1888, he and his people remained unaware that Carrington and the other men running the Protectorate were working for Cecil Rhodes. While preoccupied with Khama and Lobengula, officials largely ignored the Kgatla kgosi and played deaf to Sechele's claims on Kgatla territory. Linchwe may have even felt gratitude towards the Deputy Commissioner, who in 1886 refused to assist a Boer farmer to collect a fine from the kgosi that had been awarded by a Transvaal court.[17]

Any feelings of security the BaKgatla may have felt in the initial years of Protectorate rule were countered by their sense of isolation. The BaKgatla were still regarded as intruders by most of the Protectorate peoples with whom they had any contact, and they were being cut off from the Transvaal. Under Kruger the ZAR's new 'squatter' law was squeezing the Saulspoort BaKgatla off their old farms and driving them to Bechuanaland.[18] Only the DRC connection kept Linchwe linked to the Transvaal, but DRC missionaries lacked leverage with the British. Unlike the LMS, which aligned its religious aims with British 'protection' of BaTswana, the DRC stayed aloof from the Protectorate. Linchwe was isolated, too, by years of resistance to Sechele's rule and bad relations with J.S. Moffat and other LMS men. Sechele and the LMS had contacts that extended to British Bechuanaland, down to the Cape and all the way to Britain. Not until Linchwe came to peaceful terms with the BaKwena, in mid-1888, did he and the BaKgatla begin to enter the main arena of Protectorate politics. Though no doubt in tune with events in the region prior to that time, the BaKgatla remained alone in interpreting them.

The more firmly established and better-connected Tswana elites in the southern Protectorate were watching developments within the Protectorate and beyond its southern border with growing apprehension. The BaKwena and BaNgwaketse remained in close contact with each other during the 1885–1888 period, and through their connection with the BaRolong they would have been aware of the disturbing events taking place in British Bechuanaland. There, under the same officials who were responsible for administering the Protectorate, a series of laws were being imposed on Africans to bring the Colony in line with the Cape. These measures included the introduction of hut tax, African and European locations, and the cattle trespass system, as well as the denial to Africans of private ownership of land. The ZAR looked enlightened by comparison.[19] In 1886 Montshiwa of the BaRolong protested openly against these and other laws introduced by Sir Sidney Shippard, the Administrator, and in 1888 when rumours circulated that British Bechuanaland was to be annexed to the Cape, Montshiwa held protest meetings in Mafikeng and at Pitsani, inside the Protectorate.[20] Disquiet increased among the BaNgwaketse and BaKwena as Shippard's officials in the Protectorate befriended the BaNgwato and established their principal base at Shoshong. The Protectorate obtained Khama's loyalty by hindering Sechele's attempts to push Kgari's claim to the Ngwato chieftaincy, by awarding Khama access to the valuable Lephepe wells in Kwena territory, and by condoning a Ngwato military expedition against the BaSeleka on the ZAR border.[21]

Another source of concern to the southern Protectorate dikgosi, and one that Linchwe especially would have appreciated, was the rapidly changing role that the Protectorate had assumed since the discovery of gold on the Witwatersrand in 1886. In Mochudi and the other Tswana capitals, pressure from two new forces emanating from the South was felt almost immediately. Kgatla men, who had engaged themselves since 1877 as labourers in the diamond mines of Kimberley, readily became part of the

*Sidney Godolphin Alexander Shippard, circa 1888.
Sketch by Lemington Muzhingi.*

Tswana labour pool for extracting auriferous ore.[22] While black miners were departing from the Kgatleng and other parts of Bechuanaland and making their way south, white prospectors were passing them on the road and travelling in the opposite direction.

By mid-1887, gold was believed to exist in the Protectorate. In the granite hills around Kanye, an Australian 'gold digger' reported to Shippard that sample deposits 'showed every other sign [than actual gold] connected with gold bearing reefs'. He speculated, too, that 'there are probably a great many more reefs in the country along the Transvaal Border which we have not seen'.[23] Shippard, who then had official and missionary reports to hand, condemning the practice of slavery in the Protectorate, readily grafted moral purpose onto political control and material gain.

> The remedy [to the eradication of slavery in the Protectorate] can be prescribed in one word – Annexation – and its application is a mere question of money . . . From recent accounts which I consider trustworthy, I have every reason to believe that the revenue which could be derived from gold mines would ultimately more than cover the cost of administering the present Protectorate.[24]

Shippard's confidential report failed to elicit a response from the High Commissioner or the Cape Government, but its leaked contents aroused interest among gold-seekers already active in British Bechuanaland. By August, LMS missionary Charles Williams arrived in Taung from Molepolole to report that 'companies are being formed and prospecting parties are constantly coming up'. In December, Alfred Wookey, Williams' replacement in Molepolole, wrote that 'gold seekers are coming this way . . . [E]very man who comes wants a whole territory for himself'.[25]

Until 1887 Mochudi had been the residence of a few missionaries and storekeepers, and a stopover point for white hunters, explorers, labour recruiters, traders and the Queen's officials. Thereafter, gold concessionaires of varying backgrounds and descriptions ('some of the greatest scoundrels on earth', winced one missionary) streamed into the Protectorate from the Cape and the Transvaal, entered Mochudi and other capitals, and besieged the dikgosi with promises and pieces of paper. The white rush for gold mining concessions was the signal that Protectorate land, which had proved uninviting to generations of maBuru and maKgoa settlers, had suddenly risen in value.

Cecil Rhodes in the Protectorate

No gold was found in Bechuanaland, but the belief that it would be remained, and the Protectorate increased in importance because it stood between the legendary gold fields of Zimbabwe and a host of white men jostling their way north to lay claims in the land of King Solomon's mines. The Road to the North, established by missionaries and traders in the mid-1800s and enclosed within British Bechuanaland and the Bechuanaland Protectorate, had become the principle avenue of a new thrust for the control of the southern African interior. Beyond the Protectorate's northeast boundaries, Lobengula controlled from his capital, guBulawayo, the heart of the territory which Cecil Rhodes, along with other maKgoa, believed was destined to become a second Witwatersrand.

Between early 1887 and late 1889, Rhodes took part in the ungoverned contest among the gold seekers for control of Lobengula's territory and that of the Shona further east. The diamond magnate, who derived great financial power from De Beers and Consolidated Gold Fields, emerged victorious by buying out other concessionaires and raising the capital and influence necessary with which to obtain a royal charter for the British South Africa Company (BSA Company), for the purpose of opening up 'Rhodesia' to gold mining, white settlement and British (i.e. BSA Company) rule. The British government welcomed Rhodes's plan for personally advancing the empire northward, and they readily turned a blind eye to his methods. By accepting the legitimacy of the Rudd Concession, which Lobengula loudly repudiated, the Crown laid the cornerstone of Rhodes's future edifice, and the men Rhodes harnessed with money to his 'grand design' included not only a substantial crowd of self-seeking white concessionaires and adventurers, but Britain's own officials in the Cape Colony, the Colony of British Bechuanaland and the Bechuanaland Protectorate. From 1887, as they manoeuvred their way into Lobengula's court and obtained the crucial concessions, Rhodes's men worked along the Road to the North, between Kimberley and guBulawayo, safeguarding the avenue for Rhodes's future takeover of the country of the AmaNdebele and MaShona, as well as the Bechuanaland Protectorate.

The outer garment of Rhodes's imperial dream, which he and many of his biographers wore with pride, has been removed by historians to expose the substance of his greed and the corruptibility of the men who served him.[26] Among those who actively supported Rhodes and became central to his plan were the senior officials of the Protectorate, of whom all but one were rewarded with shares in Rhodes's financial ventures. The High Commissioner, Hercules Robinson, Deputy Commissioner S.G.A. Shippard, Robinson's former secretary and Acting Deputy Commissioner, F.J. Newton, and the Commander of the Bechuanaland Border Police, Frederick Carrington, all worked closely together and put pressure on other officials to act in Rhodes's favour. Their communication network provided Rhodes with valuable information, and they used their positions in other ways for promoting Rhodes's interests and obstructing those of his opponents. Under their authority, the Protectorate became the base for obtaining the Rudd Concession, assembling the 'Pioneer Column' and, ultimately, in 1893 the launching of a combined force against Lobengula's AmaNdebele. Only John S. Moffat remained immune to Rhodes's financial corruption, but the Assistant Commissioner fell victim instead to his imperial sales talk. Moffat's willingness to cultivate Lobengula and protect the Rudd Concession proved vital to Rhodes's success.[27]

Until 1889, when the BSA Company was in the process of being formed, the pro-Rhodes officials used the Protectorate as an avenue for advancing Rhodes's ambitions. In practical terms, this amounted to developing 'Mangwato' (Shoshong) as the primary base for influencing events in Lobengula's territory and preserving order along the major roads linking Shoshong with Mafikeng. Shoshong, the only terminal connecting guBulawayo with roads leading north through the Transvaal and Protectorate, was secured by basing a large BBP force nearby at Elebe and gaining Khama's support in patrolling the Macloutsie area, through which Transvaal Boers on horseback could slip into Ndebele country. With Moffat's posting to Shoshong in 1887, Khama's capital became Britain's northernmost station. To the south, where no stations existed, officials tried to occupy only the crevices between subject peoples. When conflict threatened to erupt between what Moffat termed the 'territorial chiefs' (Gaseitsiwe and Sechele) and the 'tenant chiefs' (Ikaneng and Linchwe), officials quickly appeared on the scene in a neutral, peacemaking role.[28] Jurisdiction within the respective territories was left almost entirely in the hands of the dikgosi. They retained a free hand in governing their peoples, granting concessions (Rhodes's people sought none in the Protectorate before 1890) and regulating the affairs of white traders in their midst. Police stationed in Kanye and Molepolole were there to intercept whites passing through and likely to cause trouble further north. Mistreatment or abuse of the locals was invariably followed by a fine or reprimand.[29]

The crowning virtue of the Protectorate scheme was that it cost Rhodes nothing. The shares Rhodes privately made available to Protectorate officials merely reduced in minute terms his looked-for profit, whereas their salaries and expenses came from the pockets of the British taxpayer. Khama's loyalty and support was freely acquired by allowing the Ngwato kgosi to help himself to important chunks of his neighbours' territory. Maintaining a large and costly police force could also be justified to the British Treasury by harping on the Transvaal Boer 'threat' or other drummed-up dangers, such as the threat of internal revolt, as was done on several occasions after the Kopong Conference in February 1889.

Sidney Shippard and the Kopong Conference

In late 1888 three dikgosi lifted the veil obscuring Rhodes's Protectorate scheme, and by the following February, at Kopong, they combined to oppose it. The three were Bathoen and Sebele, who had assumed most of the authority from their invalid fathers, and Linchwe. In 1888 the BaNgwaketse and BaKwena became even more suspicious about events that also aroused the BaKgatla. The competition at guBulawayo among concessionaires was disturbing, as was the July killing of Piet Grobler, a Boer trader passing through the disputed territory between Ngwato and Ndebele country. The revelation unfolded, however, in August that year, when Deputy Commissioner Sir Sidney Shippard entered the Protectorate for the first time. Shippard passed through Kanye, Molepolole and Mochudi en route to Baines Drift on the Limpopo to investigate the Grobler incident, and to guBulawayo for the purpose of assisting Rhodes's emissary, Charles Rudd, obtain the fateful concession from Lobengula. On his way to and from guBulawayo, Shippard's confidence and enthusiasm, filled by the recent surge in Cape colonial activity in British Bechuanaland and in Matebeleland, spilled over in his public utterances and disclosed to the southern Tswana his personal vision of the future Protectorate. In Mochudi, where he mistakenly believed BaKgatla allegiance to be firm, Shippard was especially indiscreet.

Shippard arrived in Mochudi a month following the Protectorate's resolution of another Kgatla–Kwena dispute, to Linchwe's satisfaction. At stake had been Linchwe's authority over concessions in the Kgatleng, whether

179

granted by Linchwe or Sechele. In early 1888 Linchwe had ejected from the Kgatleng one David Hume, a gold prospector to whom Sechele had granted a concession, and he angered Sechele further by awarding what appears to have been a concession to a group of white wood cutters. In March 1888 Major H.J. Goold-Adams of the BBP tried to persuade Linchwe to recognise Sechele as paramount in return for the latter's guarantee that the Kgatla could retain possession of their present territory. When Linchwe refused, Goold-Adams asked only that Linchwe refer to Government in the event of any future grievance against Sechele. Linchwe agreed. Then in Molepolole a few days later, Goold-Adams told Sechele that the Protectorate regarded Sechele as having 'sovereign rights' over the land occupied by the BaKgatla, but he added that Linchwe would have to give Hume permission to prospect in the Kgatleng.[30] In July, Moffat once more confirmed Linchwe's autonomy insofar as concessions were concerned. All concessionaires of Sechele, Moffat assured Linchwe, 'should not intrude upon ground occupied by Lenchwe's people without Lenchwe's consent'.[31] Thus, in August, when Shippard, Moffat's superior, paid his first visit to Mochudi and confirmed Moffat's decision before a large assembly, he received a cordial welcome.[32]

Like other officials at the time, Shippard had no quarrel with the BaKgatla, who had kept out of view and asserted themselves only when challenged by the BaKwena. Sechele repeatedly had pestered Shippard's men with complaints, and Gaseitsiwe, Bathoen and Sebele had given officials the impression they disliked British rule or were under the spell of the bottle. In contrast, Linchwe was regarded as well behaved and sober. The only concern with the BaKgatla was their proximity to the Transvaal and their likely use of it, in Moffat's words, 'as a background to their operations' in any future war with the BaKwena.[33] Moffat and Shippard assumed that the Transvaal had been lost to the BaKgatla since 1882 and presumed that the Kgatleng was ripe for Boer adventurers. In his remarks to Linchwe, therefore, Shippard dwelt at length on the evils of getting involved with filibusters. Without murmur the BaKgatla listened while Shippard related the story of the Kora and Tlhaping dikgosi Mosweu and Mankurwane, with whose tragedy the BaKgatla were already familiar.

Shippard, an overbearing man with set beliefs about the benefits of European rule, had arrived convinced that the BaTswana were dependent on the Border Police for protection, whether they would admit it or not.

Without asking Linchwe or his people a single question, he also assumed that the BaKgatla, wedged between the BaKwena and ZAR Boers, were the most dependent of all. Before the large assembly, gathered to receive Mochudi's most senior official visitor, Shippard had trouble resisting the temptation to overwhelm the BaKgatla with extraordinary pronouncements:

> [T]he time is probably not far distant when the whole of the country occupied by [Linchwe] on the west of the Transvaal border will, together with all the rest of the present Protectorate, be annexed to the dominions of the Great Queen, in which case magistrates will be sent to administer justice in the country and then there will no longer be any question of one chief paying tribute to another chief and people will then be equally subjects of the Great Queen and bound to pay tribute to Her Majesty Alone.

The silence that followed these words, intended by the Deputy Commissioner to arouse applause, effectively concealed their effect. Among the southern Tswana, Shippard seldom got the response he wanted. His assertion, that the dikgosi were about to be replaced with magistrates and that everyone would soon pay 'tribute', was ignored by Linchwe, who remarked only that 'he and his people desired nothing so much as to live at peace [with other BaTswana] under our protection', wrote Shippard, and expressed concern once more about Sechele's demands for tribute and sending 'men to search for gold . . . without asking [Linchwe's] permission'. Shippard asserted that he was 'opposed at present to the granting of concessions by any chiefs in the Protectorate to persons desirous of digging for gold', a statement that pleased Linchwe, and the Deputy Commissioner was afforded a warm farewell on his journey north.[34]

From this point, up to which the BaKgatla had been preoccupied with the irritations caused by Sechele's policy, Linchwe's circle became alert to the much greater dangers brewing. Shippard's appearance was the first sign that the agents of Cape colonialism were coming out in the open in the Protectorate. Wherever he happened to be, Shippard spelled trouble for Africans. His administration in British Bechuanaland had been strongly opposed by the BaRolong. Soon after Shippard departed from Mochudi for Macloutsie and guBulawayo, the BaRolong were protesting against the rumoured annexation of British Bechuanaland by the Cape Colony. Meanwhile, the nearby European community was extending a warm welcome

to a railroad survey party just arrived in Mafeking.[35] In August the Ba-
Kgatla had learned from Shippard himself that Lobengula had accepted
British protection through the agency of John Moffat, and in November
when Shippard passed back through Mochudi on his return from guBulawayo to Vryburg, they heard his disturbing reports about concessionaire activities in Matebeleland.[36]

Linchwe's conduct in Shippard's presence reveals that the BaKgatla
were aware of the significance of all these events. To the Deputy Commissioner, the kgosi expressed concern that regarding 'the ultimate preservation of peace especially in the north and northeast things looked very bad
indeed . . . In fact, he said, there is in reality no peace now in the land as
hostilities may break out at any moment'. Linchwe subtly rejected Shippard's authority by appealing to Modimo (God) for peace and by offering
to *assist* Protectorate officials 'in their efforts to secure it'. Linchwe knew,
nevertheless, that the BaKgatla, isolated as they were at that point, stood
to gain valuable time by reinforcing Shippard's assumptions of Kgatla
submissiveness, rather than by asserting their independence. Linchwe
feigned taking Shippard into his confidence by telling him that he was
'still too young for the burden of chieftainship' and left Shippard with the
impression that Linchwe 'appears to be intelligent enough to appreciate
the value of the protection afforded him . . . and he is evidently very anxious to maintain the most amiable relations with Her Majesty's Government'. Shippard responded with assurance that the 'Great Queen' –
and Shippard himself – would look after the BaKgatla.[37] For the time being
Linchwe had found the measure of Shippard.

Before leaving Mochudi, Shippard also displayed to the BaKgatla his
penchant for shifting ground while covering tracks. His August remarks
about future annexation had stirred alarm in Cape Town and London,
from which Shippard received telegraphed instructions to retract what he
had said to the BaKgatla and, as it subsequently came to light, to the Ba-
Kwena as well.[38] At their November meeting, on his return from guBulawayo, Shippard told Linchwe he had received a 'distinct intimation of the
policy of Her Majesty's Government with regard to the question'. Shippard
alleged he was now instructed

> To inform [Linchwe] that Her Majesty's Government had no inten-
> tion of annexing any portion of the Protectorate unless compelled to

> do so in the interests and at the request of the natives themselves . . .
> Her Majesty's Government desire nothing better than to see the Be-
> chuana Chiefs continue to govern their respective tribes as at present,
> that sending them European Magistrates and increased [*sic*] Police
> Force, erecting Government buildings, etc. would occasion a heavy
> outlay in a country which would yield no adequate return in the form
> of revenue, and that the British taxpayer would strongly object to any
> such expenditure.

Having issued the retraction, Shippard then took it back. Though in the Queen's service, the Deputy Commissioner preferred indulging his personal predictions in the presence of black subjects.

> Lenchwe might regard annexation . . . as out of the question except in
> one of three contingencies, viz. war with the Transvaal or filibuster-
> ing raids from the Transvaal on a large scale, civil war between the
> Bechuana Chiefs themselves and lastly the influx of a large European
> mining population . . . that while [Her Majesty's Government] would
> endeavour to preserve the protected Chiefs from the danger of attack
> from the Transvaal it remained with themselves to maintain peace with
> their immediate neighbours in the Protectorate and to refuse applica-
> tions from Europeans for mineral concessions or prospecting licences.

Apart from declaring his peaceful intentions, Linchwe responded to Shippard's words on annexation with silence.[39] At about this time, several Tswana groups adopted an unsavoury nickname for Shippard – they dubbed him *Morena Maaka* ('King of Liars'). His subsequent appearance among the BaNgwaketse, BaKwena and BaKgatla occasioned outspoken resentment among their dikgosi.

Strong feelings against Shippard surfaced three months later in a meeting at Kopong, on the border between the Kgatleng and Kweneng. Linchwe, Sebele, Bathoen, Khama, kgosi Ikaneng of the BaLete and kgosi Gaborone of the BaTlokwa, with an estimated 1,500 followers, attended. Shippard called the meeting after Sebele and his Kwena royal supporters expressed a wish of having dikgosi gather to discuss their differences. When calling the meeting, however, Shippard circulated an agenda of seven items that suggested the meeting would go far beyond the issue of reconciliation among BaTswana. Included among the topics were increasing the number of police and BBP stations, digging wells, building telegraph and railway lines and levying hut tax. Shippard downplayed these items as 'merely thrown out for discussion', and that decisions at Kopong would be restricted to the threats posed by internal disputes and filibusters.[40] The dikgosi, however, did not read it that way. Linchwe was convinced that the Kopong assembly was an excuse to announce a British takeover – which he intended to resist – and he wanted the ZAR's support. He sent two emissaries to H.P. Malan to warn ZAR president S.J.P. Kruger that Linchwe did not 'want anything to do with the English', that he was taking two mephato to Kopong to resist any attempt to force him to accept a railroad and telegraph, and that in the event of an English attack, he asked the ZAR to back him. The BaKgatla, Linchwe assured Kruger, remained loyal to the ZAR, in accordance with Linchwe's pledge to Kruger back in 1882.[41]

Shippard took for granted that the dikgosi needed him to keep out the Boers. Even if we exclude the BaKgatla, though, the BaTswana without ties to the ZAR saw in Shippard's agenda the means, not by which Boers would be kept out, but by which Shippard's people would come in. Bathoen, unaccustomed to directness, put it obtusely: 'We are very glad about peace but if Government says 'You *must* do this or that' we cannot do it.' Sebele's tone was aggressive, but his words fell shy of meaning: 'We do not know who is attacking us . . . From what are we to be defended? Have you come and found us lost? We never pay tax and we will not pay tax. Those are my last words.' Linchwe, however, put it bluntly.

> I have no one who would protect me but God. Our great protectorate is God. I have heard that you have come to protect this country . . . I have not asked you to come and assist me . . . All of us Bechuanas are under the sun, each in his own village and will fight against attack. I am close to the border and there is no war. If I were attacked I would . . . ask my people for assistance. I should wish to live at peace with the English and also to visit the Boers as we do the English . . . I do not wish either the Boers or the English to come and take our chieftainship from us . . . God will protect us if the Protectorate is withdrawn.

Once Linchwe finished, Shippard closed the day's discussions, and the following morning he announced that the meeting was terminated altogether. When Africans resisted him, Shippard became testy. 'Further discussion would be useless', Shippard declared; while he had come 'with the most kind and friendly intentions towards you', he had been 'met in a very different spirit'. '[Y]ou have evidently made up your minds on every point before coming here.' Shippard prophesied the harm that would come because Linchwe and Sebele rejected 'our assistance and flatly refuse to contribute in any way towards the necessary expenses of the Protectorate'. The railways would now be lost to the Transvaal and, with it, support in Parliament for the retention of the Protectorate.[42]

Kopong represents the first instance of opposition to Protectorate rule by a combined Tswana leadership. Shippard was struck by Bathoen, Sebele and Linchwe's 'defiant attitude . . . which is impossible to convey . . . adequate[ly] through the minutes of the meeting'. Having convinced himself beforehand that all Tswana dikgosi were divided against one another and in agreement only on the desirability of protection, Shippard discounted their opposition at Kopong as merely irrational. Sebele was 'very vain . . . given to much blustering . . . devoid of common sense and thoroughly disaffected'; Bathoen, merely 'following Sebele's lead'. They in turn, 'seemed to be greatly influenced by Lenchwe . . . a man of very limited capacity though not devoid of cunning'. Three months prior to Kopong, Shippard believed that Linchwe was 'very anxious to maintain the most amiable relations' with the Crown. After Kopong, Shippard was convinced Linchwe was 'undoubtedly maintaining a good understanding with the Boers of Marico District to whom he would readily furnish information of all our movements'. The man who had twice impressed Shippard with his loyalty was now guilty of colluding with the Boers. Shippard was guessing. He was right, but he was guessing. He had no knowledge that Linchwe had approached Pretoria to join him against England. Shippard judged Africans based on whether or not they looked up to him, and his speculation as to Linchwe's collusion with the Marico Boers – with whom Linchwe had never had cordial relations – was provoked no doubt by Linchwe's blunt rejection of Shippard's words at Kopong.[43] Shippard resented that the dikgosi would not accept the official interpretation of the dangers facing the BaTswana. Having underestimated their ability to see beneath the surface of things, Shippard resorted to threats, at Kopong and thereafter. He used their 'disaffection' in his reports to justify requests for more Border Police within the Protectorate.

At Kopong Shippard also showed his susceptibility to Khama's strategy of pitting the BaKwena and BaKgatla against the Protectorate administration. Khama strengthened his position *vis-à-vis* their own by skilfully using rumours to increase official fear of resistance from the southern Tswana. In private, Khama informed Shippard that Linchwe 'entertains no friendly sentiments towards the English or himself'. LMS missionary Rev. A.J. Lloyd was told that Sebele had attempted to involve Khama in a plan to 'open fire' on Shippard and other whites at the conference, a story that Lloyd readily passed on to Shippard.[44] For years to come, Khama planted similar types of disinformation in order to insure that, when disputes arose between himself and the two adjacent dikgosi, senior officials would decide in his favour.

Kopong marks a sudden shift in the official attitude toward Linchwe. In Vryburg and Cape Town, where he had been regarded as a minor figure when recognised at all, Linchwe's dramatic appearance at Kopong made him for years a major suspect of intrigue and opposition to Protectorate interests. Also, within the Protectorate, Linchwe became one of the principal scapegoats for police, European wagoneers and men such Khama who played on the ignorance of senior officials for the purpose of concealing their own ambitions. Next to Bathoen and Sebele, already unpopular with Shippard, Linchwe paid the heftier price for speaking out at Kopong. His boldness may have gained him the confidence of the BaKwena and Ba-Ngwaketse, whose support and knowledge the BaKgatla needed to reduce their isolation. To protect himself and his people, however, Linchwe could hardly afford to continue the defiant role performed at Kopong, lest he increase the wrath of Shippard and others like him. Nor was he prepared to act the English sycophant – as had Khama and was already Ikaneng of the BaLete – without hastening the process of Cape colonial rule and losing his chance for ZAR support. Linchwe needed the Transvaal, even though the ZAR was slowly turning its back on its old connection with the Ba-Kgatla. In 1887 the ZAR Volksraad enacted the *Plakkerswet* (Squatters Law), and ZAR officials began enforcing it the following year. In the Rustenburg District, BaKgatla and other Africans were forced out of their concentrated settlements and dispersed among Boer-owned farms. Rather than suffer living in small family groups on Boer farms, hundreds of BaKgatla migrated to Bechuanaland and streamed into Linchwe's settlements. By the time Linchwe attended Kopong, Mochudi itself had swollen by 50 percent.[45] Linchwe's defiant attitude at Kopong may have been as much an expression of anxiety over the threat of his loss of the use of the Transvaal, as it was an outburst of anger against the maKgoa who now threatened to enter the hard-won, and now over-crowded, Kgatleng. Thus, after his brief but damning appearance centre stage at Kopong, Linchwe studiously recast himself as an inconspicuous bit player. Seeking safety in the wings, he observed the flow of events, rarely voiced opinions and, when called on to speak, expressed loyalty to the Queen and the BaKgatla's desire for peace.

The British South Africa Company

At Kopong, Shippard had been aware that Cecil Rhodes was preparing to make his bid for control of the interior. In early 1889, negotiations between Rhodes, his rival concessionaires and the British government began in London. During the talks, the crown accepted Rhodes's offer to build the telegraph line from Mafeking to the Tati and to pay the salary of a British officer to be posted at guBulawayo. In October 1889, the British South Africa Company received its royal charter. Energy for the push north was released instantaneously, as the extension of the Cape railway, from Kimberley to Vryburg, got underway the same month. John Moffat, the new Assistant Commissioner for Matebeleland, was in post weeks later, and between Vryburg and guBulawayo, Colonel Carrington successfully opposed the Colonial Office's request for the diminution of the Border Police, with the justification of 'disaffection' among the Protectorate dikgosi.[46] Kopong, therefore, was a gift to senior Protectorate administrators, who were in need of a new *cause célèbre* to conceal from London the purpose of their activities. As Moffat noted, the 'Boer bogey is worn out'.[47]

Following Kopong, Linchwe sensed the danger and stayed out of view. Almost immediately he removed himself and many able-bodied men from Mochudi. Rumours circulated that the BaKgatla were preparing for war; in March Shippard dispatched Moffat to investigate. He found no cause for alarm, as 'the demeanour and conduct of the people is everything that could be desired'. Linchwe was absent, reported to be at his main cattle posts along the Madikwe, and many Kgatla men had gone to Kimberley and the Witwatersrand, 'which would certainly not be the case if hostilities were contemplated'.[48] At headquarters, however, suspicions remained strong that Linchwe and other southern dikgosi were fomenting trouble. In May, the Administration increased the Border Police numbers in the southern Protectorate. Troopers were stationed at Mochudi for the first time.[49] In the period leading up to the formation of the Company and for months thereafter, the strengthened police force was there to keep the people quiet. Linchwe murmured not a protest, but in September, when Sebele expressed dissatisfaction about police digging wells, Carrington silenced the Kwena kgosi by threatening to burn down Molepolole. In November Shippard told Bathoen his people were 'bound' to assist the police and the mail carriers.[50] The Protectorate had dispensed with the pretext of consultation.

In May 1890 the Protectorate began to apply pressure on the southern dikgosi to support the building of the BSA Company-funded telegraph line. The matter was forced on them by High Commissioner Hercules Robinson's replacement, Sir Henry Loch. A man who favoured the imperial annexation of the Protectorate, Loch was distrustful of Rhodes's company and remained immune to its corrupting influences. He was more than willing, however, to back the BSA Company and help them build their telegraph line to Macloutsie, which was becoming strategically important for the ultimate British takeover of Central Africa. Loch ordered Shippard to get Bathoen, Sechele, Ikaneng and Linchwe to agree to the line passing through their respective countries and to provide labour for its construction. Furthermore, Shippard had to get one of the dikgosi, preferably Sechele, to cede land for the erection of a police camp, 'as Khama has done'. Loch instructed Shippard to make Sechele aware that 'Her Majesty's Government protects natives at great expense to the British taxpayer', and that it was 'proper' therefore for Sechele to give freely of his land.[51]

When Shippard arrived in Kanye, Bathoen received him warmly but refused to sanction the telegraph or give away any of his land. He asserted that he had already signed over telegraph rights to the Kanya Exploration Company. A day later in Molepolole, Sechele told Shippard that permission to erect a telegraph line in the Kweneng had already been given, along with other rights, to a Johannesburg syndicate. He, too, refused to hand over any land for the use of the Border Police, and Shippard left Molepolole empty-handed.[52] Both gave Shippard friendly receptions, confident with their non-BSA Company concessions. Shippard had some success in Ramotswa, where Ikaneng offered 150 labourers. Ikaneng wanted to secede from Ngwaketse rule.

Before Shippard reached Mochudi, the construction of the telegraph had already begun. Linchwe received Shippard coolly. Untutored in the political advantages of concessions, Linchwe had brought in no syndicate or company with which to parry the thrust of the Administration and the BSA Company. Since Kopong he had shied from open quarrelling with the Administration, yet he was dead set against the telegraph line and unwilling to follow Ikaneng by offering to help the Administration as a way of asserting his authority independent of the BaKwena. His was a difficult moment. Linchwe's dilemma is revealed in Shippard's description of the kgosi as 'offhand' and his singling out Linchwe from the other dikgosi as the one who did not appear 'personally friendly'. Confronted once more with having to take a formal stand, Linchwe opted to withhold cooperation. 'He did not want a telegraph through his territory', reported Shippard, 'and [said] that he would not supply any labour for such a work from Mochudi'. Linchwe's forthrightness merely underlined his obloquy among the maKgoa.[53]

Linchwe's objections certainly did nothing to slow the telegraph's advance through the Kgatleng. Shippard and Loch regarded the intransigence of the three chiefs as troublesome roadblocks that they were obliged to remove quickly. Loch arbitrarily disallowed the concessions in order to clear the southern Protectorate for the BSA Company and open a path for the telegraph through land claimed by the BaLete and BaKgatla. Bathoen and Sechele's concessionaires went to court to challenge the legality of Loch's intervention. In response, Shippard protected the telegraph route by reviewing the jurisdiction of the various dikgosi and recommending that Ikaneng be declared a 'paramount chief' independent of Bathoen.[54]

Shippard did the same for Linchwe. In both cases the intent was to deprive Bathoen and Sechele's concessionaires of access to the territories through which the telegraph was to pass. Recognition as paramount in no way meant that Linchwe had earned the confidence of the administration. Shippard was convinced that he, Bathoen and Sechele were threats to the achievement of Cape and British imperial goals. As Shippard put it, 'one of the main difficulties in the southern Protectorate is the capacity with which the chiefs exercise the despotic power to which they cling tenaciously' and which 'policemen were a necessity to curtail'.[55] Shippard was sure that Linchwe was taking orders from Sechele on the telegraph issue and, though he and the BaKwena and BaNgwaketse had 'contemplated [no] armed resistance to the progress of telegraph construction work', Shippard suspected that Linchwe might interfere with construction if 'he could be sure of support both from Sechele and from his own people in the Transvaal'.[56] The Deputy Commissioner expected Linchwe to undercut the Administration as soon as it had its back turned. 'Should disasters occur in Matabeleland or Mashonaland', he speculated, 'Lenchwe would at once cut our wires and might even do worse'.[57]

The 'disasters', to Shippard's mind, were what Africans might precipitate now that the BSA Company's plan for the region was about to come into full view. Africans knew the telegraph was a communication device, and they also understood clearly that it pointed in the direction of future Cape expansion. Shippard was concerned that Africans might resist much more than telegraph construction, and his reports on Linchwe and others show his awareness that they regarded the telegraph as part of a larger threat. Shippard sent his 'disasters' telegram knowing, too, that Linchwe and the BaKgatla were about to witness the BSA Company's first daytime step toward establishing white settlers in 'Rhodesia'. Three days before, Shippard had been on hand when the larger part of the Company-sponsored 'Pioneer Column' left Mafeking en route to the Macloutsie, from which a march through Matabeleland to Mashonaland would be launched. In late May, the column passed through the Kgatleng. Made up of 234 wagons and 184 mounted 'Pioneers', the column stretched over three kilometres in length.[58] Among the BSA Company men were ex-Border Policemen. Moving up the Road to the North were also large reinforcements of Border Police who, along with 200 of Khama's men, met with the BSA Company column at the Macloutsie.[59]

As soon as the column reached the Macloutsie, rumours insinuating that Linchwe was preparing for war began to filter down to Shippard from the north. One, which Shippard heard from Carrington and passed on to Loch, alleged that Lobengula's envoys were in Mochudi.[60] Shippard confided to BSA Company secretary John Harris that the rumour had originated with Khama.[61] The second, which was passed on several days later by the Border Police, alleged that Linchwe had arranged for the purchase of 200 rifles 'for two oxen each' via the Transvaal from one Barney Maccabe.[62] This report originated from a Mochudi trader named August Querle, a friend of the Police and source of other false information.

It was becoming characteristic of Linchwe, whenever he sensed he was becoming the Administration's target of suspicion, that he quickly moved out of range. By the time the anti-Linchwe reports began to reach Shippard, Linchwe was heading south in an ox-wagon bound for Kimberley.[63] His trip, made on the pretext of meeting his brother Ramono, then returning from studies in Morija, was no more coincidental to the growing storm of events than had been the rumours of Khama and Querle. Linchwe journeyed south in order to undercut the campaign against him. By being absent in the safe confines of British Bechuanaland, Linchwe could not be held responsible for organising resistance in the Protectorate. Moreover, by passing through Mafeking, known since 1888 as the centre of white commercial opposition to Rhodes's ventures, he could shop for a concessionaire.

The Weil Concessions

Julius Weil, who ran a trading company in Mafeking, was one of a handful of wealthy townsmen in British Bechuanaland who looked on the Bechuanaland Protectorate as their backyard. These townsmen-traders acted as important middlemen between the Cape and Protectorate-based traders. After gold was discovered on the Witwatersrand, and before the ZAR erected custom houses next to British Bechuanaland, they also did much business supplying goods to the Reef.[64] The Mafeking group, situated as they were just outside the Protectorate and connected to long-established traders inside, were well positioned for acquiring concessions. Their fear of Rhodes and the Cape Government (the Mafeking traders and the Barolong opposed the annexation of British Bechuanaland) was an added incentive to stake their claims in advance of concessionaires from further away. In 1887 and 1888 they gained access to Bathoen and Sechele through local traders, who served as interpreters, and secured a variety of agreements governing communications and mineral exploration. When the BSA Company came into existence in late 1889, virtually all rights accruing from the Company's charter, insofar as Ngwaketse and Kwena territory was concerned, had been vested by their respective dikgosi in the hands of Mafeking concessionaires. Before the year was out, Loch tried to remove all these concessions, but his campaign met with considerable opposition from the concessionaires themselves, who took Her Majesty's Government to court.[65] One of the more determined opponents of BSA Company claims was Julius Weil, member of the Kanya Exploration Company, which had negotiated concessions with Bathoen. In late May 1890, Weil told Shippard, after the latter's return from visiting the dikgosi about the telegraph, that a 'strong legal case [exists] against the BSA to protect [our] concessions' and that we 'would fight it in the law courts in England if necessary'.[66]

While passing through Mafeking on his Kimberley trip, Linchwe met Weil and arranged for him to visit Mochudi. Within a month of Linchwe's return home, Weil arrived, met with Linchwe and his advisors before a large assembly (the translation was done by Charles Riley, Kanye trader and negotiator for the Kanya Exploration Company) and obtained two concessions, both of which were approved by all assembled. In one, Weil was given sole right in the Kgatleng to prospect for minerals 'and precious stones' and, in another, to trade.[67] In payment, Linchwe received a sum that, by 1893, totalled between £1,600 and £1,700.[68]

The political, as much as the economic, significance of the Weil concessions was apparent to all parties affected. For the BaKgatla, Weil ended their dependence on petty traders operating out of the Transvaal and, for the first time, provided them with access to an established trading network connecting Mochudi to Molepolole, Kanye and Mafeking. Of equal importance, Weil immediately shelved his mineral concession and no prospecting took place.[69] At about this time, too, Linchwe proclaimed that any shiny stone uncovered by persons digging wells was to be promptly reburied.[70] In Molepolole, where concessions had been a bone of contention between the BaKwena and BaKgatla before the BSA Company was formed, Sebele willingly gave his agreement to the Weil Concessions.[71] The Administration tried disallowing them. Within two weeks of their signing, Shippard noted to Loch that they stood 'at variance' with British Bechuanaland Notice of 27 March 1888 and with the BSA Company charter. Loch then instructed Shippard to inform Weil that the concessions had been disallowed.[72] Weil, who was aware of the legal problems the British Government were already facing on the concession issue, ignored the order and confidently established himself in the Kgatleng. 'Almost at once', Weil took over trading stations in Mochudi, Sikwane and Ngotwane Junction and invested £3,000 in buildings.[73]

Linchwe's skill in creating small but effective obstacles was not appreciated by Loch, who regarded the kgosi as an irritant rather than a rational leader. The High Commissioner had been upset with Linchwe's refusal to help with the telegraph line in May, and Loch's belief in the likelihood of a rebellion involving Linchwe was encouraged by the Border Police. In June, while Linchwe was away in Kimberley, Loch considered a proposal from Carrington, entitled 'Prospect of Trouble in the Southern Protectorate', in which the Border Police Commander outlined his troop deployment contingency plans in the event of rebels stopping mail wagons, pulling up telegraph poles and 'closing the road to the North, probably at or near Lynchwe's'. Carrington's plan to march on Mochudi if necessary involved 230 Border Police, 100 British Bechuanaland 'volunteers' and several African levies, including 1,000–2,000 BaNgwato, 'which I understand [Khama] would be willing to supply'.[74] Though Linchwe's absence between May and July reduced the ability of the Police and their supporters from implicating him, Loch received word from Mochudi in late July that the BaKgatla were disrupting telegraph construction in the area and that large numbers of armed men, including BaKgatla just over from Saulspoort, were massing in the town, taking target practice and making other signs of war.[75] The sources of this almost completely bogus report were August Querle and, it was later discovered, two Boer mail riders.

In August, after Linchwe's return, a full report revealed that the BaKgatla had done little more than open a box of telegraph materials. Capt. Fuller, who investigated the incident, reported that Linchwe was 'very civil', apologetic 'and seems quite reconciled to the telegraph, not want[ing] to interfere with or hinder it in any way'. He would not allow a telegraph *office* to be built, however, alleging that 'the other people at Makose [Mokgosi's, i.e., Ikaneng's BaLete] and those at Shoshong [Khama's BaNgwato] would hear all the news, but that we would hear nothing'.[76] Linchwe was nevertheless called on to pay compensation and, at the instruction of Loch, 'informed that Government will not countenance any opposition on his part to the erection of a telegraph office at Mochudi, should one be considered necessary'.[77]

The Weil concessions, which were signed within days of this admonition, simply drew more attention to Linchwe and increased Loch's desire to be rid of him. The advantage of the concessions to Linchwe was their legality under the principles of Protection, namely that dikgosi retained authority over matters internal to their recognised territories. As was being argued at the time in London by concession lawyers, the declaration of the Protectorate did not 'restrict the right of the chiefs to alienate their resources'.[78] With the concession cases tied up in court, Loch lacked the legal force to deal with Weil, until such time as new laws were formulated to reduce the powers of the dikgosi. Weil knew, and most probably so did Linchwe, that Loch's order of 12 September disallowing the Weil concessions was, for the time being, a dead letter.

Within a day or so of issuing his order, however, Loch was presented with an unexpected, and welcome, opportunity to gain a measure of revenge. In Cape Town the High Commissioner received an official letter, dated 11 September from ZAR State Secretary W.J. Leyds requesting that the Protectorate consider transferring half the territory of Linchwe and his people to the Zuid-Afrikaansche Republiek. 'A large portion of [Linchwe's] people live within the borders of the Republic [i.e., in Saulspoort]', Leyds wrote, 'as they are fixed by the Convention of London, while the other portion of his people are resident outside these borders'. The ZAR desired to 'get this piece of ground joined to the Republic . . . for the preservation of safety, of peace and of order.'[79] Loch promptly forwarded this request to the Colonial Office, supporting the cession of the Kgatleng 'to the Notwane River but not across it' and 'provided due compensation was given'. Loch made no secret of his reasons for wanting to hand over the heart of Linchwe's territory to the Republilc. 'The chief has for some time', he noted, 'assumed an insolent attitude towards the British authorities in the Protectorate'.[80] Within a month, the Colonial Office approved Loch's request.[81] Up to this point Loch had been prevented by Bathoen, Linchwe and Sechele from acting freely, because the dikgosi had acted within Britain's declared principles of Protection, which accorded them full authority within their respective territories. They had professed loyalty, but they had used concessions and non-cooperation within their territories to thwart the unspoken, but governing, ambitions of the top officials of the Protectorate and the BSA Company. Loch's urgent desire to dispossess Linchwe of most of his territory reflects the inability of the Protectorate to act according to its wishes within the legal framework established in 1885.

Linchwe's rising notoriety, too, was a consequence of the importance attached by the Protectorate in 1890 to the Kgatleng as a vital communication link. The line of the telegraph, and that of the envisaged railway, passed well to the east of Kanye and Molepolole, the old way stations of the Road to the North. The new BSA Company avenue, which also carried an increasing flow of ox-drawn transport, coursed instead through Lete, Kgatla and Ngwato territory. By June 1890 the Kgatleng sat astride the 'major wagon route to the North'.[82] The Administration, and particularly the Border Police, were therefore even more sensitive to Linchwe's behaviour in 1890 than they had been before, and less worried about Sebele and Bathoen. Linchwe also stood in growing contrast to Khama and Ikaneng, who were not only cooperating with the Protectorate but encouraging officials to suspect the BaKgatla.[83] The reason why Loch could contemplate transferring part of Linchwe's country, given its strategic importance, was that Mochudi and all the BaKgatla settlements lay to the east of the new road. Loch could retain the vital strip and separate Linchwe's capital from the rest of his people.

Though the transfer was duly authorised, Loch was soon forced to retract his recommendation. He was ignorant about the geography of the land under his jurisdiction. In November 1890 he realised that, were he to reduce Linchwe's territory, he would deprive his Protectorate of the Madikwe River. A steam-driven railway coursing along the fringe of the Kalahari does not forswear surface water. Loch quickly backed down. He now set about reformulating the Administration's powers so that he could control Linchwe and the other dikgosi who had 'assumed an insolent attitude towards the British authorities', and carry out more effectively the imperial plan the Protectorate shared with the BSA Company.

The Proclamations of 1891

Loch's proclamations of 10 June, 27 June and 27 September created an internal administrative and court system for the Protectorate and endowed officials with legal authority over all peoples, be they African or otherwise. Based on Orders in Council issued from London, the proclamations extended the boundaries of the Protectorate northward to the Chobe/Zambesi rivers and west of Lobengula's territory, and constituted the area of jurisdiction of the Resident Commissioner, Assistant Commissioners and Magistrates appointed under the proclamations. Much has been written about how Loch exceeded the purport of the Orders in Council and converted the Protectorate into a colony. Whereas dikgosi previously had exercised supreme authority over their people and their lands, Loch turned Bechuanaland into a Colony in all but name, whereby the Administration arrogated unto itself the power to make laws, determine land ownership and regulate trade, licences and guns.[84] Instances of direct intervention are cited to illustrate how, with new laws and officials in place, the dikgosi rapidly lost authority to the Administration. Sillery's suggestion, however, that the proclamations represent a 'watershed in Protectorate affairs', exaggerates their significance at the time.[85] Though the proclamations were a clear indication that inroads on Tswana independence were taking place, the level of interference in Tswana affairs had been on the rise long before 1891. Similarly, the ability of Tswana leaders to parry the colonial thrust was reduced in the long run by Loch's proclamations, but events in the early 1890s show that when it came to fending off the Administration, their talent – and success rate – was not seriously impaired. The proclamations were promulgated in order to change the rules of the game in favour of Loch's position, but scoring in the contest between him and the southern dikgosi, particularly those he branded as opponents, remained more or less the same.

Kgatla–Protectorate relations continued as before. Linchwe avoided confrontation though he verbally protested or declined to cooperate when discomfited or pressed by the Administration. In response, the Administration used veiled threats, rather than took direct action, against him. Soon after August 1891, when mail coaches were routed through the narrow pathways of Mochudi, Linchwe complained to the Assistant Commissioner in the new administrative post at Gaberones that the safety of children and the elderly was being put at risk. In reply, Linchwe was invited to Gaberones and there given a demonstration by the police of a 'tree being shattered by a shot from the seven pounder – range about 120 yards'.[86] Nevertheless, the Administration hesitated to assert its authority in blanket-fashion, lest it provoke combined and open resistance in the southern Protectorate. In early 1892, Assistant Commissioners John Moffat and William Surmon counselled restraint on the part of the Administration regarding 'any attempt at land settlement' and introducing 'hut tax'. They predicted 'strong opposition' from the BaNgwaketse, BaKwena and BaKgatla 'unless a display of force were made' and reported that the dikgosi would not concede the government's right to grant land', irrespective of the proclamations. Moffat and Surmon advised that the Administration should 'encourage individuals and private syndicates' rather than assert its power over the dikgosi to grant land rights and refrain from asking them to pay hut tax until the amount raised would be 'worth the expense and danger'.[87] After 1891, as before, the Administration opted to deal with dikgosi one-on-one.

Until late 1893, only once did the Protectorate attempt to exercise authority over three or more dikgosi at a time. In May 1893, the Concessions Commission, headed by Surmon, summoned dikgosi from all over the Protectorate and began hearings on the numerous concessions issued by them before and since the granting of the BSA Company charter. Against protests by Linchwe, Sebele and several concessionaires, the Commission eventually recommended disallowing the large majority, on the grounds that the Administration had the ultimate right to recognise concessions and then in accordance with the royal BSA Company charter.[88] Even then, the Administration was obliged to suffer a partial reversal at the hands of the Colonial Office, which restored a portion of the concessions.[89] More than likely the dikgosi and their concessionaires ignored the Commission's directive, confident that the courts in England would eventually rule in their favour. Linchwe continued drawing £100 a year from Julius Weil for the 1890 mineral concessions, even though the concession had been disallowed the same year and disallowed once again by the Concessions Commission of 1893. When the Colonial Office upheld the Concession Commission in 1895, Linchwe and Weil simply wrote up another mineral concession![90]

The Administration could not deal with Linchwe as long as the Colonial Office was trying to hand the Protectorate over to the BSA Company. London, which looked to the BSA Company to carry the burden of empire, reined in Loch's impulse to impose Britain's authority. Rhodes, however, confined his company's activities largely to selling land to individuals and syndicates in 'Rhodesia' as a way of financing the Mashonaland administration and boosting BSA Company shares on the London exchange. Even though its charter guaranteed the BSA Company a virtual monopoly over mineral and trading concessions in the Protectorate, and the Concessions Commission was convened to clear the Company's path in this respect, Rhodes had no capital to assume responsibility for the Protectorate, and was content to leave it in Loch's hands.[91] Insofar as the territories of Linchwe and other dikgosi were concerned, initiative remained in the hands of the older syndicates and concessionaires. The dikgosi retained much of their internal authority because the Administration feared them as enemies of the imperial advance, and hesitated turning them into subjects fit for ruling, that is, until the invasion of Matebeleland in 1893.

The BSA Company launched its attack on Lobengula's forces in order to rescue the Company's declining prospects. Loch supported the invasion, and the Bechuanaland Protectorate Border Police, supported by 1,700 armed Ngwato sent by Khama at Loch's request, provided valuable assistance to the BSA Company's mercenary force. Linchwe was asked to provide at least a token regiment, but he declined.[92] After routing the AmaNdebele and killing Lobengula, the BSA Company proclaimed Rhodesia its territory and revived the Company's capital prospects. Rhodes was now ready to assume administrative control of the Protectorate, which the Colonial Office happily encouraged. Within a year and a half of the Ndebele defeat, the Colonial Office drew up plans to hand over the lion's share of the Protectorate to the BSA Company, much of Khama's country included.[93]

The BSA Company Takeover

Between 1885 and the Colonial Office's transfer of Protectorate administration to the Company, all the linkages for mollifying the evolving imperial dispensation steadily weakened and broke. The destruction of Lobengula, friendly to all of Britain's emissaries, and BSA Company expansion heightened dikgosi's suspicion of local white officialdom and fed determination to reach Britain's men at the top, as well as the Queen. The growing certainty of some form of BSA Company takeover also sharpened each kgosi's sense of self-preservation. The loose coalition of Bathoen, Sebele and Linchwe fragmented, as Khama abandoned his accommodationist policy and used his LMS connections to appeal directly to the Colonial Office. By July 1895, he had enrolled Bathoen and Sebele in his camp. Remaining dikgosi fended for themselves.[94] Both the pro-British Lete and anti-Cape Rolong (who, in November 1892, were awarded what became known as the Barolong Farms, inside the Protectorate[95]) were manoeuvred by Shippard into making fateful land concessions to the Company. Meanwhile, Julius Weil dickered with Rhodes's men over his fee for inducing Linchwe to accept Company rule.

In 1894, the new pattern became visible. In preparation for a land dispute with Linchwe, Khama used his tried and tested method of circulating rumours of a BaKgatla war scare to lower the Administration's view of his adversary. He implicated the BaKwena and BaRolong and, by guilt of association, the BaNgwaketse.[96] The Administration doubted Linchwe's desire for war, but the Gaberones garrison prepared for an attack on Mochudi in the event of a clash between Kgatla and Ngwato regiments.[97] In addition, in the Boundary Commission set up two months after the scare evaporated, Khama was awarded all the land stated in his original claim, a large strip of territory immediately north of the Kgatleng.[98] Linchwe's evidence, which testified to the BaKgatla having taken this area from the BaKwena in the 1870s, was dismissed, as were his separate appeals to Shippard and Loch for a review. During the dispute, the BaKwena remained unhelpful to the BaKgatla case and welcomed the final arbitration, which extended the old Lephepe wells boundary, separating Ngwato and Kwena territory, all the way to the Limpopo.[99] By implication, the Administration had reopened the question of Sebele's supremacy over Linchwe. With the Ndebele threat largely eliminated, the Administration was able to treat Linchwe indifferently. While they put aside Linchwe's claims in favour of Khama's, they had assumed authority also to divest him and other of the southern dikgosi of their recognised territories. In August they had signed a contract with the BSA's construction company for extending the railroad to Palapye and had pledged 'its best endeavours to induce the several Chiefs through whose country the Railway will pass to grant to the Railway Company *free of cost* such land as may be necessary for the construction and working of the Railway' (emphasis added).[100] Linchwe's methods of fending off the Administration had ceased to be effective.

Perhaps more sensitive than others in the Protectorate to the changing mood, Linchwe and his people tried appealing their case to London via Cape Town. After two unsuccessful attempts to meet with Loch, Linchwe and his advisors sent a petition to the 'English Government, Cape town', asking to 'bring our complaints before you, dear Sir, and please let this reach the ear of Her Majesty the Queen of England the Home Government':

> When the English Government came in this country, we were told that we are now going to live in peace under its protection, and that all the quarrels which very often rises [*sic*] between us native nations shall always thoroughly be investigated before the judgment is prosecuted. But we are sorry as we do not find the same as the above promised in this protection. How is it that the Government deny us the right of this country?

After outlining the history of the colonisation of the Kgatleng and laying out evidence of Kgatla occupation of the disputed territory, the petition returned to the fundamental issue at hand:

> bought his country with the blood and lives of our fellow-men. Since the Protectorate was proclaimed in this country, we spoke nothing to the Government simply because we wanted to study the Government. We shall be heavily pressed by the Government, and feel very very discontented if that piece of ground is given to Kgama. We are frightened by the Government in this case. We are not satisfied at all that our country can be taken from us like that. We are glad to be under the English protection, as Kgama and all other nations. How is that the Government presses us like this? That is our complaint to the Government. We hope and believe that the Government will listen and take notice of our cry.

Linchwe did not know that Loch's refusal to receive him in Cape Town to discuss the border dispute had already received the approval of the British government.[101] Loch did honour Linchwe with a reply, but instructed W.H. Surmon, Assistant Resident Commissioner in Gaberones, to discourage Linchwe from pursuing the matter.[102] Linchwe, himself closely watched by a nervous Administration these past nine years, was now confidently ignored.

Linchwe's nation, as he called it, appeared to be collapsing around him. A smallpox epidemic struck, and in the midst of mounting deaths, Mochudi was cordoned off from the world for six months. Across the border in the Transvaal, the ZAR's new land policies drove 2,000 BaKgatla out of the Saulspoort area into the Kgatleng, where they placed added strain on food resources. Along the Protectorate/Transvaal border, where maBuru were establishing farms, they also began impounding Linchwe's cattle in the vicinity of Sikwane. Protectorate officials took no action.[103] By mid-year, Linchwe and the other dikgosi were aware that the BSA Company was negotiating for the assumption of control of the Protectorate. On 27 July the BaKgatla drew up yet another petition, this time directly to 'Her Majesty the Queen of England and the Home Parliament':

> It has been reported to us that the discussion is going on about our country to come in the hands of the Charter Company. We Baghatla 'Raad' are very afraid to be out of Her Majesty's Protection . . . We don't expect any good from the Company, we know that we will be slaves in their hands. We know that all the rights will be taken from us.[104]

Khama had already submitted his petition and, soon after Linchwe's, Bathoen and Sebele followed with theirs. Linchwe acted independently, however, and rejected an offer from Khama to join the three LMS chiefs and the LMS missionary, Rev. W.C. Willoughby, on their August trip to England. Linchwe's son later alleged that his father remained aloof because he distrusted the three LMS chiefs, all of whom were related.[105] In late 1895, Linchwe stood alone. By isolating himself, he had returned full circle to the point at which he had started ten years before, when first confronted with the spectre of Cape Colonial Rule.

Linchwe grabbed at another concession to keep the Company out of the Kgatleng. In October he redrafted the Weil mineral concession, which the Colonial Office had disallowed the previous year.[106] The time had passed, however, when such deterrents could be effective. With Colonial Secretary Joseph Chamberlain then negotiating with Rhodes's representatives in London, no court case over a single concession could prevent a BSA Company takeover. Weil, too, was aware that Rhodes's time in the Protectorate had come. Three weeks after he signed the new concession with Linchwe, Weil met Rhodes in Mafikeng and said he could 'guarantee Linchwe's approval of the transfer of the Administration to the Company'.[107]

The fate of the BaKgatla had slipped utterly from Linchwe's hands. In London, where the well-known story of the dikgosi's visit and Chamberlain's final deliberations regarding the BSA Company takeover was unfolding, only the BaNgwaketse, BaKwena and BaNgwato received guarantees that most, though not all, of their land would remain under the Queen's protection.[108] The remainder of Protectorate territory went to the Company. Ikaneng and Montshiwa's concessions enabled Chamberlain to maintain the fiction that the BaLete and BaRolong had consented to the Company's assumption of authority within the existing Protectorate. Regarding the BaKgatla, Chamberlain was for a while led to believe that the needed concession from Linchwe would soon be forthcoming, but by December Chamberlain had lost patience awaiting its confirmation.[109] With only the Kgatla piece left to fit into place in the overall transfer arrangement, Chamberlain cabled Cape Town to go ahead with or without the concession and tell Linchwe that he would soon come under the authority of the BSA Company.[110] Weil was then holding out for more money than Rhodes was willing to pay.[111] When William Surmon rode in to Mochudi to inform the BaKgatla of the impending transfer,

Linchwe gave the impression that he had already resigned himself to the outcome that, for the previous ten years, he and his people had exerted so much creative energy to avoid. Linchwe, came the report, 'was dissatisfied because he wished to remain under the Government . . . He expressed a hope that no township would be made in his country nor any land taken from him without his being consulted. I think', concluded Surmon, 'he will quietly submit without any further opposition'. As to Linchwe's last requests, no reply was given.[112]

Redemption

On 29 and 30 December 1895, scarcely two weeks after Chamberlain's decision, the ill-fated Jameson Raid led to a speedy eclipse of Rhodes's political influence in southern Africa and a halt to the implementation of BSA Company rule in the Protectorate.[113] Power, even when concentrated in the hands of the most successfully rapacious in southern Africa, still had a fragile base. Though cause for relief in Mochudi, the sudden official silence on the question of transfer was no occasion for celebration. The threat from the south, known by the BaKgatla in all its changing forms, was perceived to have merely retreated. Signs of its return persisted. Rhodes sent no officials to govern the BaKgatla or any other group in the Protectorate, but his railroad came, and as the rail advanced up from Mafikeng, down from Bulawayo sped the century's most devastating epizootic, the *bolawane* (rinderpest). It killed cattle along the old wagon road at rates commonly in excess of 90 percent. The BaKgatla, who lost almost their entire herd, were convinced that Rhodes had sent the disease to drive them into destitution, and from there to the rail line to exchange their labour for something to eat.[114] When the line reached the Kgatleng in May, locusts had already swarmed to feed off the crops, and miserable men queued for jobs at railhead. Linchwe complained about the low wages offered and tried to dissuade his people from working, but they worked for their pittance nevertheless, and the rail moved steadily north.[115]

ENDNOTES

1   '[I]t is a fact that a native will usually prefer to engage himself to a Boer, who underpays him and sometimes thrashes him, than to an Englishman who generally over-

pays him. The Boer appears to understand him better and to amalgamate with him; treating him like a dog at times, but at other times, gossiping with him and joking. Between the native and the Englishman there is ever a great gulf fixed, neither quite understanding the other. This is the only apparent reason for so strange a choice on the part of the Kaffir.' (Ralph Williams, 1884, MSS 5, RCS, CUL)

2   H.C. Shepstone to H. Robinson, 3 Aug. 1881, PP, C3098: 77. BaLete and BaTlokwa leaders were also present. Tshomankane had been informed of, and protested against, British plans for withdrawal several months earlier (H. Gonin to H.C. Shepstone, 7 May 1881, N74/81, SN 4A, SAA).

3   Order-in-Council of 27 Jan. 1885.

4   For the Warren Expedition, see J. Mackenzie (1969: II, 230–274), Sillery (1970: 119–135), Schreuder (1980: 166–172).

5   C. Warren to H. Robinson, 23 Apr. 1885, PP, C4588: 11. Also, in late 1881, after the BaNgwaketse attacked Ramotswa, which resulted in the burning of several houses inside the nearby ZAR border, Gaseitsiwe was fined one thousand cattle and imprisoned for three months by ZAR officials (J. Good to W. Thompson, 3 Dec. 1882, box 41, LMS).

6   PP, C4588: 37–42.

7   Mackenzie (1969: II, 245). Warren's official correspondence and reports do not mention Linchwe.

8   Linchwe and Mackenzie were probably observing one another for the first time, but for some years they would have been second-hand acquaintances. Mackenzie had been a missionary among the BaTswana since 1858 and, like Linchwe's old adversary, Moffat, had worked among people neighbouring the BaKgatla before leaving the church to serve the Queen. Linchwe's in-law, LMS evangelist Matsau Motsisi, was well known by Mackenzie, whom Matsau had served briefly as secretary. Travelling with Mackenzie and Warren was also Major Samuel Edwards, son of Rev. Rogers Edwards, the LMS missionary whom Linchwe's grandfather Pilane met at Mabotsa in 1845 (C. Lloyd to W. Thompson, 1 Jun. 1885, box 43, LMS). See ch. 1.

9   Parsons (1973: 43–45).

10   Ibid., 52; C. Warren to H. Robinson, 27 May 1885 telegraph, PP, C4588: 12.

11   Moffat Memorandum, 19 Jun. 1885, PP, C4588: 105. Khama, Sechele and Gaseitsiwe also renounced claims on their western, and in the case of Khama his northern, border.

12   Parsons (1973: 47–48).

13   Warren's report of 8 Jun. 1885 and encls. in Parsons (1973: 51–103), contains no mention of Linchwe or the BaKgatla for that matter. See also J.S. Moffat, Memorandum, 19 Jun. 1885, in Parsons (1973: 105).

14   The best account of these events is Schreuder (1980: ch. 5). See also Sillery (1965: 45–60), and Galbraith (1974: 1–16).

15   Khama learned of Salisbury's rejection of his offer to Warren by reading about it in a Cape newspaper (Gould Adams report, 8 Dec. 1885, PP, C4643: 218). At the time, Cape newspapers were also being read in Molepolole, and presumably the DRC missionaries had access to the same in Mochudi, which sat on the main road between Molepolole and Shoshong. Brink was in Pretoria when the Warren Expedition passed through

Mochudi, but he returned to his mission in June, where he remained until November 1885.

16 J. Ellenberger Memorandum, 31 Dec. 1927, S182/1, BNA. Jules Ellenberger (1871–1972) would have heard this story after joining the Protectorate administration in 1890. Carrington, who was knighted in 1887, may have been recognisable to some of the Kgatla veterans of the 1879 Pedi campaign, in which Carrington led the British cavalry (Gon 1984: 22–30, 56–69).

17 In March 1885, a month before the Warren expedition reached Mochudi, Linchwe was appearing in a Marico District court on charges of trespassing his cattle on the farms of John F. Wilsenach. Linchwe was fined an exorbitant £975 plus costs. When Wilsenach contacted Shippard to help him claim the fine, Shippard refused, writing that he had 'no coercive powers' over Linchwe, whereupon Wilsenach dropped the matter (S.G.A. Shippard to H. Robinson, 4 Feb. 1886, and enclosed extract of the court findings, HC 4/13, BNA).

18 H. Gonin to DRC, 5 Jan., 6 Mar. and all other of Gonin's letters of 1888, 15/7/2 (C), DRCA; Hasselhorn (1987: 16–17).

19 Shillington (1985: 166–180).

20 Ibid.: 176, 180; F.J. Newton to H. Robinson, 15 Oct. and 2 Nov. 1888 and R. Tillard to F.J. Newton, 25 Oct. 1888, PP, C5918: 25, 111–112.

21 J.S. Moffat to S.G.A. Shippard, 19 Oct. 1887, PP, C5090: 37–38; Sillery (1970: 137); Sillery (1965: 75–76); C. Lloyd to W. Thompson, 26 May 1887, box 44, LMS; Gumbo (1986).

22 By early 1889 it was reported from Mochudi that 'many of [Linchwe's] people are away at the Gold and Diamond Fields' (J.S. Moffat to S.G.A. Shippard, 23 Mar. 1889, HC 27/16, BNA). For the impact of gold, as well as diamonds, see Thompson (1971: 10–22, 113–126), Schreuder (1980: ch. 6).

23 J. Petersen to S.G.A. Shippard, n.d., with notes by Shippard, HC 13/40, BNA.

24 S.G.A. Shippard to H. Robinson, 21 Jul. 1887, enclosing the reports of J.S. Moffat and A.J. Wookey, HC 153/1, BNA. Shippard had been less enthusiastic about an earlier reported gold find (S.G.A. Shippard to H. Robinson, 9 Sep. 1886, HC 9/12, BNA).

25 C. Williams to W. Thompson, 17 Aug. 1887 and A.J. Wookey to W. Thompson, 16 Dec. 1887, box 44, LMS.

26 Galbraith (1974: 60, 67–68) and most importantly Maylam (1980: 50–61).

27 Galbraith (1974: 69–70), Schreuder (1980: 208). Moffat was appointed in June 1886 as Assistant Commissioner north of the Molopo River.

28 J.S. Moffat to S.G.A. Shippard, 26 Jul. 1888, HC 24/2, BNA.

29 Sedimo (1986).

30 Goold-Adams report, 5 Mar. 1888 in Schapera (1942: 37–39).

31 J.S. Moffat to S.G.A. Shippard, 26 Jul. 1888, HC 24/2, BNA.

32 S.G.A. Shippard to H. Robinson, 11 Aug. 1888, HC 24/7, BNA.

33 J.S. Moffat to S.G.A. Shippard, 26 Jul. 1888, HC 24/2, BNA.

34 S.G.A. Shippard to H. Robinson, 11 Aug. 1888, HC 24/7, BNA.

35 F.J. Newton to H. Robinson, 2 Nov. 1888 and encls, PP, C5918: 111–112; Maylam (1980: 81).

36 S.G.A. Shippard to H. Robinson, 11 Aug. 1888, HC 24/7, BNA.

37 Ibid.

38 Knutsford to H. Robinson, 4 Oct. 1888, HC 42/43, BNA; S.G.A. Shippard to H. Robinson, 6 Dec. 1888, no. 32, B.P. in SP, PP 1/3/3, BNA. (PP 1/3/3 are Schapera's notes from correspondence in the Mafeking Registry taken prior to the 1960s fire that destroyed it.)

39 S.G.A. Shippard to H. Robinson, 11 Nov. 1888, HC 24/39, BNA.

40 S.G.A. Shippard to H. Robinson, 6 Feb. 1889, CO 417/28, PRO.

41 H.P. Malan to S.J.P. Kruger, 11 Feb. 1889 (secret), SS 1833, R1588/89: 7–8, TA. Translation by Ria Groenewald.

42 S.G.A. Shippard to H. Robinson, 6 Feb. 1889, CO 417/28, PRO.

43 S.G.A. Shippard to H. Robinson, 6 Feb. 1889, HC 25/29, BNA.

44 Ibid.

45 In 1883, Mochudi's population was estimated at 8,000, and in 1889, 12,000. See P. Brink to J.H. Neethling, 2 Aug. 1883, 15/4/3/2 (B), DRCA; B. Beyer to J.H. Neethling, 15/4/3/1 (B), DRCA; and Vaughn-Williams (1941). For the 1887 Plakkerswet, see Hasselhorn (1987: 16) and all the 1888 letters of H. Gonin to DRC, 15/7/2/1 (C), DRCA.

46 Sillery (1965: 138), Maylam (1980: 115).

47 J.S. Moffat to S.G.A. Shippard, 12 Dec. 1889, HC 123, BNA.

48 J.S. Moffat to S.G.A. Shippard, 23 Mar. 1889, HC 27/16, BNA.

49 1888–1889 Annual Report, PP, C5897: 9, 23. At this time, the Administration started the new mail service by coach between Kimberley and Palapye, passing through the Kgatla capital (Hole 1968: 56–58).

50 Maylam (1980: 35–36).

51 H. Loch to S.G.A. Shippard, 19 Apr. 1890, HC 116/3, BNA; Loch Memorandum, 24 Apr. 1890, HC 81/71, BNA.

52 S.G.A. Shippard to H. Loch, 29 May 1890, HC 116/3, BNA.

53 S.G.A. Shippard to H. Loch, 29 May 1890, HC 116/3, BNA.

54 S.G.A. Shippard to H. Loch, 6 Jun. 1890, HC 139/4, BNA.

55 S.G.A. Shippard to H. Loch covering J.S. Moffat to S.G.A. Shippard, 6 Jun. 1890, HC 177/4, BNA. I am grateful to Lydia Sedimo for this reference.

56 S.G.A. Shippard to H. Loch, 29 May 1890, HC 116/3, BNA.

57 S.G.A. Shippard to H. Loch, telegraph, 20 May 1890, ibid. By then, rumours of Linchwe's hostility towards the telegraph were widespread (Mathers 1977: 333).

58 The column reached the Oodi River, south of Mochudi, on 30 May, three weeks after Shippard had visited Mochudi and been rebuffed by Linchwe. See Johnson (1972: 124–130), Brown (1970: 67–71), Molema (1966: 173). Passing through the Kgatleng with the column was Lieut. Shepstone, son of Theophilus Shepstone, past Administrator of the British Transvaal. See Mathers (1977: 335–337) for the names of the column officers, their ranks and previous regiments.

59 Maylam (1980: 115–116).

60 S.G.A. Shippard to H. Loch, telegraph, 16 Jun. 1890, HC 116/3, BNA. See also J.S. Moffat to S.G.A. Shippard, 6 Jun. 1890 covered by S.G.A. Shippard to H. Loch, n.d., HC 177/4, BNA.

61 J. Harris to C. Rhodes, 11 Jun. 1890, ibid.

62 S.G.A. Shippard to H. Loch, 21 Jun. 1890, ibid.

63 J. Harris to C. Rhodes, 11 Jun. 1890, ibid., based on a report from John Moffat.

64 F. Newton to H. Robinson, 2 Nov. 1888, PP, C5918: 111–112. For Newton's 1885 list of white male Mafeking residents, see HC 7/48, BNA. The white trading community of Mafeking, which was situated at the convergence of the Transvaal, Cape and Bechuanaland trading routes, had sprung up in the early 1880s (S.G.A. Shippard minute, 27 Jul. 1886 in the same file). A number of men listed as storekeepers, such as Edgar Rowland, William King, Edmond Gower, Emmanuel Isaacs and William Kitchen among others, later opened stores and resided in the Bechuanaland Protectorate. Weil does not appear on Newton's 1885 list but he was trading in Kanye as early as mid-1886 (S.G.A. Shippard to Gaseitsiwe, 20 May 1886, HC 5/37, BNA).

65 Maylam (1980: 99–100). H. Loch to Knutsford, 8 Jul. 1890, HC 152/4, BNA.

66 S.G.A. Shippard to H. Loch, telegram, 27 May 1890, HC 139/4, BNA.

67 The concessions were signed on 25 Aug. 1890. Concession minutes, F(a) and (b), HC 119, BNA. See also Maylam (1980: 98), citing J. Weil to W. Surmon, 3 Sep. 1890. For Weil and Riley's membership in the Kanya Exploration Company, see S.G.A. Shippard to H. Loch, telegram, 27 May 1890, HC 139/4, BNA.

68 Concession Commission Minutes, RC 3/11: 14–15, BNA.

69 Ibid.

70 Interview with Ratsegana Sebeke, Marapo Lands, Mochudi, 4 August 1982.

71 Concession Commission Minutes, RC 3/11: 13, BNA.

72 S.G.A. Shippard to H. Loch, 12 Sep. 1890 and H. Loch to S.G.A. Shippard (draft), 20 Sep. 1890, HC 158/2, BNA.

73 Concession Commission Minutes, RC 3/11: 14, BNA.

74 F. Carrington to H. Loch, 18 Jun. 1890, HC 116/3, BNA.

75 S.G.A. Shippard to H. Loch, 25 Jul. 1890, ibid.

76 J.W. Fuller to F. Carrington, 4 Aug. 1890 and S.G.A. Shippard to H. Loch, 2 Aug. 1890 quoting Fuller, ibid.

77 H. Loch to S.G.A. Shippard, 22 Aug. 1890, HC 83/76, BNA.

78 Maylam (1980: 100).

79 W.J. Leyds to H. Loch, 11 Sep. 1890, HC 157/2, BNA. The transfer request was the 'last portion' of Volksraad resolution 1204 of 11 Aug. 1890 regarding the Swaziland Convention, which would annex Swaziland to the ZAR, a move Britain supported in return for a free hand north of the Limpopo (Maylam 1980: 95–97; Bergh 1999: 200). No evidence has been found to account for the resolution's 'last portion', but it is likely to have had something to do with the fact that the Plakkerswet had already caused thousands of Saulspoort BaKgatla to remove their labour from Rustenburg District by settling in the river villages of the eastern half of the Kgatleng, that portion which Loch was prepared to transfer to ZAR authority.

80 H. Loch to Knutsford, 23 Sep. 1890, HS 157/2, BNA.

81 Knutsford to H. Loch, 27 Oct. 1890, ibid.

82 F. Carrington to H. Loch, 18 Jun. 1890, HC 116/3, BNA.

THREAT FROM THE SOUTH

83 In addition to Khama's effective rumours, Ikaneng informed the Border Police in late July 1890 that the BaLete working on the telegraph line into the Kgatleng wanted a police escort back to Ramotswa 'as they do not trust Linchwe'. This is according to Capt. J.W. Fuller reporting from Mochudi, as relayed by Standford, superintendent of construction for the Cape Telegraph Department to 'Livewright' (BSA Company, probably Rhodes's telegram monikor), telegram, 1 Aug. 1890, ibid.

84 Sillery (1965: 144–158), Maylam (1980: 37–38), Ramsay (1985).

85 Sillery (1965: 156).

86 J. Ellenberger, 'Early Days in the Bechuanaland Protectorate', MSS Afr. S. 1568 (1), RH.

87 Moffat and Surmon consultation, 14 Jan. 1892, HC 182/1, BNA.

88 RC 3/11, BNA.

89 Sillery (1965: 167n).

90 W. Surmon to Chamberlain, 5 Oct. 1895, S189/1; Concession to Weil, 4 Oct. 1895, HC 158/2; Concession minutes, F(a) and (b), HC 119; and Concession Commission Minutes, RC 3/11: 14–15, BNA.

91 Galbraith (1974: 255–286).

92 J. Ellenberger notebook, 10 Nov. 1893, EL 1/1/1/1, ZNA.

93 Only months before the 1893 war, Loch had reassured Khama that 'there is no intention of handing over your country to the British South Africa Company' (H. Loch to J.S. Moffat, 15 Dec. 1892, HC 110/4, BNA).

94 For the events surrounding Khama's decision to travel to England to resist Bechuanaland's handover to the BSA Company, and Bathoen and Sebele's role, see Parsons (1998: 59–71). The BaLete were connected to the Lutheran HMS mission, the BaRolong to the Wesleyan Methodists.

95 Comaroff (1982: 87–88).

96 Statements of Ratshosa, 23 Apr. 1894, and of Khama, 7 May 1894; Shippard to Acting High Commissioner, telegram, 20 Jun. 1894, HC 108, BNA.

97 HC 108, BNA.

98 BPBC: 2, 28; RC 9/13, BNA.

99 S.G.A. Shippard to H. Robinson, 20 Oct. 1894, HC 108, BNA.

100 Notes from British Bechuanaland Requisition No. 17, 272. Contract in connection with the Construction and Working of a Railway from Vryburg to Palapye, 3 August 1894 (London: P.S. King and Son, 1894), 16–17, Item 42.

101 Lord Ripon to H. Loch, 15 Feb. 1895, HC 108, BNA. For Linchwe's attempts to see Loch, see Linchwe to S.G.A. Shippard, 24 Oct. 1894, and Linchwe to H. Loch, 29 Dec. 1894, in the same file. The original petition, dated 'November 1894' is also found there and contains a section not included in the petition reproduced in Schapera (1942: 39–40).

102 H. Loch to Acting Administrator, 8 Jan. 1895, CO 417/138, PRO.

103 Linchwe to S.G.A. Shippard, 24 Oct. 1894, HC 108, BNA; J. Ellenberger notebook, 23 Jul. 1895, EL 1/1/1/1, ZA.

104 HC 196/1, BNA.

105 Isang Pilane interview, 29 Oct. 1932, 1/4/5, SP, BNA.

106 4 Oct. 1895, HC 158/2, BNA. In return for £100 sterling, Linchwe gave Weil 'the sole and

207

exclusive right to search, dig and win precious stones [and] minerals . . . throughout my entire territory'.

107 J.A. Stevens to G. Bower, 22 Oct. 1895, S189/1, BNA. In the previous year, the brothers Benjamin and Julius Weil were competing for BSA Company transport business between Palapye and Bulawayo by undercutting the BSA Company-linked Bechuanaland Trading Association (BTA) based in Macloutsie (G. Bower to E. Fairfield 18 Feb. 1895 minute, CO 417/138, PRO). For the BTA, see Parsons (1973: 79–81).

108 Parsons (1998), Sillery (1965: 217–231); Maylam (1980 *passim*).

109 Chamberlain to H. Robinson, 9 Nov. 1895 and 19 Nov. 1895, HC 196/1, BNA.

110 Chamberlain to H. Robinson, 10 Dec. 1895, ibid.

111 J.A. Stevens to H. Robinson, 11 Dec. 1895, ibid.

112 F. Newton to H. Robinson, 17 Dec. 1895, ibid.; See also F. Newton to W.H. Surmon, 11 Dec. 1895, ibid., and F. Newton to H. Robinson, 20 Nov. 1896, HC 158/2, BNA.

113 Sillery (1965: 233–234), Rotberg and Shore (1988: 516–550), Parsons (1998: 242–256). The Jameson Raid was launched from the Protectorate in an attempt to ignite an *Uitlander* revolt in the ZAR and enable Rhodes to gain control of the Transvaal and its gold fields. Jameson concealed this intent from his raiding party, many of whom were ex-Border Police, by letting it be known they were assembling for an attack on Mochudi. At the last moment, Jameson announced: 'Some of you lads may think we're going to attack Linchwe and his niggers. Well, that's all bosh about Linchwe. We're going into the Transvaal in support of the Uitlander' (Packenham 1982: 2).

114 Interviews with Dupleix Pilane, Gaborone, 12 Dec. 1981, Rramariba Moremi, Mochudi, 26 Jul. 1979 and Galemone Monowe, Mochudi, 24 Jul. 1979. See Van Onselen 1972.

115 J. Ellenberger notebook, 23 May 1896 and 1 Sep. 1896, EL 1/1/1/1–2, ZNA.

Chapter eight

LOVE, DUTY

His most beautiful wife was a beautiful young girl, Lekgwalo. She was one of the most beautiful girls I ever saw . . . she was a royal offspring, perfectly shaped, and beautiful black skin and beautiful teeth when she was laughing. She had one child, and it must have been quite something for Linchwe to say good bye to her. She didn't want to go, she came to me and cried. I wanted to talk to her about her soul. 'No,' she said, 'don't talk to me about your religion, that one is too cruel.' She left, and she died with a broken heart. (Deborah Retief, DRC Missionary, as told to Rev. Johan Reyneke in 1923)

* * *

Lekoalo still remained in Linchwe's house . . . I went to Linchwe and warned him to send her back, and Linchwe agreed to do this immediately. (Rev. B. Beyer, DRC Missionary, 1892)

* * *

Deborah Retief told me that Linchwe left the younger wife he loved and stayed with his older wife, after deciding to convert. (Interview by author with Mrs E.N. Reyneke, widow of Rev. Johan Reyneke, Groenkloof, Pretoria, 18 August 1982)

Sometime in 1885, or late the year before, Linchwe and his inner circle moved to adopt Christianity. The coming of the British meant that, if the BaKgatla were to contend for space in the new Protectorate, their westernisation had to be accelerated. By then it was clear, too, that Linchwe's BaKgatla were not going to return to the Transvaal and therefore must do business with the other Tswana *merafe* in Bechuanaland. As Christians they would fit in more easily. Linchwe's group also understood that such Bechuanaland Christian dikgosi as Khama and Sechele were able to rein in headstrong missionaries and their disobedient converts. They had noticed already that powerful maKgoa like Shippard had difficulty duping Bechuanaland leaders who took on Christian ways, wore western clothes and used English. Modernising Africans were more adept than others at flimflamming maKgoa. In Rustenberg district, chiefs who kept Christianity at arms' length stayed in power, but in Bechuanaland, Christian chiefs were the savvy ones. They were dealing, not with maBuru who spoke their language and formed part of the landscape, but with maKgoa, outsiders who seemed either unaware or unconcerned that they were out of place. These powerful interlopers were naïve enough to be manipulated by African, English-speaking Christians in suits. MaKgoa were apt to mistake imitation as approbation, and gloss 'civilised' chiefs as friends and allies.

Going Christian made it easier for a kgosi to use the church for his own internal agenda, regulate access to schools, put loyal African ministers in charge of outlying congregations and control the royal children's education. Missions needed African supervision. Since the 1870s the Christians in Mochudi under the DRC missionary-in-charge had been unruly and immoral. Pieter Brink (1977–1886), the white reverend, was pitifully inept at controlling his converts. Linchwe had to intervene in disputes between him and his followers and deal with Christian interference in Kgatla affairs. In Saulspoort, where African teachers operated the schools, schoolgirls fell pregnant, thereby scandalising the community. Such could not be allowed to happen in Linchwe's territory. Converts had to be placed under the authority of the royal family and a strict moral code imposed.

Yet, after the decision had been taken, it became clear to Linchwe that Christianising required from him more than he wanted to sacrifice. When the time came, Linchwe, son of Kgamanyane and grandson of the great Pilane, brave war veteran, wealthy cattle owner, supreme ruler, and a large hulking man, would have to submit to the Reverend Beyer (1886–1896), a short, stout man dependent on Linchwe for his very survival in Mochudi. Beyer had only the power over baptism, or rather setting the conditions for administering it, but it was enough. Linchwe had no choice but to accept his terms. Beyer made it clear that to qualify for baptism, the kgosi must denounce initiation, forswear traditional religious rituals and ban any practices considered inimical to Christianity – all this in public. First, though, and this was the most difficult, Linchwe would have to divorce all but one of his wives. Linchwe was thrice-married and the father of a single child with each wife.

Linchwe was not allowed to choose among the three. He must remain with Motlapele, his great wife, the *mosadi ea kgolo*, mother of Kgafela (b. 1880). Linchwe did not love Motlapele, but she had been picked for him by Linchwe's mother Dikolo, widow to Kgamanyane, and she had been married first and with the approval of the BaKgatla. When Motlapele bore Linchwe's first-born son Kgafela (1880) she became *Mma* Kgafela, mother to his heir. Soon after Motlapele, Linchwe had also married Mogaritse, the daughter of his uncle Tshomankane, thereby cementing an alliance with his principal Transvaal ally in the war against the Kwena. She bore a girl, Mosadiathebe, not long after Kgafela's birth. However, in 1885, the war was over, Tshomankane dead, and the tie between Saulspoort and Mochudi altered by events. Mogaritse was therefore dispensable. As for his third wife, Lekgwalo, their marriage in 1884 was an affair of love, with no cattle exchanged. Linchwe and Lekgwalo were deeply attached. Lekgwalo soon bore a son, Bakgatla, a name tying Linchwe's happiness to that of his people. Yet, by then, the decision to Christianise the royal family had been taken, and when Linchwe chose the time to be baptised, Lekgwalo would have to be divorced.

The plan seemed set. Linchwe's brothers Ramono and Segale were among the first to attend catechism and receive baptism. Others in the royal family soon followed, but Linchwe delayed. At the time, his hesitation seemed understandable. His people needed time to get used to the idea that those around the kgosi were entering the mission church, before he could take that step. By the late 1880s, the many BaKgatla who looked to Linchwe as their customary kgosi were resigned to seeing Christian royals around Linchwe and could be told publicly that their kgosi, like so many others in Bechuanaland, was accepting baptism. In any case, no sibling rivals to his throne were in a position to stir up public anger, because they had to demonstrate their loyalty to Linchwe by becoming Christians in advance of the kgosi. Some regarded Linchwe's half-brother Segale as the rightful successor, but Segale was the first to ask for instruction. The alacrity with which Segale learned English and made friends with the missionaries made it all the more imperative that Linchwe convert. Still, four years after the decision had been taken, Linchwe was staying away from baptism classes though attending church.

In truth, Linchwe was postponing a future in which he would be a lonely man. Finally, in 1889, Linchwe announced in the kgotla his intention to be baptised. Soon thereafter he gave Mogaritse her 'freedom'. Then, he hesitated, keeping Lekgwalo. For three more years Linchwe dilly-dallied, attending baptism class off-and-on, until February 1892, when Beyer confronted him, forced him to face Lekgwalo, and made him send her away.

Christianity and the New Politics

As Britain gained control of the region, adopting the symbols of the new order was a means by which Linchwe and other Tswana leaders held on to their power. In the 1880s, Linchwe and the Kgatla elite followed the lead of Sechele, Khama and Montshiwa by applying a veneer of suits, hats and observances in honour of the maKgoa. Linchwe's inner circle understood that in order to blend in among the other Tswana leaders, they had also to Christianise. Yet, whereas Linchwe's men understood that standing alongside other Tswana dikgosi was important, even more so was gaining Britain's recognition of Linchwe's sovereignty over the BaKgatla's newly-seized territory; for without it, the BaKgatla risked being driven back into the Transvaal or being made the vassals of the BaKwena.

Earning the recognition both of the Tswana dikgosi and British officials was a high-stakes game. Real effort, too, was needed to make it convincing, because the BaKgatla ever were in danger of being singled out – by the London Missionary Society (LMS) Tswana dikgosi, who saw them as intruders from the Transvaal, as thieves of land and cattle, and by the British, who knew of the old BaKgatla–maBuru alliance. Returning to the Transvaal had disappeared as an option. By 1885, the old Kgatla alliance with Pretoria was becoming a thing of the past. If anything, the maBuru seemed to want to have done with Linchwe's people even in Saulspoort. The BaKgatla were leaving the Transvaal as the result of ZAR's new 'squatter' law and moving into Bechuanaland.[1] The Dutch Reformed Church connection linked Linchwe to the Transvaal, but after the Kgatla–Kwena war, DRC missionaries were of questionable political value in Bechuanaland. The British who governed the Protectorate had no prior contact with DRC missionaries; only one LMS missionary had corresponded with Gonin. Whereas LMS openly aligned its religious aims with British 'protection' of BaTswana, the DRC and its Cape Afrikaaner supporters had a reputation of siding with the ZAR when it came to the white control of the interior.

Linchwe also had to overcome the isolation resulting from years of fighting Sechele, who had close ties to the LMS, and the corresponding bad relations with J.S. Moffat and other LMS men. Sechele's old LMS contacts connected the BaKwena to British Bechuanaland, to the Cape and all the way to Britain. Although the LMS connection meant little, if anything, to Rhodes and his cronies, such was not immediately apparent to the southern Tswana. So, from 1885 until 1888 the dikgosi of the South – Molema of the Rolong, Gaseitsiwe of the Ngwaketse and Sechele (effectively his son, Sebele) of the Kwena – coordinated their response to the British. Soon after the Protectorate was declared in 1885, Linchwe was made to understand that the BaKgatla leadership needed to become part of this alliance. What was made apparent, too, was that members of the Bechuanaland alliance, as well as the aloof and arrogant Khama III – the pro-British kgosi of the Ngwato – were all Christianised, westernised and monogamous men. They were convinced that establishing themselves as Christians in the eyes of the stronger British would cushion the intrusion and leave them as rulers of their own people. To become a part of this African alliance, Linchwe and his leading men would have to adopt their Christian strategy.

The declaration of the Bechuanaland Protectorate provided additional incentive for Linchwe's group to convert for the purpose of influencing, and ultimately controlling, the DRC itself. British rule enhanced the power of DRC missionaries, who, though dependent on Linchwe's permission to work in Mochudi, provided him with the only means by which his people could obtain literacy. From a young age, Linchwe had been interested in learning to read. In the brief years (1877–1881) of English annexation of the Transvaal, senior Kgatla had observed that the maKgoa stood apart from the maBuru in what appeared to be their inordinate use of the written word. In 1885 and thereafter, with each visit of officials who scribbled while the kgosi and his men talked, and with each piece of paper wielded by officials and concessionaires, this impression was reinforced. The conversions that began in 1885 among the Kgatla elite, therefore, were closely connected with their desire to read and write. In 1885 Segale started instruction with the new mission teacher, Mary Murray, and became the first descendant of Pilane to achieve literacy in English. And in 1887 Linchwe's full brother Ramono was sent, with the sponsorship of the DRC, which had no training school for Africans, to the Roman Catholic mission school at Morija in Basutoland for three years of formal training. He returned able to read and write in Sesotho and English.

In immediate terms, the decision of Linchwe's circle to embrace Christianity meant rejecting the royal institution of polygyny, which since

Pilane's day had been used to integrate commoner lineages, multiply the kgosi's children and swell the royal kgosing ward. In a successful cattle enterprise such as Kgamanyane and Linchwe's, many royal dependents could be maintained and counted on to back the kgosi in public gatherings, organise regiments and protect the kgosi from harm. Once polygyny was no longer available to tie commoners to the royal family, the kgosi would have to discern means other than marriage and kinship to build and maintain a new generation of supporters. It would also have to be done while repairing the harm done to relationships with the families shorn from the kgosi upon his Christian conversion. In Linchwe's case, only two wives had to be divorced for the transformation, and one, Mogaritse, was from the dwindling Transvaal BaKgatla. Lekgwalo was much more difficult for Linchwe, because she was Mochudi-born, of the royal Molefhe ward, and daughter of one of his closest advisors. When it came time to divorce her, Lekgwalo would move about town as a daily reminder of the divide between the converted kgosi and his inner circle and the overwhelming majority of Mochudi BaKgatla, who had no interest in Christianity. The DRC, which had been part of the Kgatla scene for twenty years, had only a handful of converts. The LMS had suffered the same level of indifference, in spite of the conversion of their dikgosi. Tswana were not blind followers of their chiefs.

Carrying Missionaries

Moreover, the DRC had demonstrated itself incapable of standing on its own without the chief's backing. After Kgamanyane departed from Saulspoort and resettled in Bechuanaland in 1870, the DRC struggled to plant a mission in Mochudi. The DRC were devastated by Kgamanyane's move, because Saulspoort was their lone mission in the western Transvaal at a time when the Hermannsburg and Berlin missionary societies were studding the region with Lutheran mission stations and monopolising conversion. The few remaining Saulspoort Christians were not so much Kgatla as inboekelinge, who found in Christianity and literacy a way out of slavery and into a cash income. The exceptions were three of Kgamanyane's brothers and their small followings that remained near Saulspoort to gain access to the mission schools. Henri Gonin, the missionary most familiar with Kgamanyane's people and their language, rather than follow Kgamanyane, remained behind to tend to his diminished Christian community.

Ramono, circa 1902. Sketch by Lemington Muzhingi.

He was anchored to Saulspoort 38, the farm where the mission stood, because he had purchased it with his (mostly his wife's) money, without permission from the DRC. The parent mission refused to reimburse him.[2] Gonin remained in contact with the Bechuanaland Kgatla, and Linchwe used him to obtain a farm north of Saulspoort for one of his brothers. Still, the Christians in Mochudi remained few, and they were not in Linchwe's good books. One included Radiphole, who had relocated from Rustenburg district to Molepolole, with Kgamanyane's estranged brother Letsebe, and fallen under the sway of the LMS mission there. Like other Christianised Kgatla under Sechele, Radiphole had come over to the Mochudi early in the war. Fearing that the BaKgatla would be lost to the English-speaking LMS, the DRC wanted to claim this mission for themselves, but it was left to the young, inexperienced Pieter Brink to keep the DRC alive in Mochudi. In 1876, during a lull in the Kgatla–Kwena war, he made his first visit, and in the following year, Brink moved with his young family to Linchwe's, at the kgosi's invitation.

Since he had been a youth of fourteen, Brink burned to join the 'armies of the King among the heathens', a strange ambition, thought his mother, for a white Dutch-speaker of the Cape DRC.[3] Prior to the 1880s, the DRC left the converting of Africans on the highveld and beyond to the Scots, Americans, Germans or Swiss, like Henri Gonin, from overseas. Determined always to be the exception, Brink studied privately, then briefly at Wellington and Stellenbosch until earning his chance, initially at Boeseman River, and then to his posting at the DRC station at Saulspoort. Placed under Gonin in 1867 and sent to an outstation (Englandskraal), Brink soon made his mark as hot-tempered, impatient, slow with languages and quarrelsome, especially with missionaries who were not Dutch. By 1870 he had married into the Rustenburg Boer community (to the daughter of Rustenburg postmaster and landdrost clerk Kroep) and set his missionary course with a stiff trekker tailwind, one that would 'make kaffirs to be servants of whites'.[4]

When Linchwe called for a missionary, Brink, who had been rankling under Gonin and having lived at a stagnant outpost for nearly nine years, jumped to volunteer. Finally, *he* would be in charge of the 'thousands of kaffirs there'.[5] Within months he was in post, writing from Mochudi that 'our work here now [is] much more important than that in Pilanesberg [Saulspoort and its outlying stations]'. Linchwe, he believed, was already in his pocket. 'I have completely won [him] over', Brink wrote home, 'now completely our friend [who] doesn't want to do anything important without asking my advice'.[6] It was typical of Brink to paint the picture he wanted to see and one that flattered himself, rather than what was there.

At the time, Linchwe needed Brink for his usefulness in communicating with ZAR officials, Linchwe's lifeline during the on-and-off Kgatla–Kwena war. Brink was suited to this role, given his Boer connections and estrangement from Gonin. The latter's difficulties with Kruger were well known, as were soon his sympathies for the British during their annexation of the Transvaal. As for Brink and his young family, however, the war caused them hardships and kept them absent from Mochudi. Between assuming his post in 1877 and his death in 1886, Brink was in Mochudi altogether three years out of the ten. Linchwe provided him more material support than Brink's missionary society, made him feel welcome, put down insurrections among his parishioners, and, sensing this white man's insecurity in a town full of black people, flattered his manhood. After the birth of Brink's third son, Brink liked it when Linchwe and others called him a 'big, strong bull'.[7] Without being aware, Brink remained throughout under the sway of Linchwe, who helped the missionary build his own house, school and church, and backed him in controlling his unruly flock. Brink relished Linchwe's support as evidence of his powerful influence among the heathen, while dismissing it as an example of 'how eager for honour the kaffirs are'.[8]

Brink penned these words in late 1885, by which time Linchwe and his men had made their move to Christianise. They were realising, however, that Brink would not compromise over the issue of baptism. Linchwe's brother Ramono entered Brink's class and tried to get baptised on the fast track. Brink resisted.

> My small and childishly obedient Christian community which I really love because they allow themselves childishly to be guided by me, has become suddenly disobedient and unruly . . . They insult me in every possible way . . . [The] reason for all this [is] a young boy who is almost ready for baptism [but] I kept him waiting . . . because [he] is not humble enough and want wanting salvation enough . . . [He] didn't want to believe me and he put the community up against me.[9]

Brink refused to budge and the protest ended to no effect. Ramono had to enter another baptism class and await Brink's approval. Soon again Brink felt the surge of authority – publicly he challenged Linchwe by removing some catechism pupils from the male initiation called by the kgosi. Now committed to Christianising his group, Linchwe was not about to expel Brink. Instead he let him alone. Brink saw this victory as testimony to his unquestionable supremacy. 'Now [Linchwe's] power has been broken', Brink preened, 'as long as he lives'.[10]

Three months later, in Rustenburg, Brink was dead of dysentery. Linchwe personally travelled to the Transvaal to visit Brink's widow Annie, entreated her to return to Mochudi and encouraged the DRC to replace her husband. Responding quickly, lest the LMS grab Mochudi, Gonin visited Linchwe, reassured Mary Murray, the first DRC female missionary in Mochudi as of October 1885, and returned to the Transvaal to find Brink's successor. By June Gonin had located an elderly German missionary, Bernard (?) Beyer, who was disgruntled with his parent BMS, looking for a mission station to run and willing to swear loyalty to DRC doctrines. Aged fifty, thickset, and five feet tall, Beyer was the more unusual too in that at his Waterberg mission he had become fluent in Northern Sotho, closely akin to SeTswana. In September, Linchwe sent an ox-wagon to Saulspoort to transport Beyer, his wife, five children and all their goods to Mochudi. At Beyer's first service, held in Linchwe's wagon house, the kgosi was among those in attendance.

Like his missionary predecessor in Mochudi, Beyer was short-fused and uncompromising, yet needing Linchwe's help to overcome his personal and religious problems. According to Deborah Retief, who joined the Mochudi mission in 1887, Beyer was 'short of money, short of person, and short of temper'.[11] He also suffered from bouts of depression, and no wonder. His wife was bed-ridden with rheumatism and his daughter had fallen into an ill-starred marriage with a local white shopkeeper named Charles Thomas Miller, who turned into a wife-beater, carouser and raging drunk. Their baby boy died young. Beyer nevertheless was indefatigable and, as a diminutive volcano, became the subject of stories retold for years. One concerned Beyer at a church gathering, where he lost his temper and was ready to storm out, until one of the Africans (recounting it over the years eventually made this Kgamanyane himself) hung Beyer's hat on a high hook. After jumping for it in vain repeatedly, Beyer calmed down and stayed.[12] Though at times more novelty than missionary, Beyer gained respect from the Kgatla as honest, even-handed, hard-working and durable. Whereas young Brink had not been up to the harsh conditions in Mochudi and absent more often than not, the elderly Beyer stuck it out. He also talked with, as well as preached to, the BaKgatla in their language. Under his administration the congregation grew also without the internal conflicts so typical of Brink's day. Such in part was the result of the growing involvement of Linchwe's brothers and advisors in the congregation and the rapid rise of Segale and Ramono in the conduct of school affairs. Linchwe was also ready invariably to help him build and underwrite the cost of accommodating his congregation in a new church and even intercede with Miller, whose shop he shut down.

For his part, Beyer had the good judgment to allow Linchwe the time he needed to reach the point of conversion on his own. Rather than to cajole the kgosi, Beyer sensed that his missionary presence alone was sufficient to draw Linchwe to him. Beyer noted only in his correspondence that Linchwe was attending services, without making too much of it. Beyer wanted Linchwe's help to build a larger church, but did not ask for it, expecting the kgosi to draw his own conclusion. He thought Linchwe would feel it necessary, because each Sunday the chief sat 'sweating in a full packed church'.[13] When construction got underway that year, it was Linchwe who decided where it would go, and who saw that it was built. Beyer felt the church site a poor choice, but kept his opinion to himself. What counted was that Linchwe was attending both Sunday services and 'listens very well to the Word'.[14] As the church building slowly went up, Linchwe gave his people the first indication that he was about to convert. In mid-1889, Beyer wrote that Linchwe had 'released' one of his three wives, Mogaritse, telling her she was 'free to go'.[15] In November he went yet further. Beyer reported to headquarters that 'King Lencoe has seriously started to give honour to the true God and mentions the wish to subdue himself to Him'. In a public address, Linchwe declared that he had converted to Christianity, that 'not he (Linchwe) but God has divine power'.[16] Though pleased, Beyer restrained himself, instead being hopeful 'that Linchwe will later on be one of them'.

Beyer sensed Linchwe's hesitation. Linchwe began to attend baptism classes but Beyer realised he had not 'registered', that is, placed his name on the formal timetable leading to baptism for the group. Beyer queried him, but in private. Linchwe told him he really desired baptism, which obliged Beyer to bring up the issue.

> When I told him about the conditions, he very well knew, he wanted to put a test to me and asked if he could be baptised if he kept more than one wife? Was I not afraid that he would cheat me by sending away his wives before baptism and taking them back afterwards? [note: Sechele of the BaKwena, the first kgosi to convert to Christianity under David Livingstone's ministry, had done so with one of his wives] And what about going to a missionary willing to baptise him on his conditions.[17]

Beyer quietly insisted on the one-wife principle as a condition of baptism, and in a discussion a day or so later, Linchwe told Beyer he would keep MmaKgafela 'as his only wife'.

In the months to come Linchwe registered for baptism, but kept his distance from Beyer and tried asserting his authority over the mission. Though still unbaptised, Linchwe had begun to issue laws banning brandy and liquor in his territory and, in Beyer's words, 'thinks he has the right, being absolute king, to interfere with church matters'. Beyer observed that while Linchwe professed to be a Christian he is 'sometimes seen with heathens'. Beyer knew, too, that Linchwe 'still has two women'. After some time, Beyer talked with Linchwe about 'those matters . . . Linchwe promises to change things but does not do so in the end'.[18] Beyer stayed quiet, though, believing that Linchwe was likely to come around, like 'the majority of the royal family [which] has turned itself away from paganism'.[19] Still hesitant to judge Linchwe openly for what the missionary felt privately as a double-standard, Beyer's letters to his superiors show that he did not know where Linchwe stood. At times, he believed that even though his attendance at services was irregular Linchwe desired to enter the church because he had registered for baptism along with Mma Kgafela. At others, Beyer speculated that Linchwe was too in love with money and cattle or that Linchwe's mother was 'the one who holds him back'.[20]

In early 1892, when Linchwe's baptism class was approaching the ultimate ritual, Beyer had no choice but to push Linchwe into a corner. Beyer refused to baptise him unless he sent Lekgwalo away. Linchwe admitted that Lekgwalo, yes, was still living with him but pleaded that 'he did not have sex with her'. Beyer would have nothing of it. He insisted that Linchwe send her away. Beyer also wanted Linchwe to issue another public statement, renouncing all 'pagan customs' and that personally Linchwe had 'completely broken from this tradition'. As Beyer recalled, 'Linchwe really had to fight with paganism and say farewell to everything which puts him on a higher plane'. 'A week passed, I wondering if Lencoe will do what he was asked to do. One day, Lencoe came to me said he was ready to do what I told him, that he reached the decision without consulting others.'

We can only imagine how Lekgwalo was told by Linchwe that the time had arrived. She had to have known it was coming, and we should, as Beyer would not, accept Linchwe's claim that he desired Lekgwalo near him even if it meant giving up sex. It rings true, and moreover explains why he and Lekgwalo ceased having children after Bakgatla's birth in 1885, while Mma Kgafela bore children at least every other year from the time the inner circle made its commitment to Christianise.[21] Whatever Lekgwalo thought of Linchwe's decision, she did not hold him responsible. Instead, she blamed the missionaries for her expulsion. She camped at Beyer's house for more than a week, pleading and crying without success, then turned to the lady missionary, Deborah Retief, in the hope that she might appeal to Beyer. Instead, Retief tried to consol her: 'She came to me and cried, and I wanted to talk to her about her soul', recalled Retief, but Lekgwalo replied, 'No, don't talk to me about your religion, that one is too cruel', and then left for good, abandoning her attempts to sway the missionaries. Lekgwalo's response to her sudden reversal is testimony to her forceful nature, and the depth of her commitment to Linchwe. Lekgwalo *had* read Retief correctly, because the lady missionary alone seems to have understood the deep personal impact conversion had made on Linchwe and Lekgwalo. Later, when relating these events to Beyer's replacement, Andrew Murray, Retief commented to him 'how heavy it must be for a convert like Linchwe to leave his wives', and Murray replied only, 'my child, you let your heart run away with your sense'.[22]

After Lekgwalo was gone, it remained for Linchwe to assemble his people and before them reject all but Christian ways. Beyer's day of triumph arrived on 28 February 1892.

> The meeting was called, one thousand were present . . . Linchwe told them that he did not have much to say, but what he came to tell them was that he has accepted the new teaching at the baptism school and

as such he has accepted to be baptized into the congregation of Christ. And therefore I want to tell you that I am doing away with all the heathen practices. And that I want to be seen as the child of God.[23]

Though a few ward heads expressed opposition, Linchwe's brothers Ramono and Segale, together with his uncle Tau and several Christianised ward heads spoke in favour of Linchwe's decision. Several days later, on 28 February 1892, Linchwe, Mma Kgafela, their four children (Kgafela, Isang, Tlhabane and Kgomotso), and thirty-one others were baptised by Beyer before a large congregation. Beyer did not give Linchwe a Christian name, allowing him to use his own 'because [Linchwe] meant "a rock" ... parallel with Peter in the Christian tradition'.

The Loss

Now a baptised Christian and monogamist, Linchwe faced a lonely future. Sympathy from his people for his personal sacrifice he would not expect, or receive. Linchwe's purpose, which foremost was to ride herd on determined and seasoned cattlemen, required that he project himself as the most daring and callous of the community while acting on their behalf at the expense of his personal needs. Linchwe's brave military deeds during the Kgatla–Kwena war and his acceptance of Beyer's conditions for baptism were like forms of public service. Little concern was expressed that Linchwe might be doing his duty at his own expense. The strain of leadership, compounded by his constant travels to the Transvaal and to meetings with other dikgosi and British representatives of the BSAC and Bechuanaland Protectorate, was to be his private personal burden to bear. Linchwe would continue depending on his inner circle of male royals, advisors and headmen to keep him abreast of developments, intrigues and problems that required his constant attention, but unburdening himself to this group was out of the question; it would merely expose weaknesses that others could exploit. Apart from his mother, who saw her role as her son's protector rather than confidante, Linchwe had no recourse, until he met and married Lekgwalo, to that private realm where his thoughts and feelings could block out the larger world pressing in on him.

Few men among the Kgatla ever expected themselves to submit to women, much less be open to them. Though polygyny was allowed, few men had the means to support more than a single wife, one invariably chosen by the parents as Mma Kgafela had been. Only a kgosi (and a handful of other wealthy men) had the privilege, once certain obligations to the people were met, of acquiring a wife or wives to assuage an inner need. Kgosi or no, Kgatla males reached maturity without contact with women their own age, without awareness of their diverse natures, characters or needs. Kgatla society was organised in such a way that the odds were tilted heavily against a man and a woman ever finding themselves in a love-match.

Cattle and women may not mix. In the mind of Kgatla determined to be men, acquiring and keeping cattle meant keeping away from town for long periods and prohibiting women from following. From youth, all boys, including Linchwe, were kept at cattle posts to help with herding, while girls stayed in town with their mothers or followed them to the lands to tend crops. Boys remained separated almost entirely from girls until initiation, performed when lads were between sixteen and twenty. Throughout this rigorous passage to manhood, foremost were stressed discipline, endurance and securing cattle: 'Let the mother's boy remain', sang the men leading the initiates to camp, 'We go to fight for cattle; Let him who remains remain, We go to fight for cattle.'[24] Initiation began with circumcision, followed by a week or two for recuperation. Then came months of hardship – repeated thrashings interspersed with hard labour, sleeping unprotected in the late autumn/early winter, and daily instruction in the 'laws' taught by songs and proverbs learned by rote. Among these were the rules of sexual conduct, which discouraged consorting with 'outside' or older women, or during a woman's period. Initiates who arrived at the camp with any sexual experience or fondness for girls were singled out for extra, indiscriminate beating. The end of initiation was anticipated by a raid into town of the initiates and attacks directed particularly at women mentioned by men at the camp as having been 'bad and rebellious'. Initiation graduates then returned to the cattle posts and spent most of their time there until their married lives began, usually the result of arrangements undertaken by the respective families.

The notion that women were a source of harm to cattle and their owners pervaded Kgatla culture. Women were chased from, sometimes physically attacked, if they wondered in the vicinity of initiation camp and were prohibited from visiting cattle posts, tending cattle or milking. They were 'hot' to cattle, threatening their health and survival, certain to undo the doctoring of kraals and infecting men tending their herds. A man who spent too much time or was too frequently in town with his wife 'in her blankets' was certain to become weak.[25] Such taboos, demeaning to females as they are, may be understood in a people whose rise to independence and prosperity was derived from men hardened to protracted physical endurance in war and cattle management in a forbidding landscape. Though more often than not on a war footing, sensitive to the well-being of their herds, and alert to their neighbours' covetousness, men with cattle were also husbands, fathers, brothers and age-mates. War and cattle keeping were an extension of their social duty. Men were civilians first, warriors out of necessity. The brutishness they endured as part of their initiation was intended to stifle their instinct for kindness, and lovemaking, and the chest-beating of initiates became their pledge that each must place the community above themselves as individuals when it came to the crunch.

Yet, it would be a mistake to conclude that the Kgatla's was a misogynist world, removed of feeling or respect across gender lines. Instead what seems to have been the case is that the sustained hardships imposed by the manner in which Kgatla earned their successes in battle and secured themselves as a group in hostile settings over generations, deepened in the mature individuals among them the need for intimacy and solace. Linchwe's grandfather, who created the aggressive, vigorous style of leadership that helped the BaKgatla expand their territory and build up their wealth, marked the beginning of his career by declaring his love for Mankube, over and against the wishes of his followers to place their nominee for Pilane's 'great wife'. Mankube had stood by Pilane in his hard times, and he declared publicly that all the BaKgatla had acquired under his leadership – cattle, children, corn, even their loinskins – belonged to Mankube, and that *she* had *shared* them with Pilane. Polygyny enabled Pilane to marry others to satisfy his followers' wishes to be tied to his bogosi, while allowing him to marry the one he loved and who offered him companionship that enabled him to keep his wits together. Linchwe, as so often with grandchildren everywhere, resembled his grandparent Pilane in having a singular, adventurous manner that concealed a soft side.

Where Linchwe differs from Pilane with regard to marriage is that Linchwe's first 'great' wife had been chosen for him and that the wife he loved, Lekgwalo, was his third, the most treasured, and, once it was decided he had to become a Christian, the one he had to divorce. His reluctance to

LOVE, DUTY

lose her, putting off her divorce for years even though he recognised the inevitable from the outset, reveals the intensity of his affection.

Linchwe's Notion of Women

Linchwe's desire for Lekgwalo may have been an expression of his longing to escape the pressures of office, perhaps even a dreamy vision of paired bliss with his young, beautiful wife. When he knew he had to divorce Lekgwalo, Linchwe was only twenty-eight, she in her supple late teens. Other of her qualities must also have made him want to put off baptism. Linchwe was drawn to strong, outspoken, independent-minded Tswana women. We need look merely at the qualities of his grandmother Mankube, of his mother Dikolo, and later to his favourite child, the headstrong and courageous daughter Kgomotso ('Kgabyana') and Seingwaeng, the wife he would eventually handpick for his meek son and heir Kgafela, to understand his notion of true womanhood.[26] The leboko Pilane sang, and which was repeated in young chief Linchwe's presence by the praise-singers on royal occasions, reminded him and others in the Pilane line, that their patriarch was 'Mankube's husband' rather than she, Pilane's wife. She partnered with him in hunting, courage, generosity, leadership and talent:

> I have slain together with my wife,
> With Mankube, Bogatsu's child . . .
> My wife helped me to make the kill;
> She took the meat alongside the head,
> My wife took the foreleg . . .
> The cattle held by the Kgatla,
> The children begotten by the Kgatla,
> The corn reaped by the Kgatla,
> The loinskins worn by the Kgatla –
> All belong to Lebe, to Bogatsu's child,
> She shares them with chief Pilane[27]

Mankube, daughter of Bogatsu, kgosi of the BaTlokwa, was an outsider among Pilane's people. Apart from her marriage to Pilane, she was free of obligations to the Kgatla. Though their respective royal lines made them eligible partners, she accepted him before the young couple knew that one day he would assume bogosi for the BaKgatla. Pilane's leboko makes it clear that each was devoted to the other outside the realm of royal status or duty. She married him when he had no cattle, much less a home. He

225

was also a hunted man. Motlotle's agents were likely to show up at any time and murder him. Mankube had picked Pilane when he could not settle down or even move in with his in-laws. He had to hide out. For a year or two, the newlyweds were on hard times, moving about in the bush like Vaalpens, keeping well away from any settlements and eating only what they could kill. We need to remind ourselves that partnerships such as this, forged through extreme hardship, would not have been exceptional in the tumultuous years of the 1820s and 1830s, when groups and individuals were dispersed and forced to make do with their wits. To be sure, the annals of this period are full of cruelties all too typical of the moments when humans, devoid of community, descend into savagery. However, when lives were cheap, and oft-times short, Pilane and Mankube represent the men and women of the time who paired up to make it through. They are testimony to Sol Plaatje's 1930 novel *Mhudi*, named for the woman who fell in love with RaThaga in the wake of the destruction of the Tshidi Rolong in the 1830s and their survival together by dint of Mhudi's courage, shrewd take on people and tenacity of spirit.[28]

Mankube and Pilane picked Dikolo, their first son's great wife (and Linchwe's mother), for similar qualities.[29] Like Mankube, Dikolo Ramontsana Tlou, wife of Kgamanyane, was an outsider. Like Pilane's mohumagadi, she came from one of the two groups – BaTlhako, BaTlokwa – that Kgatla chiefs thought of as having daughters suitable for their heirs because, in words put to me, they were 'mean, hard-hearted and courageous so that the princes could not be cowards'.[30] However, this daughter of the royal family of the BaTlhako of Mabieskraal, Dikolo was not Kgamanyane's choice. He had consorted already with Nkomeng, a local girl, who had delivered his first-born, Maganelo, before Dikolo had been married to Kgamanyane or had conceived Linchwe. The father of Dikolo's son and future king was eager to have lots of wives and children. As if to outdo his father, husband of nine wives and forty-five children, Pilane's son went on to marry forty or so more wives, and father more than 100 children.[31] Apart from the affections of Nkomeng, Kgamanyane craved the influence he gained through his wives, not their companionship. His was a dutiful marriage to Dikolo. He acknowledged her politely in the leboko he composed to celebrate his heroism in battle, and in the same poem mentioned his eighth wife Mosothwe, but not Nkomeng.[32] Yet, Dikolo's two surviving children – Linchwe and Ramono – and Nkomeng's nine, show the palpable imbalance in the attention Kgamanyane paid to his 'great wife' and to her rival.[33] Given Kgamanyane's long absences from the capital for purposes of trading, raiding with the maBuru, and attending to affairs with his brothers and other dikgosi in the Pilanesberg, it is likely that Dikolo was accustomed to living at her new home in isolation, more so that she was unrelated to the Kgatla living around her. Though her paternal relatives lived just west of the Pilanesberg, within a long day's walk, they left the area to settle near to Sechele in Bechuanaland, sometime around 1860, when Linchwe and his younger brother were toddlers.

The manner in which Linchwe was raised, until he began to spend long periods at the cattle posts with his uncles, was largely Dikolo's affair. One of the most striking characteristics formed in Linchwe's character was his charity. Although Kgamanyane's love affair with Nkomeng created a long-standing rivalry between her male children and Dikolo's for the right to inherit their father's position, Linchwe never personally felt threatened by his step-brothers. Throughout his reign, they were among his closest advisors and trusted delegates. From an early age he sometimes followed their lead. When Linchwe was a lad, Kgamanyane allowed Segale and Ramono to receive instruction from the missionaries, whereupon Linchwe thumbed the Bible surreptitiously at the cattle post and tried to read.[34] His brothers probably helped him in this regard, for who else of his age could have taught him on the sly? Somehow, Dikolo and Nkomeng had reached an understanding that influenced their sons' behaviour. Neither wife could know which of his sons Kgamanyane would declare as his successor, and as we learned in chapter four, Linchwe did not learn that he was chosen until Kgamanyane was near death.[35] How, therefore, can we acknowledge on one hand, the absence of rancour (as opposed to ambition – we know that Maganelo wanted to succeed Kgamanyane) between Linchwe and his step-brothers, from childhood, and not assume that their respective mothers lacked, or at the very least held back, similar feelings? Witchcraft, an expression of jealousy and frustration, was well known to the BaKgatla, royal and commoner alike, and to his dread, Linchwe's own children would later resort to it to advance their ambitions. However, no evidence survives to suggest that Dikolo or Nkomeng employed such services against one another's children, for then we would expect fear and resentment among siblings to have emerged.

It seems that these two women had the presence of mind to be careful, if not considerate, of one another. We may reasonably assume that Nkomeng and Dikolo, rather than being simply deep-down nice, were two women who shared a concern, or made a truce as it were, to encourage their children to respect one another (and their father) as a way of staving off the intrigues and plotting of other members of the royal family. By virtue of her royal connections, and designation as mohumagadi, Dikolo was well protected from her husband's family. Nkomeng was a commoner, though, and one of lowly status, thus her children risked being pushed aside. Of particular worry were the followers of Kgamanyane's brother Tshomankane, whose son Tau had long been publicly known as ambitious to succeed Pilane had it not been for Kgamanyane.[36] Moreover, being roughly the age of Maganelo and Linchwe, Tau had time aplenty to wait for his next turn to lay claim. To protect their sons, Nkomeng and Dikolo had to keep in mind the likelihood that no matter whom Kgamanyane designated as his heir to bogosi, the uncles and brothers who survived the kgosi would determine who succeeded, because their combined welfare depended on picking well. The character and temperament of the next kgosi, not just his legitimacy in the eyes of Kgamanyane, would matter most. Therefore, the behaviour of eligible princes were observed well in advance of the succession, particularly as the strains of living with the maBuru and *makristo* made the necessary task of keeping the BaKgatla together the more difficult.

Provision

Though forced to send away two of his wives, Linchwe continued to honour these relationships. His devotion in this regard was as true for Mogaritse as for Lekgwalo. No matter that he had become a Christian, Linchwe held fast to the traditional law governing the distribution of his property before and after his death, that is, according to his obligations to the lelwapa of each of his wives. Linchwe saw to it that the property allocated to his wives prior to their divorces remained theirs for their use until such time as it could be distributed after his death as a portion of his estate. After his baptism and until his death, moreover, Linchwe continued to recognise and support Mogaritse and Lekgwalo's children, as if they had remained married to him.

Mogaritse returned to Saulspoort but Linchwe maintained for her and their daughter Mosadiathebe the cattle post he had given Mogaritse at their marriage.[37] As for their daughter, Linchwe made it known that Mosadiathebe was a 'full sister' to Kgafela. She remained in Mochudi, where she was raised in Mma Kgafela's lelwapa, and in 1902, when Kgafela was made the head of the male regiment (Makuka), Mosadiathebe became the leader of the female regiment, of the same name.[38] She was later married into the BaTlhako at Mabeskraal inside the Transvaal, without cattle being exchanged, meaning that Linchwe afforded Mosadiathebe the option of leaving her husband and returning to Mochudi. At about the time of Mosadiathebe's marriage, Linchwe picked Seingwaeng of the BaTlhako living inside his territory, to be married to his son and heir Kgafela. In other words, Linchwe maintained Mogaritse's position as his second wife by upholding Mosadiathebe's status and demonstrating publicly at the time of female initiation – one of the very 'heathen institutions' Beyer required Linchwe to reject – that he regarded her as his senior daughter. As a result Mogaritse, who became a Christian after her return to Saulspoort, retained her position as the mother of Linchwe's senior daughter, while acknowledging the divorce as voluntary on her part through her own Christian conversion, thus maintaining her own self-respect.

As for Lekgwalo, her future became dimmer than that of Mogaritse, in spite of Linchwe's efforts to provide for her. Defiantly anti-Christian, and having to remain detached completely from Linchwe's compound, she secluded herself at her parents' home in Mochudi, until, according to Retief, she 'died of a broken heart'. In Linchwe's extended family, however, Lekgwalo continued to be regarded as *ngwetse* ('daughter-in-law'), the designation used for a junior wife attached to the senior wife's lelwapa. As with Mogaritse, Linchwe honoured Lekgwalo by maintaining a cattle post for her, as her own lelwapa entitlement, and saw that her son Bakgatla remained with the father to be raised in Mma Kgafela's lelwapa. Linchwe doted on Bakgatla. When Bakgatla reached manhood, Linchwe assigned him a lelwapa adjacent to that of Kgafela's, whereas his other sons, from Isang on down, were each given a lelwapa 'quite a distance away'.[39] Bakgatla was himself baptised, but he grew to an old age believing that Linchwe himself had never undergone this ritual.[40] No doubt for years Bakgatla circulated this myth whenever the topic of Linchwe came up, contributing to the popular notion that Linchwe's conversion was superficial. After Kgafela's death in 1915, and before Linchwe himself passed away in 1924, Bakgatla began living with Kgafela's widow Seingwaeng, as man and wife, a relationship that produced two children and lasted for years.[41]

The conscious recognition and reinforcement of traditional status within Linchwe's family, no matter that it adopted a Christian identity, could not have escaped the notice of the people. The BaKgatla would have known that Linchwe and Mma Kgafela never re-married according to the Christian rite, because such ceremonies were conducted publicly, in the church before the congregation.[42] They understood, too, that, after she and her husband underwent baptism, Mma Kgafela recognised Linchwe's children with Mogaritse and Lekgwalo as legitimate. She accepted Mosadiathebe into her lelwapa, where her step-daughter would rank above her own daughter and receive recognition by Linchwe accordingly, just as she accepted that Bakgatla be raised in her compound. After the rite of baptism, Mma Kgafela's position in traditional terms as mosadi ea kgolo of the BaKgatla, and her senior rank within Linchwe's extended family, was reinforced by her actions. By the same token, Mma Kgafela's willingness to safeguard her ex-co-wives' children made it natural for the public to regard Linchwe's divorces of his second and third wives as imposed, if not cosmetic, arrangements necessary for Christianising bogosi.

Monogamy also failed to alter Linchwe's standing obligations to the many widows of Kgamanyane and their children, as mentioned in chapter five. Thus, in addition to the three malwapa of his own, Linchwe contributed to the upkeep and increase of these wives and descendants of his father. Interestingly, Deborah Retief took notice of Linchwe's charity in this regard after he was baptised, and she alone among the missionaries seemed conscious that Linchwe had qualified his conversion in such fundamental ways. Curious and empathetic, Retief somehow came to know about Linchwe's involvement in the many compounds descended from Kgamanyane and that children had been born in these malwapa since Kgamanyane's death in 1875. Retief observed that Linchwe 'looked after forty women he inherited from his father and looked after them well'. Retief became convinced, too, that Linchwe 'never took them'.[43] Given that all children born of these wives were Kgamanyane's children in customary law, and that the actual paternal figure was not for public knowledge, what seemed to be the case is that Linchwe, or those around him, insisted that the kgosi not be understood as the physical father. If his intention of Christianising was to reduce his obligations, and hoard rather than distribute his wealth, baptism presented him with an opportunity he chose not to take. As with Lekgwalo, so with all other women in his care, Linchwe accepted the condition of monogamy in its sexual sense and as understood by the missionaries for baptism, without foregoing responsibilities arising from his father's traditional vows of marriage, or indeed, his own.

The missionaries' attitude toward marital fidelity in fact differed little from Linchwe's. Linchwe reached manhood as the product of stricter times, when sexual adventures were frowned on and made grounds for ridicule and punishment during male initiation. Whatever difficulties he had in accepting the nature of marriage as defined by the DRC (and other missionary societies he had contact with), Linchwe had converted having long adopted the principle of devotion to one's compound, in his case, to the malwapa of his three wives. At the time of his conversion, however, he and the others around him were increasingly concerned with the moral decline brought about by the new order. With European power arose the development of mining centres, and the attendant urban and compound cultures that separated men from their homes at long distances and encouraged prostitution, alcohol consumption and other symptoms alien to the traditional order common to the BaKgatla and other people whose sons spent months away from the usual controls. One of the most difficult challenges to Linchwe's authority was the wave of drunkenness, rowdiness and sexual aggressiveness (and syphilis) in Mochudi that accompanied the establishment of European-owned shops and the return of young men from the mining towns of Kimberley and the Witwatersrand – places where traditional attitudes were habitually ignored without reprimand. By becoming Christian, Linchwe's inner circle was modernising only in its most culturally conservative sense, whereby the new faith could be used to uphold traditional Kgatla codes of behaviour. In 1887, while Linchwe bided his time to convert, he nonetheless banned the selling of liquor in his kingdom. With his adoption of Christianity, the old strict code of sexual conduct was enforced by Linchwe more rigorously than ever before, and with the sjambok. In Mochudi, men found guilty of 'immorality' were strung up to wagon wheels and whipped senseless.[44]

Religion
As for Linchwe's religiousness, and of that of the men around him, it is doubtful that adopting Christianity entailed a crisis of faith. The BaKgatla

expected their kgosi to carry out certain traditional religious functions, and the non-Christians worried that his conversion might undermine his effectiveness. There is, however, no evidence to suggest that Linchwe believed baptism had robbed him of any of his powers, or for that matter, enhanced them. Among the BaKgatla and many peoples of the highveld, black and white, we are obliged to understand the powerful as more interested in using religion to influence events than for trusting spiritual explanations, just as they are more interested in attempting practical solutions than leaving matters to chance. Theirs was a world in which religion was practised in order to instil confidence, not self-doubt, and induce rather than predict such favourable results as good rains and crops or protection from an enemy or outbreak. They lived when predators – animal and human – prowled the landscape and when attacks, droughts, flooding or disease could erase in a day or two the years of hard work, sacrifice and daring that had been brought to bear to advance the corporate fortune. Good cattlemen especially were as conscious of the power of divine intervention as any, and as keen to avert its terrors. Yet they understood, too, that people without cattle knew the least about the skills in acquiring, increasing and protecting their stock, and themselves. Shrewdness, knowledge and discipline increased the odds of their success, while prayers to the forces beyond human control simply acknowledged that there were no guarantees. The Art of Rustling was practised by men who first learned to be humble.

Make no mistake, Linchwe meant that everyone take his conversion seriously. His religious activities were to take precedence among his people, his authority as a Christian to be unquestioned, lest otherwise he be thought to have abdicated. The rituals he had led heretofore to prepare the land for a successful growing season, and to celebrate the harvest, he made into Christian events, celebrated at church presided over by missionaries. Until old and decrepit, Linchwe consistently attended Christian services, honoured all observances and passed laws in tune with Christian prohibitions against drink and adultery. He attended church regularly and rigorously enforced the Sabbath in Mochudi, punishing those who worked, drank local beer, or inspanned on that day. He allowed male (bogwera) and female (*bojale*) initiation to continue, because the traditionalist public insisted, but in 1902 he withheld Kgafela from the initiation camp, even though Kgafela was denoted regimental leader. Some speculated that by

LOVE, DUTY

becoming Christian, Linchwe meant to excuse his heir from taking part in this dangerous rite of passage, where boys were known to die or be killed, but at the time Kgafela was schooling far away at Zonnebloem College, near Cape Town.[45] After the initiation of this Makuka regiment, Linchwe prohibited future bogwera and bojale camps, allowing only a naming ceremony.[46]

Linchwe's Christianity was an acquired set of rituals and symbols that could be carried out without requiring the many BaKgatla who stood outside the church to convert. Linchwe had been curious about Christianity since he was a boy at the cattle post, and years before he converted, bogosi remained his to invest with religious meaning. A kgosi had to demonstrate his religious powers rather than apply a set of traditional prescriptions to be carried out mechanically. What mattered most to the people was the degree to which Linchwe's religious conduct advanced and safeguarded their lives, and in this regard Linchwe strove to demonstrate his prowess in magical as well as religious terms. Where his personal ritual powers were most closely identified with bogosi – in the realm of rainmaking – Linchwe continued to practise his traditional craft and for which he was remembered fondly after his death as having been particularly effective.[47] Linchwe's rainmaking powers, though dismissed by missionaries, were respected by the Kgatla, by Christians and non-Christians alike. It was known, too, that Linchwe had taught his children Kgafela and Kgomotso his secret rain-making process and passed on to them his paraphernalia. Linchwe understood rain-making as a special form of potent knowledge that he alone had taken the initiative to obtain. Rather than a part of his inheritance, Linchwe had 'bought it', pieced it together as it were, from several noted rain-makers after his installation. His was a personally acquired power, controlled only by himself, and one he made Kgafela purchase in turn. Linchwe's bogosi, in other words, had acquired a Christian content without shedding any religious substance in the traditional sense, or any of its power.

In the years following Linchwe's conversion, Linchwe's position inside his territory remained intact, even though the BaKgatla entered extremely difficult times. Drought, disease and locust invasions punctuated the seemingly endless seasons of hardship, while the stress felt inside Linchwe's circle was intensified by the threat posed by the British South Africa Company. Even the eclipse of the Company's fortunes occasioned by the Jameson Raid in 1895, gave Linchwe little respite. The 1896 rinderpest devastated their cattle and the drought that persisted edged them toward starvation. The BaKgatla had reached their lowest point since the days of Pilane's exile, seventy years earlier. Linchwe's role, like that of his grandfather, was to lead his people in the direction of opportunities that would enable them to rebuild their herds and reclaim their self-respect. Redemption for cattlemen would not be found by working on rail-lines, in the mines, or seeking jobs that paid in cash, and little of that. What the Kgatla needed was cattle, many cattle, for their nourishing milk, their steady increase as wealth for distribution, and the constant demands they placed on disciplined, abstemious men. The BaKgatla were aware that Linchwe's powers, and that of the other dikgosi, paled in comparison with the maKgoa, and that the hardships they faced were no greater than that faced by the other BaTswana in the Bechuanaland Protectorate, but they looked to Linchwe to find a way to rescue them from an increasingly desperate situation.

ENDNOTES

1 H. Gonin to DRC, 5 Jan., 6 Mar. and all other of Gonin's letters of 1888, 15/7/2 (C), DRCA; Hasselhorn (1987: 16–17).
2 Mbenga and Morton (1997), Morton (1998a). See ch. 3.
3 According to his mother, the widow of J.J. Malan, in an undated letter to DRC missionary in Mochudi, Miss M.E. Murray, DRC 15/4/3/2 (B), DRCA.
4 Brink to DRC, 1 Nov. 1880, ibid.
5 Brink to Neethling, 1 Dec. 1876, ibid.
6 Brink to Neethling, 15 May 1877, ibid.
7 Brink to Neethling, 1 Nov. 1880, ibid.
8 Brink to Neethling, 9 Nov. 1885, ibid.
9 Brink to Neethling, 21 Oct. 1885, ibid.
10 Brink to Neethling, 9 Nov. 1885, ibid.
11 Reyneke (1923: 42).
12 Ibid.
13 B. Beyer to Neethling, 20 Jan. 1888, 15/4/3/1 (B), DRCA.
14 Beyer to Neethling, 14 Dec. 1888, ibid.
15 Beyer to Neethling, 6 Jul. 1889, ibid.
16 Beyer to Neethling, 29 Nov. 1889, ibid.
17 Beyer to Neethling, 6 Jun. 1890, ibid.
18 Beyer to Neethling, 11 Oct. 1891, ibid.
19 Beyer to Neethling, 11 Sep. 1891, ibid.

20 Beyer to Neethling, 11 Oct. 1891, ibid.

21 Linchwe also stopped having children with Mogaritise. Mmakgafela bore Isang, Linchwe's second son, in 1885, his third Tlhabane in 1887, and his first daughter, Kgomotso, in 1890 (Birth register, 15/4/2/1, DRCA; Kgatla: Baptisms, SP, BNA).

22 Renyeke (1923: 43).

23 Beyer to Neethling, 4 Mar. 1892, ibid. Beyer's account is mirrored in Retief's recollections as told thirty years later to Rev. Reyneke (Reyneke 1923: 43).

24 Sung by the men leading the initiates to their first camp (Schapera 1978: 4).

25 Schapera (1934).

26 Morton (1998b: 25).

27 Schapera (1965: 60).

28 Plaatje (1930), Willan (1984: 349–371).

29 Komane Pilane, interviewed 9 Dec. 1929, PP 1/1/1, SP, BNA.

30 Interview with Selogwe Pilane, Masiana ward, 19 Dec. 1981. Selogwe's words echo those of DRC missionary Deborah Retief, who described Dikolo as 'such a hard-hearted heathen, whom none of us could reach' (Retief to J. Neethling, 26 Jun. 1895, 15/4/3/13 [B], DRCA). Dikolo's mother was a MoFokeng (Interview with Seikgokgoni Pilane, Kgosing ward, 16 Dec. 1981). Selogwe was the adoptive son of Kgafela, Linchwe's eldest son and Seikgokgoni was the daughter of Ramfolo Pilane, Linchwe's younger brother.

31 Kgatla royal family lists, PP 1/3/9, SP, BNA. An undetermined number of the 110 reckoned as Kgamanyane's surviving children were conceived after the kgosi's death in 1874. See ch. 6.

32 *Makgadimotse yoofega sankwe, otlhoma katau, mogatsa-Dikolwe, kemogatsa-Dikolwe ka Mosothwe* ('Dodger who wears a leopard-skin but steps like a lion, Dikolo's husband; he's the husband of Dikolo and Mosothwe') (Schapera 1965: 67, 69). The reference to these two wives in particular emphasises his marriage to royal families, including his own. Mosothwe was the daughter of Kgamanyane's great uncle Motlotle (Pheto's younger brother and son of Molefhe), whose murder made way for Pilane's succession. See ch. 1.

33 Dikolo's first child, a daughter Ntshadi, died in infancy.

34 Interview with J. Ramodisa Phiri and England Kgamanyane Pilane, Tribal Office, Saulspoort, 6 Jan. 1982; H.Gonin to DRC, 5 Dec. 1866, 15/7/2(A), DRCA.

35 According to Thomas Phiri, Linchwe's one-time secretary, Linchwe was heard to say that, as a young man, 'I knew myself only as Kgamanyane's son, not knowing that one day I would be a BaKgatla chief' ('On Kgosi Lentsoe K. Pilane', *Lesedi la Batswana*, nd., PP 1/1/17, part I: 5–6, SP, BNA).

36 For Tau, see chs. 2 and 5. Nkomeng was a Motsomi, from the Masiana (Tlagadi) ward, which was attached to the Kgatla during either Pheto or Pilane's reign. BoMasiana were of lowly, Kgalagadi origin (Schapera 1952: 113–114). Nkomeng's paternal genealogy was Radibeela-Molatlhegi-Motsomi-Matlhage (PP 1/3/9, SP, BNA). Molatlhegi-Motsumi is not to be confused with Molatlhegi-Mosome of the BaKwena a Modomosana ba Malthaku of Pella location. See Breutz (1953: 128–130).

37 Isang testimony, Linchwe Estate Commission, 1935, S343/24: 5f, BNA.

38 Interview with Sebele Motsitsi, Baekgedi Nkele et al, Lentswe-le-Moriti, 26 Feb. 1986.
39 Interview with Linchwe II, Cumberland Hotel, 11 Jul. 1995.
40 Bakgatla's statement, 3 Dec. 1947, DCM 6/7, BNA.
41 Morton (1998b).
42 Isang testimony, Linchwe Estate Commission, 1935, S343/24: 5f, BNA
43 Retief, according to Neethling (1923: 43).
44 Reyneke (1924: 93).
45 Kgafela Linchwe Kgamanyane to J. Neethling, 14 Oct. 1901, 9 Aug. 1902, 15/4/3/18, DRCA.
46 Schapera (1970, *passim*).
47 Schapera (1971: 1f).

Chapter nine

THE LAST RAID[1]

Red-faced people with jutting noses,
Indunas of the white man Makopye . . .
He turned them back at Makalakala . . .
Ramelora and company fled, the cowards . . .
As they fled they turned into baboons,
Become male baboons, inmates of caves.
(Linchwe's praise song, composed by Rammhi)

* * *

Someone reported to Linchwe that in Waterberg at Modubyane river
was a Boer laager with many cattle and they were worrying people very
much. Linchwe decided to go there and Government did not agree, not
good for him to go so far into the Transvaal, but he went; he said, they're
there, some of my people are there, too, suffering, I'm going to punish
these Boers. (As recalled by Thomas Phiri, 1931)

Atop Phuthadikobo, standing in front of the rondavel Kgamanyane had
planted amidst the rocks, Linchwe's view surveyed his father's vision.
Below, on the lower slopes of Phuthadikobo and the expanse beyond, a
stony space where twenty-five years before was a habitation of lions, were
spread snugly together hundreds of the homes and courtyards of his people. The wall surrounding Mochudi, built to defend against the Kwena,
no longer stood, its stones now part of house foundations and courtyard
walls. Peace had become routine. To the west, in the distance, where the
Kopong hills once marked the approach of Kwena armies, small villages
of Linchwe's subjects had sprouted. To the north and east were located
hundreds of Kgatla cattle posts, awaiting replenishment from the rinderpest, for new herds to savour the grazing and slake at wells and along the
long, thin Ngotwane. Linchwe's view to the south spanned the fertile lands
of Talane, wanting only rainfall, and took in Tshwene-tshwene, 40 kilometres distant, his father's last stopping point in the Transvaal. On his
side of Tshwene-tshwene, the river villages sat along the Madikwe, facing
across the border into the South African Republic.

This panorama of accomplishment, the Kgatleng, yielded by wiliness

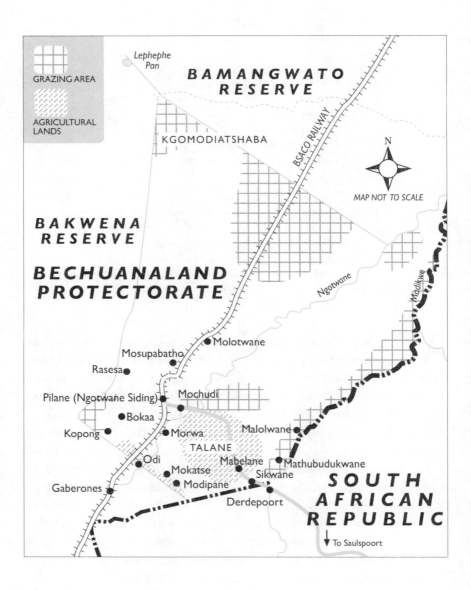

and sacrifice, had become a snare. In 1899 the maKgoa enclosed his people. Now Linchwe was 'chief' of the 'Bakgatla Reserve' they had demarcated. For generations, Linchwe's cattlemen and their forbearers had understood boundaries as bendable, as a range line extending until others had the will to challenge. Territory for cattle, like a herd, naturally needed to expand. After 1882, when peace was struck with the BaKwena after BaKgatla had driven them from their eastern land and water, the Kgatla continued pressing slowly west into the Kweneng along the Kopong foothills. In this borderland, they welcomed refugees resentful of the drunken Kwena kgosi, Sebele, and allowed them to settle as Linchwe's subjects. The famine-ridden Kwena were unfortunate losers. Linchwe's people then looked north and northwest, nudging their cattle into *GamaNgwato*. In 1894 they ventured beyond Kgomodiatshaba to the perennial wells of Lephepe and its grassy surroundings, which Khama of the Ngwato protested was his. Protectorate officials backed Khama, and Linchwe retreated.[2] By 1895, officials, tired of entangling territorial disputes, sent surveyors to make straight lines and separate 'tribe' from 'tribe'. In 1899 'tribal reserves' were proclaimed to settle matters once and for all. Inside, 'natives' became subject to 'hut tax', for collection by the 'chief'.[3] These beaconed lines, and the job of tax collection, Linchwe accepted quietly. Acquiescence gained him formal recognition as 'chief' of his land and people and deafened the maKgoa to Sebele's beery though honest complaints that the Kgatla had swiped his territory. What Linchwe had lost from Khama, the British allowed him to keep of Sebele's. Linchwe, too, knew that protest on his part over the reserve boundaries would be used by Khama to put grist into the old rumour mill that Linchwe was anti-British, ready to revolt in sympathy with the Ndebele,[4] and that he ought to be run back into the Transvaal. So Linchwe played humble and professed loyalty to the Queen.[5] Yet, doing so meant stifling his people's impulse to find more space for their cattle. After twenty years, the powerful momentum set in motion by Kgamanyane's exodus from Saulspoort, inexorably extending the Kgatla's reach from the Pilanesberg to the Kalahari, had spent its force.

Meanwhile, pestilence and drought had tested their strength. Smallpox came, and dysentery, then the bolawane. Dying cattle, whole bellowing herds climbing atop one another to make heaps of carcasses, abandoned their human families. A three-year drought lay in waiting, joined by malaria, typhus, locusts and famine. Long used to milk, meat and porridge, the Kgatla now ate roots, berries and locusts. These few endless years were a reminder, a revisiting crisis of endurance, rather than of faith. Only the number of DRC faithful and the appeal of Christianity shrivelled. The heathen hunkered down. Questions were taken to older sources, pragmatism brought to the fore. Men against their wishes trekked off to the mines in Kimberley and Witwatersrand to work for their families' survival. Those who went or remained knew that the Kgatla of Pilane had endured worse, and had revived, by looking for opportunities in all forms. As smallpox spread, Linchwe's brothers and headmen were seen sitting beside Linchwe, with their painful, seeping inoculation sores in plain view.[6] Cattlemen understood the heavy hardships that could befall them and, if first self-inflicted in near-fatal amounts, be turned to their defence.

In these awful times, the durability of Linchwe's team attracted streams of adherents. In 1899 Linchwe was the leader of 23,000 souls in Bechuanaland. His inelastic Bakgatla Reserve was being crowded with refugees. Over the previous fifteen years, the river villages, along the ZAR border, of Sikwane, Malolwane, Mabalane and Mathubudukwane had swollen to 5,000. Recently villages had taken root nearer to Mochudi – Morwa, Bokaa, Rasesa, Modipane, Odi and Molotwane. Mochudi itself, a mere 8,000 in 1882, had grown to 15,000. Newcomers were fleeing the ZAR crackdown on 'squatters' (persons who exceeded five families per farm) in the Pilanesberg. Others were coming into Linchwe's reserve from neighbouring reserves in the Protectorate after falling afoul of one kgosi or another. None were turned away. Linchwe's generosity made the Kgatla more than the descendants of settlers who trekked with Kgamanyane. Others from Saulspoort had come over, as had Tlokwa from Kolontwane in the Transvaal, and Lete from Bamalete Reserve, and Kaa, Taung and Kwena from the Bakwena Reserve.

Trade had helped them endure. Through Derdepoort, opposite Sikwane, and up from Mafeking, the roads entering the Protectorate allowed the Kgatla to straddle the trade routes. Since the Kgatla–Kwena war, traffic along the wagon routes had flourished, and the demand for transport increased dramatically. Kgatla acquired oxen and wagons for hiring out, earned wages as drivers and ox-team leaders, sold produce to traders and travellers passing through, and sustained a growing number of European shop owners. White traders also established themselves in the Kgatleng. Resident Mochudi trader Charles Thomas Miller was the first of many in the post-war period. An increasing flow of wagon traffic, goods and post from the south to Shoshong and Matabeleland was passing along the Mochudi route, which in the mid-1880s the Protectorate discovered had reliable water.[7] Before the railroad came, a small community of whites and 'coloureds' had emerged in Mochudi, as storeowners and their employees, petty traders, and blacksmiths. The DRC held special services for their children on the Sabbath, and railed against their fathers for getting drunk during the week and on Saturday.[8] The railroad killed the victualling trade and reduced demand for ox transport, but the shops remained and multiplied. In spite of loses suffered from rinderpest, the Kgatla remained consumers in their own right by exporting their labour to the mines and bringing back cash to the Kgatleng. By 1899, six stores operated in the Bakgatla Reserve, five owned by Mafeking-based Julius Weil, to whom Linchwe had given a mining and trading concession in 1890.[9] Weil remained partners with Linchwe after the Jameson Raid. In 1896, after losing £5,000 in an unsuccessful bid to break the BSA trading monopoly in Khama's country, Weil rejected a BSA offer to buy him out in the Kgatleng.[10] The Protectorate recognised Weil's concession, which gave him exclusive trading rights in the Bakgatla Reserve, except on land granted to the BSA-owned Bechuanaland Railway Company. Weil failed to convince officials that Linchwe's jurisdiction, like that of Khama, extended to the railway strip.[11] At Mochudi Station, Weil had to compete with

The European Business Community, Bakgatla Reserve (1899)

Site	Business	Owner	Employee
Mochudi	1. General Trader	Julius Weil	H.O. Osbourne
	2. Trader	Harbour	
Pilane's	Blacksmith	Horron ('Lenake')	
Mochudi RR Station	1. General trader, liquor dealer	Charles Riley	R.K. Wheare
	2. General trader	Julius Weil	R.A. Wheare
	3. Blacksmith	Phillips	
Sikwane	General Trader	Julius Weil	Sidney Engers
Notwane Junction	General Trader	Julius Weil	Armstrong

Charles Riley, who held the upper hand with a liquor store and an 'accommodation house', but Linchwe reserved the rest of the Kgatleng for Weil to operate his stores. Weil's monopoly, after all, was Linchwe's, who used it to enforce a ban on brandy, restrict the export of locally produced grain and prevent the sale of breeding stock after the rinderpest.[12] Weil profited from the retail trade but Linchwe required him to sell at low margins for the sake of Kgatla buyers. For the use of the land on which his five stores stood, Weil also paid Linchwe an annual fee of £400.

As for the Protectorate government, since the disastrous Jameson raid put paid to BSA ambitions to rule Bechuanaland, the Kgatla had been left to rule themselves. Not a single official or policeman resided in the Reserve. The nearest official post, for the Assistant Commissioner and Magistrate, Southern Protectorate, was located at Gaberones, 30 kilometres from Mochudi. The lone symbol of British power inside the Reserve was a small BSA police presence at Mochudi and Sikwane, placed there to monitor the road into the Transvaal and prevent guns and ammunition from being smuggled north into Matabeleland.[13] The Assistant Commissioner in Gaberones, William H. Surmon, was agreeable enough though slow, aging and in poor health. He was the first Protectorate official without ties to the LMS able to speak to Linchwe in his own language, albeit with a SeSotho accent. Surmon arrived in Bechuanaland after nearly a quarter-century's service in the Basutoland police and magistrate's offices.[14] Surmon's young aide, Jules Ellenberger, was soft-spoken and likeable. Born and raised on the Paris Evangelical Missionary Society station at Masitisi in Basutoland and educated as a teenager in Paris and Lovedale, Jules was the son of Swiss missionary and collector of Sotho historical traditions Rev. D. Frédéric Ellenberger. Jules spoke fluent SeSotho and, soon after arriving in Bechuanaland in 1890, he was fluent in SeTswana. As important to the Kgatla, he practised African etiquette with deference to elders, and the BaKgatla took to him. Ellenberger was unlike any *leKgoa* they had ever encountered. He spoke respectfully. BaKgatla gave him the nicknames, *Ramariba* and *Ramaebana* (father, or keeper, of pigeons), acknowledging Jules' hobby and their liking of his gentle eccentricity.[15]

Unthreatened by such officials living at a distance, and with unrestricted authority over his people in the Reserve, Linchwe exercised it to show his obedience to the Protectorate. In 1899, the year hut tax was introduced and chiefs charged with its collection, Linchwe delivered up a respectable

242

£646, on a par with the Ngwaketse and £100 in excess of that which was turned in by the more numerous Kwena.[16] Linchwe's vigour was particularly marked when collecting tax from people who tried sneaking into his Reserve to hunt. After Linchwe's men tortured several Kwena and Kgalagadi and impounded their arms, Surmon intervened to restrain Linchwe with a fine. Linchwe paid it and admitted wrong, but redacted government's orders by claiming to follow 'instructions'. What, Linchwe asked playfully, 'will government do if [I] failed to collect tax?'[17]

However, relations with the BSA, who operated the trains crisscrossing the Reserve, remained tense and difficult. Quarrels over access to water, the use of land and employing outsiders to work along the line were constant, reaching a breaking point in 1899. Using tax collection as a pretext, Linchwe's men raided a railway camp and looted guns, skins and food, briefly took women and children hostage, and threatened coloured ganger G. Hill to keep clear and remain inside. 'If I dared put my head out', Hill reported, '[they said] they would shoot it off'.[18] Within weeks, up the line in Khama's country, the word was out that Linchwe was among a group plotting with the Boers to 'shoot up the English'.[19] The South African (Anglo-Boer) War, which would put these rumours to a test, was only a few weeks away.

Meanwhile, in the Transvaal, Linchwe had managed to maintain de facto authority over the BaKgatla in the Pilanesberg. About 5,000 lived in and around Saulspoort.[20] He was their sole lifeline to land. In the 1890s Linchwe purchased from DRC missionary Henri Gonin three farms: Saulspoort 38, Kruidfontein 40 and Holfontein 361. Though insufficient for all, the farms served the needs of many and kept them anchored next to the DRC mission, available to surrounding Boer farmers, and near to Linchwe's cattle posts along the Oodi (Krokodil). Moreover, as of 1898 two of these farms, and a third (Modderkuil 39), were held in trust by the Superintendent of Natives and recognised by the ZAR as a *kafferlokasie* in which large numbers of Kgatla were entitled to reside.[21] The Saulspoort location formed a buffer against the Plakkerswet (squatters law), which limited Africans to five families per farm. Not all Kgatla could be accommodated in the location, however, and at least two thousand Kgatla moved over to Bechuanaland rather than disperse themselves among the maBuru.

Impoverished by the bolawane, Linchwe's resources to purchase additional farms, or use Gonin for the purpose, had reached an end. Gonin's own orbit, too, which for three decades had revolved around his Saulspoort mission and DRC outstations, was fast coming to ground. Leading Kgatla Christians in Saulspoort could now defy his rules, and often did, because he had sold Saulspoort to them. The Plakkerswet broke up the communities on the outstations and sent whole Christian communities to Bechuanaland. Without Kgatla subject to him, Gonin was isolated, and alone. The Pilanesberg and Rustenburg Boers had never befriended this Swiss interloper, or the other DRC male missionaries, who quarrelled among themselves. Gonin's seven children were grown and, save Fannie, living weeks or months away. Also, Henri's wife of 36 years, Jenny de Watteville-Gonin, of Swiss royalty (granddaughter of Count Zinzerndorf), died in 1897, malaria-ridden. Sympathy from the Kgatla, long sufferers in the extreme in their own right, was not forthcoming. Linchwe, the DRC's most celebrated convert, Gonin grumped, 'does not behave toward me well', is 'dishonest' and 'very insincere'. Linchwe's 'ungratefulness', and his finagling of Gonin to buy him Holfontein 361, rankled. Worse, over Gonin's objections, Linchwe supported 'heathen' practices such as female initiation. Girls from Saulspoort, some in the mission, were stealing away to Bechuanaland for the ceremony.[22] The evangelists Gonin had groomed – Phiri, Maribe, Mariri, Molefi – were now in Bechuanaland with large congregations out of reach of white missionaries, and under *Linchwe's* control.[23] In the Bakgatla Reserve, Linchwe was shoring up bogosi among his heathen and Christian followers.

In the ZAR, building his *bona fides* with the state had been Linchwe's first priority. He meant his Saulspoort Kgatla to be submissive and loyal. Linchwe picked Mokae, son of Pilane's ninth house, to rule in Saulspoort, and Native Commissioner Harklaas P. Malan readily recognised Mokae as the local kapitein and as Linchwe's deputy. In the 1890s, as in the past, Linchwe, Malan and the local Boers were on good working terms, meaning that when the Commissioner wanted labourers for public works and for commando support, the kapitein sent him the men.[24] During rinderpest, Linchwe's people were instrumental, too, in quarantining infected *kafferbeeste* in the Pilanesberg, to the survival of Boer herds. In return, Linchwe's credentials got him into high places. When Linchwe worried over the effects of the Plakkerswet on his Transvaal subjects, he visited Pretoria and met with ZAR President Paul Kruger to discuss the subject. Soon Malan and neighbouring Boers backed Linchwe and the 'heathen party' in pressuring Gonin to sell Saulspoort, and Kruger's son, Hex River veldkornet Piet Kruger, and son-in-law Teunis Eloff, then sold Linchwe the adjacent farm Modderkuil 39 to enlarge the Saulspoort location. Malan also got Pretoria's permission for Linchwe to sign a lucrative lease with shopkeeper Pieter Morris, over Gonin's protests about allowing a 'canteen' at Saulspoort, especially one run by an 'unscrupulous and immoral' Jewish *smous*.[25] Gonin had no clout, though, whereas Linchwe had what his followers believed was a 'great friendship' with *Oom* Paul.[26]

In truth, Linchwe had no friends. Whether regarded by maKgoa or maBuru, missionary, official, farmer or BSA employee, whether Kwena or Ngwato or any other of his African neighbours in the Protectorate or Pilanesberg, he and his people had become a singular object of distrust. Sebele's Kwena were bitter over the loss of their best land and water resources to the maBuru-backed Tswana filibusters from the Transvaal. Khama of the Ngwato believed the Kgatla were in cahoots with rebel factions such as Khamane and Seleka, and aiding the Boers to encroach on his territory. In spite of his Christian, modernising leadership, Linchwe had failed to shake his notoriety among English-speaking whites. With the possible exception of the young Acting Assistant Commissioner in Gaberones, Jules Ellenberger, all other Protectorate and BSA officials, and the LMS missionaries, suspected Linchwe of harbouring rebellion against British rule and being loyal to the Dutch Reformed Church and the Transvaal Boers. Moreover, notwithstanding Linchwe's good relations with ZAR officialdom, the Boers had an old reputation for cruelty. To the Kgatla, Malan was 'the spoiler of the country, [who] used to make life hard for us'.[27] While ready to support Linchwe for their own ends, Malan and his fellow Boers suspected him of lying in wait to overthrow white rule and perpetrate racial murder. Kruger and Malan, who had failed famously to force Linchwe's father to kowtow to them, feared the Kgatla's bent for assertiveness. The Kgatla posed as *meekkaffers* in the Transvaal to keep the line open between Bechuanaland and the Pilanesberg, and the *maBuru* postured as all-powerful to conceal their dread of a Kgatla onslaught, should it come.

They had good reason to fear. Beyond the boundaries of their little towns, Boers were scattered about on farms among far more numerous Africans. BaKgatla had long known this. Among the people of Bechuanaland, they alone were familiar with the Transvaal, its African and Boer peoples, its resources and its passageways. The open, rolling thorn-treed grassland between their new home in Bechuanaland and their old one in Pilanesberg was thinly settled by Boer farmers and barely defended. Armed Kgatla mephato could transverse this stretch in little more than a day. As their defeat of the Kwena had demonstrated, the Kgatla were well armed and experienced in war. By dint of their assistance to the Rustenburg commandos over the past four decades, moreover, Linchwe's seasoned troops were familiar with Boer methods of fighting. The best, really the only, defensive strategy the Boers had against the Kgatla, the region's most powerful group and most likely to foment an African rebellion in the ZAR, was sharing with their 'friend' today the *proposition* that, in a fight, should the Kgatla become their adversary, the Boers would come out on top. The older Boers, youngsters of the *trek* and veterans of many commandoes, like Kruger and Malan, had learned to avoid inciting kaffers or engaging them in a fair contest, lest the proposition be exposed as an *illusion*. The older generation, meanwhile, were concerned that the younger Boers – raised to lord it over kaffers without having been around when they were subdivided and subdued – did not know the difference. All Boers talked to and about kaffers as beneath them. However, the old, wiser heads knew full well that Africans did not like it that way one bit, while others, the young and headstrong, believed that kaffers had no choice but to accept lowliness as a plain fact.

War

Opposite Sikwane, across the Madikwe River, stood the ZAR government outpost of Derdepoort. Since 1890 it had been manned by P.J. (Hans) Riekert, tax collector on the western border and from 1898, landdrost and border kommandant. Previously the veldkornet of Elands River, Riekert was the brother-in-law of Harklaas P. Malan, the man who had whipped Kgamanyane and who was now Native Commissioner of Rustenburg.[28] The Kgatla knew Riekert as 'Matlabane' ('Rustenburger'). In the first few days of October 1899, before President Kruger declared war against Great Britain and the siege of Mafeking began, veldkornet Piet Kruger arrived at Derdepoort with a Rustenburg commando and instructions to laager atop the hill next to Riekert's place and the few houses nearby.[29] There they waited until October 11, when Boer offensives were launched in Natal, the Cape and in the northern Cape, where a force under General Piet Cronje lay siege to Mafeking, just outside the southern Protectorate border. In order to prevent relief from arriving from Rhodesia, a joint Marico-Bosveld commando under Zeerust veldkornet Piet Swart moved north from Mafeking into Bechuanaland, sacking the terminal at Lobatse, then moving up the line to Ramotswa, where Swart's force of 300 or so was joined by 170 men under Caspar (Kas) du Plessis. As of the 18th, Swart was dug in at Crocodile Pools south of Gaberones, when a Bechuanaland Police force under Capt. Hoel Llewellyn was moving down from Palapye in an armoured Panzer train equipped with a Maxim gun and a 7-pounder gun. Llewellyn's barrage dislodged Swart's men, who retreated south, but Llewellyn moved back north out of fear of attacks on the line from the Derdepoort laager, as well as from a Pietersburg commando under General F.A. Grobler mustering in the northwestern Transvaal near the Macloutsie, passageway to stations at Mahalapye and Palapye. Within a week, a Boer force under General J.P. Snyman had returned to Crocodile Pools with cannon and explosives, blew the bridge nearby, and headed for Gaberones. Grobler's forces entered the Macloutsie area on the 23rd, and on the 25th Surmon and Ellenberger abandoned Gaberones and joined Llewellyn, who moved his train north – moving between the Bakgatla Reserve and Palapye – where they awaited a BSA contingent coming south from Rhodesia. Snyman and his men entered Gaberones on the 26th without resistance and destroyed both railway bridges. Emboldened, the Rustenburgers at Derdepoort, now under Kas du Plessis, began forays into the Bakgatla Reserve, disrupted the railway line and blew up a bridge north of the station.

Men at the laager also began to pressure Linchwe to join them. Harklaas Malan, recently arrived at Derdepoort, was tapped for the purpose, and Linchwe was sent an invitation to meet Malan at the river. Linchwe rode over. According to Thomas Phiri, Linchwe's personal secretary and evangelist at Sikwane, Linchwe and his headmen had already reached the conclusion that the Boers were going to defeat the British.[30] Apart from being fully informed of the quick successes of Snyman's forces, as reported by Ellenberger and BaKgatla passing through the southern Protectorate returning from the mines,[31] Linchwe recalled the failure of the English to subdue the Boers in the Transvaal during Annexation (1877–1881) and how effortlessly the Jameson invasion of the Transvaal had been handled less than four years before. In fact, thanks to the Boers who snuffed that raid, the BSA was denied its chance to confiscate most of Linchwe's land and get rid of him. The man he was about to meet once again was in the group that arrested Jameson himself. Not to mention also the Rustenburg Superintendent of Natives, who held the fate of his Saulspoort people in the ink of his pen.

At that moment, Linchwe was hedging his bets. Through Ellenberger he knew that the BSA police were expected soon, coming down from Matabeleland, where twice they had crushed the AmaNdebele. Word had arrived, too, that Khama had rejected an ultimatum from Grobler to remain neutral and had welcomed BSA troops under Plumer arriving at Palapye. Any hint that Linchwe favoured the Boers would be an invitation to the BSA, with Khama's help, to declare him an enemy and his Reserve hostile territory. At the meeting Linchwe told Malan that the Kgatla wished to stay out of the fight, that they had no grudge against the Boers and that the Kgatla would not oppose the Boers if Malan's men did not 'worry him'. Malan, though, wanted a commitment. He boasted of the Boers' strength and, according to Phiri, claimed they 'could drive the British into the sea'.[32] Linchwe would give no answer. Malan agreed to wait, but an answer should come soon. The sign that the Kgatla would assist the Boers was to be a gift of slaughter oxen to the laager.

Meanwhile, ignorant of the Linchwe–Malan meeting, Protectorate officials and their meagre police force retreated up the railway line and encouraged Linchwe to defend his Reserve against the Boers. Overnight, the Bakgatla Reserve had become central to British survival in the region. Loss of the Reserve, which straddled a hundred-kilometre stretch of the railway above Gaberones, could mean the loss of the southern Protectorate and a further, perhaps fatal, delay in relieving Mafeking. Desperately undermanned, the British suddenly found themselves dependent on Linchwe for their own protection. While the Rhodesians were delayed in the north, in anticipation of an invasion by Grobler not only into Macloutsie but into southern Matabeleland, Llewellyn plied Linchwe with ammunition, promised him that support from BSA troops from Rhodesia was imminent, and reminded him of his duty as a chief of the Protectorate. Yet, Llewellyn stationed no men in Linchwe's reserve and visited Mochudi only to remove furniture and goods from the stores of British traders.[33] Instead of giving Linchwe direct support, Llewellyn's men rode their armoured train up and down the line playing cat-and-mouse with mounted Boer parties, who were attempting to damage the rails. Privately the British doubted Linchwe's willingness to fight and were convinced he was

THE LAST RAID

Hercules (Harklaas) Malan and associates, 1896. Seated from left: Hercules P. Malan, Johannes Cornelis Brink, Piet Riekert. Standing from left: Oom Jan Heystek, Johannes Izak Eloff. Sketch by Lemington Muzhingi.

being influenced by the DRC missionaries in Mochudi, who were telling Linchwe to remain 'neutral'. The Boers, Linchwe told Ellenberger, 'were too many for him'.[34]

Linchwe was stalling for time. In the fortnight following the sack of Gaberones, the Boers possessed the initiative in the Protectorate, and without British support Linchwe had little choice but to give the Rustenburgers the run of his reserve. Though pretty much convinced that the Boers ultimately would win, his future and that of his people would be better off with their defeat. To side with the retreating British, however, was to invite swift retaliation or, in the peace following a Boer victory, a more pervasive revenge. Until the British committed themselves in force, however, Linchwe's only defence was, as one of his messenger-spies later put it, 'to blind the Dutch' by giving them the impression that the Kgatla sympathised with their cause.[35] In response to Malan's request for tribute as a sign of Linchwe's readiness to assist them, Linchwe instructed his men to drive cattle, sheep and goats to the Derdepoort laager and to help the Rustenburgers strengthen the drift across the Madikwe River connecting Derdepoort with Sikwane.[36] All this Linchwe concealed from the British, whose anger he feared much less than the Boers, but whose intentions were much more ambiguous. Instead, his aides and messengers paid daily visits to Ellenberger and prodded him, Surmon and Llewellyn with selected intelligence in order to discover how far they were prepared to take the fight to the maBuru.

While waiting for a reversal in the general trend of military events, Linchwe was losing face in front of his own people. With seemingly little to fear from the Kgatla, the Rustenburgers began stealing cattle in the Bakgatla Reserve and galloping through Mochudi without regard for the safety of children and the elderly. Linchwe did nothing about the cattle theft. When he politely asked a party of Boers passing through Mochudi to rein in their mounts, leader Hendrick Riekert, son of Hans Riekert, head of the police at Derdepoort, delivered Linchwe a public insult of the first order. 'Riekert picked up a handful of dirt and said that the dirt was cleaner than the chief of the Kgatla, then he threw his handful of dirt in the air and said that the little stone falling was bigger than the chief of the Kgatla'.[37] Linchwe bore Riekert's cocksure display in silence. The chief's helplessness was made to appear the more acute by the behaviour of Segale, his half-brother and leading advocate of Kgatla control of the DRC, who was now

250

using the growing threat of war to promote his ambitions. Outspokenly anti-Boer, Segale clamoured for an attack on the Derdepoort laager, busied himself reconnoitring Boer positions, and made frequent visits to the British, whom he impressed as being the man in the Reserve most eager for a fight.[38] Linchwe had nothing to gain by following Segale's lead, but the need to maintain Kgatla regiments at battle readiness in Mochudi kept the atmosphere tense, lent importance to Segale's conspicuous activities and, to Linchwe's even greater disadvantage, risked giving the Boers the impression that the Kgatla were in league with the British. On 8 November Segale compromised Linchwe's position even further when he and his men joined Llewellyn's armoured train in a surprise attack on Riekert's party then attempting to tear up the railway at Mosupabatho, five kilometres northwest of Mochudi.[39]

Linchwe had little choice now but to act. That night, after welcome reports were received that the BSA troops had reached Mahalapye and were preparing to move south, the war horn was sounded on the hill above the DRC church. On 10 November Linchwe told Surmon that the Kgatla were ready to fight and wanted firearms.[40] Promised a new supply of rifles, Linchwe dispatched his regiments to patrol the countryside north of Mochudi. No skirmishes resulted, but within days Hendrick Riekert and a corider from the laager rode into Mochudi unaware that Linchwe had placed the Kgatla on a war footing. Linchwe had the two arrested and turned over to the British. Word of young Riekert's arrest, which amounted to a declaration of war, spread quickly. On or about 22 November, when Colonel J. Holdsworth's Rhodesian 7th Hussars were coming down the rail from Mahalapye, one of Linchwe's principal loyalists in Saulspoort, Dikeme Mantirisi, galloped into Mochudi with disturbing news: Boer troop reinforcements had left Rustenburg for Derdepoort in preparation for a major offensive against the Kgatla, and they were coming with a price on Linchwe's head.[41]

At this point, the Rhodesians arrived. On 23 November, Llewellyn and the Rhodesians steamed into Mochudi station, where Llewellyn and Holdsworth met with Linchwe and Segale. A sketch of Derdepoort, based on information brought in from Kgatla scouts, lay before them. Two laagers were situated atop two ridges in Derdepoort, above the small village below. According to Klaas Segogwane, Linchwe's spy, all the cannons at Derdepoort had been removed. Holdsworth told Linchwe that a hundred of his mounted Rhodesians, together with a maxim gun, would march the following evening to Sikwane for the purpose of launching an attack on the Derdepoort laager and that Linchwe's regiments should be stationed in Sikwane ready to defend the Kgatla Reserve if the attack suffered a reverse. The Kgatla were enjoined to refrain from firing or entering into the battle and told to follow orders quickly.[42] Surmon insisted that the Kgatla simply stand by in Sikwane while Holdsworth's men attacked Derdepoort. All agreed, and Segale was to accompany Holdsworth. Linchwe sent word to the cattle posts along the riverine border and in the southern part of the Reserve that all Kgatla stock be removed to the Mochudi area.[43] Then, on the evening of the 24th, as Segale and two regiments (maKoba and maFatlha) set out with the Rhodesians towards Sikwane/Derdepoort, Linchwe quietly moved south with three other regiments (maJanko, maThukwi and maThakana) and camped the night at Odi, in preparation for stopping the Boers at Gaberones, where Malan was now laagered, to come to the relief of Derdepoort.[44] Meanwhile, Segale led the other force through the darkness.

Before dawn, as they neared Sikwane, Holdsworth ordered Segale to see that Kgatla regiments were positioned on a ridge overlooking the enemy laager from the east. In effect, this order required the Kgatla to cross the Madikwe and enter the Transvaal, contrary to Surmon's wishes and against the agreement struck at the railway station.[45] However, Holdsworth had told Segale before departing Mochudi that 'he and his people should obey orders at once'. With less than an hour awaiting daylight and no time to question, Segale obeyed Holdsworth, and Ramono, Linchwe's brother, led the Koba and Fatlha regiments across the Madikwe and on to the ridge above the laager, while Segale remained with other troops on the Protectorate side to assist Holdsworth. Then, with the clock ticking, Holdsworth was induced by Klaas Segogwane, who came from Sikwane to meet the contingent, to abandon his plan to position himself on a ridge near the beacon and northwest of laagers and move his cavalry and maxim instead onto a ridge above the river, inside the ZAR border, to get a shorter and more direct view of the laager.[46] When dawn arrived, therefore, Ramono's forces were positioned on a ridge northeast and adjacent the two Boer laagers and Holdsworth was atop a ridge directly opposite, i.e. southwest of the laagers, with the Madikwe River between him and the Boers. The signal for attack was to be a Rhodesian bugle and Holdsworth's whistle, but after reaching his position, Holdsworth claims he saw smoke and heard shooting north of his position and immediately began discharging the maxim gun, after which all began firing.[47]

Only after Kgatla guns came into action, so Holdsworth claimed later, did he realise that the Kgatla had crossed into the Transvaal. Holdsworth also felt himself badly placed. The bullets and shot of Kgatla fire were passing through the laager and landing at Holdsworth's position and he claimed the angle of the maxim put the Kgatla at similar risk. Within minutes, Holdsworth withdrew his maxim and cavalry out of the range of the Boer Mausers and beat a retreat, leaving the Kgatla in the thick of battle. For the next three hours, Ramono's men held their position and fired their Martini-Henrys and muzzle-loaders into the laager. According to one account, the Koba and Fatlha 'attacked the laager in a Boer way' and shot with accuracy.[48] Word was sent to Holdsworth that 'the laager almost taken. . . [we] wanted a little assistance to take the laager' but Holdsworth accused the Kgatla of disobeying his orders by entering the Transvaal and stated he had 'instructions to go back to Mahalapye'. 'And so', Ellenberger recorded in his diary later that day, 'we left Sequane village while the Bakhatla were still fighting for the Queen'.[49] Ramono's forces struggled on, but eventually retreated carrying their dead and wounded past Derdepoort houses and rounding up Boer women and children. Crossing the river to Sikwani, they wagoned their captives and casualties back to Mochudi and handed over all eighteen Boer women and children, unharmed, to the British.[50]

Linchwe was furious. At Mochudi station, in the presence of Surmon and Ellenberger, he confronted Holdsworth:

> Linchwe asked how many men he had killed and how many wounded, and [Holdsworth] replied 'none' at which Linchwe told him he had fourteen men killed and sixteen wounded and told him that Colonel Holdworth had gone not to fight but to see a fight – that when a native Chief went with another chief to battle they won together or fell together, but that one never abandoned the other in the field.

Linchwe wanted another attack, immediately, to drive out the surviving Boers and protect his grain supplies near the river.[51] The Boers had already begun to retaliate against his people by shelling Sikwane. But the Rhodesians, expecting to push south and begin the overland drive to relieve

Mafeking, remained at Mochudi station awaiting the arrival of a column from Plumtree and leaving Linchwe alone with the task of protecting the river villages.

The Kgatla had been set up. As Klaas Segowane put it, 'the British were satisfied that with these shots they had involved Linchwe, whom they apparently distrusted, as a friend of the Boers'.[52] The Rhodesians had long thought of Linchwe as an opponent of British expansion, and considered Derdepoort a threat to the railway as long as Linchwe claimed he was neutral. Holdsworth was not prepared to risk the lives of his own men while Linchwe's men watched out of harm's way; his major objective was the relief of Mafeking. Better to arm Linchwe's men and push them into battle against the Boers.

In the coming weeks, Linchwe's regiments along the river struggled to hold their ground. Days after the Derdepoort attack, the Boers launched an attack on Sikwane, but were driven back by armed BaKgatla lining the river bank.[53] In early December, Boer reinforcements began arriving from Rustenburg and Pietersburg until the number at the laager reached two hundred or more.[54] During their build-up the Boers sacked Sikwane on 14 December and, after the Kgatla attacked Derdepoort on 21 December, resumed their reprisals on 22 December with attacks on Malolwane, Mathubudukwane and Sikwane, the last of which they burned on Christmas Eve. The villagers vacated to Mochudi.[55] On 29 December Linchwe's men again tried to dislodge the Boers in a battle that one report said lasted seven hours. The result was inconclusive, but after 1 January 1900 the Boers ceased their raids into the Bakgatla Reserve, allowing the BaKgatla to take the offensive.[56]

In January, too, the tide of the war in South Africa began to shift in favour of the British. Early that month, British troop reinforcements began flooding into South Africa, reversing the balance of strength in the south. From the Cape, Roberts and Kitchener's forces marched inland and, in February and March, they relieved Kimberley and Ladysmith and in turn captured Bloemfontein. Boer forces retreated north deeper into the Orange Free State and the Transvaal, putting up modest resistance before the British advance. While these events were unfolding, the Boers continued their siege of Mafeking and reinforced the laagers at Derdepoort and at Crocodile Pools in an effort to prevent the relief of Mafeking by Rhodesians entrained from the north. In mid-January, Plumer's column of Rhodesian mounted infantry was engaged in trying to destroy the Boer laager at Crocodile Pools and establishing an overland base at Kanye.[57]

As soon as the Boer effort to obstruct Plumer was concentrated at Crocodile Pools, the Derdepoort laager became fair game for Linchwe. In early December Linchwe had been instructed by Surmon to refrain from moving his forces into the Transvaal, an order Linchwe threatened to ignore should the Kgatla suffer another attack. 'If they cross', he cautioned Ellenberger, 'I shall cross and shall not stop at Sequani'. Already he had word from the Pilanesberg that his people were being targeted in retaliation for Derdepoort. 'I hear they intend to kill my people at Saul's Poort, and I do not want them to', he upbraided Surmon through Ellenberger, 'you give them every possible chance'.[58] After the Christmas sack of Sikwane, however, Linchwe checked his men from retaliating beyond Derdepoort, while sending scouts to reconnoitre behind Boer lines. With Holdsworth in Mochudi and the laager receiving reinforcements, his hands were tied. However, when Plumer passed through Mochudi station in January, the British military were preparing to employ Africans in the war effort. Colonel Baden-Powell at Mafeking had been informed of the Derdepoort attack of 29 November and received complaints from General Snyman – and Baden-Powell defended Linchwe's actions. Baden-Powell was then within weeks of threatening an invasion of the Transvaal with armed Bechuanaland Tswana regiments.[59] It also appears that Linchwe was given permission to enter the Transvaal and received additional arms for the purpose.[60] Plumer may have had in mind that Linchwe's men challenge the Derdepoort laager while Plumer's troops moved on Crocodile Pools. By early February Linchwe had grouped 800 men at Sikwane, as the *Times* reported, to 'defend borders from Boer invasion'. These men included reinforcements from Saulspoort.[61] Soon, on 16 February, two regiments circled around Derdepoort and marched into the Transvaal to Kaeye, at mid-point on the road between Derdepoort and the Dwarsberg. There the maKoba under Ramono and maJanko under Motshwane lay in wait for a large convoy of wagons, troops and supplies heading for Derdepoort. A third regiment, maNtwane under Mochele, remained closer to Derdepoort to prevent the commandos there, estimated at 300 men, from breaking out of the laager.[62] When the convoy passed between Ramono and Motshwane's men, a vicious crossfire surprised the Boers, several of whom died on the spot, while others fled on foot leaving behind their horses and supplies.[63]

Linchwe, for weeks the object of insults and threats from the maBuru at Derdepoort, now had his turn to taunt. He sent Thomas Phiri to the laager to meet Kas Du Plessis and Piet Kruger and deliver the message:

> So works a man. I have had a good fight at Kaye Pit, I have got the wagons and all that was on them, if you want to come here you can, you only stand at Sikwane and destroy food of children (crops) in the lands, and I thought you came to fight BaKgatla. I'm here at Mochudi, why don't you come?

Du Plessis and Kruger asked Phiri:

> What had Linchwe done with all the food and cases of brandy and clothes on the wagon? [I] replied that all were divided at the kgotla, brandy anyone could drink. And they shook their heads and sent word to Linchwe that [they were] finished with him and wished to return to the Transvaal, but surprised that Linchwe, as a member of the Dutch Reformed Church, could treat them like that, kill people, use spears and axes, beat heads in with [knob]kirries. This was not Christian-like and yet [we] belong to one church and one belief.

In seBuru minds, what Linchwe's people had done to them at Derdepoort and Kaeye was *moord* ('murder'), a sentiment, fuelled by the rumour that BaKgatla had killed Boer women, that spread throughout budding Afrikanerdom and survived in the retelling for another century.[64] Acknowledgment of the commando's own treatment of Kgatla civilians, of course, or recollections in decades past of the slaughter of African men and women and the enslavement of their children, had not taken root in their heads. Theirs was not a land of remorse. When Phiri returned to Mochudi and related Du Plessis and Kruger's comments to Linchwe, 'he only laughed'.[65] Soon afterwards the Boers abandoned Derdepoort laager, which remained unoccupied for the duration of the war.[66]

Offensive

Now the road into the western Transvaal lay open to Linchwe's regiments. Plumer's column moved steadily south, drawing Boer troops tighter around Mafeking, where the next drama of the war was building to a climax. For the next three months, Plumer's forces made their way west of the rail past Kanye, slowly approaching Mafeking from the northwest. Desperate to gain a British surrender before Plumer could arrive, the Boers under General Snyman intensified pressure on the besieged town and began arming some of their BaRolong allies.[67] Snyman acted in response to what he considered the British violation of an early agreement to fight a 'white man's war', when Linchwe's regiments were armed and used at Derdepoort. The Kgatla victories at Derdepoort and Kaeye, however, gave Mafeking commander Baden-Powell a pin with which to skewer Snyman and weaken his men's morale, while Plumer's relief column pressed nearer to Mafeking. 'If the armed natives are not withdrawn [from the Mafeking area]', Baden-Powell wrote to Snyman, 'steps will be taken for carrying into effect an invasion of the Marico and Rustenburg districts by Linchwe, Khama, Batheon, etc.'[68] By the time this letter was delivered to Snyman, word had arrived of Linchwe's entry into the Transvaal and his regiments' victory at Kaeye over the convoy trying to relieve Derdepoort and the abandonment of Derdepoort itself, leaving the Transvaal undefended.

The largely empty bushveld around the Pilanesberg and north up to the Limpopo was known by the BaKgatla more intimately than it was by other Africans, more so than by the maBuru. Before the Voortrekkers arrived the Kgatla had occupied it, and it remained largely theirs to use even after they came under Boer rule. They kept cattle there all year round, hunted, and traded along routes they had pioneered generations before Pilane. The Boers took their cattle into this zone during the winter months from May to September, and spent time hunting, but their herds were governed most of the time by servants while the baasen were back at their farms in the Rustenburg district. The territory between the Pilanesberg and the new Kgatla home in Bechuanaland was a veritable private highway connecting Linchwe's people around Mochudi with his subjects at Saulspoort. When the Boer commandos arrived in Derdepoort, they came with Kgatla guides.[69] Below the Derdepoort–Saulspoort line lay scattered Boer farms and the villages of Mabe's Tlhako, Mphoto's Tlhatlherwa, and Sehume's Kwena, well known to and fearful of Linchwe's people. In other words, the terrain for the new conflict, now in the Boers' backyard, favoured the BaKgatla. What remained uncertain was whether the British wanted Linchwe in the Transvaal enough to supply him with more arms and ammunition.

Linchwe could not wait. Already he was a declared enemy. Sometime in March 1900 word arrived in Mochudi that Linchwe's cattle posts, located well north of the Pilanesberg, at the edge of the Waterberg at Modubyane, were targeted by a Boer commando. Rather than listen to officials who advised him to hold back, Linchwe sent his men straight away. 'They're there [and] some of my people there are suffering . . . I'm going to punish these Boers.'[70] Three regiments reached Modubyane, 130 kilometres directly east of Mochudi, by which time the Rustenburgers had moved out of the Waterberg and moved southwest towards the Pilanesberg, where Linchwe's men found them at Makalakala (Buffelshoek), in the Mfete Valley. They were riding behind veldkornet Piet Swart, who had been in the Derdepoort laager. The Kgatla knew him as 'Rameolora' (blondie), for his long light-yellow hair.

> . . . the Kgatla fired on them with a Martini,
> With a Martini, the Kgatla of Kgafela's tribe,
> He turned them back at Makalakala
> At the hillock of Siloagae;
> Ramelora and company fled, the cowards
> Carting away their goods by night;
> As they fled they turned into baboons
> Becoming male baboons, inmates of caves.[71]

Linchwe's men captured 36 oxen and returned with them to Mochudi.[72]

Meanwhile, the war had turned against the Boers. The siege of Mafeking ended on 17 May 1900, and immediately the British advanced into the Transvaal heartland. In quick succession, British troops captured all the main centres: Johannesburg in May, Pretoria in June and Rustenburg in July. As British control extended steadily along the major roads and centres, Linchwe's regiments were issued more Martini-Henrys and advanced into the hills and mountains north of Rustenburg where small commandos were keeping their hopes alive for an assault on vulnerable British positions. In May 1900 word reached Linchwe in Mochudi that the Boers, in retaliation for his Makalakala attack, were commandeering and thrashing his people in Saulspoort. Again, Linchwe requested and received formal permission from Surmon for his men to enter the Transvaal.[73] Linchwe's men, however, had already gone ahead. In Tlhako country, 30 kilometres west of Saulspoort, the Kgatla ambushed a Boer convoy at Moreteletse, at the foot of the Matlapengsberg and not far from the commando camp at Ruighoek 169. The Kgatla, led by Linchwe's uncle Kgari Pilane, captured

300 oxen and three wagons.[74] By then the Kgatla had already begun to loot cattle from Boer farms either abandoned or undefended. All this stock was driven back to the Bakgatla Reserve and into the Bamangwato Reserve for safekeeping. Khama, Linchwe's old adversary, was happy to lend a hand to stick it to the Boers, whom he loathed. Just as Pretoria had allowed Linchwe's regiments to empty the eastern Kweneng of its cattle during the Kgatla–Kwena War and send them into the Transvaal for the duration of the conflict, now Khama was doing his part to punish the citizens of the expiring South African Republic. Largely on account of Kgatla raiding, much of the western Transvaal north and west of Rustenburg was abandoned by the time Smuts passed through the area in mid-1900.[75]

By this time, the British had decided to rein in Linchwe. British confidence in full victory rose in step with their advance along the main roads, and their need for Linchwe's assistance dwindled. Soon after the capture of Pretoria in early June, Linchwe was warned to recall all his men from the Transvaal and turn over all stock captured to the officer at Gaberones.[76] In July, however, Linchwe's men were still in the Transvaal when Kitchener's troops marched into Rustenburg. Kitchener summoned the Kgatla regiments into the town, demanded back all the rifles issued to the Kgatla when Britain needed an ally and, as the Kgatla watched, set their 250 Martini-Henrys on fire.[77]

Little time passed, however, before Kitchener needed the Kgatla again. After the capture of Rustenburg, the British found it difficult to hold the town and keep lines of communication open. Between July 1900 and the end of the year, Boer forces under De Wet and De la Rey drove the British to distraction in and around the Magaliesberg range between Rustenburg and Pretoria.[78] De la Rey's forces also moved about the bushveld north of the line between Rustenburg and Swaartruggens, striking at weak points in British lines. For two weeks in August, they besieged Hore's column at Elands River and exacted a heavy toll.[79] As Kitchener shored up his defences along the main lines of communication, he called on the Kgatla to attack De la Rey's food supply, namely the cattle grazing on farms to the north in the bushveld. This arrangement, clandestinely administered by military intelligence through Mafeking, fitted into Kitchener's plan of divesting guerrilla zones of food and draught resources without risking British lives. The Protectorate employed a white civilian to enlist Linchwe's support and offered as a reward 25 percent of the stock captured. Linchwe's men were supplied with tickets to be sewn into the collars of their jackets as a warrant for safe passage when returning through British lines.[80] Linchwe went along but soon lost interest. Without rifles, the risks were too great. In November, Linchwe lost forty men while bringing one hundred head out of commando territory. When offered prize money, he tossed off the reward. 'Linchwe handed over the cattle', reported a Mafeking transport official, 'and refused to have anything more to do with [them]'.[81] Complaints, though, began to arrive from Africans in the Transvaal that the Kgatla were helping themselves to *their* cattle.[82]

Bonokwane

Without awaiting any instructions, Linchwe attempted to control the Pilanesberg and the area between it and Bechuanaland. As a *de facto* surrogate British force, the Kgatla had been operating north of Rustenburg intermittently since mid-1900. They were particularly effective in moving into unprotected Boer farms, dispersing laagers of Boer children, women and elderly, shooting their guards, and looting goods and stock.[83] Delicious pleasure was had in spending the night at Piet Kruger's abandoned house and helping themselves to his stores, and in carting back to Bechuanaland symbols of Boer elegance. Segale was especially proud of his new pump organ. In early 1901, small Kgatla bands became an even more determined presence. They took control of the Saulspoort area and raided for stock among the Fokeng, Kwena and Phalane. These groups Linchwe later painted as Boer collaborators: keeping their cattle, feeding them, and providing them with scouts. He would know.[84] Linchwe no longer mobilised regiments for the purpose; instead he doctored the bullets of men from wards who reckoned their own opportunities. Kgatla began combing the area in twos and threes, on the loose with their own ambitions *tla bonokwane*, to rustle cattle from the most vulnerable, and bring them back to Mochudi.

> When men went looting, they did so as members of dikgotla (wards). They moved [as] swiftly as possible, lest they be detected by maBuru, and not only that but by other BaKgatla of other wards 'stealing a march' from others . . . people were even killing fellow Bakgatla to get at the cattle first.[85]

Once back with the cattle in the Kgatleng, Linchwe took his share of those brought to his kgotla.

Virtually unchallenged in the Transvaal, the Kgatla extended their reach over an area extending from Palla camp on the Oori River, along Limpopo south beyond the Kgetleng (Elands) River and east well into the Pretoria district.[86] Because men were eventually needed back in Bechuanaland to attend the harvest, this territory again reverted to the Boers, leaving the Saulspoorters at their mercy.

> [T]here were 44 cases of what, to use an euphemism, one might call 'summary executions' by the Boers, all of which were due to the well known Anglophile tendencies of the tribe [Kgatla]. Numberless cases of cruelty by Boers took place in public at Saulspoort, amongst which the flogging to death of an invalid, Mosogae Segogoane, is the worst.[87]

In August 1901 Linchwe's regiments stormed back into the Transvaal. Pushing all the way to the Pretoria area and north to Thabazimbi, Kgatla parties sacked Boer farms and took cattle which they alleged had been seized on earlier commando raids.[88] In September, the Rustenburgers retaliated, sending 300 against the Bechuanaland Kgatla, but Linchwe's men turned them back at the border, killing several men and capturing 133 oxen and other stock.[89] Then, in December, the commando took its revenge by attacking Saulspoort and raiding cattle from Kgatla posts all the way to Bierkraal.[90]

After receiving, at last, a new consignment of rifles on Kitchener's instructions, Linchwe's men returned to the Transvaal and secured the territory for the British until the end of the war. Between December 1901 and May 1902, two lots of rifles were supplied to the Kgatla, who fought two pitched battles near the Pilanesberg, one at Draaiberg and another at Janskop, before the Boers surrendered to the British on 31 May 1902.[91] In the closing months of the war, the Kgatla claimed they had received additional inducements to fight that went well beyond a stack of Martini-Henry rifles. A British official reported,

> The Bakhatla seem to have been under the impression that the Government relied on them to hold the country, north of the Elands River, and that if they were successful, they would receive in return, all the country held, or the farms at Saulspoort claimed as tribal territory by Kgamanyane, the father of Linchwe.[92]

Four months before the war ended, the Kgatla effectively controlled the country between Rustenburg and the Protectorate border and 'protected for us', noted the Resident Commissioner, 'a long frontier without the aid of a single man'.[93]

The Cost

At the end of the war, the accumulated cost to the Kgatla in driving the Boers back into the Transvaal and pinning them there was heavy. In 1903 the Transvaal commissioner at Pilanesberg placed the total number of Kgatla killed in action at 52, but this was much too low a figure. Fourteen died at Derdepoort and forty in the September 1900 cattle raids alone, and four deaths and twenty-two casualties at Kaeye were reported at Gaberones.[94] In addition Linchwe lost men at Moreteletse, where his advisor Tlhatsi was slain, and at Derdepoort again in November 1901. Adding Draaiberg and Janskop, the Kgatla–Boer skirmishes in August–September 1901 and the December 1901 commando raid against Saulspoort and surrounding cattle posts, would suggest that at least 200 fighting men were killed in action or on raids, and 500 casualties were the consequence. Seventy years later, old men in Mochudi recalled the many men who survived the war disfigured: amputated limbs, ears blown off and other permanent losses. With an estimated population of 30,000 Kgatla at the beginning of the war, probably 3,500 men would have been battleworthy.[95] Seven hundred dead or wounded, therefore, represents 18 percent of the adult male population between eighteen and forty, or roughly one in five.[96]

Other means can help to estimate the suffering. The civilian population in Saulspoort lived in constant insecurity in what was guerrilla territory from August 1900 to February or March 1902. The Saulspoort Kgatla who sided with the Boers for a time did not fear reprisals from Linchwe's regiments, but Linchwe also could not command loyalty from the Saulspoorters without exposing them to retaliation by the maBuru. Some of his own people acted as scouts or spies for the Rustenburgers, but none were victims of recrimination. Mokae, kapitein of Saulspoort, cooperated with the Boers and was eventually captured by Linchwe's men, and spent the war in 'house arrest' in Mochudi. He was allowed to return to Saulspoort after the war.[97] Forty-four known executions by Boers in Saulspoort alone came to light after the war, not to mention unreported killings at cattle posts during commando raids.[98] To these costs may be added the difficulties of getting enough to eat. Cultivating and harvesting on both sides of the border declined greatly in Kgatla areas during the war, in spite of good rainfall. Insecurity and the scarcity of men and cattle reduced agriculture to hoe-cultivation by women. Boys were needed to safeguard the herd deep into the Bakgatla Reserve and in Khama's country, and the men too old or too tired for regimental duties were organised, by ward, for standby defence in Mochudi and the villages. Surplus cattle were sold to purchase grain, equipment and supplies for Linchwe's people and regiments: the British were giving out only ammunition.[99]

Mosunyane

As for cattle, that was another story. Linchwe claimed losses of more than seven thousand head, one of the few exaggerated Kgatla laments after the war.[100] The Boers did seize many Kgatla cattle during the conflict, but Kgatla regiments and raiding parties more than restored the balance. Such facts Linchwe concealed from Protectorate officials, who before the war was over were attempting to restore stock to Boers claiming to be non-combatants or pro-British.[101] Linchwe had the same apprehension about cattle his men had taken from Africans collaborating with the Boers.

The truth is that, between Derdepoort and the Boer surrender, the Kgatla expanded the national herd enormously. In 1904 officials estimated the Kgatla herd at 16,091, which was probably as much as ten times the number of cattle the Kgatla possessed after the rinderpest and before the war. In 1911, when officials had fuller appreciation of the extent of Kgatla holdings, the number was 36,301, a figure that subsequent stock censuses show could not have been far off the mark.[102] In the years after the war, cattle were so plentiful in the Reserve that beasts were slaughtered almost nightly in Mochudi for feasting.[103]

Linchwe distributed the cattle spoils of war generously among the Kgatla, especially to those men who had distinguished themselves in war. During the conflict, Linchwe controlled the cattle arriving from the Transvaal with his regiments. These were the *mosunyane*, cattle that were needed to feed his men while on duty and to sell for grain, clothing and other supplies. After the war, Linchwe gave beasts to sons of men who died while fighting, as well as to the poor. To the gallant men, such as Molemane Monametse ('ugly mug') and Lebotse Motsete Phetu among many others, went the core of a new personal herd. Headmen of the main wards received gifts, and to reliable wardsmen Linchwe offered generous loans of up to ten head. During the war Saulspoort Kgatla brought cattle over to the Bakgatla Reserve and at the end those who fought with Linchwe returned to the Transvaal with their reward in kind. The flooding of the Reserve with cattle from the Transvaal transformed the Kgatla herd as well as resurrected it. Before the war, Kgatla cattle were tall beasts with huge horns and little carrying weight; afterwards, the herd carried an unmistakable Afrikander stamp.[104]

Linchwe's people had also dealt a telling blow to the Rustenburg maBuru. Battling with the commandos lost more Kgatla than Boers, because for much of the conflict the Kgatla had muzzle-loaders while the Boers had the latest Mauser rifles. Nevertheless, the pressures of war, the guerrilla campaign and the exposure of the bushveld to Kgatla attacks led to the Boer evacuation of much of the area. Boer rule in these areas came to an end, at least for the time being. Hundreds of Boer families departed, and their farms stood vacant or unsold for years. The First World War came and went before the second Boer colonisation of the Transvaal north of Rustenburg got underway. In that time, the Kgatla had more space than three generations before them. After the war, Kgatla cattle grazed undisturbed on both sides of the Madikwe and Oori rivers, and Kgatla in Saulspoort had much land available for agriculture. The post-war Saulspoorters had a reputation for being rich, even among the few Boers still farming in the area. Before the war, white farmers had no difficulty in getting abundant black labour at no cost to themselves. After it, they had trouble hiring a single man at the going rate. 'I know of one particular occasion', reported the Sub-Native Commissioner at Pilanesberg,

> When a farmer told me that he was working on his land, putting in tobacco, and he saw some natives passing at the end of his land. As he wanted labour he went up to them and offered them 2s 6d a day to work for him, but they simply turned round to him and said 'If you would like to work for 2s 6d a day, baas, we shall be only too pleased to employ you.'[105]

As late as 1914, Boer women and children gathering the harvest alone was another common scene.[106]

For their sacrifices in the war, the Kgatla achieved much of what they had set out to accomplish. Linchwe's regiments and free-lancing bands recovered far more cattle than the rinderpest had taken away, and the defeated Boers of the Transvaal had ceased, or so it seemed, to farm or reign supreme. 'Not one family of farmers has returned to the Pilansberg', reported a local British official first on the scene after the cessation of hostilities, 'and I fear the natives exult in the consciousness that the Boers are afraid of them'.[107] Prosperity, an experience unknown to Kgatla living before the war, became commonplace at the beginning of the twentieth century. The hand of the Protectorate government remained light, and in the Transvaal a similar policy of British administration was being implemented. In 1902 Linchwe installed Ramono as deputy chief in Saulspoort, and in the Kgatla Reserve Linchwe enjoyed greater and firmer control over his people than perhaps any kgosi before. He governed without fear of Malan, now dead, or supplication to Kruger, now exiled.

The Kgatla did fall short of attaining one important objective: reclaiming ancestral land in the Transvaal. Kgatla gained immediate access to much land in the Saulspoort area and elsewhere, not because they owned the property, but for the simple reason that the Boers had vacated it. The promise, that in peace the Kgatla would be given the territory they had controlled in war, was disavowed. The Kgatla considered them their own 'by right of conquest', but the farms owned by Boers, whether British enemy or friend during the war, remained their property under the new administration, and Kgatla who had been using these properties were run off. British protection of Boer interests upset the Kgatla and the others who had helped Kitchener's forces; it was reported that the 'natives are greatly disappointed at not being made grants of land in consideration of the services they rendered . . . they full expect that the farms would be taken from the Boers and given to them'.[108] The Transvaal administration also postponed changes in their predecessor's land policies, namely that land so purchased was tribal property held in trust in the name of the 'Native Commissioner'. No demarcation of reserves along Protectorate lines was undertaken, and in terms of legal occupation the Saulspoort Kgatla ended the war where they had started – with Saulspoort 38, Modderkuil 39, Kruidfontein 40 and Holfontein 361.[109]

Linchwe, though but 44 years old, was worn out from the war, and disinclined to budge from Mochudi. His travelling days were over, his reclusion setting in. His mind now dwelt on delegation. Linchwe took the titles of 'Kgosi eKgolo ea Bakgatla' and 'Paramount Chief of the Bakhatla Na-

Linchwe, 1902. Sketch by Lemington Muzhingi.

tion', and placed his brothers in administrative control of his two territories; Ramono became 'Chief of the Bakhatla Tribe in the Transvaal' and in the Bakgatla Reserve his half-brother Segale became 'Kgosi Segale Kgamanyane Pilane, Mochudi'. Already Linchwe's thoughts were turning towards succession. His eldest son, the phlegmatic Kgafela, was arranged to be married to the staunch Tlhako, Seinwaeng, in the new DRC church built for the purpose. His second son, Isang, brilliant and assertive, sat next to his father in the kgotla soaking up customary law and tradition, and was sent to the Cape to study at Zonnebloem College and learn English ways and laws. When Linchwe wanted the British in the Transvaal to hear a firm Kgatla voice from Bechuanaland, he sent Isang. In addition, to safeguard Kgafela from Isang's ambitious nature, Linchwe tutored his eldest daughter Kgomotso (Kgabyana – 'little monkey' – affectionate for the Kgatla totem) in the ways of rainmaking, Linchwe's primal source of regal power, for transmission to Kgafela or his son.

Securing the future, too, meant unwrapping wealth built up in recent years to offset the growing restrictions on his people in the Transvaal and coming to grips again with their need for more land. The persistent press for territory, a task as old as his father and grandfather, was again beset with new obstacles. With the compromise of 1906, between Boer and Briton, to restore Boer rights and move towards a new Union government for white people only and in which a Boer majority would be assured, yet another new set of Kgatla strategies must come into play if honour was to be paid to Pilane, Kgamanyane and the many others who had found ways to make Linchwe's 'nation' a reality, so far.

ENDNOTES

1   Based in part on Morton (1985b).
2   BPBC 1894; correspondence in AC 2/2/1 and HC 108, BNA.
3   Proclamation 9 of 1899.
4   Twice, in 1893 and 1896, the Ndebele rose against the rule of Cecil Rhodes's British South Africa Company, Linchwe's old nemesis. Khama sent a token force to assist the BSA, but Linchwe demurred (Ellenberger diary, 10 Nov. 1893, EL 1/1/1/1, ZNA; Ranger 1967). See ch. 7.
5   Surmon to Goold-Adams, 21 Apr. 1899, RC 4/11, BNA.
6   '[They] have inoculations on their forehead in the habit of the kaffirs and [which] really hurt them' wrote Henri Gonin, 24 Apr. 1895 (C), DRC. The method of small-pox

inoculation had been developed at least a quarter-century earlier. 'For small-pox the natives employed in some parts inoculation of the forehead with some animal deposit; in other parts they employed the matter of the small-pox itself' (*Précis of Information* 1881: 35–36).

7   Goold-Adams report, 8 Dec. 1885, C4643, 218–220, and map.

8   Ellenberger diary, 24 Oct. 1891, EL 1/1/1/1, ZNA; Concession Commission Minutes, 13–14, RC 3/11, BNA; Beyer to Neethling, 27 Jul. 1893 and 22 Aug. 1894, 15/4/3/1 (B), DRC; Hargreaves to Thompson, 18 Mar. 1894, box 51, LMS.

9   See ch. 7.

10 Newton to Milner, 19 Nov. 1896 and J. Weil to B. Weil, 29 Mar. 1897, HC 158/2, BNA.

11 Newton to Milner, 16 Oct. 1897 and Milner to Chamberlain, 6 Dec. 1897, HC 158/2, BNA.

12 The ban on brandy began in 1891 when Linchwe granted Weil the concession (Beyer to Neethling, 11 Sep. 1891, 15/4/3/1[B], DRC; Schapera 1943a: 203; Schapera (1943b: 90–91).

13 1898–99 Annual Report, 31 Mar. 1899, RC 4/20, BNA; Form A, Annual Report of Personnel, B.S.A., BP division, 31 Dec. 1898, HC 163/2, BNA. As recently as July 1897, a Boer wagon en route to Mochudi and loaded with Martini-Henry ammunition and two rifles was impounded (Ellenberger diary, 23 Jul. 1897, EL 1/1/1/2, ZNA).

14 Surmon to Williams, 25 Mar. 1902, CO 417/343, No. 372, PRO.

15 Ellenberger to Williams, 3 Apr. 1902, CO 417/343, No. 482, PRO; Ellenberger, 'Early Days in the Bechuanaland Protectorate', 1966. MSS Afr. S. 1568 (1), RH; Edwin Gare notes, 1982; Schapera (1965: 107n3).

16 Southern Protectorate returns, RC 9/7, BNA.

17 Ellenberger diary, 12 Oct. 1899, EL 1/1/1/2, ZNA.

18 Hill to McEntee, 30 Jul. 1899, in McEntee to Acting District Engineer, Mafeking, 31 Jul. 1899, RC 4/1, BNA.

19 Parsons (1973: 186).

20 Gonin to Neethling, 17 Jul. 1897, 15/7/2 (D), DRC.

21 De Villiers minute, 29 Jun. 1898, NA 761/03, SNA 119, TA.

22 Gonin to Neethling, 5 Jan. 1898 (D); Stofberg annual report, 4 Jan. 1899, 15/4/5/1 (A), DRC.

23 Morton (1998a).

24 Malan et al. to Mokae, 1894, 1897 *passim*, A1/59, ZRB, vol. 4 (189, 219, 288, 598), vol. 5 (16, 28, 152, 256), TA.

25 Rustenburg Magistrate Court, 7 Mar. 1897, ibid., vol. 5 (325–331), TA. Gonin to Neethling, 22 Nov. 1895, 12 Sep. 1896, 17 Jul. 1897 (D). Gonin objected to Morris because of his 'adultery' – sleeping with local women – and Malan noted for the record his 'unmannerly' behaviour and that 'there already are two large bastards on Saulspoort' (Malan to Joubert, 3 May 1897, NA 761/03, SNA 119, TA). Malan got Pretoria's approval by arguing that white farmers 'are living at a distance from town [Rustenburg] it is very inconvenient for us to be without a good shop'.

26 Gonin to Neethling, 7 Sep. 1895 (D); Recollection of Thomas Phiri, 6 Jul. 1931, SP, BNA.

268

THE LAST RAID

27 From Linchwe's praise song (Schapera 1965: 94).

28 DSAB IV: 503.

29 The following account of Boer activities in the Derdepoort laager relies in part on Botha (1969). I am grateful to Barry van Wyk for his assistance in translation.

30 Interview, 6 Jul. 1931, Boer War, SP.

31 Ellenberger diary, 19 Oct. 1899, statement of Jacob Rakhole, EL, 1/1/1/3, ZNA.

32 Thomas Phiri interview, 6 Jul. 1931, Boer War, SP. If another report is to be believed, Malan also dangled before Linchwe the promise that 'if he sided with the Republic and obeyed the Boer government . . . the Boers [would] restore to him a portion of his Father's country in the Pilandsberg' (H.R. deBertadano, Capt. Intelligence, Pretoria and Northern districts, to Acting Commissioner of Native Affairs, Pretoria, n.d. [1902], SNA 26, NA 857/02, CAD, SAA).

33 Ellenberger diary, 4 Nov. 1899, EL 1/1/1/3, ZNA.

34 Ibid., also 18 Oct. 1899.

35 Klaas Segogwane interview, 2 Sep. 1932, Boer War, SP.

36 Interviews, Klaas Segogwane 2 Sep. 1932, and Thomas Phiri, 6 Jul. 1931, Boer War, SP.

37 As related to the author by Amos Kgamanyane Pilane of Mochudi, 20 Jul. 1982. Kgatla traditions have other variations on the encounter, but all agree on the substance of the insult. As A.S. Hickman learned when talking to an Afrikaner of Rustenburg in 1967, Boer traditions also register this event and assign it key importance in the Kgatla decision to fight the Boers at Derdepoort (Hickman 1970: 233).

38 Ellenberger diary, 2 Nov. 1899, ZNA. Ellenberger, 'The Bechuanaland Protectorate and the Boer War', MSS Afr. S. 1568 (5), RH; Schapera (1942a: 44).

39 Ellenberger, 'The Bechuanaland Protectorate and the Boer War', MSS Afr. S. 1568 (5), RH. Ratsegana Sebeke, Marapo Lands, Mochudi, interviewed by the author on 4 Aug. 1982, gave a florid account of the surprise of Mosupabatho, on the Kalakane rivulet.

40 Ellenberger diary, 10 Nov. 1899, EL 1/1/1/3, ZNA.

41 Interviews with Selogwe Pilane, son of Dikeme (22 Jul. 1982), Amos Kgamanyane Pilane (20 Jul. 1982) and Ratsegana Sebeke (4 Aug. 1982). According to Selogwe, Dikeme had been arrested by the Transvaal Boers as a Linchwe sympathiser and used as a horse caretaker.

42 Ellenberger diary, 23–25 November, EL 1/1/1/3, ZNA; J. Ellenberger, 'The Bechuanaland Protectorate and the Boer War', MSS Afr. S. 1568(5), RH; Schapera (1942a: 47); and Ellenberger to Hunt, 8 Jul. 1937, MSS. Afr. S. 1568 (6), RH.

43 Schapera interviews with Rakabane and Maribe Mokotedi, 6 Aug. 1929, Boer War, SP. Amos Kgamanyane Pilane, at the time a 10-year-old herd boy near the junction of the Ngotwane and Oodi, received the order to move the cattle in his care most likely on the morning of 24 November. He says he drove his cattle hard the entire day ('there was no time even to let calves suck their mothers'), stopped that night, and, just before dawn, heard the guns in the direction of Derdepoort (Interview 7 Jul. 1982).

44 Rakabane/Mokotedi, Segogwane and Phiri interviews, Boer War, SP; Schapera (1965: 99).

45 Ellenberger diary, 25 Nov. 1899, EL 1/1/1/3, ZNA.

46 Ellenberger diary, 25 Nov. 1899, EL 1/1/1/3, ZNA.

47 Holdsworth, 'Report on Reconnaissance in Sequani', Nov. 26th (*sic*) 1899, 10 Dec. 1899, HO 3, ZNA.

48 According to 1940 recollections of DRC missionary Peter Stofberg as quoted in Botha (1969: 62).

49 Ellenberger diary, 26 Nov. 1899, EL 1/1/1/3, ZNA.

50 Boers claimed to have killed many more of their opponents than they admitted had died of their own. They asserted that only 6 died at Derdepoort and claimed to have killed as many as 90 Kgatla, whereas Linchwe had nothing to gain by reducing the death toll among his own men when complaining to Holdsworth. The Kgatla, using various sources, including a grave digger, reported between 25 and 54 Boer dead. These did not include 16 Boers killed during a Kgatla ambush near Gaberones on the same day. According to Tom Phiri, Harklaas Malan was among them (Interview of Phiri, 6 Jul. 1932, Boer War, SP). The *Dictionary of South Africa Biography* claims Malan died at about this time in nearby Ramotswa, 'of a stomach complaint' (IV: 339). For varying claims on Derdepoort fatalities, see Botha (1969: 63–64); Ellenberger diary, 26, 27, 30 Nov. 1899, EL 1/1/1/3, ZNA; Weil papers, vol. 2, f.44, 46849 D.112, BM.

51 Williams, quoting Ellenberger's report in Williams to Lagden, 23 May 1902, SNA 59, NA 2104/02, TA.

52 Interview of 2 Sep. 1931, Boer War, SP.

53 Weil papers, vol. 2, f.44, 46849 D.12, BM.

54 Ellenberger diary, 7 Dec. 1899, EL 1/1/1/3, ZNA; Truschel (1972: 189).

55 Ellenberger diary, 18–25 Dec. 1899, EL 1/1/1/3, ZNA; Amery (1905); W. van Everdingen, *De Oorlog in Zuid Afrika*, quoted in Schapera (1942a: 42–43, 45).

56 *The Times* (London), 1 Jan. 1900. I am grateful to Neil Parsons for this and other references in the British press. Small groups of Boers on reconnaissance continued to penetrate the Bakgatla Reserve, exacting reprisals on people and crops, and trying to attack the railway (Ellenberger diary, 17 Jan. 1900, EL 1/1/1/3, ZNA; *The Times*, 22 Jan. 1900).

57 Gardner (1966: 141–144).

58 Ellenberger diary, 2 and 7 Dec. 1899, EL 1/1/1/3, ZNA.

59 Baden Powell to Snyman, 8 Dec. 1899, vol. 3, f.73, 46850 D.13; and Baden Powell to Snyman, 28 Feb. 1900, vol. 2, f.119, 46849 D.12, Weil Papers, BM. See also Warwick (1983).

60 Edmeston to Native Commissioner, 27 Apr. 1903, SNA 116, NA 762/03, TA. Linchwe received 100 Martini-Henry rifles before the battle at Derdepoort in November 1899 and the following July the Kgatla turned over to the British 250 rifles (Linchwe et al. to Lawley, n.d., in the same file).

61 23 Feb. 1900, as per report from Gaberones, dated 16 Feb. 1900; Interview with Amos Kgamanyane Pilane, 20 Jul. 1982.

62 Edmeston to Native Commissioner, 27 Apr. 1903, SNA 116, NA 672/03, TA; Interview with Ratsegana Sebeke, 4 Aug. 1982; Interviews with Klaas Segogwane, 2 Sep. 1932, and Thomas Phiri, 6 Jul. 1931, Boer War, SP. Mochele was the youngest brother of Segale.

63 According to Thari Pumetse, whose father fought in this battle, many Kgatla were killed or wounded (Interview, 3 Aug. 1979).

64　See for example, Jan Smuts to Stead, 4 Jan. 1902, Hancock and Van der Poel (1966, I: 482); ibid., Smuts, 'Memoirs of the Boer War', I: 585–586; Botha (1969); Pretorius (1999: 15, 281, 297).

65　Phiri interview, 6 Jul. 1931, Boer War, SP.

66　*The Times*, 19 Mar. 1900; Edmeston to Native Commissioner, 27 Apr. 1903, SNA 116, NA 672/03, TA.

67　Pretorius (1999: 297).

68　28 Feb. 1900, Public Announcement in Weil Papers, vol. 2, 46849 D.12, BM. The letter was sent on 17 Feb. 1900 (Plaatje 1990: 107). Plaatje was Baden-Powell's interpreter.

69　Who were subsequently apprehended by Linchwe's men and turned over to Ellenberger and Surmon for incarceration in Bulawayo.

70　Thomas Phiri interview, 6 Jul. 1931, Boer War, SP.

71　Linchwe's praise, as composed by Rammhi and recited by Klaas Segogoane in 1932. Schapera (1965: 94). Linchwe had been issued 100 Martini-Henry rifles prior to the battle at Derdepoort in November 1899. The commandos in the Rustenburg hinterland, as were others at this time, probably were raiding cattle for food (Pretorius 1999: 31–34). Reference to caves likely pertains to Boers known as *kaboutermanne* (gnomes), who hid out to avoid service in commandos or capture by the British (Carruthers 1990: 313).

72　Warwick (1983: 45).

73　Truschel (1972: 189); Harbor to Nicholson, n.d., RC 5/4, BNA.

74　Schapera (1942a: 20); Edmeston to Native Commissioner, 27 Apr. 1903, SNA 116, NA 672/03, TA.

75　Smuts, 'Memoirs of the Boer War', in Hancock and Van der Poel (1966, I: 597–598).

76　Ellenberger's judgement, 20 Jun. 1901, RC 4/17, BNA. Two orders were issued to Linchwe, on the 14th and 25th June, respectively. See also Ellenbeger diary, 22 Jun. 1900, EL 1/1/1/3, ZNA.

77　Linchwe et al. to Lawley, n.d. (1903), SNA 116, NA 672/03, TAD.

78　Carruthers (1990: 289–321).

79　Ibid., 305n4; Wulfsohn (1984).

80　Williams to Lagden, 23 May 1902, SNA 59, NA 2104/02, TAD; Edmeston to Lagden, 27 Apr. 1903, SNA 116, NA 672/03, TAD. By October 1900 the commission for looting had risen to 30 percent (Mellwyn to ADT, Mafeking, 30 Oct. 1900, RC 4/14, BNA).

81　Telegram (n.d.) with Ryan to Acting Resident Commissioner, n.d. (received 20 Nov. 1900), RC 4/14, BNA.

82　Ellenberger diary, 31 Aug., 2 Oct. and 26 Nov. 1900 and 27 Mar. 1901, EL 1/1/13, ZNA.

83　Smuts, 'Memoirs of the Boer War', in Hancock and Van der Poel (1966, I: 586) regarding the 'looting and murdering' done by Kgatla regiments under Ramono (Linchwe's brother).

84　Linchwe et al. to Lawley, n.d. (1903), SNA 116, NA 672/03, TAD; Griffith to Lagden, 10 Nov. 1903, SNA 71, NA 2482/02, TAD; Warwick (1983: 45–46). For the Boer use of Africans in the war in general, see ibid.; Pretorius (1999: 282–299).

85　Interview with Ratsegana Sebeke, 4 Aug. 1982. Sebeke's father Piet was among the raiders.

86 In February 1901, General Botha was guided at night from Waterval to Nylstrom 'through the armed hordes of Linchwe' (Smuts, 'Memoirs of the Boer War', in Hancock and Van der Poel 1966, I: 627).

87 *Times*, 23 Dec. 1901.

88 Truschel (1972: 189). See also Linchwe to Ellenberger 26 Nov. 1911, RC 6/13, BNA.

89 Truschel (1972: 189–190); Draft to Williams' letter 7 Nov. 1901 covering Perry to Kitchener, 30 Nov. 1901, RC 6/3, BNA, also Williams to Milner, 7 Nov. 1901 in the same file.

90 Linchwe claimed the loss of between six and seven thousand head (Edmeston to Lagden, 27 Apr. 1902, SNA 116, NA 672/03, TAD); the *Times*, 27 Dec. 1901, reported Linchwe's losses at '60,000' head. Bierkraal is 32 kilometres from Saulspoort on the northwest side of the Pilanesberg.

91 Linchwe et al. to Lawley, n.d. (1903), SNA 116, NA 672/03, TAD; Williams to Lagden, 27 May 1902, SNA 59, NA 2104/02, TAD.

92 Edmeston to Lagden, 27 Apr. 1903, SNA 116, NA 672/03, TAD; statement of Kgatla grievances, Driver to Griffith, 26 Sep. 1902, SNA 62, NA 2160/02, TAD; Transvaal Administration 1903: B27 Annexure D.

93 Williams to Lagden, 23 May 1902, SNA 59, NA 2104/02, TAD.

94 Ellenberger diary, 27 Feb. 1900, EL 1/1/1/3, ZNA.

95 Assuming that 14,000 were males, half of whom were under age and a quarter over.

96 Most of these casualties were suffered by two regiments – maKoba and maJanko. Another regiment, maNthwane, spent most of the war inside the Protectorate at the border 'guarding the chief'. Casualty percentages for the two most active regiments are, therefore, likely to have been well above 18 percent.

97 Interviews with Amos Kgamanyane Pilane, 20 Jul. 1982, and Selogwe Pilane, 22 Jul. 1982.

98 Edmeston to Lagden, 27 Apr. 1903, SNA 116, NA 672/03, TAD.

99 Linchwe et al. to Lawley, n.d. (1903), SNA 116, NA 672/03, TAD. The Ellenberger diaries contain several references to imported grain for sale to Linchwe and other chiefs (29 Nov. 1899, 2 and 7 Feb. 1900, EL 1/1/1/3, ZNA). Linchwe was also required to submit Hut Tax returns throughout the war (see ibid., 11 Jan. 1900, 1 Mar. 1901, 18 Jun. 1902).

100 Linchwe et al. to Lawley, n.d. (1903), SNA 116, NA 672/03, TAD.

101 '[Linchwe] said that his principal grievance was that the Govt. took cattle from him and gave them back to the Boers under the impression that they were giving them up to the Boers who had surrendered . . . You think they are surrendered Boers, but they have fought against you' (Williams covering Perry to Kitchener, 30 Nov. 1901, RC 6/3, BNA).

102 Cattle censuses, 1904 and 1922, S295/2, BNA. In 1921, the figure was 33,231, in 1931, 30,000, and in 1946, when the first accurate census was conducted, 74,695. See Daniel to Stanley, 1 Dec. 1922, S4/9, and Neal to Schapera, 15 Aug 1933, S182/1, BNA; Bechuanaland Protectorate, *Bechuanaland Protectorate Government Census*, 1946 (n.p., n.d.) iv: 66.

103 Interview with Selogwe Pilane, 7 Aug. 1979.

104 The 1948 'Report on the Cattle Industry', noted that the Kgatla owned good cattle

'which they admit owe their origin largely to the cattle acquired from the Transvaal during the Anglo-Boer War. Today there are in this Reserve a number of cattle that would rank high as Afrikander amongst Union cattle breeders' (V, 1/5/2, box 1, BNA). For Linchwe's distribution of *Mosunyane* cattle, see interviews with Amos Kgamanyane Pilane (23 Jul. 1979), Gabriel Palai (24 Jul. 1979), Selogwe Pilane (19 Dec. 1981), Kgamanyane Pilane, J.R. Phiri and England M.T. Pilane (5 Jan. 1982), and Ratsegana Sebeke (4 Aug. 1982).

105 Statement of H.D.M. Standford, *Report Select Committee* 1911: 90–91.

106 Statement of P.G.W. Grobler, *Report of the Natives Land Commission* 1916, II: 264.

107 Driver to Griffith, 26 Sep. 1902, SNA 62, NA 2160/02, TAD.

108 *Annual Report* 1903: B.27, Annexure D. See also Driver to Griffith, 26 Sep. 1902, SNA 62, NA 2160/02, TAD.

109 New farm numbers: Saulspoort 38, Modderkuil 39, Kruidfontein 40 and Holfontein 361.

Epilogue[1]

THE ECLIPSE OF ISANG

Linchwe realised that [European] civilisation was coming to stay [and that] in adapting ourselves to the same civilisation lay our future as a nation. (Isang Pilane)

* * *

During his rule [Isang] burned huts of Malebi whilst children were in them; inspanned people with yokes, thrashed people for several hours, one woman named Motsei died as a result of injuries, and another who was tied to a boy named Intlasi had a miscarriage, having been flogged for two hours with a whip, and I myself was also hit with a knobkerrie and sustained a broken arm . . . During Isang's rule no one dared to advise him for fear of being killed. (Lebotse Moneng)

* * *

The Lord only knows what it means to live in Mochudi under Isang. (W.W. Hibbert)

September 1931, Part One

After waving off William Ballinger, Margaret Hodgson and Leonard Barnes, Isang Pilane had business to turn to. *Ramalebanya* ('the farsighted one') was forever thinking ahead. He should be driving over to Rustenburg, where papers for the purchase of Kraalhoek 399 were being drawn up, but he had to attend to matters in Mochudi regarding kgosi Molefi. In the months since Isang took the law into his own hands and gave Kgari Pilane a beating that put him in hospital, public grumbling about the ex-regent undermining the chief and trying to run things on his own had been on the rise. It was true that he wanted to be in charge, because Isang knew that his strong hand, more than ever, was needed to keep the BaKgatla from ruining themselves. Since Isang's elder brother's death in 1915, Linchwe's health had steadily declined. In 1921 the ailing Linchwe handed over to him, and since then Isang alone had shouldered the responsibility of keeping the Kgatla together. During his regency Isang exerted all his energies to develop new strategies for offsetting the forces threatening Pilane's descendants and to marshal among them new habits and skills. Yet, the more projects he initiated, and the more he compelled the BaKgatla to work for the good of their community, the less his subjects proved willing to go along.

All of Isang's efforts to ignite his people seemingly came to naught in November 1929, when the Kgatla forced Isang to step down as regent and install his young nephew Molefi as the new kgosi. The BaKgatla wanted Molefi in the chair because they feared Isang might otherwise find a way to stay there. Most of all they wanted an end to his curfews, strict measures, harsh judgements and demands on their time. Claims of all sorts were piled on Isang to bring him down. He was held to be incompetent (as a rainmaker), ambitious (for the chieftaincy), corrupt (stealing other peoples' property), autocratic (personal in his judgements) and ready to kill those who stood in his way. Among Isang's intended victims was supposedly the heir to *bogosi* himself. Molefi's mother Seingwaeng accused Isang of wanting to do away with her son through witchcraft and seize the chieftaincy. The deaths of two other of her children she said were proof of Isang's evil power.[2]

Isang knew what was taking place. The people who thought they wanted Molefi mostly wanted Isang off their backs, if not out of their lives, and to accomplish their aim, they would install a boy-chief who was sure to let them alone. This just-turned-twenty youth, who fancied the urban tastes of the new South Africa and dressed like a 'Johannesburg mine boy',[3] appealed to the young, semi-educated generation who had seen something of township life across the border. Molefi's hardiest supporters were wage earners and their hangers-on, living for the moment. Like most of his generation, Molefi not only was too young to be chief but too ill-equipped to grow up. They had escaped being tested by their elders. True, Linchwe was known to be immature and rowdy as a young chief, but leading the BaKgatla into combat against the BaKwena transformed him. Molefi had no battle to fight, no call to action against imminent dangers threatening him or his people. He had not led his peers through the crucible of initiation. His entitlement to office as Kgafela's eldest son was his only qualification, his willingness to stay in office and draw the chief's sinecure his only necessity. This mere lad, ill-schooled and ill-disciplined, was already a carouser and drinking like his alcoholic father. He had returned to Bechuanaland as the imminent chief, just as he had entered South Africa as a schoolboy – for his own indulgence. This carefree, inconstant fellow had no knowledge of the BaKgatla: their laws, their history, their cattle. The achievements of the past, and the skills honed and sacrifices accumulated over three generations to realise them, were scarcely known and of little consequence to him. Plenty of celebrating marked Molefi's coronation, but Isang did not join in. He could feel disaster looming.

Within a year, all the signs were there. Molefi sat idly and indifferently in the *kgosi*'s chair, spending most of his time away socialising with his young cronies, pleasing himself by riling the elders and taking special delight in provoking his incendiary uncle. For months, Isang held his temper while urging (some thought it badgering) his nephew to shape up, but eventually he had to explode. The spark was lit in kgotla, by Molefi, in a September 1930 case brought by Isang against Kgari Pilane. The scoundrel of Sikwane, Kgari, who once assisted Isang and fellow conspirators to smuggle cattle into the Transvaal, Isang had caught cheating *him*. Isang's charges, however, were dismissed; Molefi allowed in a white man's evidence favouring Kgari and let Kgari go unpunished. Isang had no choice but to deliver the justice that Molefi had denied him in court. 'I was going to the cattle post and saw Isang chasing me', reported Kgari in Gaberones after his release from hospital. 'He caught me and flogged, punched and kicked me till I fainted'.[4] Others were sitting at the kgotla when Isang hauled Kgari in. '[Isang had] beaten him unconscious, blood flowing from his ears and nose, had dragged him to his car and brought him back into the kgotla, where he had thrown him at the chief's feet saying "There is your dog".'[5]

Already Isang was regretting that Kgari had lived, for now that he had recovered, skelm Kgari had joined up with Molefi's weaklings, gone to white officials in Gaberones with stories about Isang and threatened to bring down the whole smuggling operation. In September 1931 Isang's treatment of Kgari was up for discussion in the kgotla, a reprimand of the ex-regent in its own right. The time had arrived to get rid of Molefi and rally support for Isang's reinstatement as regent. By winter's end it was all coming to a head: Molefi's accumulated misbehaviour had forced others of Isang's generation to lose their patience. While Molefi's followers complained that Isang was the root of the young's chief's problems, older BaKgatla were voicing their discontent with the kgosi. Isang headed for the kgotla, this time not to be humiliated but to relish the chief's chastisement.

Wealth and Money

The generations born after the South African (Anglo-Boer) War and reaching maturity in the 1920s were not initiated into regiments by their elders in the old, hard way. After Linchwe abolished bogwera in 1911, young men and women were kept out of the initiation camps and were merely assembled and named. They came of age from experiences shaped largely through association with their peers and, apart from their schoolteachers and tax collectors, away from authority. They were accustomed to far more freedom than the Kgatla before them and had more time to do things for themselves. By their mid-teens, girls and boys alike were walking across the South African border and getting above-ground work on Transvaal farms or in white homes and white-owned businesses in Rustenburg and the Witwatersrand. There they earned cash, milled with wage-earners from all over South Africa, and got a taste for township life. Few boys were staying behind in the Reserve, where they had only herding chores to do and had to put up with being ordered about, if not by their parents and uncles, then by Isang and his headmen who assigned them regimental tasks without compensation.

While regent, Isang had tried a host of wealth-generating initiatives for the Kgatla in the Reserve and the Saulspoort Location, but few of his subjects were interested. They grew weary of compulsory cooperatives, tribal levies, community development projects, and civic undertakings, and they increasingly resisted Isang's attempts to get them to comply. He chalked it up to ignorance and what he called 'laziness'.

> This laziness has been encouraged by the suggestion that no man should be employed for nothing and that some payment should be made for whatever he does . . . We who have had some education can draw the line between compulsory labour and labour which is for one's own good. But in so far as commoners are concerned they cannot draw the distinction between enforced labour and labour which is beneficial to one's self.[6]

Isang failed to mobilise the BaKgatla as a whole to support his community projects, but during and after his regency he did persuade men of his own generation to follow him in creating groups and syndicates that pooled their investments in land, grazing, breeding, water development and irrigation, mechanised and fertilised vegetable and grain farming, marketing, and cattle smuggling, in order to increase their individual wealth.[7] The other Kgatla, who had been raised in the twentieth century and made up Molefi's generation, thought that being with the times meant generating cash from jobs available in South Africa. Like Molefi, they thought their future depended on bringing wealth in from outside as cash in their pockets, not creating wealth where they lived. From their point of view, the compulsory community projects of Isang's regency were a form of unpaid labour that created no paying jobs in their wake. The growing wealth of Isang and his syndicate members was proof that Isang and his like were living off the backs of others, through coercion, extortion or medicine. They were convinced as well that Isang had eaten Molefi's inheritance. Theirs was a zero-sum notion of who had and who had not. Molefi's refusal to submit to Isang and his uncles, while ignoring the Protectorate's wishes to be a good chief and listening to his own drummer, spoke to their hearts.

Yet, Molefi and Protectorate officials had similar, static mindsets. Both needed the tribal system. In spite of his lack of interest in chieftaincy, Molefi needed the chief's salary and tax commission to sustain his lifestyle, having little education or flair for generating independent income. He tried at times to escape the chieftaincy with money-making schemes that were based on sudden inspirations and thoughts of quick returns. All failed. Similarly, officials needed even uninterested chiefs such as Molefi to run their administrations and afford the cost of the Protectorate through tax collection. Their willingness to abide Molefi for years and uphold 'customary law' in his interest was intended to sustain a system that suited their purposes.[8]

Meanwhile, Isang and his followers were discarding a 'tribal' modus operandi and developing a corporate one. As entrepreneurs they could increase their wealth and control over their lives even while remaining subjects of Molefi and the Protectorate 'native administration'. Though he knew how to get around the law, such as when smuggling cattle into the Union, Isang was openly deferential to white officials, accommodating his behaviour to, rather than challenging, their tribal mentality.[9] Isang and his like could not conceal their disgust, however, for Molefi and his profligate minions, who in their view had no vision save self-indulgence and escape from obligation. Isang's group was self-disciplined, abstemious and tight with money. 'Free spirits' like Molefi and his younger group were mere consumers dependent on wages, loans or sinecures.

The Saulspoort Location

Isang's corporate approach was learned from Linchwe, who with Isang's uncle Ramono established the joint administration of the BaKgatla in the Protectorate and the Union after the South African War. The thinly staffed Protectorate permitted Linchwe almost unrestricted self-government in the Bakgatla Reserve, where he was content to maintain his headquarters. Yet it was crowded with people and cattle, and the Reserve and the Protectorate were bereft of opportunities for development or investment. Blocks of private farms (Tuli and Lobatse) along watercourses existed at either end of the Reserve, but the Protectorate restricted their ownership to whites. Across the border in South Africa where the rest of the BaKgatla lived, however, the picture was much more promising. Although subject to legal segregation and the colour bar, 'natives' were permitted to purchase or lease certain farms that became available after the War. Between 1903 and Ramono's death in 1917, Linchwe and Ramono purchased fifteen farms in the Rustenburg (the portion later known as Pilansberg) district. After Ramono's death, when Linchwe gradually retired from public life from failing health and Isang assumed authority, more property was added. Before he stepped down as regent in 1929, Isang had purchased another nine farms and set in motion the purchase of two more, acquired in 1931 (Kraalhoek 399) and 1933 (Welgeval 171).[10] Altogether, the three men acquired twenty-six farms, and they leased an as-yet-undetermined number of farms along the Oodi (Crocodile) and Madikwe (Marico) rivers for their cattle posts.

It is worth recalling that when the War ended in 1902, BaKgatla in South Africa were living, apart from the four farms they owned and those held in trust by the Native Commissioner, entirely on white-owned farms. Nearly thirty years later, at the end of Isang's reign, all but a few Kgatla resided at one of the twenty-two villages located on their own properties. The combined territory used or occupied by the Kgatla was 61,000 morgen, or 320 square kilometres. The Saulspoort Location represented the single largest African-owned set of properties in the western Transvaal. This was a staggering achievement.

While they helped the South African Kgatla establish themselves, Linchwe, his brother and his son bought farms for themselves and their families. Of the twenty-four Location farms, eleven farms or portions thereof were the personal property of Linchwe, Ramono, Ofentse and Isang.[11] Three were Linchwe's (Witfontein 396, Middelkuil 8 and Cyferkuil 330), two Ramono's (portions of Koedoesfontein 42 and Doornpoort 57), one Ofentse's (Welgevaagd 133 portion B), and five Isang's (Vogelstruiskraal 400, Application 398, Nooitgedacht 406, Zwaartklip 405 and Varkensvlei 403, portion B).[12] Altogether, these five chiefs owned 16,520 morgen or 87 square kilometres.[13] Also, Linchwe, Ramono and Isang contributed substantial sums toward the purchase of farms owned by the Kgatla in their own right (and in trust with Minister for Native Affairs), judging from the scattered record.

The chiefs' and Kgatla-owned farms formed what was known, after the Land Act of 1913, as the Saulspoort Location. They enabled the Kgatla to establish large villages, build dams and irrigation works, develop agriculture and sustain large cattle holdings. The location farms were semi-arid and too short of surface water, particularly in drought years, to be able to support their entire populations, but villages were close to roads connected by bus to Rustenburg and the Witwatersrand, where work above ground was readily available. The Saulspoort Location became more prosperous than the Bakgatla Reserve in the Protectorate, more capable of supporting its population, and less dependent on white employment. As of 1949, the Location and the Reserve each supported around 20,000 people, although the Location, by then nearly reaching its maximum extent, was one-tenth the size of the Reserve.[14] A 1949 survey of the Rustenburg and Pilanesberg districts also revealed that

> labour migration seems to take place on a smaller scale [among the Saulspoort Kgatla] than among other tribes. While work in towns is preferred, a few men work on the Thabazimbi mine and on the Witwatersrand, and very few on farms in the Brits district. A number of people produce enough to have a surplus of maize and sorghum for sale, while others obtain the cash they need by selling cattle.[15]

About 40 percent of Kgatla men in the Reserve worked in South Africa, and about 50 percent of the 'working population [of the Location] appear to live in towns for periods'.[16] Though the percentage of wage-earners in the Reserve and Location were roughly equal, once the nature of work contracts, the distance between home and work and the cost and strain on families are compared, it becomes clear that Location residents were much less beleaguered than their Reserve counterparts. In terms of cattle holdings, Location residents owned far fewer cattle than those in the Reserve: 10,000 head versus 75,000, but with the 1924 weight restrictions, cattle in the Reserve were effectively cut off from South African markets.[17] Most strikingly, however, the Location easily outperformed the Reserve in agricultural commodities:

	Reserve	Location
Maize (bags)	230	1,513
Sorghum (bags)	1,097	6,236
Beans (bags)	371	68
Millet (bags)	795	---
Orange trees	---	79
Fruit trees	---	285

The advantage from gaining access to property in the Transvaal was even greater with regard to cattle. Soon after the South African War the Ba-Kgatla moved large herds into the Transvaal. By 1905 they had established at least 25 cattle posts on white-owned farms leased along the Oodi and Madikwe rivers. Others were found. By 1910, 'the herds of cattle owned by the Bakgatla', stated the Transvaal Native Affairs Department, 'are immense'.[18] The Union government attempted to lure white farmers into the dry area north of the Kgetleng (Elands) River by sinking boreholes, but many owners appear simply to have leased them to the Kgatla.[19] The irony was sweeter still for the Kgatla, whose herds were replete with the progeny of beasts they had rustled from unprotected Transvaal farms during the South African War.

As with acquiring land, so with enlarging cattle holdings: the lead was taken by Linchwe. Many of the initial posts along the Oodi and Madikwe were his.[20] Ramono, whose role in the Saulspoort Location was representing Linchwe in Kgatla affairs and maintaining agreeable relations with Pretoria, was not permitted to be a cattleman. His estate revealed slightly more than 100 head. As Linchwe explained, 'Ramono's cattle were not his own property, but belonged to various people'.[21] After Linchwe handed all his chiefly responsibilities to Isang, attempts were made to purchase farms strictly for grazing. In 1921 alone, Isang applied to buy twelve farms for this purpose.[22]

Coincidentally, or perhaps not, seven of the fourteen farms acquired in the Rustenburg district between 1908 and 1919 proved of interest to prospectors. In 1922, soon after Isang assumed authority from his father, the Saulspoort Bakgatla passed a resolution granting prospecting rights on these seven farms to Potgietersrust Platinum, and in the next several years Isang purchased two more as his personal farms (Zwartklip 405 and Nooitgedacht 406) where platinum was later discovered.[23] Garnering prospecting rights had been well understood since the 1880s, when Linchwe had negotiated several contracts applicable to the Bakgatla Reserve with Benjamin Weil, but then the purpose was to keep large mining companies *out* of the Reserve, not bring them in.[24] The consequences were likely to be transfer of authority over the territory where minerals were discovered from the Protectorate to the respective mining company.[25] In contrast, the purchase of title deeds to farms in South Africa placed Linchwe and Isang in a position to arrange for prospecting rights or leasing farm portions to mining companies, for substantial fees, without risking loss of the whole. For the five farms involved in the prospecting contract in 1927, Isang received £625 per year on behalf of the Saulspoort Bakgatla.

Linchwe and Isang retained their administrative headquarters in the Protectorate for reasons that merged the practical with the political. The Bakgatla Reserve in the Protectorate contained the standing capital, Mochudi, the Kgatla's largest town. Linchwe, who was Britain's strongest Protectorate ally during the South African War, was allowed then and later to govern the Bakgatla Reserve without any direct colonial supervision. Linchwe also got Protectorate backing to be recognised as the paramount chief of the Kgatla in Saulspoort and to be allowed to designate the chief there. Even though they remained residents of the Protectorate, Linchwe and Isang were able to buy farms in the Transvaal in their own names, and keep their cattle there. As Christians married in common property, Ramono (Linchwe's brother and first chief in Saulspoort) and Isang were also able under South African law to bequeath their Transvaal property, including cattle, to their widows and heirs. Thus, transferring capital, in the form of cattle or coin, into South Africa for long-term investment was easily managed from Mochudi. Only after the cattle weight restrictions of 1924 did Isang's pipeline begin to dry up.

Even after this point, Isang had more opportunities in the Union to generate personal wealth than he did in the Protectorate. He bought farms for himself in the Transvaal, whereas in the Protectorate private property was restricted to whites. Africans lacked title to land also in the Reserves, which permitted only communal land ownership in accordance with customary law. Until 1930, by which time Isang was no longer chief, attempts to use co-operative approaches to wealth accretion in the Reserve went unsupported financially or technically by the Protectorate. The lack of results increased public resistance to Isang's leadership in this regard, and more of his people sought their fortunes in South Africa. At the end of Isang's reign, an estimated 40 percent of the residents of the Reserve were working for wages outside in order to meet the annual tax.[26]

September 1931, Part Two

By the time Isang reached the kgotla, hundreds of men had gathered, awaiting the ex-regent. All knew that, without Isang present, what was about to take place could not resolve itself. Either Molefi must accept the criticisms sure to come and welcome his uncle's assistance, or Isang must apologise to his nephew and submit to the kgosi's judgement in future.

The kgotla, where elders and headmen took turns expressing their opinions on the subject of the day, as a prelude to the kgosi's decision, was an unpredictable forum when the main issue was the kgosi's own competence. In the past, serious questions about leadership were dealt with in private by a select group, usually uncles of the kgosi, who had the power to take his life if necessary. It was said that not long after his installation, Linchwe himself was threatened with execution for being irresponsible. In those days, too many other lives were at stake to risk waiting until a kgosi matured. The fact that Molefi's misbehaviour, likewise that of his uncle, had become the subject of open discussion, in kgotla, showed that BaKgatla had long ceased depending on their leaders, in a life-or-death sense. Rather, bogosi had become 'chieftainship', a role they needed Molefi to fill in regulating the semblance of order that had survived from the days of rustling. To the BaKgatla, Isang was still living in the past, unwilling to let go of force as the instrument for binding the community to his purview. Since Pilane, it had always been about force – of circumstances, of necessity, of combined might – that kept men in line behind the kgosi, or so Isang believed. Whereas BaKgatla resisted Isang's attempts to impose on them a legacy, they mourned that Molefi seemed to have given up on the future, for in him the BaKgatla saw their sons and daughters, fleeing their homes and responsibilities. Thus, they wanted Molefi to remain in the chair, and they cared to nurture him until he was capable of fending for himself. Otherwise how could they believe they had sacrificed themselves for good? The kgotla was the only space left for them to educate their royal son and through him, their children.

After Isang arrived at kgotla, Molefi listened to complaints about his absence from Mochudi, his behaviour with his young pals, public outbursts, the general lack of direction of the BaKgatla under his chieftainship, and especially the beating of girls by the chief as of late. Molefi then stood to answer. Molefi suffered not from any lack of will to be a good chief. He was as determined as ever to serve his people. All troubles stemmed, he claimed, from his uncle who had undermined him at every turn. The assembly was hushed, and in dread. They yearned for his supplication, but saw another dodge. Molefi's claim of blamelessness was for show. There was no doubting his resentment toward Isang, however, and Molefi drove it home: 'I have no confidence in my uncle because in earlier years he did not co-habit with my mother. I should have had stepbrothers'.[27]

Hundreds of men seated round rose in an uproar. No indecency exceeded mentioning a mother's intimate life in public. Again, Molefi had outdone himself in performing the outrageous. Yet it was Isang, now beyond self-control, who followed his instinct to triumph over his nephew, even in obscenities. 'Why don't you listen to me', he snapped, 'is it because you are hurt that I am not riding your mother?'[28]

From that moment, Isang's cruel and mean-spirited insult, and this from the ex-regent-who-would-be chief, a person of enormous talent, intelligence and ideas, lost him for good the support he needed to reclaim the chieftaincy, resurrect the tradition of Pilane and refashion the BaKgatla as a modern version of their once-expanding cattle enterprise. For years he attempted to transfer the essence of his patriline to fend with what he called 'the beast the white man calls civilization', by garnering knowledge and applying it to practical goals that advanced the BaKgatla's wellbeing. His capacity to throw himself into a struggle was gargantuan, as large as the furnace that fuelled the wild diminutive Pilane, propelled Kgamanyane alongside Boer commandos, and threw Linchwe to the front of the regiments advancing on Molepolole. Skilful beyond question and adept as he was in making himself into a modern leader, in truth, Isang was born for the previous century.

Postscript

In 1934 Protectorate officials banned Isang Pilane from the Reserve for undermining Molefi. There was no protest, from Isang or anyone else. In 1935 Isang was brought before the Linchwe Estate Commission to answer claims by Molefi that Isang had seized Linchwe's cattle and other properties that rightfully belonged to Molefi. Isang was acquitted on all counts and was found to have safeguarded carefully all the inheritance of his father, on behalf of Molefi and other of Linchwe's descendants. He produced detailed and accurate information in all respects. Isang died in 1942 at the age of 57. Molefi remained chief but was suspended in 1937 for continued failure to perform his duties and causing widespread mayhem. A small but determined resistance to his suspension continued for years. He was restored to the chieftaincy in 1945 but died in 1957 in a car accident. He was only 46 years old. He was succeeded as chief by his son, Linchwe Molefi Kgafela, otherwise known as Linchwe II. Molefi's mother Seingwaeng and uncle Bakgatla, who had been Molefi's main supporters over the years and leading figures in the protest over his suspension, were publicly humiliated and expelled from Mochudi by Molefi after he resumed the chieftaincy. He denounced them and other members of the Zion Christian Church. The ZCC exiles from Mochudi settled at Lentswe-le-Moriti in northeastern Botswana, immediately north of the Tuli block.

The farm Saulspoort, owned by DRC missionary Henri Gonin, though purchased earlier, was not legally transferred to the BaKgatla until 1922, following the death of Henri Gonin in 1910 and the division of his estate.

The Dutch Reformed Church remained the principle Christian faith adhered to by the BaKgatla both in the Transvaal and in the Protectorate.

ENDNOTES

1 Based in part on Morton (2006).

2 Molefi's mother Seingwaeng became a rallying point for the anti-Isang forces. Since Kgafela's death in October 1915, his widow had been convinced that Isang wanted to rob her son of his power and inheritance. She kept Molefi away from Isang and his group, played down her son's faults, and allowed his formal education to slide. She would pay her own price (Morton 1998b).

3 Germond diary, 27 Aug. 1934, DCM 2/6, BNA.

4 Kgari's statement, recorded in pencil by an anonymous official, undated, attached to Kgari Pilane to Resident Magistrate, Gaberones, 21 Mar. 1931, DCM 2/6, BNA.

WHEN RUSTLING BECAME AN ART

5   F. Rey report, kgotla meeting, 22 Nov. 1934, S402/13, BNA. Missionary Johan Reyneke told Rey that the incident had taken place, and that he had 'seen the man brought in and had been told by the doctor that he very nearly died' (ibid.).

6   Minutes, African Advisory Council, Bechuanaland Protectorate, 19th session (1938), p. 18.

7   Ramsay and Morton (1987: 23–29), Peters (1994: 51–59).

8   Resident Commissioner Charles Rey (1930–1937) emphasised development, but without permitting private property, which Isang noted and opposed (Peters 1994).

9   For an account of how the Kgatla created a tribal identity to gain concessions from the British after 1885, when the Protectorate was declared, see Morton (1995).

10 Old numbers: Kraalhoek 516, Welgeval 749.

11 Privately-owned land by Africans was legal after 1904.

12 Old farm numbers: Witfontein 215, Middelkuil 564, Cyferkuil 372, Koedoesfontein 818, Doornpoort 251, Welgevaagd 535, Vogelstruiskraal 679, Application 984, Nooitgedacht 9, Zwaartklip 988 and Varkensvlei 903.

13 In 1935 the South African Government overruled the Linchwe Estate Commission's recognition of the farm Application 984 as Isang's personal property. Though Isang had purchased it with his own money, the South African government declared it legally only tribal land, because it had been Crown land when Isang purchased it and therefore entitled only for tribal ownership, in trust with the Minister of Native Affairs. Isang was not reimbursed.

14 Breutz (1953: 247); Bechuanaland Protectorate, *Bechuanaland Protectorate Government Census, 1946* (n.p., n.d.): 4, table II (c) and 7, table II (f).

15 Breutz (1953: 284).

16 Ibid., 247; Schapera (1933: 652). Schapera made no estimate of women migrant labourers, but oral evidence collected in 1982 makes it clear that many young girls in the Bakgatla Reserve walked across the border to obtain jobs in farms and in the towns. See the interviews of Leah Moagi and Motlapele Molefi, in Morton (1982: 36–37, 52–53, 65–66).

17 Ettinger (1972); Breutz (1953: 280); *Bechuanaland Government Census, 1946*: 66.

18 Transvaal Native Affairs Department Annual Report, June 1910, State Library, Pretoria.

19 Union of South Africa, *Report of the Natives Land Commission* 1916: 305, 327–328; Union of South Africa, *Report of the Natives Land Committee* 1918: 8, 20, 22, 48, 57.

20 Linchwe to R. Williams, 30 Jan. 1904, and 'Native Cattle Posts on the Crocodile River', 26 Aug. 1905, LTG 124, 110/38, 41, TA.

21 H. Williams to Acting Government Secretary, 20 Oct. 1917 and Inventory of the Late Chief Ramono Kgamanyane Pilane, 29 Oct. 1917, NTS 61/55, vol. 333, part I, SAA.

22 Tussenkomst 241 (old number 448), Turfbult 404 (989), Gomkiri 131 (982), De Kameelkuil ? (813) Elandskuil 126 (814), Mosqietdoorens 127 (981), Zwartklip 405 (988), Pieterse ? (106), Vaaldraai ? (202), Haakdornbult ? (302), Bethanie 112 (190) and Donald 37 (93). E.R. Osborne to Secretary for Lands, 24 Feb. 1921, and Magistrate, Rustenburg to Secretary for Native Affairs, 23 Feb. 1921, NTS B98/308, vol. 3454, SAA. Because they did not adjoin the Location, Isang's request was denied.

23 Old numbers: Zwartklip 988 and Nooitgedacht 9. Cranko and Schaffer to Secretary, Native Affairs, 12 Sep. 1929, NTS 293, 162, vol. 1170; 25 May 1922 resolution by Ofentse Pilane et al., Agreement between Bakhatla tribe and Potgiersrust Platinum signed by Isang, 27 Jul. 1927, NTS 6853, 55/319, Part I, SAA; Manson and Mbenga (2003: 27).

24 See ch. 7.

25 Rhodes' British South Africa Company and the Tati Mining Company had been given such authority in the Protectorate.

26 Schapera (1933: 652).

27 Isang to Govt. Secretary, Mafeking, 24 Sep. 1931, DCM 2/3, BNA. The Kgatla were accustomed to observing the levirate principle, whereby a younger brother 'raised up seed' in the deceased elder brother's widow, in this case Seingwaeng. Isaac Schapera was given, as was Molefi, an earful by Seingwaeng and Isang's sister Kgabyana about Isang in this regard. They claimed that Isang had used Seingwaeng for *coitus interruptus* but refused to impregnate her, because Isang feared having yet another heir to the throne than Molefi and his brother Musi, who might stand in his way of securing the chieftaincy for himself. Schapera passed on this information to J.D.A. Germond, clerk of Gaberones, who was in Mochudi in August 1934 investigating the Molefi–Isang conflict. See 'Domestic Relations between Isang and Molefi', n.a., n.d., S305/19, BNA. For Germond's diary, see especially entry 24 August 1934, DCM 2/6, BNA.

28 Testimony of Moti Pilane, kgotla minutes, 12–17 Nov. 1934, S402/12, p. 34, BNA.

KGATLA MEPHATO (Male regiments)

Name	Year of formation	Leader
maChechele ('Fleas'?)	n.d.	Mmakgotso Kgwefane
maFatshwana ('Snakes'?)	n.d.	Pheto Molefe
maDima ('Extinguishers')	n.d.	Senwelo Molefe
maGata ('Tramplers')	n.d.	Dikeme Molefe
maChama (?)	n.d.	unknown
maFiri ('Hyenas')	1805?	Letsebe Pheto (and **Pilane** Pheto)
maThulwa ('Gorers')	1813?	Thari Pheto
maNgope ('Bleeders')	1820?	Molefi Molefe
maLomakgomo ('Cattle Stealers'?)	1826?	Kgotlamaswe Pheto
maDingwana ('Cannibals'?)	1837?	Sebele Pheto
maNoga ('Snakes')	1842?	Letsebe Pilane
maSoswe ('Large Ants')	1847?	**Kgamanyane Pilane**
maNgana ('Obstructers')	1856?	Tshomankane Pilane
maThukwi ('Small hyenas')	1863?	Bogatsu Pilane
maFatlha ('Dazzlers')	1869	Maganelo Pilane
maTlakana ('Vultures')	1873	**Linchwe Kgamanyane**
maKoba ('Chasers')	1878	Ramono Kgamanyane (and Segale Kgamanyane
maJanko ('Nose Eaters')	1883	Modise Kgamanyane
maNtwane ('Fighters')	1892	Mochele Kgamanyane
maKuka ('Up-enders')	1901	**Kgafela Linchwe**
maChechele ('Fleas'?)	1911	Isang Linchwe

Pilane's Line
(Eldest son of each lelwapa, by rank)

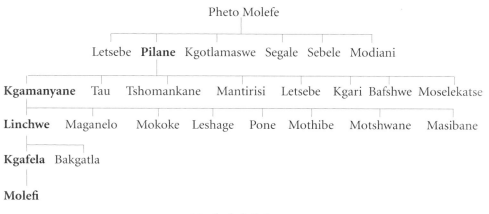

Mankube's Lelwapa

PILANE = **Mankube Bogatsu Tuakobong**

KGAMANYANE Mathudi Mmamorema BOGATSU

Dikolo's Lelwapa

KGAMANYANE = **Dikolo Ramontsana Tlou**

LINCHWE RAMONO

Nkomeng's Lelwapa

KGAMANYANE = **Nkomeng Radibeela Molatlhegi Motsomi Matlhage**

MAGANELO SEGALE MODISE MOCHELE Tsebe Senewe Mmapidiwe Tselane Botlhoko

Motlapele's Lelwapa

LINCHWE = **Motlapele Poonyane**

KGAFELA ISANG OFENTSE KGAMANYANE Kgomotso RADIKOLO BOGATSU BANA

GLOSSARY OF KGATLA TERMS

badimo	ancestors, ancestral spirits
bafaladi	immigrant settlers, outsiders
Bahibidu	red-skinned people (see maBuru)
bogadi	bridewealth, usually cattle
bogosi	the institution of kingship, chiefship; see kgosi
bogwera	male initiation
bojale	female initiation
bojalwa	fermented millet beer
bolawane	rinderpest (lit. 'of Bulawayo')
bonokwane	raiding, terrorising; also raiders, terrorists
borra	sirs, gentlemen
dikgafela	tribute from the first harvest, rendered to the kgosi
dikgosi	see kgosi
dipathusi	cloth
dithaka	age mates (fellow initiates)
GamaNgwato	Ngwato territory (lit. where the Ngwato are)
inkosi	king, senior lineage head; Nguni (e.g. Zulu) term
kgabo	vervet monkey; also the totem of the Kgatla
Kgatleng	Kgatla territory (lit. 'where the Kgatla are')
kgoro	ward, section of a settlement
kgosi	king, senior lineage head, 'chief' pl. dikgosi (see kapitein below)
kgosing	the royal ward, where the kgosi and members of his agnate lineages are located
kgotla	meeting place for public discussions and hearing legal cases, both at the ward level and at the main kgotla, where the kgosi presides
kwena	crocodile, the Kwena totem
Kweneng	Kwena territory (lit. 'where the Kwena are')
lapa	also lelwapa, pl. malwapa; compound of a wife and her children
le	and
leboko	praise poem, recited publicly

GLOSSARY OF KGATLA TERMS

leBuru	see maBuru
leKgoa	see maKgoa
lelwapa	see lapa
leBuru	see maBuru
maBuru	Boers, 'ma-' making it derisory, sing. leBuru
madodo	veterans
mafisa	loan cattle
maKgoa	Europeans, 'ma-' making it derisory, sing. leKgoa
maKoni	outsiders, (lit. 'northerners'), 'ma-' making it derisory
makristo	Christians, 'ma-' making them outsiders
malome	mother's brother
malwapa	see lapa
maSetedi	persons of mixed heritage, e.g. Griqua, Korana
matlaba	eastern, sandy part of Ngwaketse territory
mephato	see mophato
merafe	see morafe
meraka	see moraka
meratswane	refugees
mfecane	a period of drought, conflict, and turmoil in southern Africa, in the 1820s–1830s
mma	Madame, Mrs, may also mean 'mother of' when prefixing a child's name
Modimo	the supreme spirit, God
mohumagadi	queen, senior wife of a kgosi, mother of the future heir to bogosi; see mosadi ea kgolo
mophato	regiment, pl. mephato
morafe	all those who accept the authority of the kgosi; a kingdom, chiefdom; pl. merafe
moraka	cattle post, pl. meraka
moruti	priest (Christian)
mosadi ea kgolo	'great', i.e. senior wife of a kgosi; see mohumagadi
mosunyane	Kgatla name for the cattle captured from the Transvaal Boers during the South African (Anglo-Boer) War and kept under the authority of Linchwe
ngwetse	'daughter-in-law', or a junior wife attached to a senior wife's lelwapa
phiri	duiker

Rre	Sir, mister
seantlo	a substitute wife, usually the sister of the deceased wife
seBuru	the Dutch language; also an adjective referring to things, matters Boer
seKgoa	the English language; also an adjective referring to things, matters English
seTswana	the Tswana language (in South Africa often referred to as Northern Sotho)

GLOSSARY OF NINETEENTH-CENTURY DUTCH TERMS

baas	master, pl. baasen
dorp	town
Dorslanders	Boer emigrants from the trans-Vaal who in the 1870s passed through the Kalahari (lit. 'Thirstlanders')
hoofdkapitein	head or paramount chief
Hoofdkom- mandant	Head commander, Commander-in-chief
inboekeling	a 'registered' person, or 'apprentice', euphemism for slave; pl. inboekelinge
kaffer, kaffir	black person, showing repugnance
kafferbeeste	African-owned cattle
kafferkaptein	see kapitein
kafferkom- missie	Commission on African labour and administration
kafferlokassie	African locations
kafferwet	law governing black persons
kapitein	an African who could control a following, a 'chief'; pl. kapi- teins, kapiteinen
kleurling	a 'coloured', i.e. black, person; pl. kleurlingen
kloof	ravine, gorge
Kommandant	Commander
Kommandant- generaal	Commander-in-chief
Kommando/ commando	an armed expedition led by horse riders

GLOSSARY

kopje	hill
kraal	large cattle enclosure, often located near to the chief's residence
landdrost	magistrate, pl. landdrosten
mampoer	fruit liquor
meekkaffers	submissive, meek Africans
moord	murder
Oom	'Uncle', euphemism for an elderly authority
oorlamse, oorlamse kaffers	'civilised' black people, i.e., those who had adopted Dutch, had Christianised and wore Dutch-style clothing
plakkerswet	squatters' law
riem	rawhide strip, thong
rondavel	a round hut, usually with a thatched roof
sjambok	rhinoceros hide whip
skelm	rogue, crook
smous	trader, often itinerant
stoep	stoop, porch
trekker	one on the move, a migrant, emigrant; see also voortrekker
Vaalpens	BaKgalagadi or Bushman foragers, servants
veldkornet	field-cornet, pl. veldkornetten
vervlugte	misspelling of vervloekte, 'cursed'
volksraad	parliament (lit. people's council)
voortrekker	one of the early Boer emigrants from the Cape into the trans-Vaal

BIBLIOGRAPHY

Archival Sources

Botswana National Archives, Gaborone (BNA)
  Assistant Commissioner (AC)
  District Commissioner, Mochudi (DCM)
  Hermannsburg Missionary Correspondence Typescripts (HMSR)
  High Commissioner (HC)
  Native Advisory Council minutes (NAC)
  Resident Commissioner (RC)
  Secretariat (S)
  Schapera Papers (SP)

British Musuem (BM)
  John Bolton Papers ADD MS.46, 152.
  Julius Weil Papers, vols. I–IV, VIII (46848–46851, 46855), 1899.

British Parliamentary Papers (PP)
  C. 2220 (1876–1878), C. 3841 (1884), C. 4141 (1884–85), C. 4588 (1884–85), C. 4643 (1886), C. 5090 (1887), C. 5918 (1890), C. 5897 (1890)

Cambridge University Library (CUL), Royal Commonwealth Society Collection (RCS)
  Frederick J. Newnham manuscripts. MSS 55/MSS 55V
  Sir Ralph Champneys Williams, 'The Native Races of Central South Africa', submitted to the Royal Colonial Institute, 1884, MSS5
  Accounts of Papers. 'Khame, King of the Bamangwato', LS-1877

Dutch Reformed Church Archives, Cape Town (DRCA)

Baptism Register 1	5/4/2/1 (A–D)	1877–1905
B. Beyer	15/4/3/1 (B)	1886–1894
P. Brink	15/4/3/2 (A–B)	1867–1886
H. Gonin	15/7/2 (A–E)	1861–1907
F. Gonin	15/7/2 (E)	1884–1888
H.M. Gonin	15/7/2 (E)	n.d.
J. Horak	15/7/2 (E)	1877–1882
W.W. Hibbert	15/4/2/4 (B)	1917
Journal, Mochudi	15/4/7/1 (A)	1916–1929
J. Meeuwsen	15/7/2 (E)	1875–1883
Molefi et al.	15/4/3/1 (A–B)	1901–1926
M.E. Murray	15/4/3/8 (B)	1895–1898
Reports, Mochudi	15/4/5/1 (A)	1898–1937
D. Retief	15/4/3/13 (B)	1889–1919
J. Reyneke	15/4/3/14 (A)	1922–1929

294

BIBLIOGRAPHY

London Missionary Society Records (Microfiche), (LMS)
Boxes 36–44 (1870–1887), 51 (1894)

Public Record Office, Kew Gardens, London (PRO)
Colonial Office, 417 series
Confidential Prints, Colonial Office, 879/7/61

Rhodes House, Oxford University (RH)
Jules Ellenberger Papers

Selly Oak Colleges Library, Birmingham (SO)
William Charles Willoughby Papers (WP)

South African Archives (SAA), National Archives Repository, National Archives of South
Africa, Pretoria
Governor General, 1907–1974 (GG)
Native Affairs, 1880–1972 (NTS)

South African Musuem, Cape Town (SAM)
Andrew Smith Journals

State Library, Pretoria.
Transvaal Native Affairs Department Annual Report, June 1910.

Transvaal Archives (TA), National Archives Repository, National Archives of South Af-
rica, Pretoria
Administrator of the Transvaal Colony, 1877–1881 (ATC)
Auditor General, 1867–1900 (AG)
Attorney General, 1902–1939 (ATG)
British Resident, Transvaal, 1880–1885 (BR)
Colonial Treasurer, Transvaal, 1900–1910 (CT)
Dorsland Trek Documents (A.779), 1876–1877
Kommandant General, 1880–1900 (KG)
Landdrost, Rustenburg, 1873–1890 (ZRB)
Landdrost, Rustenburg, 1902–1980 (LRB)
Law Department, Transvaal, 1900–1925 (LD)
Lieutenant Governor of the Transvaal Colony, 1902–1907 (LTG)
Military Governor, Pretoria, 1900–1902 (MGP)
Native Commissioner, Rustenburg, 1910–1968 (KRB)
Postmaster General, 1892–1904 (PMG)
Public Works Department, 1901–1914 (PWD)
Secretary of the Governor of the Transvaal, 1900–1910 (GOV)

295

Sir Owen Lanyon Papers (A.596)
State Attorney, 1864–1900 (SP)
State Secretary, ZAR, 1829–1900 (SS)
State Secretary, Foreign Affairs Section, 1894–1900 (SSA)
Superintendent of Native Affairs, 1877–1900 (SN)
Superintendent of Native Affairs, 1900–1911 (SNA)
Supreme Court of the SAR and of the Transvaal Colony, 1877–1910 (ZTPD)
Transvaal Agricultural Department, 1900–1919 (TAD)

University of Pretoria
Theophilus Shepstone papers (SPUP)

Published Government Sources

Alphabetical List of Farms in the Province of Transvaal. Pretoria: Government Printer, 1980. (ALFPT)

Annual Report by the Commissioner for Native Affairs for the Year Ended 30th June, 1903, Pretoria: Government Printers, 1903.

British Bechuanaland. Proceedings of the Bechuanaland Protectorate Boundary Commission. Vryburg: Townshend and Son, 1894. (BPBC)

Colonial Office Confidential Prints (COCP)

Précis of Information Concerning the Transvaal Territory Prepared in the Intelligence Branch of the Quartermaster-General's Department, Horse Guards, War Office. London: Harrison and Sons for HMS Stationery Office, 1881.

Report by the Commissioner for Native Affairs Relative to the Acquisition and Tenure of Land by Natives in the Transvaal. Pretoria: Government Printing and Stationery Office, 1904.

Report of the Natives Land Commission, 2 vols. Cape Town: Government Printers, U.G. 22–1916, 1916.

Report of the Select Committee on Native Affairs. Cape Town: Cape Times, 1911.

South African Archival Records, Transvaal (SAAR). *Notule van die Volksraad van die Suid-Afrikaanse Republiek (volledig met alle bylae daarby), Vol II (1851–1853).* Edited by J.H. Breytenback. Cape Town, n.p., 1949.

Topo-Cadastral Maps, Surveys and Mapping, Mowbray.

Transvaal Administration, *Annual Report by the Commissioner for Native Affairs for the year ending 30 June 1903.* Pretoria: Government Printing and Stationery Office, 1903.

Union of South Africa, *Report of the Natives Land Commission,* II. Cape Town: Government Printers, 1916.

Union of South Africa, *Report of the Natives Land Committee, Western Transvaal.* Cape Town: Government Printers, 1918.

Newspapers

Bulawayo Chronicle
Die Gereformeerde Kerkbode
Graham's Town Journal

Hermannsburger Missionsblatt
Die Koningsbode
Natal Mercury
The Times (London)
Transvaal Argus
De Volksstem

Interviews

Gaborone:
   Dupleix Pilane (12 Dec. 1981)
   Ernest Sedumedi Moloto (22 Feb. 1982)

Lentswe le Moriti:
   Sebele Motsitsi, Baekgedi Nkele et al. (26 Feb. 1986)

Mochudi:
   Amos Kgamanyane Pilane (23 Jul. 1979, 20 Jul. 1980, 7 and 20 Jul. 1982)
   Bakgatlabatsile Pilane (18 Dec. 1981)
   Edwin Gare (5 Jan. 1983)
   Francis Phiri (23 Dec. 1981)
   Gabriel Palai (24 Jul. 1979)
   Galemone Monowe (24 Jul. 1979)
   Harris Thulare, (28 Jul 1982)
   Leitshole Letshole (9 Aug. 1979)
   Linchwe Molefi Kgafela (11 Jul. 1995)
   Molefhe Motsisi (10 Jul. 1995)
   Ratsegana Sebeke (26 Jul. 1982)
   Ratsegana Sebeke and Harris Thulare (4 Aug. 1982)
   Rramaiba Moremi (26 Jul. 1979)
   Seikgokgoni Pilane (16 and 21 Dec. 1981)
   Selogwe Pilane (30 Jul. and 7 Aug. 1979, 19 and 21 Dec. 1981, 22 Jul. 1982)
   Thari Pumetse (3 Aug. 1979)

Saulspoort (Moruleng):
   Kgamanyane Pilane, J.R. Phiri, and England M.T. Pilane (5 Jan. 1982)
   Rev. J. Phiri and England Kgamanyane Pilane (6 Jan. 1982)

Unpublished Materials, Theses

Erasmus, D.J. 1995. 'Re-thinking the Great Trek: A Study of the Nature and Development of the Boer Community in the Ohrigstad/Lydenburg Area, 1845–1877', M.A. Thesis, Rhodes University.

Gumbo, G. 1986. Chronological list of officials, chiefs, Bechuanaland Protectorate, handwritten.

Huffmann, T.N. et al. 1996. 'Achaeological Survey of Madikwe Game Reserve, North West Province. A Phase 1 Report Prepared for North West Parks Board', Paper. Archaeology Department, University of Witwatersrand.

Legassick, M.C. 1969. 'The Griqua, the Sotho-Tswana, and the Missionaries, 1780–1840: The Politics of a Frontier Zone', Ph.D. dissertation, University of California, Los Angeles.

Morton, R.F., comp., ed. 1982. 'Interview Notes on Bakgatla History.' Mimeograph. Department of History, University College, Botswana.

Okihiro, G.Y. 1976. 'Hunters, Herders, Cultivators, and Traders: Interaction and Change in the Kgalagadi, Nineteenth Century', Ph.D. dissertation, University of California, Los Angeles.

Parsons, Q.N. 1973. 'Khama III, the Bamangwato, and the British, With Special Reference to 1895–1923', Ph.D. dissertation. University of Edinburgh.

Ramsay, F.J. 1985. 'Better Red than Dead, Some Observations on the British Occupation of Kweneng, 1885–1895', University of Botswana Seminar Commemorating the Centenary of the Founding of the Bechuanaland Protectorate.

—. 1991. 'The Rise and Fall of the Bakwena Dynasty of South-Central Botswana, 1820–1940', Ph.D. dissertation, Boston University.

Sedimo, L. 1986. 'The Border Police and the Bechuanaland Protectorate, 1885–1895', B.A. Thesis, Department of History, University of Botswana.

Van der Merwe, W.J. 1934. 'The Development of Missionary Attitudes in the Dutch Reformed Church in South Africa', Ph.D. Thesis, Kennedy School of Missions of the Hartford Seminary Foundation.

Volz, S. 2006. '"From the Mouths of our Countrymen": The Careers and Communities of Tswana Evangelists in the Nineteenth Century', Ph.D dissertation, University of Wisconsin, Madison.

Published Sources

Agar-Hamilton, J.A.I. n.d. [1928]. *The Native Policy of the Voortrekkers: An Essay in the History of the Interior of South Africa, 1836–1858*. Cape Town: Maskew Miller.

Alpers, E.A. 1975. *Ivory and Slaves: Changing Pattern* [sic] *of International Trade in East Central Africa to the Later Nineteenth Century*. Berkeley: University of California Press.

Amery, L.S., ed. 1905. *The Times History of the War in South Africa*, III. London: Samson Low, Marston.

Anderson, A.A. 1974. *Twenty-five Years in a Waggon: Sport and Travel in South Africa*. Cape Town: Struik.

Baines, T. 1964. *Journal of Residence in Africa, 1842–1853*. 2 vols. Edited by R.F. Kennedy. Cape Town: The Van Riebeeck Society.

'Bamangwato'. 1868. *To Ophir Direct: or, the South African Goldfields: with a map showing the route taken by Hartley and Mauch, in 1866–67; and an Account of the 'Transvaal' or South African Republic*. London: Edward Standford.

Bergh, J.S. 1999. *Geskiedenis Atlas van Suid-Afrika: Die Vier Noordelike Provinsies*. Pretoria: J.L. van Schaik.

Bergh, J.S. and Morton, F. 2003. *'To Make Them Serve': The 1871 Commission on African Labour*. Pretoria: Protea Book House.

298

BIBLIOGRAPHY

Bloemhof Arbitration Court. 1871. *Evidence Taken at Bloemhof Before the Commission Appointed to Investigate the Claims of the South African Republic, Captain N. Waterboer, Chief of West Griqualand, and Certain Other Native Chiefs, to Portions of the Territory on the Vaal River, Now Known as the Diamond-fields.* Cape Town: Saul Solomon.

Boeyens, J.C.A. 1994. '"Black Ivory": The Indenture System and Slavery in Zoutpansberg, 1848–1869.' In *Slavery in South Africa: Captive Labor on the Dutch Frontier*, edited by E. Eldredge and F. Morton, 187–214. Boulder: Westview Press.

Bonner, P. 1983. *Kings, Commoners and Concessionaires: The Evolution and Dissolution of the Nineteenth-century Swazi State.* Cambridge: Cambridge University Press.

Boshier, A.K. 1969. 'Mining Genesis.' In *Mining Survey No. 64.* Johannesburg: Chamber of Mines of South Africa: 18–31.

Botha, H.J. 1969. 'Die Moord op Derdepoort, 25 November 1899. Nie-blankes in oorlogs-diens', *Militaria*, 1, 2: 3–98.

Breutz, P.-L. 1953. *The Tribes of Rustenburg and Pilansberg Districts.* Pretoria: Department of Native affairs, Ethnological Publications No. 28.

—. 1987. *A History of the Batswana and Origin of Bophutatswana: A Handbook of a Survey of the Tribes of the Batswana, S.-ndebele, Qwaqwa and Botswana.* Ramsgate: private publication.

Broadbent, S. 1865. *A Narrative of the First Introduction of Christianity among the Barolong Tribe of Bechuanas, South Africa.* London: Wesleyan Mission House.

Brown, J.T. 1875. 'The Bechuana Tribes.' In *Cape Monthly Magazine*, XI: 1–5.

—. 1926. *Among the Bantu Nomads: A Record of Forty Years Spent Among the Bechuana A Numerous and Famous Branch of the Central South African Bantu, With the First Full Description of Their Ancient Customs, Manners and Beliefs.* Philadelphia: J.B. Lippincott.

Brown, W.H. 1970. *On the South African Frontier. The Adventures and Observations of an American in Mashonaland and Matabeleland.* New York: Negro Universities Press.

Bryden, H.A. 1893. *Gun and Camera in Southern Africa.* London: Edward Standford.

Carruthers, V. 1990. *The Magaliesberg.* Johannesburg: Southern Book Publishers.

Child, D., ed. 1979. *A Merchant Family in Early Natal: Diaries and Letters of Joseph and Mariaane Churchill, 1850 to 1880.* Cape Town: A.A. Balkema.

Chirenje, J.M. 1977. *A History of Northern Botswana, 1850–1910.* Rutherford: Fairleigh Dickinson University Press.

Collins, W.W. 1965. *Free Statia: Reminiscences of a Lifetime in the Orange Free State.* Cape Town: C. Struik.

Comaroff, J.L. 1978. 'Rules and Rulers: Political Processes in a Tswana Chiefdom.' *Man*, 13: 1–20.

—. 1982. 'Dialectical Systems, History and Anthropology: Units of Study and Questions of Theory.' In *Journal of Southern African Studies*, 8, 2(April): 143–172.

Cory, G.E. 1940. *The Rise of South Africa: A History of the Origin and South African Colonisation and of its Development Towards the East from the Earliest Times to 1857.* 6 vols. Cape Town: The Archives of the Union of South Africa/*Cape Times*.

Crowder, M. 1990. 'Legitimacy and Faction: Tswana Constitutionalism and Political

Change.' In *Succession to High Office in Botswana*, edited by J. Parson, 1–31. Athens: Ohio University Center for International Studies.

Cumming, R.G. 1906. *The Lion Hunter of South Africa: Five Years' Adventures in the Far Interior of South Africa, with Notices of the Native Tribes and Savage Animals.* 8th edition. London: John Murray.

Davenport, T.R.H. 1981. *South Africa: A Modern History.* 2nd ed. Johannesburg: Macmillan South Africa.

De Kiewet, C.F. 1965. *The Imperial Factor in South Africa.* London: Frank Cass.

d'Elegorgue, A. 1844. 'Brief Outline of an Expedition into the Interior of South Africa.' In *Graham's Town Journal.* 8 August.

—. 1847. *Voyage dans l'Afrique Austale, Notamment dans le Territories deNatal . . . Durant less Annees 1838, 1839, 1840, 1841, 1842, 1843 & 1844.* 2 vols. Paris: A Rene et Cie.

Delius, P. 1984. *The Land Belongs to Us: The Pedi Polity, the Boers and the British in the Nineteenth-century Transvaal.* Berkeley: University of California Press.

Delius, P. and Trapido, S. 1983. 'Inboekselings and Oorlams: The Creation and Transformation of a Servile Class.' In *Town and Countryside in the Transvaal: Capitalist Penetration and Populist Response*, edited by B. Bozzoli, 53–81. Johannesburg: Ravan Press.

De Vaal, J.B. 1953. 'Die Rol van Joao Albasini in die Geskiedenis van die Transvaal.' In *Archives Year Book for South African History*, XVI, 1.

Du Plessis, J. 1911. *A History of Christian Missions in South Africa.* London: Longmans, Green.

Du Toit, A. 1983. 'No Chosen People: The Myth of the Calvinist Origins of Afrikaner Nationalism and Racial Ideology.' In *American Historical Review*, 88, 4: 920–952.

Du Toit, A and Giliomee, H. 1983. *Afrikaner Political Thought: Analysis and Documents. Volume One: 1780–1850.* Berkeley: University of California Press.

Eldredge, E. 1993. *A South African Kingdom: The Pursuit of Security in Nineteenth-Century Lesotho.* Cambridge: Cambridge University Press.

—. 1994a. 'Delegoa Bay and the Hinterland in the Early Nineteenth Century: Politics, Trade, Slaves, and Slave Raiding.' In *Slavery in South Africa: Captive Labor on the Dutch Frontier*, edited by E. Eldredge and F. Morton, 127–165. Boulder: Westview Press.

—. 1994b. 'Slave Raiding Across the Cape Frontier.' In *Slavery in South Africa: Captive Labor on the Dutch Frontier*, edited by E. Eldredge and F. Morton, 93–126. Boulder: Westview Press.

Eldredge, E. and Morton, F., eds. 1994. *Slavery in South Africa: Captive Labor on the Dutch Frontier.* Boulder: Westview Press.

Ellenberger, V. 1937. 'History of the Ba-Ga-Malete of Ramoutsa (Bechuanaland Protectorate).' In *Transactions of the Royal Society of South Africa*, xxv, 4: 1–72.

—. 1939. 'History of the Batlokwa of Gaberones (Bechuanaland Protectorate).' In *Bantu Studies*, 13: 166–198.

Engelbrecht, S.P., ed. 1925. *Paul Kruger's Amptelike Briewe, 1851–1877.* Pretoria: Volkstem-Drukkery.

Etherington, N. 1991. 'The Great Trek in Relation to the Mfecane: A Reassessment.' In *South African Historical Journal*, 25: 3–21.

BIBLIOGRAPHY

Ettinger, S.J. 1972. 'South Africa's Weight Restrictions on Cattle Exports from Bechuanaland, 1924–41.' In *Botswana Notes and Records*, 4: 21–29.

Eybers, G.W. 1969. *Select Constitutional Documents Illustrating South African History, 1795–1910*. New York: Negro Universities Press.

Freeman, J.J. 1851. *A Tour in South Africa, with Notices of Natal, Mauritius, Madagascar, Ceylon, Egypt, and Palestine*. London: John Snow.

Galbraith, J.S. 1974. *Crown and Charter: The Early Years of the British South Africa Company*. Berkeley: University of California Press.

Gardner, B. 1966. *Mafeking: A Victoria Legend*. London: Cassell.

Gillmore, P. 1876. *The Land of the Boer, or Adventures in Natal, the Transvaal, Basutoland and Zululand*. London: Cassell, Petter, Galpin.

Gon, P. 1984. *Send Carrington! The Story of an Imperial Frontiersman*. Craighall: A.D. Donker.

Goodfellow, C.F. 1966. *Great Britain and South African Confederation, 1870–1881*. Cape Town: Oxford University Press.

Gray, R. 1975. 'Southern Africa and Madagascar.' In *The Cambridge History of Africa. Volume 4: c. 1600–1790*, edited by R. Gray, 384–468. Cambridge: Cambridge University Press.

Grobler, J.E.H. 1997. 'Jan Viljoen, the South African Republic and the Bakwena, 1848–1882.' In *South African Historical Journal*, 36: 240–255.

Hall, S. 1995. 'Archaeological Indicators for Stress in the Western Transvaal Region between the Seventeenth and Nineteenth Centuries.' In *The Mfecane Aftermath: Reconstructive Debates in Southern African History*, edited by C. Hamilton, 307–321. Johannesburg: Witwatersrand University Press.

Hamilton, C, ed. 1995. *The Mfecane Aftermath: Reconstructive Debates in Southern African History*. Johannesburg: Witwatersrand University Press.

Hancock, W.K. and Van der Poel, J., eds. 1965. *Selections from the Smuts Papers*. Cambridge: Cambridge University Press.

Hasselhorn, F. 1988. *Bauermission in Südafrika*. Erlangen, Bayern: Erlanger Monographien aus Mission und Ökumene.

Hickman, A.S. 1970. *Rhodesia Served the Queen: Rhodesian Forces in the Boer War, 1899–1901*. Salisbury: Government Printer.

Hinchcliffe, P., ed. 1971. *The Journal of John Ayliff, 1821–1830*. Cape Town: A.A. Balkema.

Hodgson, M.L. and Ballinger, W.G. 1932. *Britain in Southern Africa. No. 2. Bechuanaland Protectorate*. Alice: Lovedale Press.

Holden, W.C., ed. 1963. *History of the Colony of Natal, South Africa*. Cape Town: C. Struik.

Hole, H.M. 1968. *Old Rhodesia Days*. London: Frank Cass.

Holub, E. 1880. 'Journey through Central South Africa, from the Diamond Fields to the Upper Zambezi.' In *Proceedings of the Royal Geographical Society and Monthly Record of Geography*, 2: 166–182.

——. 1976. *Seven Years in South Africa*. Vol. II. Johannesburg: Africana Book Society.

Human Sciences Research Council. 1968–1987. *Dictionary of South African Biography*. 4 vols. Cape Town and Pretoria: Nasional Boekhandel Bpk. for National Council for Social Research, Dept. of Higher Education.

Jackson, A.O. 1983. *The Ndebele of Langa*. Department of Co-operation and Development Publications No. 54. Pretoria: Government Printer.

Johnson, F. 1972. *Great Days*. Bulawayo: Books of Rhodesia.

Jordan, W.W. 1881. 'Journal of the Trek Boers.' In *Cape Quarterly Review*, I, I: 145–175 with map.

Keegan, T. 1996. *Colonial South Africa and the Origins of the Racial Order*. Cape Town: David Philip.

Kirby, P.R., ed. 1939. *The Diary of Dr. Andrew Smith, director of the 'Expedition for Exploring Central Africa', 1834–1836*. 2 vols. Cape Town: The Van Riebeeck Society.

Kistner, W. 1952. 'The Anti-slavery Agitation against the Transvaal Republic, 1852–1868.' In *Archives Yearbook for South African History*, II: 194–278.

Kruger, S.J.P. 1902. *The Memoirs of Paul Kruger, Four Times President of the South African Republic, Told By Himself*. London: Unwin.

—. 1969. *The Memoirs of Paul Kruger, Four Times President of the South African Republic, Told By Himself*. New York: Negro Universities Press.

Landau, P.S. 1995. *The Realm of the Word: Language, Gender, and Christianity in a Southern African Kingdom*. Portsmouth: Heinemann.

Lemue, P. 1834. 'Voyage de M. Mellen.' In *Journal Des Missions Evangeliques*: 266–276.

Livingstone, D. 1959. *David Livingstone: Family Letters, 1841–1856*. 2 vols. Edited by I. Schapera. London: Chatto and Windus.

—. 1960. *Livingstone's Private Journals, 1851–1853*. Edited by I. Schapera. London: Chatto and Windus.

—. 1961. *Livingstone's Missionary Correspondence, 1841–1856*. Edited by I. Schapera. London: Chatto and Windus.

—. 1974. *David Livingstone South African Papers, 1849–1853*. Edited by I. Schapera. Cape Town: Van Riebeeck Society.

Lye, W.F., ed. 1975. *Andrew Smith's Journal of His Expedition into the Interior of South Africa/ 1834–1836. An Authentic Narrative of Travels and Discoveries, the Manners and Customs of the Native Tribes, and the Physical Nature of the Country*. Cape Town: A.A. Balkema.

Mackenzie, W.D. 1969. *John Mackenzie: South African Missionary and Statesman*. New York: Negro Universities Press.

Manson, A. and Mbenga, B. 2003. '"The Richest Tribe in Africa": Platinum-mining and the Bafokeng in South Africa's North West Province, 1965–1999.' In *Journal of Southern African Studies*, 29, 1: 27.

Maree, W.L. 1965. *Uit Duisternis Geroep die Sendingwerk von die Nederduitse Gereformeerde Kerk onder die Bakgatla von Wes-Transvaal en Betsjoenaland*. Johannesburg: N.G. Kerk Boekhandel.

Marks, S. and Gray, R. 1975. 'Southern Africa and Madagascar.' In *The Cambridge History of Africa. Volume 4: c. 1600–1790*, edited by R. Gray, 384–468. Cambridge: Cambridge University Press.

Mason, R.J. 1982. 'Prehistoric Mining in South Africa, and Iron Age Copper Mines in the Dwarsberg, Transvaal.' In *Journal of the South African Institute of Mining and Metallurgy*, 82: 134–142.

Mathers, E.P. 1977. *Zambesia: England's El Dorado in Africa*. Bulawayo: Books of Rhodesia.

Mathews, Z.K. 1945. 'A Short History of the Tshidi Barolong.' *Fort Hare Papers*, June: 9–28.

Maylam, P. 1980. *Rhodes, the Tswana and the British: Colonialism, Collaboration and Conflict in the Bechuanaland Protectorate, 1885–1899*. Westport, CT: Greenwood.

Mbenga, B.K. 1997. 'Forced Labour in the Pilanesberg: The Flogging of Chief Kgamanyane by Commandant Paul Kruger, Saulspoort, April 1870.' In *Journal of Southern African Studies*. 23(1): 127–140.

Mbenga, B.K. and Morton, F. 1997. 'The Missionary as Land Broker: Henri Gonin, Saulspoort 269 and the Bakgatla of Rustenburg District, 1862–1922.' In *South African Historical Journal*, 36: 145–167.

McCarter, J. 1869. *The Dutch Reformed Church in South Africa with Notices of Other Denominations. An Historical Sketch*. London: J. Nisbet.

Meeuwsen, J.P. 1879. 'Customs and Superstitions Among the Betshuana.' In *Folk-lore Journal*, I: 33–34.

Methuen, H.H. 1846. *Life in the Wilderness: or Wanderings in South Africa*. London: Richard Bentley.

Mientjes, J. 1974. *President Paul Kruger: A Biography*. London: Cassell.

Mignon, A. 1996. *The 19ᵗʰ Century Lutheran Mission in Botswana*. Gaborone: The Botswana Society and the National Archives and Records Services.

Moffat, R.U. 1969. *John Smith Moffat, CMG Missionary: A Memoir*. New York: Negro Universities Press.

Mokgatle, N. 1971. *The Autobiography of an Unknown South African*. Berkeley: University of California Press.

Molema, S.M. 1966. *Montshiwa, 1815–1896: Barolong Chief and Patriot*. Cape Town: C. Struik.

Moodie, G.P. 1878. 'The Population, Prospects, and Future Government of the Transvaal.' In *The Journal of the Royal United Service Institution*, XXII: 583–611.

Moodie, T.D. 1975. *The Rise of Afrikanerdom: Power, Apartheid, and the Afrikaner Civil Religion*. Berkeley: University of California Press.

Morton, B. 1993. 'Pre-1904 Population Estimates of the Tswana.' In *Botswana Notes and Records*. 25: 89–99.

——. 1994a. *Pre-colonial Botswana: An Annotated Bibliography and Guide to the Sources*. Gaborone: The Botswana Society.

——. 1994b. 'Servitude, Slave Trading, and Slavery in the Kalahari.' In *Slavery in South Africa: Captive Labor on the Dutch Frontier*, edited by E. Eldredge and F. Morton, 215–250. Boulder: Westview Press.

Morton, F. 1982. *Interview Notes on Bakgatla History*. Gaborone: Department of History, University College of Botswana.

——. 1985a. 'Chiefs and Ethnic Unity in Two Colonial Worlds: The Bakgatla baga Kgafela of the Bechuanaland Protectorate and the Transvaal, 1872–1966.' In *Partitioned Africans: Ethnic Relations Across Africa's International Boundaries, 1884–1984*, edited by A.I. Asiwaju, 126–153. London: C. Hurst.

—. 1985b. 'Linchwe I and the Kgatla Campaign in the South African War, 1899–1902.' In *Journal of African History*, 26: 169–191.

—. 1994a. 'Captive Labor in the Western Transvaal after the Sand River Convention.' In *Slavery in South Africa: Captive Labor on the Dutch Frontier*, edited by E. Eldredge and F. Morton, 167–185. Boulder: Westview Press.

—. 1994b. 'Slavery and South African Historiography.' In *Slavery in South Africa: Captive Labor on the Dutch Frontier*, edited by E. Eldredge and F. Morton, 1–9. Boulder: Westview Press.

—. 1994c. 'Slavery in South Africa.' In *Slavery in South Africa: Captive Labor on the Dutch Frontier*, edited by E. Eldredge and F. Morton, 251–269. Boulder: Westview Press.

—. 1995. 'Land, Cattle and Ethnicity: Creating Linchwe's BaKgatla, 1875–1920.' In *South African Historical Journal*, 33 (November): 131–154.

—. 1998a. 'Cattleholders, Evangelists and Socioeconomic Transformation among the BaKgatla of Rustenburg Dstrict, 1863–1898.' In *South African Historical Journal*, 38 (May): 79–98.

—. 1998b. 'The Politics of Cultural Conservatism in Colonial Botswana: Queen Seinwaeng's Zionist Campaign in the Bakgatla Reserve, 1937–1947.' In *Pula: Botswana Journal of African Studies*. 12 (1 and 2): 22–43.

—. 2003. 'Perpetual Motion: Resettlement Patterns in the Western Transvaal and Southeastern Botswana since 1750.' In *Historia: Journal of the Historical Association of South Africa*, 48, 1 (May): 265–282.

—. 2005. 'Female *Inboekelinge* in the South African Republic, 1850–1880', *Slavery and Abolition*, 26, 2 (August): 199–214.

—. 2006. 'Cattle, Land, and Entrepreneurship: Creating the Saulspoort Location after the Anglo-Boer War.' In *Historia: Journal of the Historical Association of South Africa*, 51, 2 (November): 95–118.

—. 2007. 'Female *Inboekelinge* in the South African Republic, 1850–1880.' In *Women and Slavery*, Vol. I, edited by G. Campbell, S. Miers and J.C. Miller, 191–212. Athens: Ohio University Press.

Nathan, M. 1941. *Paul Kruger: His Life and Times*. Durban: Knox.

Notes from British Bechuanaland Requisition No 17, 272. Contract in connection with the Construction and Working of a Railway from Vryburg to Palapye. 3 August 1894. London: P.S. King and Son, 16–17, Item 42.

Omer-Cooper, J.D. 1966. *The Zulu Aftermath: A Nineteenth-century Revolution in Bantu Africa*. Burnt Mill, Harlow: Longman.

Orpen, J.M. 1979. *History of the Basutos of South Africa*. Mazenod: Mazenod Book Centre.

Packenham, T. 1982. *The Boer War*. London: Macdonald.

Parsons, Q.N. 1995. 'Prelude to Difaqane in the Interior of Southern Africa, c. 1600–c. 1822.' In *The Mfecane Aftermath: Reconstructive Debates in Southern African History*, edited by C. Hamilton, 322–349. Johannesburg: Witwatersrand University Press.

—. 1998. *King Khama, Emperor Joe and the Great White Queen: Victorian Britain through African Eyes*. Chicago: University of Chicago Press.

Peters, P. 1994. *Dividing the Commons: Politics, Policy and Culture in Botswana*. Charlottesville: University Press of Virginia.

Plaatje, S.T. 1930. *Mhudi: An African Romance*. Alice: Lovedale Press.

——. 1990. *Mafeking Diary: A Black Man's View of a White Man's War*, edited by J. Comaroff. Cambridge: Meridor.

Précis of Information concerning the Transvaal Territory Prepared in the Intelligence Branch of the Quartermaster-General's Department, Horse Guards, War Office. London: Harrison and Sons for HMS Stationery Office, 1881.

Pretorius, F. 1999. *Life on Commando during the Anglo-Boer War, 1899–1902*. Cape Town: Human and Rousseau.

Price, E.L. 1956. *The Journals of Elizabeth Lees Price*. Edited by Una Long. London: Edward Arnold.

Proceedings of the Bechuanaland Protectorate Boundary Commission, October 1894. Vryburg: Townshend and Son.

Ramsay, J. and Morton, F., eds. 1987. *Birth of Botswana: A History of the Bechuanaland Protectorate from 1910 to 1966*. Gaborone: Longman Botswana.

Ranger, T.O. 1967. *Revolt in Southern Rhodesia, 1896–97: A Study in African Resistance*. Evanston: Northwestern University Press.

Rasmussen, R.K. 1978. *Migrant Kingdom: Mzilikazi's Ndebele in South Africa*. London: Rex Collings.

Readers' Digest. 1988. *Readers' Digest Illustrated History of South Africa: The Real Story*. Pleasantville: The Readers' Digest Association.

Reyneke, J. 1923. 'Mochudi lets uit die oue doos.' In *Die Kongingsbode Kerstnummer*, 23: 41–43.

——. 1924. 'A Remarkable Tribe.' In *Native Affairs Departmental Annual* (Salisbury): 2 (Dec): 93.

Ross, R. 1976. *Adam Kok's Griquas: A Study in the Development of Stratification in South Africa*. Cambridge: Cambridge University Press.

Rotberg, R.I. and Shore, M.F. 1988. *The Founder: Cecil Rhodes and the Pursuit of Power*. New York: Oxford University Press.

Sadler, C., comp. 1967. *Never a Young Man: Extracts from the Letters and Journals of the Rev. William Shaw*. Cape Town: Haum.

Sanderson, J. 1860. 'Memorandum of a Trading Trip into the Orange River (Sovereignty) Free State, and the Country of the Transvaal Boers, 1851–1852.' In *Journal of the Royal Geographical Society*, 30: 233–255.

Saunders, P. 1975. *Moshoeshoe: Chief of the Sotho*. London: Heinemann.

Schapera, I. 1933. 'Economic Conditions in a Bechuanaland Native Reserve.' In *South African Journal of Science*, XXX: 633–655.

——. 1934. 'Herding Rites of the Bechuanaland BaKxatla.' In *American Anthropologist*, N.S. 36: 651–584.

——. 1941. *Married Life in an African Tribe*. New York: Sheridan.

——. 1942a. 'A Short History of the Bakgatla-bagaKgafela of Bechuanaland Protectorate.' Cape Town: University of Cape Town, Communications from the School of African Studies, New Series No. 3 (mimeograph).

——. 1942b. 'A Short History of the Bangwaketse.' In *African Studies*, I: 1–26.

—. 1943a. *Native Land Tenure in the Bechuanaland Protectorate*. Alice: Lovedale Press.

—. 1943b. *Tribal Legislation Among the Tswana of the Bechuanaland Protectorate: A Study in the Mechanism of Cultural Change*. London: London School of Economics.

—. 1945. 'Notes on the History of the Kaa.' In *African Studies*, 4, 3: 109–121.

—. 1947. Migrant Labour and Tribal Life: A Study of Conditions in the Bechuanaland Protectorate. London: Oxford University Press.

—. 1952. *Ethnic Composition of Tswana Tribes*. London: London School of Economics and Political Science.

—. 1963. 'Kinship and Politics in Tswana History.' In *Journal of the Royal Anthropological Institute*, 93, 2: 159–173.

—. 1965. *Praise Poems of Tswana Chiefs*. Oxford: Oxford University Press.

—. 1970. *Tribal Innovators: Tswana Chiefs and Social Change, 1795–1940*. London: Athlone Press.

—. 1971. *Rainmaking Rites of Tswana Tribes*. Leiden: Afrika-Studiecentrum.

—. 1977. *A Handbook of Tswana Law and Custom*. 2nd edition. London: Frank Cass.

—. 1978. *Bogwera: Kgatla Initiation*. Mochudi: Phuthadikobo Museum.

Schreuder, D.M. 1980. *The Scramble for Southern Africa: The Politics of Partition Reappraised*. Cambridge: Cambridge University Press.

Sillery, A. 1952. *The Bechuanaland Protectorate*. London: Oxford University Press.

—. 1964. *Sechele: The Story of an African Chief*. Oxford: G. Ronald.

Smith, A. 1836. *Report of the Expedition for Exploring Central Africa, from the Cape of Good Hope, June 23, 1834, Under the Superintendence of Dr. A. Smith*. Cape Town: Government Gazette Office.

Smith, A.K. 1970. 'Delegoa Bay and the Trade of South-eastern Africa.' In *Pre-colonial African Trade: Essays on Trade in Central and Eastern Africa before 1900*, edited by R. Gray and D. Birmingham, 265–289. London: Oxford University Press.

Smith, E.W. 1956. 'Sebetwane and the Makololo.' In *African Studies*, 15, 2: 49–74.

—. 1957. *Great Lion of Bechuanaland: The Life and Times of Roger Price, Missionary*. London: London Missionary Society/Independent Press.

Struben, H.W. 1920. *Recollections of Adventures: Pioneering and Development in South Africa, 1950–1911*. Cape Town: Maskew Miller.

Tabler, E.C. *The Far Interior*. Cape Town: Balkema.

Tema, B. 2005. *The People of Welgeval*. Cape Town: Struik (Zebra Press).

Templin, J.A. 1984. *Ideology on a Frontier: The Theological Foundation of Afrikaner Nationalism, 1652–1910*. Westport: Greenwood.

Theal, G.M. 1964. *The History of South Africa from 1795 to 1872*. Vol. 4. Cape Town: C. Struik.

—. 1969. *The History of South Africa from 1795 to 1872*. 5 vols. Cape Town: C. Struik.

Thompson, L. 1969. 'Co-operation and Conflict: The High Veld.' In *The Oxford History of South Africa: I: South Africa to 1870*, edited by M. Wilson and L. Thompson, 391–446. Oxford: Clarendon Press.

—. 1975. *Survival in Two Worlds. Moshoeshoe of Lesotho, 1786–1870*. Oxford: Clarendon Press.

BIBLIOGRAPHY

Trapido, S. 1980. 'Reflections on Land, Office and Wealth in the South African Republic, 1850–1900.' In *Economy and Society in Pre-industrial South Africa*, edited by S. Marks and A. Atmore, 350–368. Burnt Mill, Harlow: Longman.

Truschel, L. 1972. 'Nation-building and the Kgatla: The Role of the Anglo-Boer War.' In *Botswana Notes and Records*, 4: 185–193.

Van Coller, H.P. 1942. 'Mampoer in die Stryd om die Bapedi-troon (die Mapoch oorlog, 1882–1883).' In *Historiese Studies* III (3–4), October–December: 97–152.

Van Onselen, C. 1972. 'Reactions to Rinderpest in Southern Africa, 1896–1897.' In *Journal of African History*. 13: 473–488.

Van Rooyen, T.S. 1951. 'Der Verhoudinge Tussen die Boere, Engelse en Naturelle in die Geskiedenis van die Oos-Transvaal tot 1882.' In *Archives Year Book for South African History*, XIV, I.

Van Warmelo, N.J. 1935. *A Preliminary Survey of the Bantu Tribes of South Africa*. Department of Native Affairs Ethnological Publications No. 5. Pretoria: Government Printer.

Vaughn-Williams, H. 1941. *A Visit to Lobengula in 1889*. Pietermaritzburg: Shuter and Shooter.

Wagner, R. 1980. 'Zoutpansberg: The Dynamics of a Hunting Frontier, 1848–1867.' In *Economy and Society in Pre-industrial South Africa*, edited by S. Marks and A. Atmore, 313–349. Burnt Mill, Harlow: Longman.

Walker, E.A. 1962. *A History of Southern Africa*. London: Longman.

Wallis, J.P.R., ed. 1945. *The Matebele Journals of Robert Moffat: 1829–1860*. Vol. 1. London: Chatto and Windus.

——. 1946. *The Northern Goldfield Diaries of Thomas Baines*. 3 vols. London: Chatto and Windus.

Warwick, P. 1983. *Black People and the South African War 1899–1902*. Johannesburg: Ravan.

Willan, B. 1984. *Sol Plaatje: A Biography. Solomon Tshekisho Plaatje 1876–1932*. Johannesburg: Ravan.

Willoughby, W.C. 1909. 'Notes on the Initiation Ceremonies of the Becwana.' In *The Journal of the Royal Anthropological Institute of Great Britain and Ireland*, XXXIX: 228–285.

Worger, W.H. 1987. *South Africa's City of Diamonds: Mine Workers and Monopoly Capitalism in Kimberley, 1867–1895*. New Haven: Yale University Press.

Wulfsohn, L. 1984. 'Elands River: A Siege Which Possibly Changed the Course of History in South Africa', *Military History Journal*, 6, 3. http://rapidttp.com/milhist/vol063lw. html accessed 20 January 2007

INDEX

AmaNdebele *see* Ndebele
AmaSwati *see* Swazi
AmaZulu *see* Zulu
Annexation (Transvaal)
    128-138, 168, 213
Anglo-Boer War 246-267
Apies River *see* Tshane
Application 280
BaBididi *see* Bididi
Baden-Powell, [Robert S.] 255,
    257
BaFokeng *see* Fokeng
Bafshwe, son of Pilane 119,
    154, 157
Bahibidu *see* Boers
BaHurutshe *see* Hurutshe
BaHwaduba *see* Hwaduba
Bailie, Alexander C. 127, 128, 130
Baines, Thomas 18, 41
BaKaa *see* Kaa
BaKalanga *see* Kalanga
BaKgalagadi *see* Kgalagadi
BaKgatla (baga Kgafela) *see*
    Kgatla
BaKgatla baga Mmanaana *see*
    Mmanaana Kgatla
Bakgatla Reserve xix-xx, 239-
    242, 244, 250, 259, 263, 264,
    279, 280, 282
Bakgatla, son of Linchwe 211,
    221, 229, 285
BaKololo *see* Kololo
BaKwena *see* Kwena
BaKwena baga Moletse *see*
    Moletse Kwena
BaKwena ba Mogopa *see*
    Mogopa Kwena
Bakwena Reserve 240
BaLaka *see* Langa Ndebele
Ballinger, William xix-xxii,
    xxv, 274
BamaLete *see* Lete
Bamalete Reserve 240
BaNgwaketse *see* Ngwaketse
BaNgwato *see* Ngwato
BaPedi *see* Pedi

BaPhalane *see* Phalane
BaPhiring *see* Phiring
BaPo *see* Po
Barnes, Leonard xix–xxii, xxv,
    274
BaRokologadi *see* Rokologadi
BaSarwa *see* Sarwa
BaSeleka *see* Seleka
Basetsane 33
BaSotho *see* Sotho
Bastaards 7, 10
Basutoland 16
BaTaung *see* Taung
BaTlhalerwa *see* Tlhalerwa
BaTlhaping *see* Tlhaping
Bathoen 179, 180, 183, 185, 186,
    188, 189, 191, 194, 195, 198
Battle of Mochudi 110-119
Bechuanaland xxv, xxviii, 10, 19,
    30, 89, 92, 100, 163, 176, 209, 210,
    214, 240, 242, 244, 245, 260
Bechuanaland Border Police
    (BBP) 172, 173, 178, 180, 185,
    187, 190, 193, 198
Bechuanaland Protectorate xix,
    167, 169, 172-174, 176, 177-179,
    181, 186, 188, 191, 195, 196, 197,
    200-202, 213, 234
Beerfontein 42, 53n50, 68, 71, 76,
    84n42
Beestkraal 52n48
Berends, Berends 7-10, 14, 23n35,
    24n52
Berlin Missionary Society
    (BMS) 82n14
Bethanie 65, 76
Beyer, Bernard (?) 210, 211, 218-
    221, 229
Bididi 23, 51n33, 53n58
Bierkraal 42, 261
Bloem, Jan Jr 7, 9, 15
Bloemhof 30
Boekenhoutfontein 52n50
Boers xxvi-xviii, 12-16, 18-20,
    28, 29, 31, 32, 34, 35, 37-39,
    41-43, 46, 48, 55, 60, 61, 64-67,

70, 76, 89, 91, 92, 97, 102,
    104, 111, 119, 123, 128-130, 136,
    138, 139, 150-152, 162, 167, 168,
    170, 178, 181, 185, 227, 244-246,
    248, 250, 253, 254, 257, 258,
    264, 265
Boetsap 7, 9
Bogatsu (Tlokwa) 4
Bogatsu, son of Pilane 64, 92,
    100, 101, 119, 122, 126, 127, 154,
    156, 168, 225, 288
Bogopana 5, 14, 22n28, 24n61
Bopitiko (Bopitikwe) 50n10,
    101, 162
Boschfontein 42
Botha, G.S. 79, 80
Botswana xix, 4, 5
Bottman (Bothman)
    86ns85&86
Boundary Commission 198
brass 18
bronze 37
Breutz, Paul-Lenert 20n1
Brink, Rev Pieter 71, 76, 102,
    104, 127, 129, 130, 131, 132, 134,
    135, 145n76, 152, 160, 161, 162,
    173, 210, 216, 218
British Bechuanaland 172, 174,
    177, 181, 191, 209, 212
British South Africa Company
    168, 177, 178, 187-192, 194, 195,
    197, 198-202, 233, 241, 242,
    243, 247
Buffel's drift 99, 124
Buffelshoek 13
Burgers, T.F 102, 120, 123-128,
    130, 132, 142n44, 152
Bushmen *see* Sarwa
Buys brothers 37 *see also* De
    Buys
Cape government 168f
captives 10, 14, 30, 37, 38, 39, 41,
    47, 52ns43&44, 69
Carrington, Col Frederick 173,
    178, 187,188, 193, 204n16
Cashan mountains 23n46

308

INDEX

Chamberlain, Joseph 201, 202
Christelijke-Gereformeerde Kerk (CGK) 59
Christianity 47, 61, 75, 120, 170, 209-234
Colley, Sir George 138
Commandos xxvi, 9-11, 12, 23n38, 30, 31, 36f, 59, 66, 69, 70
concessions 188, 189, 197 see also Weil
copper 6, 11, 16, 37
Crocodile River see Oodi
Cronje, Piet 246
Cyferkuil 279
David 61, 82n17
D'Elegorgue, Adulphe 6, 7, 18, 19, 24n61
De Buys, Coenraad 7, 14
De la Rey, Jacobus Herculaas (Koos) 259
Delagoa Bay 5, 6, 8, 12, 16, 17, 22n16, 67, 83n38
Derdepoort xix, 153, 246f
De Wet, Christiaan 259
diamond fields 100, 122, 127, 129, 145n70, 152, 159, 174
Dikeme, son of Mantirisi 251
Dikgatlong xxixn5
Dikolo Ramontsana Tlou (wife of Kgamanyane) 34, 35, 118, 211, 155, 220, 222, 225-228, 235n30, 289
Dimawe 30, 52n44, 93, 117
Dingane 11
Dinokana 82n14
Diphokwe, son of Pilane 154
disease, epidemics 36, 50n16, 152, 200, 202, 231, 233-234, 239-240, 244, 267n6
Dithakong 8
Dithubaruba 82n14
Doornhoek 50n10, 86n85
Doornpoort 280
Doppers, Dopper Church 49, 59, 73, 122, 146n85
Dorslanders 123, 124, 143ns46&51, 171
Draaiberg 261, 262
Dreifontein 86n85

drought 36, 69, 74-75, 112, 122, 135, 158, 233, 239
Du Plessis, Caspar (Kas) 247, 256
Du Plessis, Louw 124
Dutch Reformed Church (DRC) xxii, 37, 59, 61, 65, 67-69, 71-73, 104, 127, 161, 162, 173, 212-214, 216, 218, 231, 241, 245
Du Toit, S.J. van Kervel 77, 85n55
Dwarsberg 5, 97, 159
Edwards, Rogers 18, 26n96
Edwards, Samuel 26n96, 203n8
Elands River see Kgetleng
Ellenberger, Jules 242, 245, 247, 248, 250, 253, 255
Eloff, Sarel 53n58, 64, 78, 86n85, 104
Eloff, Teunis 245
emigration see Kgatla emigration
Engers, Sidney 241
evangelists (DRC) 161-162
Enslin, J.A. 81n8
Esterhuyse, J.A. 76
Ferreira, Ignatius Phillip 136
field-cornets see veldkornetten
firearms 8, 16, 17, 19, 25n74&78, 67, 70, 80, 83n38, 94, 106, 116, 127, 145n79, 159, 190, 242, 251, 255, 258, 259, 261, 264, 270
Firi 3
Fokeng 1, 8, 13, 16, 19, 21n5, 30, 36, 42, 44, 45, 50n16, 149, 150, 260
Frere, Sir Bartle 134
Gaberones (Gaborone) xxii
Gaborone, Tlokwa kgosi 183
Gare, Edwin 138n3
Gasebonwe 42
Gaseitsiwe 121, 170, 171, 178, 180, 203n5
Gladstone, William 138, 171
gold 97, 98, 100, 107n25, 108n45, 174-176, 181
Gonin, Jenny 62, 72, 73, 85n60, 244
Gonin, Rev. Henri Louis 54n72, 58, 60-61, 62, 63 -67, 68,

69, 70-75, 78, 80, 81, 82n14, 84ns43, 45&46, 85n60, 87n93, 92, 95, 98, 99, 101, 102, 120, 122, 129, 130, 151, 157, 162, 212, 214, 216-18, 243-245, 285
Goold-Adams, H.J. 180
Goshen 163, 168
Griqua 7, 8, 9, 10, 24n52
Griqualand West 129, 130, 162, 168
Grobbelaar, Wilhelmus Petrus 24n58
Grobler, F.A. 247, 248
Grobler incident 179
Groep, Annie 129
Harris, John 190
Harts River see Dikgatlong
Hermannsburg Missionary Society (HMS) 44, 65, 68, 71, 73, 76, 82n14, 207n94
Hex River see Matsukubjana
High Commission Territories xix
Hodgson, Margaret xix – xxii, xxv, 274
Holdsworth, Colonel G.L. 251-253, 255
Holfontein 122, 130, 157, 243, 244, 265
Hurutshe 1, 7, 10, 21n1, 22n28, 26n8, 63, 82n14, 153
hut tax 136, 174, 196, 242, 243, 283
Hwaduba 26n90
Ikaneng 178, 183, 186, 188, 189, 193, 201, 207n83
inboekelinge 17, 38, 41, 46-48, 214 see also captives, slaves, slavery
Inglis, Walter 25n86
Inhambane 17, 18, 26n93
initiation 73, 102, 103, 223, 231
iron 11, 16, 21n8,
Isang, son of Linchwe xii,xx, xxi, xxii-xxvi, xviii, 222, 267, 274-285, 287n27, 288
ivory 6, 8, 11, 16, 41, 43, 44, 53ns54&58, 57, 69, 94
Jameson Raid 202, 208n113, 233, 242, 247

309

Janskop 261, 262
Jerusalem Pilgrims 59, 81n8
Joubert, Petrus Jacobus (Piet) 60, 104, 120, 121
Kaa 7, 96, 112, 115, 240
Kaeye 255, 256, 257, 262
Kafferwet 1866 70, 78-80
Kalahari sandveld xxvi, 93, 94, 100
Kalanga 22n29
Kalkfontein 92
Kanya Exploration Company 191-192
kapiteins 15, 16, 20, 45, 47, 49
Keate, Robert 97, 98
Keate Award 102
Kekana Ndebele 38, 44, 51n25, 69
Kekana, Matlhodi *see* Matlhodi Kekana
Kgabotshwene, son of Pilane 96, 119, 154
Kgafela 2
Kgafela, son of Linchwe 89, 211, 222, 225, 229, 233, 267, 274, 275, 288
Kgalagadi xviii, 19, 27n104, 118, 132, 141n28, 159
Kgamanyane, son of Pilane xxv, xxvii, 6, 14, 20, 21n12, 24n64, 28, 30-40, 43, 46, 49, 50n10, 51ns32&33, 53ns58&59, 54n66, 55, 57, 58, 60, 61, 63-68, 71, 73, 74-80, 83n36, 88n99, 89, 91-93, 96-102, 103-105, 119, 129, 154, 156, 168, 226, 227, 267, 284, 288
Kgari, son of Pilane 33, 36, 101, 119, 154, 162, 258
Kgari, son of Molefi (aka Kgari Pilane, "Mussolini") xxiv-xxv, 274, 276
Kgatla
auxiliaries 19, 36, 37-38, 43-44, 66, 132, 140n25, 143n56
bridewealth, marriage 26n102, 34, 209f
chieftaincy, succession 2, 31f, 118-120, 154f
emigration 80, 81, 89-106

labour migration 159, 187, 231, 240, 241, 277, 280
praise songs (maboko) 1, 10, 19-20, 28, 39-40, 55, 66-67, 110, 225, 235n32, 237, 258
rain-making 75, 233, 267
regiments, initiation 3, 21n3 & 9, 35, 66, 73-74, 102-103, 118, 147n103, 218, 223, 229, 232-233, 244, 277, 288
river villages 153-154, 156, 240
totem 2, 23n36, 267
Kgatla-Kwena War 103-106, 110-138, 150-154, 157, 159, 217
Kgetleng river xxixn5, 1, 55, 281
Kgomotso, daughter of Linchwe 225, 233, 267
Kgosidintsi 112
Kgosing ward 100, 157
Kgotlamaswe, brother of Pilane 5, 11, 21n10, 23n48, 32, 50n10, 288
Khama III, 113, 117, 121, 123, 130, 170, 171, 173, 178, 185, 186, 190, 191, 198, 199-201, 209, 239, 245, 248, 257, 259
Khamane 123, 245
Kleinsdoornspruit 42B
Kobedi 108n36, 156
Koedoesfontein 280
Koedoesspruit 42
Kololo xxvi, 5, 35, 98
Komane, son of Pilane 85n66, 108n36, 156
Kookfontein 13, 42
Kopong, Kopong hills 112, 152, 185, 186, 189, 237, 239
Kopong Conference 179-187
Kora 7, 9, 10, 24n52, 180
Kraalhoek 274, 279
Krokodil River *see* Oodi
Kruger, Caspar Jan Hendrik 37
Kruger, Gerrit Johannes 16, 17, 18, 37, 52n52
Kruger, Piet 245, 246, 256, 260
Kruger, Stephanus Johannes Paulus (Paul) 17, 20, 29, 36-38, 39, 40-44, 46, 47, 49, 53ns58& 59, 55, 57, 58, 59, 60, 61, 64, 66,

68, 69, 70-3, 76, 77-79, 84ns43, 45&46, 86n83, 87n93, 88n95, 89, 92, 93, 101, 128, 149, 150, 152, 173, 244, 245, 265.
Kruidfontein 243, 265
Kwena xxviii, 1, 3, 4, 7, 17, 30, 36, 42, 77, 93, 94, 97, 105, 106, 111-113, 117, 118, 120-122, 126, 127, 132, 133, 150-153, 160, 167, 170, 174, 179, 180, 183, 186, 189, 191, 196, 199, 201, 212, 237, 245
Langa Ndebele 11, 12, 16, 30, 31, 37-40, 42, 44, 47, 51n19, 69
Lanyon, Sir Owen 135, 136
Lekgwalo 157, 211, 214, 220-222, 224, 225, 228, 229
Lekwakwe 104, 105
Lephepe wells 174, 199, 239
Lete 8, 95, 97, 105, 111, 121, 136, 151, 153, 183, 193, 194, 198, 201, 207n94, 240
Letlhakeng 5
Letsebe, son of Pheto 2-4, 21n4, 288
Letsebe, son of Pilane, 21n9, 33, 36, 57, 92, 96, 119, 130, 141n31, 154, 288
Lewis, Fred J. 123-125, 129, 130, 143n50, 160
Leyds, W.J. 194
Limpopo river 1, 6, 99
Linchwe, son of Kgamanyane xxii, xxv, xxviii, 1, 21n4, 33-35, 89, 101, 102, 104, 105, 112, 113, 118-137, 141n28, 149-153, 155, 156-163, 167, 168, 170, 173, 179, 180-184, 187-202, 239, 240, 243, 245, 248, 250, 251, 254, 255-265, 266, 279, 280, 283, 284, 288
Linchwe II, son of Molefi xvii, 89, 285
literacy in the Kgatleng 160-163
Livingstone, David 16, 17, 19, 25ns74&86, 37, 50n10, 61, 133
Llewellyn, Noel 247, 248, 250, 251
Lloyd, Rev A.J. 186
Lobengula 177, 179, 182, 190, 195, 197, 198

INDEX

Loch, Sir Henry 188, 189, 191-195, 197, 199
locusts 74
London Missionary Society (LMS) 17, 18, 19, 95, 96, 98, 120, 127, 128, 130, 133, 139n11, 163, 173, 174, 176, 212-214, 216
Losperfontein 42, 76
Lydenburg 37
Mabalane 8, 153, 154
Mabe 4, 86n84, 96, 104
Mabieskraal 4, 23n48, 34, 53n59, 96, 103, 104, 118
Mabine 19-20
Mabodisa ward 1, 100, 112, 115, 116, 122, 139ns13&16
Mabotsa 18, 19, 25n86, 26n87, 30
Mabule Hill 2, 4, 57, 81n2
maBuru see Boers
Macheng 98, 113, 117
Mackenzie, Rev. John 98, 130, 133, 169-173, 203n8
Madibana
Madikwe river xxixn5, 1, 4, 5, 11, 12, 13, 55, 99, 158, 159, 195
Madisa, Joseph 162
Mafeking (Mafikeng) xxii, xxiv, 192, 206n64, 246-248, 254, 258
Mafikeng see Mafeking
Magaliesberg 7, 13, 14, 17, 19, 20, 23n46, 24n58, 37, 44, 51n21
Magaliesberg oxen 46, 58
Magalikwena xxixn5
Magomeng 4, 5
Maganelo, son of Dikeme 96, 107n15
Maganelo, son of Kgamanyane 85n62, 118, 119, 122, 142n41, 154-156, 165n23, 226, 228, 288
Magathashoek 13
Magobye 24n58, 76
Magomeng 3, 5
Mahura 42
Mainole, son of Pilane 85n66
Makapansberg 11, 12, 37, 38
Makgophana ward 100
Makopane 47
Malan, Hercules (Harklaas) Phillipus 66, 68, 69, 76, 78, 80,

87n93, 104, 121, 184, 244-246, 247, 248, 249, 252, 265, 269n32, 270n50
Malebye ward 100
Malolwane 254
Malok 24n58
Mamoanwana 42, 52n43
Manamakgothe ward 100, 157
Mankodi 95
Mankopane 37, 51n25
Mankube, great wife of Pilane 4-6, 19, 20, 21n9&11, 31, 32, 34, 49n9, 224-226, 289
Mankurwane 130, 163, 180
Mantatee 8, 22n30
Mantirisi, son of Pilane 13, 14, 24n59, 33, 39, 50n10, 101, 107n15, 119, 123, 154, 157
Maomogwe, Andries 92
Mapela 11, 12, 30, 42, 51n25, 69, 83n36, 121
Mapotsana ward 116
Maree, W.L. 87n85
Maremapoong 57
Marico district 30, 92
Marico River see Madikwe
Mariri, Leoke 162
Maritz, Gert 12, 24n52&54
Maruatona 16
Masellano 57
MaSetedi see Setedi
Matabeleland 57
Mathibe Kgosi 26n90
Mathubudukwane 153, 154, 254
Matlapeng 4, 6, 18, 22n16, 92, 97, 134
Matlhodi Kekana (Paulina) 46, 47
Matsau (Matsawi), David 130, 142n37, 145ns80&81, 163, 166n46, 203n8
Masiana ward 1, 19, 100
Matsukubjana xxixn5
McCabe, Joseph 19, 25n67, 26n99
McKidd, Alexander 61, 82n14
Melvill, Samuel 133-138
Melvill-Ferreira Commission 135-138

Melvill-Van Staden Commission 132-136
Methuen, George 19
Mfatlha Maila 51n33
Mfatlha Ndebele 18, 39, 51n33
mfecane 2, 5, 36
Middelkuil 42, 43, 57, 279
migrant labour 28, 159, 160
Miller, Charles Thomas 218, 219, 240
missionaries 11, 48, 133 see also Beyer, Brink, Edwards, Gonin, Inglis, Livingstone, Lloyd, Moffat, Murray, Price, Retief, Schröder, Schulenberg, Williams and Wookey; also Berlin Missionary Society, Dutch Reformed Church, Hermannsburg Missionary Society and London Missionary Society
Mma Kgafela 211, 220-223, 229, 230 see also Motlapele
Mmadipitse 33
Mmagotso, son of Kgwefane 1
Mmakgabo wife of Pilane 13, 26n101, 33,
Mmamitlwe 57
Mmamodimokwana 5, 22n28
Mmamogale Sekwati 16, 24n58, 25n70&71, 65, 76, 80
Mmampana 4
Mmanaana Kgatla 18, 21n1, 96, 98, 107n22, 112, 115, 116, 122, 139n11, 152
Mmantselana 32, 33, 49n9, 85n66
Mmasebudule 1, 14, 18, 19, 27n105, 44, 55
Mmatau 1
Moatshe Ramokoka 18, 24n58, 41, 60, 63, 65, 75, 80, 162
Mochela Mfatlha 26n90, 51n33
Mochele, son of Kgamanyane 157, 255, 288
Mochudi xix-xx, 20n1, 89, 91, 99-105, 110-112, 117, 123, 124, 127, 130, 131, 136, 137, 150, 152-154, 156, 158, 160, 161, 168, 173, 174, 176, 179, 182, 186, 187,

311

192, 193, 196, 214, 218, 231, 237, 241, 250, 253, 255, 257, 258, 260, 265

Mochudi National School xxii

Modderkuil 42, 43, 52n48, 57, 80, 243, 245, 265

Modie 21n9, 33

Modimosana 1

Modise, son of Kgamanyane 157, 288

Moetlho 104, 105, 108n42

Moffat, John S. 128, 131-133, 137, 138, 170, 174, 178, 180, 182, 187, 196, 212

Mogale Masite 8, 14, 16, 24n58, 25n68, 80

Mogaritse, wife of Linchwe 157, 211, 214, 219, 228-230

Mogemi 69

Mogopa Kwena 1, 21n5, 42

Moilwa 26n86, 65, 82n14

Mokae, son of Tshomankane 244, 262

Mogkatle, Naboth 46

Mokgatle aThethe 8, 13, 16-19, 24n58, 25n74, 30, 41-47, 49n1, 52n50, 63, 65, 68, 71, 76, 80, 83n36, 84n42, 101, 148

Mokgethi, wife of Kgamanyane 154

Mokgosi 8, 105, 107n13, 108n52, 134, 152

Mokopane (Makapan) 38, 39, 42, 47, 51n25, 52n43, 69

Molatlhegi Dikobe 18

Molefe, son of Kgwefane 1, 3, 11, 119, 157, 275, 276, 278, 283

Molefi, son of Molefe 5, 11, 119, 288

Molefi, son of Pheto 24n64, 50n10, 119

Molefi, son of Kgafela xx, xxiv, 274, 275, 283-285

Molepolole (Ntsweng) 67, 92, 94, 103, 104, 106, 112, 113, 118, 119, 122, 126-128, 150-152, 154, 168, 178-180, 194, 95, 192

Moletse Kwena 16, 30, 36, 37, 50n19, 54n71

Molitsane 9

Molopo River 7

Moloto, Ernest Sedumedi 54n71

Monamaneng 5

Montshiwa 18, 26n91, 42, 121, 152, 163, 201,

Mooi River 18, 24n58, 53n53

Morelle, wife of Pilane 3, 5, 11, 32, 33, 49n9

Moruleng 57, 87n93 *see also* Saulspoort

Mosega 11, 12, 13

Morris, Pieter 245, 268n25

Mosadiathebe 211, 228, 229

Moselekatse, son of Pilane 14, 26n101, 76, 86n85, 101, 119, 151, 154, 157

Mosenyi 96, 112, 115

Moshoeshoe 12, 23n52, 41, 66, 69, 77, 83n36, 129

Mosielele 18, 19, 26n87, 30, 42, 52n44, 96

Mosinyi 112

Mosothwe 158

Motlapele, great wife of Linchwe 157, 210, 211, 289 *see also* Mma Kgafela

Motlotle, son of Pheto 4, 5, 7, 34

Motshodi 97, 98

Motshwane, son of Kgamanyane 255

Motswasele 3, 4

Mozambique 6, 17

Murray, Andrew 61, 218, 221

Murray, Mary 213, 218

Mzilikazi xxvi, 7-12, 14, 15, 30, 36, 44, 49

Ndebele xxvi-xxvii, 7-13, 15, 30, 31, 35, 40, 95, 167, 171, 177

Nederduitsch Hervormde Kerk (NHK) 59

Nederduitse Gereformeeerde Kerk *see* Dutch Reformed Church

Neethling, J.H. 88n93

Newton, F. J. 178

Ngotwane River xx, 11, 99, 158, 159

Ngwaketse 1, 3, 4, 7, 11, 111, 136, 152, 174, 179, 183, 186, 188, 189, 191, 196, 198, 201, 203n5

Ngwako Sekgotlela 4

Ngwato xxvii, 7, 10, 44, 82n14, 95, 111, 117, 123, 193, 194, 198, 199, 201, 239

Nkomeng, wife of Kgamanyane 34, 118, 154, 155, 226-228, 235n36, 289

Noge 8

Nooitgedacht 280, 282

Ntereke *see* Rakgobatana

Ntletleng 158

Ntshaupe 24n58

Ntsweng *see* Molepolole

Nylstrom River *see* Magalikwena

Ohrigstad 16, 17

Oodi river xxixn5, 1, 55, 99

oorlamse 47, 48, 61, 64, 69, 73, 76, 81, 92 *see also* inboekelinge

Orpen, J.M. 41

Osborn, Melmouth 131, 132

ostrich feathers 11

Paris Evangelical Missionary Society 162, 242

Pedi xxviii, 3, 4, 12, 16, 19, 21n5, 23n52, 30, 31, 42, 77, 121, 125, 135, 136

Penzhorn, Christof 44, 68, 71, 84n42, 101, 102, 149

Phalane 18, 63, 162, 260

Pheto, son of Molefe xxv, 1, 2, 4, 5, 19, 21n10, 26n100, 288

Phiri, Franz 75

Phiri, Thomas 144n60, 247, 256

Phiring 8

Phokeng 13, 45, 46, 53n50 *see also* Beerfontein

Phuthadikobo Hill xx, xxii, 89, 97, 99-103, 110-112

Pienaars River *see* Tlokwe

Pilane, son of Pheto xxv, xxvii-xxviii, 1-27, 31-34, 36, 49n9, 50n10, 51n33, 57, 119, 168, 224, 226, 267, 283, 284, 288

Pilanesberg xxv, 1, 2, 9, 26n99, 36, 44, 55, 73, 74, 150, 153, 245, 260, 280

INDEX

Pioneer Column 178, 190
Plaatje, Sol 226
Plakkerswet 244
Po 8, 14, 31, 36, 42
polygyny 213, 214, 222, 224
Postma, Dirk 59, 60, 122, 123
Potchefstroom 20, 41, 52n43, 53n53
Potchefstroom district 30, 92
Potgieter, Andries Hendrik 12, 13, 16-20, 24ns52-58, 25ns71, 78&83, 30, 36-38, 41, 43, 51n19, 52n50, 68
Potgieter, Hermanus 37, 38
Pretoria Convention 138
Pretorius, Andries 37, 38
Pretorius, M.W. 42, 48, 60, 69, 70, 77, 92, 94, 97, 102, 132
Price, Rev. Roger 88n100, 96, 135
Querle, August 190, 193
Radipholo, Samuel 161, 216
railway 187, 199, 202, 241
Rakgobatana Molefi (Ntereke) 154
Rakgole, Jakob 161
Ramodibe 124
Ramokoka see Moatshe Ramokoka
Ramono, son of Kgamanyane 156, 157, 191, 211, 215, 217, 219, 222, 226, 227, 253, 255, 265, 267, 279-281, 288
Ramotshedisi 19-20
Ramotswa 95, 97, 134, 152, 203n5
Rantseo 124
Rasubaas 77, 78, 79
Ratsegana Sebeke 113, 117, 138n3, 164n20
Retief, Deborah 87n93, 218, 221, 230
Rhenosterfontein 55, 105
Rhodes, Cecil John 168, 173, 177-179, 187, 188, 197, 198, 201
Riekert, Hendrick, 250, 251
Riekert, P.J. (Hans aka Piet) 246, 249, 250, 251
Riley, Charles 192, 241, 242
rinderpest 202
Robinson, Hercules 173, 178, 188

Roets, Nicolaas 80, 88n94
Rokologadi 61, 63, 65, 86n85, 95
Rolong 7, 10, 22n28, 30, 37, 42, 152, 163, 168, 181, 191, 198, 201, 204n94
Rooiberg 22n28
Rudd Concession 177-179
Rudd, Charles 179
Ruighoek 86n85, 106n13, 258
Rustenburg xxiv, 1, 14, 41, 46, 51n21, 129
Rustenberg district 31, 37, 41-46, 51n21, 57-59, 65, 69-71, 101, 111, 280, 281
Sakalengwe 2
Salisbury, Robert Cecil 171-173
Sand River see Thokwe
Sand River Convention 37, 67, 70, 97
Sanderson, John 41, 45, 53n53
Saron 76
Sarwa xviii, 118, 159, 141n28, 159
Saulspoort 2, 42, 43, 44, 49, 55-81, 89, 91, 92, 100-102, 105, 111, 119, 120, 126, 153, 154, 157, 161, 200, 216, 239, 243, 244, 257, 262, 265
Saulspoort Location 277, 279-283
Schaapkraal 86n85
Schapera, Isaac xxiv, 20n1, 39, 287n27
Schoeman, Stephanus 60
Schoemansdal 17, 36, 41, 77
Scholtz, P.E. 30, 37, 93, 117
Schröder, Heinrich 82n14
Schulenberg, Heinrich C. 106, 108n52, 109n54
Sebele, son of Sechele 104, 105, 108n42, 111-118, 122, 138ns4&5, 140n22, 170, 179, 180, 183-186, 188, 192, 195, 197, 198, 201, 239
Sebetwane xxvi, 5
Sechele 16, 17, 25n78, 26n87, 30, 37, 42, 51n19, 52n44, 65, 75, 77, 82n14, 86n84, 91, 92, 94-98, 100, 103-106, 108ns38&39, 112-115, 117, 118, 121, 123-128, 130-135, 137, 150, 152, 170, 171, 173, 174, 178, 180, 188, 191, 194, 209, 212, 216

Sefikile Hills xxv, 1
Segale 5
Segale, son of Kgamanyane 156, 157, 211, 213, 219, 222, 227, 251, 252, 260, 267, 288
Segogwane, Klaas 251, 252
Seingwaeng, wife of Kgafela 225, 229, 267, 275, 284, 285&n2, 287n27
Sekgoma 44, 53n59, 82n14, 83n38
Sekhukhuni 46, 125, 128, 129
Sekwati 12, 23n52, 30, 36, 42, 77
Seleka 1, 174, 245
Selogwe Pilane 50ns10&11
Selolweng 158
Sentshu see Sentswe
Sentswe 63-65, 86n84, 95
Senwelo 3, 4, 26n101, 288
Seruruma valley 118
Setedi xxvi, 7-10, 12, 13, 15, 35
Shepstone, Henrique Charles 131-133, 135, 136
Shepstone, Theophilus 128, 129, 131-135, 205n58
Shippard, Sidney Godolphin Alexander 174, 175, 176, 178-186, 187-190, 192, 198, 199, 209
Shona 177
Shoshong 44, 57, 67, 82n14, 83n38, 117, 124, 171, 174, 178
Sikwane xix, 153, 154, 162, 200, 250f
slaves 16, 17, 118 see also captives, inboekelinge
slavery 28, 41, 42, 44, 46-49, 70, 97, 176
Smit, A. 77
Smit, N.J. 79, 80
Smith, Andrew 7, 12, 23n46
Snyman, J.P. 247, 257
Snyman, T.J. 53n58
Soswe 36
Sotho xxviii, 8, 12, 23n52
South African (Anglo-Boer) War xxv, 237f
South African Republic see Zuid Afrikaansche Republiek

313

Southey, Nicholas 127
Soutpansberg mountains xxvi, 12, 38, 69, 70
Stellaland 163, 168
Surmon, William H. 196, 197, 200, 201, 242, 247, 250, 251, 253, 255
Swart, Piet 247, 258
Swartruggens 13, 69, 92
Swaziland xix, 41
Swazi xxviii, 30, 41
Synodale Mission 61
Tau, son of Pilane 32, 33, 49n9, 73, 74, 75, 85n66, 108n36, 119, 127, 154-156, 222, 228
Taung 9
telegraph 188-190, 193, 194
Tema, Botlhale 54n71
Thaba Bosiu 24n52
Thaba Nchu 12, 24n52
Thabazimbi 53n58
Thamaga 112
Thari, son of Pheto 2, 4, 288
Thokwe xxixn5
Thulare 3
Tidimane, son of Ramono 87n93
Tin 11, 37
Tlagadi ward 27n104
Tlhabane, son of Linchwe 222
Tlhako 1, 4, 26n101, 34, 96, 103, 258
Tlhako ba Leema 86ns84&85, 96, 106n13
Tlhalerwa 34, 51n33
Tlogwane see Bottman
Tlokwe xxixn5
Tlhaping 7, 30, 42, 129-130, 152, 163, 168, 180
Tlhokwane hill 4
Tlokwa 4, 6, 92, 97, 111, 121, 126, 134, 136, 153, 183, 240
tobacco 11
Tonga 41
trans-Vaal xvi, xxvi-xvii, 28, 29, 35, 36, 40, 41, 43, 46, 57, 58, 69, 97, 100, 103, 118, 120, 123, 127
Transvaal xvi, 128, 128-131, 135, 137, 138, 159, 160, 163, 168, 186, 247

Tregardt, Louis 12, 13
Tshane xxixn5, 7
Tshidi Rolong 18
Tshomankane ('England'), son of Pilane 33, 50n10, 86n85, 101, 119, 122, 132, 135, 146n94, 147n107, 154, 157, 162, 168, 203n2, 211, 228, 288
Tshonwane 26n87, 30
Tshwene-tshwene xvi, 5, 92, 93, 96-99, 107n16, 237
Tswana 11, 12, 31, 180, 181, 185, 196, 209, 212, 214,
Turffontein 52n50, 68, 71, 84n42
Tweedepoort hills 92, 159
Uitvalgrond 86n85
Uys, Piet 12
Vaalpens 80, 88n95, 98, 226
Vaal River xxvi, 7
Van Der Merwe, D.J. 76
Van der Hoff, Dirk 59
Van der Walt, Petrus J. 66, 79, 92
Van Rensburg, Johannes 80
Van Rensberg, W.C.J. 60, 63
Van Staden, Petrus Johannes 58, 77-80, 91, 93, 100, 121, 123, 130, 133, 134, 143n48
Varkensvlei 280
veldkornetten (field-cornets) 20
Venda 77
Venter, Jacobus 49
VhaVenda see Venda
Vieland (Stephanus Moloto) 48-49, 54n72, 64, 69, 75
Viljoen, Jan 82n14, 94
Vleeschfontein 92
Vogelstruiskraal 280
Volksraad 70, 78, 80, 98, 101
Warmbaths 53n58
Warren Expedition 169-172
Waterberg mountains xxvi, 11, 19, 23n41, 38
Warren, Sir Charles 169, 170-173
Weeber, O.C. 86n83
Weil Concessions 191-195, 197, 201
Weil, Julius 191, 192, 197, 198, 200, 208n107, 241-242, 282

Welgeval 64, 65, 71, 76, 82n27, 96, 103, 279
Welgevaagd 280
Welgevonden 42
Williams, Charles 105, 106, 109n54, 125, 112, 125, 127, 128, 176
Willoughby, Rev W.C. 201
Wilson, J.W. 19
Winburg 41
Witfontein 5, 123, 124, 279
Wodehouse, P.E. 70, 97, 98
Wolseley, Sir Garnet 135, 136, 170
women 44, 162, 209f, 286n16
see also Kgatla bridewealth, succession, Dikolo, Kgomotso, Lekgwalo, Mankube, Matlhodi, Mogaritse, Morelle, Motlapele, Nkomeng and Seingwaeng
Wookey, Alfred 176
Zeerust 129, 134, 138
Zuid-Afrikaansche Republiek (ZAR) 59, 60, 63, 63, 67, 68, 77, 89, 91, 93, 94, 97, 98, 100-102, 111, 118, 120-123, 125-128, 131, 142n44, 159, 160, 162, 163, 173, 174, 184, 194, 200, 212, 240, 246
African locations 101, 102
and the English press 70
and missionaries 82n14
and slavery 47-48, 69, 70
borders, boundaries 97, 98, 102, 194, 203n5
labour polices 78, 79-80, 101
land polices 42, 53n51, 68, 70, 173, 186, 200, 243, 265
pass laws 70, 78, 80, 152
refugees from 94
tax laws 70, 78, 79, 80, 88n100, 101
Zulu 135, 136
Zwaartbooi 18, 26n90, 51n33, 53n58
Zwartklip 282
Zwartkoppies 60